Vladimir Latinovic ·
Jason Welle
Edito

Catholicism Opening to the World and Other Confessions

Vatican II and its Impact

palgrave
macmillan

Editors
Vladimir Latinovic
University of Tübingen
Tübingen, Baden-Württemberg
Germany

Jason Welle, O.F.M.
Pontifical Institute of Arabic and
  Islamic Studies
Rome, Italy

Gerard Mannion
Department of Theology
Georgetown University
Washington, DC, USA

Pathways for Ecumenical and Interreligious Dialogue
ISBN 978-3-030-40479-6   ISBN 978-3-319-98581-7   (eBook)
https://doi.org/10.1007/978-3-319-98581-7

Library of Congress Control Number: 2018951557

This Palgrave Macmillan imprint is published by the registered company Springer Nature
Switzerland AG
The registered company address is: Gewerbestrasse 11, 6330 Cham, Switzerland

For John O'Malley, S.J.—with gratitude—
Who reminded the world just how much happened at Vatican II

FOREWORD

THE GOLDEN SIGNIFICANCE OF VATICAN II AT 50

The Jubilee of the Second Vatican Ecumenical Council provided extraordinary opportunities for scholars, theologians and others to reflect, engage in lively conversations, and study further the importance of this monumental meeting and the initiatives flowing from it. Pope John XXIII announced Vatican II on January 25, 1959, with the dual purpose of "the spiritual good and joy of the Christian people but also an invitation to the separated communities to seek again that unity for which so many souls are longing in these days throughout the world."[1] His dual purpose of renewal and promotion of ecumenical relations expanded to three discernable goals by the time the Council convened on October 11, 1964: the spiritual renewal of the church; *aggiornamento* or updating church discipline to the needs and conditions of the present; and the promotion of Christian unity.[2]

John O'Malley, S.J., has suggested that Pope John's announcement launched a process that led and to "quite possibly the biggest meeting

[1] John XXIII, alloc. *Questa festiva*, AAS 51 (1959): 65–69, at 69; *L'Osservatore Romano*, January 26/27, 1959; see also comments by Thomas F. Stransky, C. S. P., "The Foundation of the Secretariat for Promoting Christian Unity," *Vatican II Revisited by Those Who Were There*, ed. Alberic Stacpoole (Minneapolis: Winston Press, 1986), 64.

[2] Joseph A. Komonchak, "Is Christ Divided? Dealing with Diversity and Disagreement," 2003 Common Ground Initiative Lecture, published in *Origins: CNS Documentary Service* 33, no. 9 (July 17, 2003), 141.

in the history of the world."[3] Whatever its size in comparison with other world convocations, Vatican II was a religious event of major portions and probably the most important and influential religious event of the twentieth century.

Its Jubilee began tentatively in 2009, much like the process that Pope John launched, with few, if any, having any real idea of what would happen over the next few years.

Already in 2012, there were some conferences marking the anniversary of the opening of Vatican II. Dialogue was much to the forefront of such commemorations. For example, at Georgetown University, 300 scholars, church leaders and interested people gathered around the theme "Vatican II after Fifty Years: Dialogue and Catholic Identity," beginning on the anniversary of the Council's opening day, October 11. Attention was also given to the council in April, earlier that same year, when the EI Network, itself, gathered over 250 scholars and interested persons in Assisi on the same theme of dialogue: "Where We Dwell in Common: Pathways for Dialogue in 21st Century." While many enjoyed reliving the exciting times of the Vatican II era, few seemed to know with much certainty in 2012 that its initiatives were about to become lively again.

VATICAN II RE-ORIENTED AND RE-ENERGIZED: PARALLELS IN PAPAL TRANSITION

Then, a major shift occurred and the Jubilee took on new energy. This shared some striking parallels with what had taken place at a crucial juncture of the council, itself. During Vatican II, there had been a shift between the first and second sessions that provided a more certain direction for the future, so a similar change took place during the Jubilee. In June 1963, Pope John succumbed to cancer and Pope Paul VI was elected to take his place. Pope John did his part to envision a council, to establish the mechanisms for it to become a reality, to provide inspiration for its work, and to offer trust that the assembled bishops would find a way to make the meeting effective. Pope Paul VI gathered the disparate efforts and suggestions, somewhat disorganized after the first period of meetings, and sought to provide a direction for the future. He organized

---

[3] John W. O'Malley, S.J., *What Happened at Vatican II* (Cambridge: The Belknap Press of Harvard University Press, 2008, 18.

the themes around the nature and mission of the church and outlined them for the council fathers in his truly remarkable and substantive opening address for the second period on September 29, 1963.[4] Later, Pope Paul developed a new vision of the church around the theme of dialogue in his first encyclical, *Ecclesiam Suam* (August 6, 1964). Paul VI used the term "dialogue" over 70 times in the text, a term that had been absent from church documents before Vatican II.

Similarly, nearly 50 years later, in February 2013, Pope Benedict XVI resigned as pope, in what some considered to be an extraordinary gesture of humility, ecclesiological insight, and service to the church universal. Pope Francis was elected to take his place two weeks later. The first Jesuit, Latin American, and successor bold enough to take the name of the poor little saint of Assisi, Jorge Bergoglio as Pope Francis brought a new confidence to the Catholic Church and around the world with his novel style of living and acting as pope. The Jubilee of Vatican II also took on a new character of hope and direction. At first, Pope Francis with his many surprises reminded everyone of Pope John—getting out of the Vatican on quick trips around Rome, acknowledging the advantages of living simply, showing a sense of humor, and willing to change the way things were done by 180 degrees; but by the time of Pope Francis's first major writing, *Evangelii Gaudium*, comparisons with Pope Paul were also becoming significantly obvious.[5]

A HALF-CENTURY OF OPEN DOORS

By default, the annual gatherings of the Ecclesiological Investigations International Research Network (EI) to date have been ecumenical in orientation and participation. And several of these gatherings (as detailed in the volume introduction, see p. 6), have taken explicit ecumenical themes, challenges, aspirations and opportunities for their focus. These

---

[4] Paul VI, alloc. *Salvete fratres*, AAS 55 (1963): 841–859. The address is published in translation in its entirety in several places, for example, in Xavier Rynne, *The Second Session* (New York: Farrar, Straus & Company, 1963), 347–363, and *"The Church in the World,"* *Inaugural Address of Pope Paul VI at the Second Session of the Second Vatican Ecumenical Congress*, ed. Vincent Yzermans, and pub. Most Rev. Leo Binz, Archbishop of St. Paul (Saint Paul: North Central Pub. Co., 1963).

[5] Many have commented at length on the wide-ranging and striking parallels between Pope Francis and John XXIII, somewhat fewer on the parallels with Paul VI.

gatherings have always been intentionally about engaging participants in dialogue as much as having them listen to and present scholarly papers about ecumenical dialogue. So, also, have these gatherings been aimed toward reflection upon and the engagement in interreligious dialogue and engagement.

The 2015 EI Network conference, "Vatican II: Remembering the Future—Ecumenical, Interfaith and Secular Explorations of the Council's Legacy and Promise," was an event which placed such intentions very much to the forefront, along with promoting reflection upon Catholicism's dialogue with and engagement in the wider world.

These three strands come together—ecumenical and interreligious dialogue and encounter, as well as dialogue with and engagement with the wider world have social and practical outcomes.

What was distinctive about this gathering was that it also sought to both mark the fiftieth anniversary of the monumental church council that was Vatican II and to hear from voices throughout and from far beyond the Catholic Church with regard to the council's achievements, legacy and ongoing energy and power.

So the gathering out of which this volume arose primarily hosted at Georgetown University itself reflected both the achievements of the council in transforming the church's understanding of and relationship with other Christians, other religions and the wider human family, as well as the promise and hope that the Pontificate of Francis offers for the church and all people of good will.

While volume II explores the transformation of Catholicism's relationship with people of other faiths, this first volume of papers touches broadly on the important themes of ecclesiology and ecumenism, along with the church's relationship with the wider world. Collectively, its chapters demonstrate that Vatican II was a fresh start for the Catholic Church, offered both doctrinal statements and pastoral direction, engaged the laity as never before, especially encouraging women to grasp leadership roles in the church, challenged all churches to consider both their identity and their relationship with other churches, gave new hope and direction to an already vibrant ecumenical movement, and launched a new creativity among theologians and church leaders in envisioning a church that was more human, more spiritually alive, more consequential to the lives of all people, and more open to improvement than in previous centuries.

This volume discerns the church's present and looks forward as much as, indeed, for most contributors, even more so than it looks back.

In considering some aspects of what the contributors envisage as the future unfolding of the council's mission, let us turn to offer some reflections on how the wider mission of the church has been unfolding of late and what the signs of the present times signs might be pointing toward in years to come.

THE FRANCIS ERA AND THE COUNCIL'S LEGACY AND FUTURE

With all humanity, Christians, including Catholics, are being drawn into an unknown future of tumultuous change (see GS 5–8). At the time of the Second Vatican Council, it was revolutions in the sciences, a new historical consciousness, the advance of economic development, migrations to cities, the expansion of means of communications, the networking of peoples across societies and nations, and the spreading aspirations for greater liberty. The Council tutored us on reading "the signs of the times" (GS 4), finding the hand of God in those changes (GS 11); and it counseled us on exercising our freedom to direct the course of history in the midst of tumultuous change (GS 9).[6]

Today the world experiences the pervasive presence of social media, cyber insecurity, the rise of populist authoritarianism, the return of great power rivalries and increased threat of nuclear war, global climate change, commercial integration through a new wave of trade agreements without the US, and the expansion of global institutions. People today find themselves being drawn back first into the future, trying to keep their bearings amidst a host of daunting challenges. Others include: the collapse of vast ecosystems like the oceans and the staggering loss of plant and animal species; the unwitting capture of the human world by artificial intelligence and the invasion of internet security by social media giants, national adversaries and predatory hackers; the loss of political order across wide areas, especially the Middle East, and the consolidation of Chinese and Russian power. All this takes place when the post-1945 liberal political order has been enfeebled and cooperation among the leading states is at low ebb.

Such are "the dangers, toils and snares" through which Pope Francis leads the Vatican II Church in its ongoing dialogue with the world. If the Council took place in a time of optimism with a sense of possibility, today's world is marked by a sense of uncertainty and loss of human

---

[6] "[Humanity] is becoming aware that it is [its] responsibility to guide aright the forces which [it] has unleashed..."

control in face of the dangers human ingenuity has unleashed. The dialogue the Council initiated with the world and with other churches requires a new imaginative, flexible style of leadership.

GUERRILLA PASTORING AS THE WORLD MOVES BACK FIRST INTO THE FUTURE

With so many complex problems, Francis's leadership style is not that of a supreme pontiff reigning above the fray or a commander leading an assault. He is like an inventive guerrilla pastor, sometimes acting on his own, sometimes engaging others, like Pax Christi International, in extended dialogue, at others summoning the crowds to join him, as in his convening of meetings of popular movements. As the Vatican II Church matures, Pope Francis has the subtlety to rouse the energies of the People of God in direct and indirect ways and to martial the resources of the Holy See and the hierarchy in new ways. He leads with indirection, tacking into the wind, edging forward against breaking waves.

When it came to family life, he summoned a pair of synods to gather the collective wisdom of the Church, first through encouraging the bishops to poll the laity and then drawing on the collective wisdom of the world's bishops to draw up *Amoris Laetitia*, the apostolic exhortation concluding the synod, but then in the critical chapter eight laying out his own discernment model for pastoral care of divorced and remarried Catholics.[7] Notably, he identified it as his own approach, acknowledging others within the church might address it differently. He acknowledges that "those who prefer a more rigorous pastoral care which leaves no room for confusion. But, I sincerely believe that Jesus wants a Church attentive to the goodness which the Holy Spirit sows in the midst of human weakness ..."[8]

Francis addressed the issue of climate change, in *Laudato Si'*, his environmental encyclical, published in advance of the Paris Climate Summit, where the encyclical and his message were greeted with appreciation by world leaders.[9] The letter itself was assembled with input from secular

---

[7] Francis, Post-Synodal Apostolic Exhortation *Amoris Laetitia*, AAS 108, no. 4 (2016): 311–446, see esp. Chapter 8, "Accompanying, Discerning, and Integrating Weakness," nos. 291–312.

[8] Ibid., 308.

[9] Francis, Encyclical Letter *Laudato Si'*, AAS 107, no. 9 (2015): 847–945.

scholars, presented with the collaboration of nonbelieving scientists and environmental activists, and published as a letter not just to the Church but the whole world. Under Francis the engagement with the world has grown in intensity and depth. It has become clear that, as the Council hoped, in this time of crisis the Church can be "a leaven in the world" (LG 31).

A similar process can be seen in the field of nuclear disarmament. Senior statesmen, like George Shultz and William Perry, have united to urge the abolition of nuclear weapons. The Vatican diplomatic corps has been at the vanguard of the abolition movement. Its presence was quite visible in the 2017 UN Conference that negotiated the Treaty to Prohibit Nuclear Weapons. The Conference opened in March with a message from the Holy Father; and he was the first head of state to ratify the treaty. In November, that same year, at a Vatican conference on integral disarmament and development he openly condemned deterrence in contradistinction to the just-war thinkers who normally address these issues; and in his 2017 address to the diplomatic corps he called for "serene and wide-ranging debate on the subject.[10]

The Vatican policy on nuclear abolition is a case of moving back first into the future. While Pope Francis announced his condemnation of deterrence at the November 2017 Vatican symposium, saying "the threat of [the] use [of nuclear weapons], as well as their very possession, is to be firmly condemned," the Vatican is only gradually preparing the ground for preachers and teachers to educate the faithful and the public on its updated teaching on the morality of nuclear weapons and training pastoral workers to accompany Catholic military and national security personnel in the vocational decisions posed by that condemnation and for the wider church to receive this teaching.[11] Given the accelerating nuclear arms race and the threat of nuclear war on the Korean Peninsula, the papal condemnation was timely, but it will take time to reach even those whom this teaching will impact most directly, military and defense personnel and national security specialists.

[10] See Pope Francis, 2018 Address to the Diplomatic Corps at https://w2.vatican.va/content/francesco/en/speeches/2018/january/documents/papa-francesco_20180108_corpo-diplomatico.html.

[11] See Pope Francis, Address to the Symposium "Prospects for a World Free of Nuclear Weapons and for Integral Disarmament," at https://w2.vatican.va/content/francesco/en/speeches/2017/november/documents/papa-francesco_20171110_convegno-disarmointegrale.html.

GOSPEL ECUMENISM

There are surprises on every front, including ecumenical relations, one of the principal areas discussed by several contributors to this first volume. Francis's meeting with Russian Patriarch Kirill at the Havana Airport in February, 2016, with their 14-point declaration on world affairs was a major step forward in the long-blocked relations with the largest Orthodox Church.[12] While it was not a formal ecumenical encounter aimed at church unity, it was nonetheless a significant moment of mutual recognition and shared exercise of responsibility toward the world.

The observance of the Quincentennial of the Reformation in 2017 represented a long step forward in the relation between the Lutheran and Catholic churches. Earlier anniversaries had been occasion to note differences and expose old wounds. The 2017 anniversary, by contrast, was occasion to own historic faults, offer hope-filled expressions of mutual respect and to demonstrate comfortable, open relations between church leaders and the faithful of the respective churches.[13] Pope Francis, in a private exchange with parishioners at Rome's Lutheran church, expressed his impatience with theological quibbles on the question of Eucharistic sharing.[14] Likewise, the Holy Father's familiarity in annual meetings with Pentecostals, Methodists and Waldensians

---

[12] See "The Historic Meeting of Pope Francis and Patriarch Kirill: Havana, 20 February 2017," Information Service of Pontifical Council for Promoting Christian Unity, no. 147 (2016/I), at http://www.vatican.va/roman_curia/pontifical_councils/chrstuni/information_service/pdf/information_service_147_en.pdf.

[13] The complete documentation may be found at "The Journey of His Holiness Pope Francis to Sweden for the Commemoration of the 500th Anniversary of the Reformation," Information Service of Pontifical Council for Promoting Christian Unity, no. 148 (2016/II), 18–26 at http://www.vatican.va/roman_curia/pontifical_councils/chrstuni/information_service/pdf/information_service_148_en.pdf.

[14] The Pope's actual remarks are reported here, https://w2.vatican.va/content/francesco/en/speeches/2015/november/documents/papa-francesco_20151115_chiesa-evangelica-luterana.html. For samples of the commentary and interpretation they generated, see https://www.ecumenicalnews.com/article/pope-francis-prayers-at-service-with-romes-lutherans-hailed-by-lwf/35865.htm; and especially David Gibson, "Did Pope Francis Say that Lutherans Can Take Communion at Catholic Mass?", *National Catholic Reporter*, https://www.ncronline.org/news/vatican/did-pope-francis-say-lutherans-can-take-communion-catholic-mass.

witnesses to the growing intimacy between Christians of different denominations at the grassroots, an unheralded fruit of fifty years of ecumenism, but real nonetheless, and pregnant with promise for the future.[15]

In his closing address to the conference that inspired this volume, presented at the Episcopalian Washington National Cathedral, Cardinal Walter Kasper, the longtime president of the Vatican's Council for Promoting Christian Unity, imagined these less formal communal interchanges, especially with Evangelicals and Pentecostals, as "a Gospel-oriented" ecumenism of the future.[16] For these less traditional churches, fitted by their individualism to post-modernity, Kasper noted "the church is an event."[17] His Gospel-oriented ecumenism understands that "the path to unity is not the path to institutional merger." The new ecumenism sprung from the Gospel, Kasper argues, is found in the *sensus fidei* shared by all believers and expressed in a catholicity that will be concretely realized in synodality (the communal governance of the several churches).[18] "Catholicity involves all," he writes. "The laity are not merely recipients but also actors, not only objects but above all subjects in the church." For this reason, he asserts, Pope Francis "wants a listening magisterium that makes its decisions after it has heard what the Spirit says to the churches (Rev 2:7, etc.)."[19]

WOMEN AND THE MAGISTERIUM

Nowhere is a listening magisterium as necessary as with women in the Church.[20] Pope Francis's record with respect to women has been modest at best. He called off the investigations of American religious women and

---

[15] For a list of identifiable fruits of Vatican II Ecumenism, see Walter Kasper, *Harvesting the Fruits: Basic Aspects of Christian Faith in Ecumenical Dialogue* (New York and London: Bloomsbury, 2010).

[16] See Cardinal Walter Kasper, 'Church and Churches Remembering the Future: Towards Multi-Faceted Unity', Chapter 20 of the present volume at 329–346, esp. 340–346.

[17] Ibid., 337.

[18] Ibid., 341–344.

[19] Ibid., 344.

[20] On the attitudes of US Catholic women, see the recent *America*/CARA survey, "Proud to be Catholic? A groundbreaking *America* survey asks women about their lives in the Catholic Church," *America*, January 16, 2018 at https://www.americamagazine.org/faith/2018/01/16/proud-be-catholic-groundbreaking-america-survey-asks-women-about-their-lives.

met in person with their representative leaders. He appointed a committee to advise him on opening the diaconate for women[21] and appointed a couple of women to curial positions, though in the Dicastery of Laity, Family and Life, where traditional women's concerns for children and family would make them an easy fit.[22]

Since 1970 the Church has named four women doctors of the church: Teresa of Avila, Catherine of Siena, Therese of Lisieux and Hildegaard of Bingen.[23] Teresa had run-ins with the male religious leaders of her day, Catherine took it upon herself to lecture the pope on his weakness, and Hildegard, a polymath mystic, had been adopted as a model by feminists and New Agers before Benedict XVI named her a doctor. It is no big stretch, then, for Gerard Mannion to offer reflections on "Women and the Art of the Magisterium." Of the contribution of women to post-Vatican II theology, Mannion writes, "Much needs to be done to increase awareness, acknowledgement and appreciation of the contribution of women to church teaching authority, and, most importantly of all, to increase their participation in the same."[24]

Teaching authority (*magisterium*), Mannion argues in a bold move, is a matter of what people teach, not who they happen to be.[25] It is more about action and particular activities than the actors and their positions within the church. Mannion traces the history of the women who have taught the church "with authority" from Saint Clare of Assisi to Mary Ward, or famous women dissenters who brought the church to greater insight through their dissent—from Catherine of Siena who chastised a pope, to Australia's first saint, Mary MacKillop to the countless activists such as Dorothy Day."[26] The modern exercise of this role includes the

[21] See "Francis Institutes Commission to Study Female Deacons," *National Catholic Reporter*, August 2, 2016 at https://www.ncronline.org/news/vatican/francis-institutes-commission-study-female-deacons-appointing-gender-balanced.

[22] See "Francis Appoints Two Laywomen to Key Positions in the Roman Curia," *America*, Nov. 7, 2017 at https://www.americamagazine.org/faith/2017/11/07/pope-francis-appoints-two-laywomen-key-positions-roman-curia.

[23] See Mary T. Malone, *Four Women Doctors of the Church* (Maryknoll, NY: Orbis, 2015).

[24] See Chapter 9 of the present volume, Gerard Mannion, 'Women and the Art of Magisterium: Reflections on Vatican II and the Postconciliar Church', 119–147 at 120.

[25] Ibid., 133–134.

[26] Ibid., 137.

women observers at Vatican II, like Mary Luke Tobin and Rosemarie Goldie, who ultimately served also as *periti and* members of subcommissions. (Pope Paul referred to Rosemarie Goldie as *nostra collaboratrice*, "our collaborator.") Mannion backs the historical argument with the growing appreciation of the Council's teaching of the *sensus fidei* as a gift of all the faithful.[27] He concludes, Women "have taught the church much and will continue to do so" and "Magisterium deserves aggiornamento as much as any other part of the church and its theological enquiries."[28]

Clearly, integrating the multifold gifts of women into the life of the church is essential to its future vitality. Given the variety of cultures the Catholic Church embraces, there will be differences in the pace, the direction and even the content of that integrative process. But, given the changing status of women in society to which the church has given repeated support, the activism even of poor and less-educated women, and the enormous service of women to the church's pastoral activities, there is no doubt the future phases in the unfolding of the Vatican II church will involve women and their gifts. The time of "prudent" hesitation, symbolic action and progress by indirection will pass. The time when the church and especially its women of faith are drawn back-first into the future is fast passing.

After more than half a century of a concerted effort by this global church to throw open its doors, it is right and fitting, indeed necessary, that we discern and explore the implications and outcomes of what was set in motion by John XXIII back in January, 1959, when he announced the council. All in all, this volume demonstrates that the Golden Jubilee of the council was not just a remembrance of a creative period fifty years ago but also an occasion to reflect creatively on the present, now fully a post-Vatican II period, and, above all, to look toward the future. While pointing toward remaining challenges, unfinished business and much

---

[27] Ibid., 146. On the central role of the *sensus fidei*, see International Theological Commission, "Theology Today: Perspective, Principles and Criteria" (2009) at http://www.vatican.va/roman_curia/congregations/cfaith/cti_documents/rc_cti_doc_20111129_teologia-oggi_en.html, nos. 33–35. The text is important for resting the teaching authority of the bishops on the *sensus* possessed by all the baptized. Similarly, see Pope Francis' comments on "thinking with the church" as thinking with the whole church, faithful and bishops together in Antonio Spadaro, S.J., *A Big Heart Open to God: A Conversation with Pope Francis* (New York: HarperCollins, 2013).

[28] Mannion, 'Women and the Art of Magisterium', 147, 144, respectively.

work to be done, these essays collectively demonstrate the impact, legacy and future promise of Vatican II. They point to bright future indeed.

Washington, DC, USA   John Borelli
                              Special Assistant to the President
                                 for Catholic Identity and Dialogue,
                                         University of Georgetown

                                          Drew Christiansen S.J.
                              Berkley Center for Religion, Peace,
                      and World Affairs, University of Georgetown

John Borelli is special assistant Catholic Identity and Dialogue to President DeGioia of Georgetown University. Returning from a tour in Vietnam, Borelli finished his doctorate in the history of religions and theology in 1976 while teaching full-time. After 11 years of teaching in New York, he accepted a position with the National Conference of Catholic Bishops, promoting ecumenical and interreligious relations. Since 2003, Borelli has been at Georgetown University. Borelli has B.A. from St. Louis University and Ph.D. from Fordham University.

Drew Christiansen, S.J. is Distinguished Professor of Ethics and Global Human Development in Georgetown's School of Foreign Service and a senior research fellow at the Berkley Center for Religion, Peace and World Affairs. His current areas of research include nuclear disarmament, nonviolence and just peacemaking, Catholic social teaching and ecumenical public advocacy. He is a frequent consultant to the Holy See and a member of the steering committee of the Catholic Peacebuilding Network.

ACKNOWLEDGEMENTS

First of all, our deep gratitude once again to all at Palgrave Macmillan and their associates for the smooth and professional way in which they have worked with us yet again in bringing to print two further important volumes in the Ecclesiological Investigations Series—Pathways for Interreligious and Ecumenical Dialogue. Special thanks to Phil Getz, Amy Invernizzi and also to Sridevi Purushothaman, Rachel Taenzler, Redhu Ruthroyoni and all at SPS for their thorough and diligent commitment at all stages of production for this particular volume. It has been a pleasure once again working with you. Thank you also to the peer reviewers who shared such enthusiastic feedback on the proposal for these volumes.

It is only fitting that we should here thank those who helped make the commemorative event out of which these volumes emerged such a special one that has brought forth the impressive collection of essays you have in your hands. Thank you to all who were part of this very special gathering, especially to all of our presenters and speakers, particularly those travelled so far, including our ecclesial keynotes, Cardinal Kasper, Cardinal Tagle and Cardinal Tauran, Archbishop Fitzgerald, Archbishop Machado and Bishop Hiiboro who took time out of such busy schedules to be us.

That event could not have taken place without the hardwork and support of many people and organizations, above all else the organizing committee which comprised of John Borelli, Special Adviser to the President on Interreligious Initiatives, Georgetown University; Mark D. Chapman, Vice Principal, Ripon College, Cuddesdon and Reader in Historical Theology, Oxford University; Drew Christiansen S.J., Distinguished Professor of Ethics and Global Development, Georgetown University; Brian Flanagan, Assistant Professor of Systematic Theology, Marymount University, VA.; Miriam Haar, then of Trinity College, Dublin and Evangelische Landeskirche in Württemberg, Germany (now at the Lutheran World Federation in Geneva); Peter Herman, one of our Graduate Students in Religious Pluralism at Georgetown University, USA; Leo Lefebure, Matteo Ricci, S.J., Chair in Theology, Georgetown University; Peter De Mey, Professor of Ecclesiology and Ecumenism and Director of the Center for Ecumenical Research, Katholieke Universiteit Leuven, Belgium; Peter C. Phan, Ignacio Ellacuria Professor of Catholic Social Thought, Georgetown University; and Sam Wagner, Special Assistant to the President, Georgetown University. Among this band of heroes, a special word of acknowledgement for supererogatory efforts must be said also to John, Brian, Peter De Mey, Peter Herman and Sam who did so much heavy lifting behind the scenes throughout.

We had so much great support in multiple ways from Georgetown University's community most especially from John J. DeGioia, Georgetown's 48th President, whose office afforded remarkable support from start to finish, especially in the person of Joe Ferrara, Chief of Staff to the President, as did Chester Gillis, Dean of Georgetown College and Richard Cronin, the Senior Associate Dean of Georgetown College; deep gratitude for invaluable support is also expressed to Thomas Banchoff, Georgetown's Vice President for Global Engagement and then Director of the Berkley Center for Religion, Peace and World Affairs; Fr. Joe Lingan S.J., Rector, Wolfington Hall Jesuit Community; Fr. Kevin O'Brien S.J., Vice President for Mission and Ministry; William Treanor, Dean, Georgetown Law; Fr. Leon Hooper S.J., Librarian and Amy Phillips, Rare Materials Cataloger, the Woodstock Theological Library; James Wickman, Director of Music, Liturgy and Catholic Life. We also received great support from Lyndsay B. Taylor, Deputy to Joe Ferrara, Chief of Staff and Communications Manager, Alexandra McCarthy, Andrew Koenig, Melissa Bennett and Susan Cruden—all of the Office of the President. Others of the Georgetown community whose tireless efforts really helped make the whole thing possible and who deserves a very special mention include Karen Lautman, Michael Friedman, Taraneh Wilkinson and especially Linda Ferneyhough who graciously came out of retirement to help with preparations. A huge thank you is also owed to Patrick Ledesma, Director and Sonam Shah, Program Coordinator at the Healey Family Student Center, where so much of the program was memorably staged.

Beyond Georgetown, enormous debts of gratitude are equally due first and foremost to Matt Shank, President of Marymount University and his staff; Dean Gary Hall, Canon Gina Campbell, Ruth Frey, Mitchell Sams and all at the National Cathedral; and also David Pennington, the pastoral Associate for Liturgy, Holy Trinity Parish Georgetown, Aaron Hollander, Nicolas Mumejian, Scott MacDougall, Craig Phillips and Joshua Ralston. Our sincere and deep gratitude also to all at the Study Centre for Church & Media (Belgium) which allowed us to produce an English version of their informative films about the Council (see www.volgconcilie.be), for the opening session and the event website.

Among our numerous benefactor institutions, in addition to the many Georgetown and Marymount administrators named above, special words of deep gratitude should also said for Joseph and Winifred Amaturo and the Amaturo foundation; for the Church and World Program, Berkley Center for Religion, Peace and World Affairs (as well as the Center in general for such great support on many fronts); to Fr. Johan Verschueren, S.J., Provincial, and Fr. E. J. J. M. Kimman S.J., of the Dutch and Flemish Province of the Society of Jesus and all members of that community; Mark David Janus and Bob Byrns at Paulist Press; the National Jesuit Advisory Board on Interreligious Dialogue and Relations; Prof. George Demacopoulos, Director of the Orthodox Christian Studies Center, Fordham University; Woodstock Theological Library and the Jesuit Community of Wolfington Hall, Georgetown University; Michael Bloom, Now You Know Media Inc.; Ian Markham, President, Virginia Theological Seminary; Dale Irvin, President, New York Theological Seminary; Ripon College, Cuddesdon, Oxford; the Scalabrini International Migration Institute, Rome; Fr. James Wiseman, St. Anselm's Abbey; Leonora Mendoza, President, and all members of the Philippine Nurses Association of Metropolitan DC; Mr. & Mrs. Dennis Lucey. Our greatest debt of gratitude here of all is to a foundation which wishes to remain anonymous and above all to its Director.

Thank you one and all!

Gerard Mannion
Jason Welle, O.F.M.
Vladimir Latinovic

CONTENTS

NOTES ON CONTRIBUTORS

Agnes M. Brazal is co-founder and past President of the Catholic Theological Society of the Philippines, former Coordinator of the Ecclesia of Women in Asia, and professor at St. Vincent School of Theology. She is co-author of *Intercultural Church: Bridge of Solidarity in the Migration Context* (Borderless Press, 2015), and co-editor of several books, including *Living With(Out) Borders: Catholic Theological Ethics on the Migration of Peoples* (Orbis, 2016), *Feminist Cyberethics in Asia* (Palgrave, 2014) and *Body and Sexuality* (AdMU Press, 2008).

Mark D. Chapman is Reader in Modern Theology at the University of Oxford, Visiting Professor at Oxford Brookes University and Vice-Principal of Ripon College, Cuddesdon, Oxford. His most recent books include *Theology and Society in Theology and Society in Three Cities: Berlin, Oxford and Chicago, 1800–1914* (James Clarke, 2014); *The Fantasy of Reunion: Anglicanism, Catholicism and Ecumenism, 1833–1882* (Oxford, 2014); and *Anglican Theology* (T & T Clark, 2012).

Charles E. Curran is the Elizabeth Scurlock University Professor of Human Values at Southern Methodist University. He has written extensively in moral theology and Catholic social ethics, especially in the Moral Traditions series from Georgetown University Press. He has served as president of three national academic societies—the American Theological Society, the Catholic Theological Society of America and the Society of Christian Ethics.

Agnes de Dreuzy teaches Church history and ecclesiology at St. Mark's College, the Catholic Theological College at the University of British Columbia in Vancouver. She holds her Ph.D. in Church History from the Catholic University of America in Washington, DC and is also a graduate from the Institut d'Etudes Politiques de Paris, France, where she specialized in foreign affairs. Her research interests are interdisciplinary and include the history of papal diplomacy in the modern period as well as interreligious dialogue and diplomacy. She recently published *Vrai et saint: Ecritures chretiennes et autres religions* (Lit Verlag, 2017), the French translation of Leo Lefebure's *True and Holy*.

Brian Flanagan is Associate Professor in Theology/Religious Studies at Marymount University. He completed his Ph.D. in 2007, writing a dissertation on the ecumenist and theologian Jean-Marie Tillard, O.P. He continues his research in ecclesiology, ecumenism and Jewish-Christian dialogue, particularly through the Ecclesiological Investigations Network and the Ecclesiological Investigations Group of the American Academy of Religion. At Marymount University, he is able to indulge both his research and his passion for teaching. He draws upon the diversity of his students' experiences and his own study of Christian theology to create a classroom focused on shared critical inquiry.

Mary McClintock Fulkerson teaches theology at Duke Divinity School. Her books include *A Body Broken, a Body Betrayed: Race, Memory, and Eucharist in White-Dominant Churches*, co-authored with Marcia W Mount Shoop (Cascade, 2015); *Places of Redemption* (Oxford, 2010); and *Changing the Subject: Women's Discourses and Feminist Theology* (Wipf and Stock, 2001). Her co-edited volumes include *The Oxford Handbook of Feminist Theology* (Oxford, 2013) and *Theological Interpretation for Life, Liberty and the Pursuit of Happiness: Public Intellectuals for the 21st Century* (Palgrave, 2013).

Patrick J. Hayes is the archivist for the Redemptorists of the Baltimore Province and an active church historian. He is the editor of several books and the author of *A Catholic Brain Trust: The Catholic Commission on Intellectual and Cultural Affairs, 1945–1965* (University of Notre Dame, 2011), and most recently, a monograph on a Philadelphia parish, *St. Peter the Apostle, A History: 1842–2017* (Custombrook, 2017).

Dagmar Heller is ordained in the (United) Protestant Church in Baden, Germany and, since 2007, has been a lecturer of Ecumenical

Theology at the Ecumenical Institute in Bossey, Switzerland and Programme Executive for the Commission on Faith and Order of the World Council of Churches in Geneva. Since 2014 she has also served as Academic Dean at the Bossey Institute.

Dale T. Irvin is President and Professor of World Christianity at New York Theological Seminary. His publications include *History of the World Christian Movement, Volumes 1 & 2,* written with Scott W. Sunquist (Orbis, 2001), as well as several other books and numerous articles. He is also a founding editor of the *Journal of World Christianity.* Among his various academic interests, he lists ecumenical studies, multifaith studies and global Pentecostalism.

H. E. Cardinal W. Kasper is a native of Heidenheim-Brenz, Germany. He both studied at and later was Professor of Dogmatic Theology at the University of Tübingen. He was ordained for the Diocese of Rottenburg-Stuttgart in 1957, and became bishop of that diocese in 1989. He is the author of many influential and ground-breaking books including *Pope Francis' Revolution of Love and Tenderness* (Paulist, 2015) and *Mercy: The Essence of the Gospel and the Key to Christian Life* (Paulist, 2014), which Pope Francis started reading during the conclave and has praised repeatedly. A veteran of many ecumenical and inter-faith initiatives, he served as a Catholic member of the World Council of Churches' Faith and Order Commission, as co-chair of the Lutheran-Catholic Commission of Unity, and as secretary and later president of the Vatican's Pontifical Council for Promoting Christian Unity. Under his leadership, the Pontifical Council advanced the cause of dialogue between Roman Catholics and many different Christian traditions and he equally left a deeply positive impression on Christian–Jewish relations.

Vladimir Latinovic is a lecturer in Patristics and Church History at Tübingen University, where he previously was a research fellow at the Institute for Ecumenical and Interreligious Studies. He is also project manager of the project "Treasure of the Orient," which seeks to improve the integration and visibility of Near Eastern and Orthodox Christians in Germany. As an undergraduate, he studied Orthodox Christian theology at the University of Belgrade and did his doctorate at the Catholic Theological Faculty at Tübingen University on homoousian Christology and its repercussions for the reception of the Eucharist (the first volume of the fruits of these researches, *Christologie und Kommunion,* was published by the Aschendorff-Verlag in 2018). He is vice-chair of the Ecclesiological Investigations International Research Network.

Patricia Madigan, O.P. is the Executive Director of CIMER, the Dominican Centre for Interfaith, Ministry, Education and Research (www.cimer.org.au). She lectures regularly in Australian universities and has worked on research projects with organisations such as the Australian Human Rights Commission and the Australian Catholic Bishops' Conference. Her publications include *Women and Fundamentalism in Islam and Catholicism* (Peter Lang, 2011) and *Iraqi Women of Three Generations* (San Antonio, 2014).

Gerard Mannion holds the Joseph and Winifred Amaturo Chair in Catholic Studies at Georgetown University, where he is also a Senior Research Fellow of the Berkley Center for Religion, Peace and World Affairs. Educated at the Universities of Cambridge and Oxford, he has held visiting professorships and fellowships at universities such as Tübingen (Germany), the Dominican Institute for Theology and University of St Michael's College, Toronto (Canada), the Australian Catholic University, the Institute of Religious Sciences in Trento (Italy) and at the Katholieke Universiteit Leuven (in Belgium). He serves as chair of the Ecclesiological Investigations International Research Network and has published numerous books and articles particularly in fields such as ecclesiology, ecumenical and interreligious dialogue, ethics and social justice. He is the current President of the International Network of Societies for Catholic Theology (INSeCT).

Paul G. Monson is Assistant Professor of Church History at Sacred Heart Seminary and School of Theology in Wisconsin. He holds a doctorate from Marquette University, where he defended a dissertation on transatlantic monasticism. His research and publications focus on the relationship between theology, history and culture in American Catholicism, with a distinct transnational lens.

Jan Nielen has served as program officer at CORDAID for almost 30 years. He received his Ph.D. in social sciences from Free University in Amsterdam, specializing in the anthropology and sociology of South Asia. During the last 10 years he has focused on the role of religion in conflict transformation and peacebuilding. He initiated several linking and learning programs on interreligious dialogue in close collaboration with the church in and of Asia.

John O'Malley, S.J. is University Professor in the Theology Department at Georgetown University. A specialist in the religious culture of early modern Europe, his best-known book is *The First Jesuits* (Harvard, 1993), now in thirteen languages. For more than four decades, he has written extensively on Vatican II, including his monograph, *What Happened at Vatican II* (Harvard, 2008), now in six languages.

Anne E. Patrick, S.N.J.M. was William H. Laird Professor of Religion and Liberal Arts, at Carleton College in Northfield, Minnesota, and a Sister of the Holy Names of Jesus and Mary. A former president of the Catholic Theological Society of America, her books include *Conscience and Calling: Ethical Reflections on Catholic Women's Church Vocations* (Bloomsbury/T & T Clark, 2013) and *On Being Unfinished: Collected Writings* (Orbis, 2017). She passed away in 2016.

Dorothea Sattler professor of Ecumenical Theology and Dogmatics at the University of Münster since 2000, obtained her doctorate in 1992 with an ecumenical thesis on the Sacrament of Reconciliation and habilitated in 1996 with a study of the Doctrine of Salvation. She is the Scientific Director of the Ecumenical Study Group of Protestant and Catholic Theologians in Germany and delegate of the German Bishops' Conference in the National Council of the Churches.

Matthew A. Shadle is Associate Professor of Theology and Religious Studies at Marymount University in Arlington, Virginia. He has been published in journals such as *Horizons*, the *Journal of the Society of Christian Ethics*, the *Journal of Catholic Social Thought*, and *Political Theology*. He also serves as the editor of the Catholic Social Ethics section of the *Political Theology Today* blog, and also writes for the *Catholic Moral Theology* blog.

Jason Welle, O.F.M. is Dean of Studies at the Pontifical Institute for Arabic and Islamic Studies in Rome. His teaching and research focus on interreligious dialogue, Muslim-Christian relations, the Franciscan intellectual tradition and Islamic mysticism, particularly in the medieval period. He has published articles in a number of scholarly journals, including *The Muslim World, Islamochristiana*, and the *Journal of Ecumenical Studies*. He is presently engaged on a major project focusing on the notion of companionship in the writings of the eleventh-century Ṣūfī master Abū ʿAbd al-Raḥmān al-Sulamī, including English translations of some of his treatises. He holds a Ph.D. in Theological and

Religious Studies from Georgetown University and master's degrees from the University of Notre Dame and the Catholic Theological Union.

Susan K. Wood S.C.L. is a professor at Marquette University in Milwaukee, Wisconsin and a past president of the Catholic Theological Society of America. Very active in ecumenical work, she serves on the International Lutheran-Catholic dialogue, the US Lutheran-Catholic dialogue, and the North American Orthodox-Catholic Theological Consultation. Her most recent book is *A Shared Spiritual Journey: Lutherans and Catholics Traveling Toward Unity* (Paulist, 2016), co-authored with Timothy J. Wengert.

Anastacia Wooden defended her doctoral dissertation on the ecclesiology of Fr. Nicholas Afanasiev at The Catholic University of America, Washington, DC., in late 2018. She researches the theological and historical aspects of ecumenical interactions between the Catholic and the Russian Orthodox theologians on the eve of Vatican II. A native of Belarus, she resides with her husband and four children in Maryland, USA.

ABBREVIATIONS AND WORKS FREQUENTLY CITED

Documents of the Second Vatican Council

AA   *Apostolicam Actuositatem*, Decree on the Apostolate of the Laity (1965)
AG   *Ad Gentes*, Decree on the Mission Activity of the Church (1965)
CD   *Christus Dominus*, Decree Concerning the Pastoral Office of Bishop (1965)
DH   *Dignitatis Humanae*, Declaration on Religious Freedom (1965)
DV   *Dei Verbum*, Dogmatic Constitution on Divine Revelation (1965)
GE   *Gravissimum Educationis*, Declaration on Christian Education (1965)
GS   *Gaudium et Spes*, Pastoral Constitution on the Church in the Modern World (1965)
IM   *Inter Mirifica*, Decree on the Means of Social Communication (1963)
LG   *Lumen Gentium*, Dogmatic Constitution on the Church (1964)
NA   *Nostra Aetate*, Declaration on the Relation of the Church to Non-Christian Religions (1965)
OE   *Orientalium Ecclesiarum*, Decree on the Eastern Catholic Churches (1964)
OT   *Optatam Totius*, Decree on Priestly Training (1965)
PC   *Perfectae Caritatis*, Decree on Renewal of Religious Life (1965)
PO   *Presbyterorum Ordinis*, Decree on the Ministry and Life of Priests (1965)
SC   *Sacrosanctum Concilium*, Constitution on the Sacred Liturgy (1963)
UR   *Unitatis Redintegratio*, Decree on Ecumenism (1964)

GENERAL

AAS   *Acta Apostolica Sedis*
ASS   *Acta Sanctae Sedis*

CDF	Congregation for the Doctrine of the Faith
CELAM	Consejo Episcopal Latinoamericano (Latin American Bishops' Conference)
CJC, CIC	*Codex Juris Canonici* (Code of Canon Law)
D, DZ, DS	H. Denzinger: *Enchiridion Symbolorum, Definitionum et Declarationum de Rebus Fidei et Morum*
H/V	*History of Vatican II*, eds. Giuseppe Alberigo and Joseph Komonchak, 5 vols
FA:ED	*Francis of Assisi: Early Documents*, 3 vols
ITC	International Theological Commission

The proceedings of the Second Vatican Council are collected as Acta synodalia sacrosancti concilii oecumenici Vaticani II, 32 vols. (Vatican City: Typis polyglottis Vaticanis, 1970–1999). Various English translations of these documents are regularly used. Among the most common are:

Walter M. Abbott, ed., *Documents of Vatican II* (New York: America Press, 1966)

Austin Flannery, ed., *Vatican Council II - The Conciliar and Post Conciliar Documents*, Revised Edition (Dublin: Dominican Publications, 1992)

Giuseppe Alberigo and Norman Tanner, eds., *Decrees of the Ecumenical Councils* (Washington, D.C.: Georgetown University Press, 1990)

Contributors have been free to choose their own preferred translations. The majority have employed those from the Vatican's web archive, publicly available at http://www.vatican.va/archive/hist_councils/ii_vatican_council/index.htm.

In all essays, biblical references occur with parenthetical, in-text citations according to the standard chapter and verse numbering, and contributors have chosen their preferred translations. Citations of the documents of the Second Vatican Council also occur in-text according to the paragraphs of the document, not according to the page numbers of a specific edition. Citations of all other sources occur in notes. References to papal writings, speeches, or other ecclesial documents generally cite the official text published in *Acta Apostolicae Sedis or Acta Sanctae Sedis*; English translations of many of these documents are available on the Vatican's web archive as well as in a variety of volumes of collected documents.

PART I

Introduction

CHAPTER 1

How a Church Opened Its Doors

Gerard Mannion

2015 marked the 50th anniversary of the close of one of the most important events in the history of the Roman Catholic Church: The Second Vatican Council, which took place between 1962 and 1965. This is the first of three volumes that originated from a major international conference to commemorate that milestone.[1] These events were staged at Georgetown University as well as at the National Cathedral, Washington, DC, and Marymount University in Virginia. It took as its theme *Vatican II: Remembering the Future—Ecumenical, Interreligious and Secular Perspectives on the Council's Impact and Promise.*

Staged across several days, this constituted the 9th international gathering of the *Ecclesiological Investigations International Research Network* (EI).[2] The Network was founded in 2005—its *raison d'être* arising out of the realization that many different churches and religious

---

[1] The second volume was published simultaneously with this present one, and is entitled *Catholicism Engaging Other Faiths*. The third volume is edited by Peter De Mey on the 'hard sayings' of Vatican II— passages and conceptions in conciliar texts that remain stumbling blocks for dialogue.

[2] See www.ei-research.net. The full program as well as films and images from many of the conference sessions can be accessed at http://dc2015.ei-research.net.

G. Mannion (✉)
Department of Theology, Georgetown University, Washington, DC, USA
e-mail: gm751@georgetown.edu

© The Author(s) 2018
V. Latinovic et al. (eds.), *Catholicism Opening to the World and Other Confessions*, Pathways for Ecumenical and Interreligious Dialogue,
https://doi.org/10.1007/978-3-319-98581-7_1

communities from other traditions share common concerns and challenges, as well as hopes and aspirations. The network came into being to help facilitate the dialogue necessary to help diverse church and faith communities come to understand one another better, to understand themselves better, to engage and interact with the wider society in which people live out their faiths better and to help work toward common constructive ends.

EI, then, is an ecumenical venture established to promote dialogue, scholarship and collaboration in an open, pluralistic and inclusive spirit throughout the different churches, between Christianity and other faith communities, and between the church and secular societies. In particular, EI promotes collaborative ecclesiology in national, international, intra-ecclesial and ecumenical contexts. In addition to ecumenical and interreligious encounter and understanding, EI's work has an equally central and ongoing commitment to promoting dialogue toward the ends of enhancing social justice. The Network initiates research ventures and tries to help break new ground through making conversations, scholarship and education in these fields happen.

The commemorative Vatican II event received worldwide media attention, with highlights including keynote addresses from the late Cardinal Jean-Louis Tauran (President of the Vatican's Pontifical Council for Interreligious Dialogue and who announced to the world the election of Pope Francis back in March 2013), who opened the event, from Cardinal Luis Antonio Tagle, Archbishop of Manila and a leading voice on many key committees in Rome, and a hugely significant address on the future of ecumenical dialogue, delivered during a moving ecumenical prayer service at Washington National Cathedral, by Cardinal Walter Kasper, President Emeritus of the Vatican's Pontifical Council for Christian Unity and a key adviser to Pope Francis, particularly on ecumenism.

The aim of this gathering was not merely to have academic reflections on dialogue but for participants to engage one another in dialogue during and beyond the gathering itself.

It was a gathering of people from all around the world, featuring well over 300 regular participants from different continents, churches, religions and multiple different academic disciplinary perspectives. Those speaking alone numbered around 133 different perspectives.

For the organizers, at times along the way, it felt as if we were not so much commemorating Vatican II as reconvening it!

WHY THIS COUNCIL?

For readers perhaps less familiar with the story of the council, the name—Vatican II—points to the fact that it was assembled at the Vatican, itself, as well as that it was only the second such council to be held there (after the first in 1869–1870). The main council sessions were held in St. Peter's Basilica itself. The council was a gathering of bishops, heads of religious orders, accompanied by an army of theologians and related specialists, along with many there to 'observe' proceedings from within and without the church. At the close of the council, the most substantive outcomes were the sixteen final documents agreed upon by varying majority votes among those assembled, the end result of painstaking preparations, discussions, arguments, revisions and finally promulgations over the course of its four sessions. Of varying degrees of importance, significance and length, these included four constitutions, three declarations and nine decrees. The council's true and lasting significance, however, would be with regard to the implementation of the ecclesial vision and reforms outlined in those documents and the resultant impact upon the church, its subsequent teaching and the life of Catholics worldwide.

Thanks to this council, day-to-day life for Catholics would be transformed in many ways. The church's organization, liturgy, outlook, teaching and self-understanding were all left transformed in deeply significant ways. The church became a more open church in many respects and it embraced the modern world, at last, vowing to learn from the 'signs of the times'. And the lives and ministry of priests, religious and bishops would equally be transformed. The Catholic Church's understanding of relations with other Christians, other religious traditions, as well as communities and people of no faith were likewise radically changed for the better.

But the story is neither as exclusively positive nor radically revolutionary as some accounts suggest. The conciliar documents contain much compromise, ambivalence and ambiguity on vital issues at multiple junctures. And, as with earlier councils in the church's history, many opposed the changes which Vatican II brought in and have continued to challenge aspects of its legacy down to this day.

Having allowed time for the dust of the cycle of fiftieth anniversaries to settle (and it was also judged prudent to wait some time to allow 'Vatican II anniversary fatigue' to subside), we believe it is a good moment to publish these volumes. This is particularly so because further time has now also passed to allow Pope Francis's agenda to further implement the spirit and intentions of Vatican II with regard to contemporary church-world, ecumenical and interfaith relations to become further consolidated and so better understood. As with the EI event out of which they arose, these volumes bring together an internationally renowned and diverse group of scholars and church leaders, alongside many exciting emerging voices to explore the Second Vatican Council, just as the cycle of sixtieth anniversary commemorations of the council dawns.

Remembering the Future of Vatican II

Why *this* theme, why these areas of focus, why the people involved who were there? The EI Network chose this theme to further expand and deepen the dialogue engaged in throughout its work since 2005, particularly through its previous eight international conferences. Following the original 2007 gathering at St. Deiniol's in Hawarden, Wales, invitations to which were sent out to a carefully selected global group of leading figures in ecclesiology and ecumenical dialogue and research, further past themes have included *Religious Pluralism*, held in Kottayam, India (2008); *The Household of God and Local Households* in Leuven, Belgium (2010); *Ecclesiology and Exclusion* in Dayton, Ohio (2011); *Religion Authority and the State* in Belgrade, Serbia (2013); *Hope in the Ecumenical Future* in Oxford, England (2014); *Christianity and Religions in China* in Hong Kong (2016); *The Reformation and Global Reconciliation* in Jena, Germany (2017); and *The Church and Migration: Global In-difference?* in Toronto, Canada (2018). In 2012, we broached a broader and more ambitious program in Assisi, Italy: *Pathways for Dialogue in the Twenty-First Century*, where we encouraged 'thinking outside the ecumenical box' in developing new methods and practices for ecumenical, interreligious and church-world dialogue. Since 2005, Ecclesiological Investigations has also organized multiple sessions each year as part of the American Academy of Religion's Annual Meeting which have proved further venues for groundbreaking dialogue, encounter and research. More recently, the Network has also been a regular part of the annual program for the European Academy of Religion which, to date, has met each year in Bologna, Italy.

The primary genesis for the precise theme of these volumes, and the event of which they reflect many of the fruits, was obviously the fiftieth anniversary of the conclusion of the Second Vatican Council. But its genesis was more than that. At times it seemed as if every institution and organization were marking Vatican II—our intention was to do something distinctive, something truly different. The core flash of inspiration that made this gathering something different came from Professor Brian Flanagan of Marymount University who conceived of the great idea of exploring what people from other churches, other religions and secular standpoints made of Vatican II. Thus EIDC 2015 was born. And there was also a feeling that it would enhance the quality of the conversations we hoped to encourage all the more if a still further distinctive dimension was added to the theme in order to channel the focus of this event, given the plethora of conferences marking Vatican II in recent times. The solution was to place the emphasis upon the *future*, rather than simply the past or indeed the present—this proved the final piece in the jigsaw. And so we embarked upon the road to *Vatican II, Remembering the Future: Ecumenical, Interfaith and Secular Perspectives on the Council's Impact and Promise*. It was not the most succinct and catchy of titles, but it was evocative of what we wanted to achieve across four days of what would become a packed and, we hoped, inspirational program.

Most distinctively, then, as with the original EI event, these volumes assess the council, its legacy and promise through the eyes of scholars and practitioners from beyond the Roman Catholic world, alongside perspectives from a wide variety of Catholic scholars, practitioners and church leaders within the Catholic tradition. So multiple Catholic assessments are brought into dialogue with contributions on the council and its key documents from Christians belonging to other churches, figures from other faith traditions and wider perspectives informed by secular-oriented research. The contributors come from a wide range of different disciplinary backgrounds and different contexts. The volumes include contributions from most continents and feature many contributions from pioneering and leading figures in their respective fields. They feature the voices of those who were around during the council itself as well as voices from scholars not yet born when the council closed. These volumes are dialogue in action. Each contribution has been substantially revised and expanded in the light of the gathering itself. All in all, each volume draws together a range of perspectives with international, disciplinary and experiential breadth and depth.

The pioneering film director, Christopher Nolan, has spoken of the score to the 1981 multiple Academy Award winning film, *Chariots of Fire*, as among his all-time favorites. Nolan described the electronica genre music by Vangelis—for a film set in the 1920s—as 'nostalgia for the future'. We hereby declare our unapologetic nostalgia for the future of Vatican II in these volumes.[3] So how and even why should we continue to go on remembering Vatican II in these volumes and into the future? The simple answer is because no matter what historical or rhetorical perspectives that have been put to the contrary—it was a monumental event of significance that changed the Roman Catholic Church and indeed helped change the world—in a positive sense—forever. This despite the opinion of the Archbishop of Dublin, John Charles McQuaid, who, returning from Vatican II in December 1965 famously told the people of Ireland that nothing had happened at the council and reassured his flock that 'You may have been worried by talk of changes to come. Allow me to reassure you: no change will worry the tranquility of your Christian lives'.[4] How wrong he would be proved to have been! On the contrary, Vatican II, was a monumental event in history, period, and arguably the most significant council ever in terms of its global impact upon Catholicism. These volumes bear testimony to the fact that the council continues to be an event of transformative power and influence throughout today's church and the world alike.

In the period of anniversaries relating to the council—especially the fortieth then fiftieth anniversary periods, there were many debates about whether the council's teachings and reforms primarily constituted continuity or discontinuity with earlier, particularly more recent periods of the church's history. This led to an especially rather pointed debate in recent years about whether anything really did happen at the council or not. A clear answer was given by the eminent church historian and Jesuit, John O'Malley, S.J.,

> the questions recur: Is there a "before" and an "after" Vatican II? Is there any noteworthy discontinuity between the council and what preceded it? Did anything happen? When the council ended in 1965 …, practically everybody would have answered those questions with a resounding

[3] 'Christopher Nolan', *Desert Island Discs* (Feburary 18th, 2018), BBC Radio Four, https://www.bbc.co.uk/programmes/b09rwygm.

[4] From a sermon reported in *The Irish Times*, December 10, 1965.

affirmative, to the point that ... Archbishop Lefebvre condemned the council as heretical and led a group into schism. Today, however, there are learned, thoughtful, and well-informed people who are responding in the negative. ... As a historian ... I believe we must balance the picture by paying due attention to the discontinuities. When we do so, one thing at least becomes clear: the council *wanted* something to happen.[5]

History will judge the council as a decisive era when the church sought to turn away (i.e., to embrace *metanoia*) from the monolithic world-renouncing character and style of magisterium and the ecclesial mindset that had begun in the late eighteenth century and been entrenched in the second half of the nineteenth century, early twentieth century and in an ongoing battle against totalitarian regimes in the mid-twentieth century. The church had for too long been characterized by a siege mentality against modernity and its ideas and social impact. With Vatican II that came to an end.

In calling the council, Pope John XXIII was essentially presenting the church with a series of daunting yet empowering challenges—how do we bring the church up to date? How do we engage the wider world in a constructive and positive fashion? How do we better discern the signs of *these* times? And how do we advance the cause of unity among the religions and churches of the world?

The church needed to move into a process of transition before those tasks could even begin to be addressed. In many ways, Catholicism is still in that period of transition. Anyone who wants to know how long processes of genuine reform and renewal can take has only to look at the Kyoto agreement from 1992—still awaiting implementation in so many ways, with some steps forward being achieved and yet intermittent steps backward along the way, too. A church council, of course, should be thought of as something even more long term and long range in scope and ambition.

Indeed, instead of asking what, if anything, happened at the council, a more fruitful approach today is to explore what is *happening* with Vatican II. This is a core task that these volumes give attention to, just as it was at the EI gathering *Vatican II: Remembering the Future*. Pope

---

[5] John O'Malley, S.J., "Vatican II: Did Anything Happen?" in *Vatican II: Did Anything Happen?*, ed. David G. Schultenover (New York and London: Continuum, 2007), 52–85 at 84–85. This passage admirably sums up O'Malley's now classic study, *What Happened at Vatican II* (Cambridge, MA: Harvard University Press, 2008).

Francis has also helped lead the way here. Very early on in his pontificate, he spoke of Vatican II as a 'beautiful work of the Holy Spirit'.[6] He also said that throughout the church we must ask whether we have we done enough to actualize what the Holy Spirit was willing the church to do through the vision of the council. Answering his own rhetorical question in the negative, he cut to the heart of the clashes over the council in recent decades, stating that 'We celebrate this anniversary, we put up a monument but we don't want it to upset us. We don't want to change and what's more there are those who wish to turn the clock back'.[7] His point was that those who resist the vision of the council are resisting the presence and work of the Holy Spirit in the church.

In some countries, particularly on the European continent and in North America, the first decade and a half of the twenty-first century is a period that has been termed the 'Battle for the Council', as differing interpretations of the conciliar documents jostled for supremacy. But this also follows from a process that has been going on since the late 1960s and which gathered pace in the '70s and which became an almost fanatical obsession for some groups in the church in recent decades.

Yves Congar once remarked in an interview that it would take thirty to fifty years for the council to really begin to bear fruit.[8] And if we are to agree with him, as opposed to Abbot B. C. Butler, who returned from the Second Vatican Council to his Benedictine brethren at Downside to enthuse about the council's decisions but also to caution them that those same teachings would take 'half a millennium' to implement (causing at least one brother to lament that that was far too long for him...!), then we are now living in the key period during which Vatican II's true and enduring legacy will hopefully become ever-more apparent.

---

[6] In a homily preached on April 16, 2013, as reported widely, for example, https://www.catholicnewsagency.com/news/rejecting-holy-spirits-work-in-vatican-ii-is-foolish-pope-says and https://www.ncronline.org/blogs/ncr-today/francis-vatican-ii-beautiful-work-holy-spirit. Alas, the report on the Vatican's own news website no longer features the original page on which it was reported: http://www.news.va/en/news/pope-2nd-vatican-council-work-of-holy-spirit-but-s. Furthermore, the summary record of the pope's homily that day also no longer records those words, see http://w2.vatican.va/content/francesco/en/cotidie/2013/documents/papa-francesco-cotidie_20130416_spirit.html.

[7] Ibid.

[8] The interview, 'Trente ans de souvenirs' (30 Years of Memories), was conducted in 1964, as cited in Joseph A. Komonchak, "On Yves M.-J. Congar, O.P. (1904–1995)," *Proceedings of the Catholic Theological Society of America* 59 (2004): 162–66 at 163.

Therefore, Vatican II is not simply ever more ancient history—its effects are only just starting to come into their own. There is much 'unfinished business' of the council and, in many ways, as Paul Lakeland has memorably said, it is 'a council that will never end'.[9]

DISCERNING THE FRUITS

So these volumes explore Vatican II's story and history, yes. They explore what mark it has left upon different communities and parts of the globe, yes. But above all else, their intention, in sum, is to relate those foregoing explorations to considering what is *going* to happen to Vatican II and to what will be its legacy in the future. *To such ends, each contributor was asked to consider and explore the council in general and/or particular conciliar documents in retrospective and prospective fashion: what difference did the council/particular documents make? What difference do they continue to make? What difference could they make in the future?*

Both of these first two volumes are broken down into key thematic sections as well as featuring treatments of major council documents and of questions, challenges and prospects ahead for the council's ongoing legacy and impact into the future. The intention is not simply for these all three volumes to mark the end of the cycles of conciliar anniversary programs in relation to the Second Vatican Council. But, and perhaps even more importantly, the essays contained throughout this trilogy genuinely aspire to contribute to the ongoing interpretation and advancement of the mission and legacy of the council through furthering discourse and understanding about Catholicism in relation to the wider world, to social justice, to ecumenical and interreligious dialogue.

CATHOLICISM OPENING TO OTHER CHURCHES, TO THE WIDER WORLD

This first volume explores how Catholicism began and continues to open its doors to the wider world and to other churches in embracing the ecumenical imperative. Who more fitting to offer a most hope-filled foreword then, than *John Borelli* and *Drew Christiansen, S.J.*, two veterans

---

[9] Paul Lakeland, *The Council That Will Never End* (Collegeville: Liturgical Press, 2013).

of so many initiatives to promote dialogue, ecumenism and peace, across many decades. Both were also vital members of the planning that made the original gathering out of which these volumes emerged possible and the fruitful event it became. This present chapter is followed by a masterfully incisive overview of the council's overall significance and substantive character by John O'Malley, S.J., that giant of conciliar history whom some of us are so privileged to call a colleague and friend.

Following a study of the twentieth century context preceding the council (and of the legacy of Pope Benedict XV as a surprising precursor of the inspiration for the council—*Agnes de Dreuzy*), the first thematic part of the volume then turns to engage the legacy of Vatican II in relation to issues such as ethics, social justice, church-world dynamics and economic activity (*Charles E. Curran* and *Matthew A. Shadle*). The focus then turns to a series of explorations of women and the church—before, during and after Vatican II (opening with *Patricia Madigan, O.P.*), including an ecumenical and feminist perspective on the council (*Mary McClintock Fulkerson*), as well as examinations of those tensions between women religious and the Vatican in recent decades (the late, much lamented *Anne Patrick, S.N.J.M.*), alongside a study of how the women at the council provide inspiration for the continued exercise of magisterium by women in the church, in line with Pope Francis's call for women to be involved in the highest decision-making processes in the church today and beyond (*Gerard Mannion*).

The following section is concerned with *inculturation* and the council via three in-depth studies of contextualized receptions of Vatican II that have received lesser attention to date—respectively in Papua (*Jan Nielen*), a study of the reception of *Lumen Gentium* among Asian women (*Agnes M. Brazal*) and a thought-provoking and original study of the ongoing fascination with the council of the movie industry in Hollywood (*Paul G. Monson*).

The first volume next turns to explore a range of *ecumenical readings of Vatican II*, including a Free Church perspective from one of the leading pioneers of the study of World Christianity (*Dale T. Irvin*), an analysis of the council vis-à-vis the churches of the Protestant Reformation from a veteran of the World Council of Churches (*Dagmar Heller*), a study of the role of Russian Orthodox conciliar observers in the context of Soviet-era politics (*Anastacia Wooden*), and an intricate account of how Vatican II helped to transform global Anglicanism (*Mark D. Chapman*).

Continuing with the ecumenical vein, the volume turns to consider *the fruits and the future of Vatican II's ecumenical opening*, beginning with a survey of the impact of *Unitatis Redintegratio* on actual processes of dialogue and what questions remain for the future (*Dorothea Sattler*), an historian's account of how Marian devotion in the light of the Council can continue to further the cause of church unity (*Patrick J. Hayes*) and one of the leading US ecumenists rounds off this section with an assessment of how the ecumenical imperative stands after Vatican II, surveying the greatest achievements and the most pressing challenges that remain (*Susan Wood, S.C.L.*).

This volume concludes with two inspiring and especially future-oriented contributions. First, that groundbreaking address on *the future of ecumenical dialogue* and of unity among churches and the human family in wider terms, delivered by *Cardinal Walter Kasper* at Washington National Cathedral, the wonderfully imposing Episcopalian center of worship in the USA's capital city. This address was reported widely around the globe and made a huge stir in ecumenical discussions across differing continents, providing much encouragement for the decades of dialogue ahead. It is equally fitting, then, that we have *Brian Flanagan* provide the volume's epilogue, as the voice of a younger generation of ecumenists and as the person who conceived of the idea of bringing together perspectives on Vatican II from beyond Roman Catholicism and who was equally vital in making the original gathering happen.

When Pope John XXIII opened Vatican II with that memorable address, *Gaudet Mater Ecclesia* ('Mother Church Rejoices'), he uttered the following words which encapsulate why it is important to go on remembering the future of Vatican II,

> … and they behave as though they have learned nothing from history, which is, nonetheless, the teacher of life. They behave as though at the time of former Councils everything was a full triumph for the Christian idea and life and for proper religious liberty. We feel We must disagree with these prophets of gloom, who are always forecasting disaster, as though the end of the world were at hand.[10]

---

[10] John XXIII, alloc. *Gaudet Mater Ecclesia*, AAS 54 (1962): 786–96; English translation from "Pope John's Opening Speech to the Council," in *Documents of Vatican II*, ed. Walter M. Abbott (New York: America Magazine, 1966), 710–19 at 712.

Indeed, today we have so very much to learn from history. We hope all three volumes will help further that task of allowing the history of the church not simply to be studied or even celebrated, as well as, where necessary, challenged, but also to allow that past to impact the present and the future in multiple positive and creative ways. Pope John's watchword for the council, *aggiornamento*, sums up such an aspiration in the most apt way possible.

CHAPTER 2

Deconstructing and Reconstructing a Cliché—Vatican II as a "Pastoral Council"

John O'Malley, S.J.

Dictionaries define a cliché as a trite or overused expression, a truism, a platitude. This definition implies that the cliché might well express a truth but that it at the same time distorts it, trivializes it or misdirects our attention. We generally recognize clichés when we hear them, but sometimes we are less alert than we should be. We take them at face value and then move on to something else.

From the moment Vatican II opened it has consistently been described as a pastoral council. The basis for the description is unassailable. Pope St. John XXIII on the day he opened the council, October 11, 1962, thus designated it. In his address that day, *Gaudet Mater Ecclesia*, he told the assembled prelates that the council was to be "predominantly pastoral in character."[1] The prelates heard the message. From that

---

[1] John XXIII, alloc. *Gaudet Mater Ecclesia*, AAS 54 (1962): 786–96; for an English translation, see "Pope John's Opening Speech to the Council," in *Documents of Vatican II*, ed. Walter M. Abbott (New York: *America* Magazine, 1966), 710–19.

J. O'Malley, S.J. (✉)
Washington, DC, USA
e-mail: jwo9@georgetown.edu

© The Author(s) 2018
V. Latinovic et al. (eds.), *Catholicism Opening to the World and Other Confessions*, Pathways for Ecumenical and Interreligious Dialogue, https://doi.org/10.1007/978-3-319-98581-7_2

point forward, speaker after speaker at the council, especially those from the so-called majority, insisted on the council's pastoral character and intent. The speakers from the majority sometimes used the term to calm the fears of those who opposed the direction the council seemed to be taking.

Without a doubt, Vatican II was a pastoral council, and it had a pastoral impact in the conventional sense of the term. To mention only one example, *Nostra Aetate* in effect gave the church a new pastoral mission, the mission to be an agent of reconciliation among the religions of the world. The popes, beginning with Paul VI himself, have faithfully carried that mission forward. In that regard, Pope John Paul II and now Pope Francis have been outstanding. On a broader scale, *Nostra Aetate* made clear to all Catholics that the Church could never again tolerate pogroms against Jews or promote crusades against "the infidels."

So, where is the cliché? What is wrong with designating Vatican II a pastoral council? In response, I will say that in essence there is nothing wrong with it. In fact, I want to vindicate this designation, but before it can be vindicated it must be deconstructed. Once deconstructed, it can be reconstructed and then emerge with greater force and deeper meaning.

The cliché must be deconstructed as it is currently understood because it tends to trivialize the council. This principally occurs in two ways. First, the label seems to imply that Vatican II is special in being pastoral, as if other councils were not. Secondly, it seems to imply, at least for some commentators, that the council's decrees are less substantial, more contingent, more subject to reform or even dismissal than the decrees from the supposedly great doctrinal councils of the past. Vatican II, like certain beers and soft drinks, is Council Lite.

Even more importantly, the cliché as currently understood misdirects our attention from what is utterly unique about the council's pastoral character. Vatican II was pastoral in such a radically new mode when compared with previous councils that before we can correctly use the expression "pastoral," we must purify it of the conventional understanding, reconstitute it in its proper breadth and depth, and only then let it return to its rightful place in the world with its head held high.

Let us begin to examine these issues by first comparing Vatican II with the Council of Trent, which is itself one of the history's greatest victims of our penchant for cliché. Even in the good old days before Vatican II, when the Council of Trent reigned supreme in the Catholic imagination,

Trent was known, in so far as it was known at all, only through excerpts of its decrees that appeared in theological textbooks. Through this medium, Trent became the exemplar *par excellence* of a doctrinal council. Our attention was thereby misdirected from the great pastoral accomplishments of the council, which in their importance for the church at least rival, and perhaps surpass, Trent's doctrinal accomplishments.

Without doubt, as Hubert Jedin argued over fifty years ago, the doctrinal masterpiece of the Council of Trent was its decree on justification, that is, its decree on the relationship between grace and free will. The council labored over the decree for seven long months. The result shows it. In so far as a decree on a profound mystery can be intellectually satisfying, the decree on justification is just that, but this means that the decree is complex and lacking in rhetorical punch. Tellingly indicative of the problem is that after the council, the persons who constructed the so-called Tridentine Profession of Faith could not summarize it in a few lines. They resorted instead to the vacuous expression, "I embrace and accept each and all the articles defined and declared by the most holy Synod of Trent concerning Original Sin and justification." The decree was a masterpiece but pastorally untranslatable.

Trent's decrees on the sacraments, which in terms of sheer quantity constitute by far the largest percentage of the council's doctrinal decrees, did little beyond ratifying standard medieval teaching, teaching which itself was no less complex than the treatment of justification. Yet, in some instances, as with Penance and the Eucharist, these decrees had a pastoral impact by giving preachers grist for promoting more frequent use of those sacraments, which became a hallmark of modern Catholicism.

We thus see how misleading the distinction between pastoral and doctrinal can be, as we, with Trent, without awareness slide from doctrinal to pastoral. But for Trent, we need not slide. Trent spent at least as much time on pastoral issues as it did on doctrinal ones. Pastoral issues were more hotly contested during the council and had a less ambiguous result. By its decrees forbidding bishops to hold more than one diocese at a time and pastors to hold more than one parish, by requiring bishops to reside in their dioceses and pastors in their parishes, and by requiring them once they were there to perform their traditional pastoral duties, Trent had a pastoral impact of immense import, whose fruits we enjoy today. By adding to bishops' list of duties the obligation of establishing a seminary in their diocese, Trent had a pastoral impact of similarly immense proportions.

Nonetheless, if we judge a council's dignity and *gravitas* by the number and importance of its doctrinal decrees, does not Vatican II still qualify as Council Lite? After all, Vatican II did not define a single doctrine. This absence, however, does not mean that Vatican II was not a teaching or doctrinal council. Nor does it automatically mean that the council's teachings are less important or less binding, solemnly approved as they were by the largest and most diverse gathering of prelates in the whole history of the Catholic church and then solemnly ratified by the Supreme Pontiff, Paul VI. If indeed, we look at the number and importance of Vatican II's teachings, Vatican II is not Council Lite but the very opposite.

The key themes of the Second Vatican Council are well known, but to consider the council's doctrinal character, we do well to briefly identify some of the highlights. Certainly toward the top of the list is the council's teaching that what God has revealed to us in Jesus Christ is not a set of propositions but his very person. In the same *Dei Verbum* the council taught that the Bible is truly inerrant but only in "the truth that God for the sake of our salvation wished confided to the sacred Scriptures" (DV 11), or as this constitution says elsewhere, inerrant only in what "serves to make the people of God live their lives in holiness and increase their faith" (DV 8). That last statement highlights the council's teaching, repeated again and again after it first appeared in *Lumen Gentium*, that the purpose of the church is to promote the holiness of its members. No previous council had taken the trouble to state that. Holiness became a leitmotif in the council's teaching.

The council taught that the church is constituted by the people in it, so that "the people of God" is a valid, crucially important, and, moreover, traditional expression of the reality of the church (LG 9–17). Since the people of God are everywhere on the face of the earth, the council, therefore, taught that the church was at home in every culture and needed to incarnate itself in each of them. Because the council also taught that the sacred liturgy was an act of the whole community at worship and was therefore essentially a participatory action, the liturgy itself had to admit into it symbols and customs of every culture. The council likewise shifted emphases on church structures, teaching that, while the structure of the church is hierarchical, it is also collegial, that is participatory (LG 18–29). In particular, it taught the traditional but formerly unexpressed doctrine that bishops when acting as a body with and under the Roman Pontiff have a responsibility not only for their own dioceses but for the church at large. It taught that just as the Roman Pontiff has a collegial relationship to other bishops, bishops were to foster a collegial relationship with their priests and priests with their people.

Vatican II taught that while the church has the heavy responsibility of proclaiming the Gospel to the world, it also has the responsibility of exerting itself for the well-being of the world as such, that is, to exert itself for the well-being of the so-called temporal order—to be concerned about social justice, about the heinousness of modern war, about the blessing of peace, and about the advance of every aspect of human culture (GS 76). It taught that it is incumbent on Catholics to work with others, even non-believers, in promoting such goals. It at the same time taught that this proclamation was not a one-way street, but that, just as the church benefited the world, the world benefited the church. The church must, therefore, listen to the world and, learn from it—a remarkable and utterly unprecedented teaching (GS 4, 11, 44, et passim).

The council taught that it was the duty of the church and of every Catholic to respect the religious beliefs of others (DH 15) and to work for reconciliation among the Christian churches (UR, esp. 4, 15, 24). It taught, as I mentioned earlier, that the church had the further and perhaps more difficult mission to seek reconciliation even with other religions, a mission so desperately needed in the world today. It in that regard taught that, although proclamation was the privileged Christian form of discourse, dialogue was also a legitimate form and, in some instances, a more appropriate one (AG 11–12).

The council taught the dignity of marriage (GS 47–52). It taught that marriage was essentially a partnership in love (GS 48). It further taught that, while children were the great blessing of marriage, for appropriate reason couples could limit the number of their children (GS 50–51). It taught that women had a right to "legitimate social advancement" (GS 52).

In the temporal order, the council taught the dignity and excellence of political freedom. It taught the right of persons to follow their consciences in the choice of religion, and, more generally, it taught in some of its most moving words the dignity of conscience, "that most secret core and the sanctuary of the human person, where they are alone with God whose voice echoes in their depths" (GS 16). In that regard, the council explicitly taught that grace and the Holy Spirit were operative outside the visible confines of the Catholic Church and that salvation was, therefore, possible outside those confines (LG 16).

The council taught, to use its own words, that "any discrimination against people or any harassment of them on the basis of their race, color, condition of life or religion," was, "foreign to the mind of Christ" (NA 5). Vatican II taught, moreover, that "the church reproves every form of persecution against whomsoever it may be directed" (NA 4).

Finally, the council taught that "The joys and hopes, the grief and anguish of the people of our time, especially of those who are poor or afflicted, are the joys and hopes, the grief and anguish of the followers of Christ as well. Nothing that is genuinely human fails to find an echo in their hearts. For theirs is a community of people united in Christ and guided by the Holy Spirit in their pilgrimage towards the Father's kingdom, bearers of a message of salvation for all humanity" (GS 1).

These and other teachings of the council are not trivial. They are not of a secondary level of importance. They are not platitudes or pious palaver. True, they are not of the same constitutive level of Christian belief as are the doctrines of the Trinity and Incarnation, but they are nonetheless truths of the utmost importance for understanding the practical implications of those doctrines and for understanding what it means to be a Christian in the world today. If we understand them in that sense, they become pastoral truths and pastoral teachings. Even that phrase illustrates the problem with our conciliar cliché. "Pastoral teachings": as opposed to what? What is the alternative to pastoral teachings? Did God reveal academic teachings or academic truths? I do not think so.

I find it difficult to name an alternative to pastoral teaching, especially if we agree with *Dei Verbum* that what God revealed was truths pertinent to our salvation. God revealed, in other words, "the message of salvation." Put in still other words, as does *Dei Verbum*, God revealed "what serves to make the people of God live their lives in holiness and increase their faith" (DV 8). Does not this mean, then, that by definition all Christian truths are pastoral truths? Are we then saying that Vatican II is a pastoral council by means of its teaching, by means of its doctrine? I think we are.

All the councils before Vatican II operated as essentially legislative and judicial bodies. This pattern was set long before the Council of Nicaea, but Nicaea provides the classic exemplar of it. Virtually all these councils, both hundreds upon hundreds of local councils and the twenty-one ecumenical councils, had a pastoral component. In some, perhaps in most of the medieval councils, that component was the dominant one. But as legislative bodies, those councils pursued their pastoral goals by passing laws that prescribed or proscribed certain behaviors, and they usually attached penalties for failure to observe the prescription or proscription. That is, after all, how laws operate. The Council of Trent effected its great pastoral reform of the episcopate precisely in this way. We must remember too, that prior councils pursued their doctrinal agenda in precisely the same way, by prescribing or proscribing certain behaviors. Councils were not directly concerned with what persons might believe in the secret of their hearts but in what they *say* and in what they *taught*. "If anyone should *say* such and such, let him be anathema." Does not this mean that even the so-called doctrinal decrees are in fact pastoral decrees in that their most direct and most obvious aim is proper public order in the church, which is what pastoral means in this legislative-judicial context?

Be that as it may, we must realize that with Vatican II we are in a brand-new situation. When the council implicitly but categorically rejected the legislative-judicial model of discourse and adopted a different one, it made a decision with the most radical implications. In the first place, the new model redefined what a council is and what it is about, which therefore demanded a new hermeneutic for interpreting and understanding it. Moreover, the new model dismantled whatever might have been valid in the classic—or clichéd—distinction between a doctrinal and a pastoral council. Vatican II was pastoral through its teachings, that is, through its doctrine. Ah, the cliché that Vatican II was a pastoral council has returned to us vindicated, vindicated but radically redefined. Deconstructed it now returns reconstructed. Vatican II was a pastoral council not in the conventional sense of ensuring proper public order in the church but in teaching the truths that "serve to help people live their lives in holiness and to increase their faith." In a word, Vatican II was pastoral by being doctrinal.

When during the first year of the council Cardinal Alfredo Ottaviani introduced the now infamous draft document, "On the Sources of Revelation," he spoke for only five minutes, less as presenting a text for consideration than as defending it even before the discussion began. He said, in part, "You have heard many people speak about the lack of a pastoral tone in this document. Well, I say that the first and most fundamental pastoral task is to provide correct doctrine... Teaching correctly is what is fundamental to being pastoral." I have argued here that the Second Vatican Council can be described as a pastoral council precisely by virtue of being doctrinal. One can only hope that Cardinal Ottaviani would be pleased with me.

PART II

Opening to the World—The Turn to Moral Mission and Social Justice

CHAPTER 3

Benedict XV: A Most Unexpected Architect of Vatican II

Agnes de Dreuzy

INTRODUCTION

The short reign of Pope Benedict XV (1914–1922) has been little appreciated and largely overlooked by scholars; to quote one, Benedict's contributions have been "fading into almost complete obscurity."[1] However, the often invisible but real influence that Benedict exerted on the Second Vatican Council demands a reappraisal of his pontificate. His understanding of the role of the church in the new world order that emerged from the Great War informed John XXIII, Paul VI, and the Council Fathers in their discussion regarding the opening of the church to the modern world. His pontificate was foundational in developing a new spirit of openness to the world that was embraced by the Council. Benedict's farsighted vision of the church manifested itself in his defense of international peace, his actions in favor of Christian unity,

[1] John F. Pollard, *The Unknown Pope: Benedict XV (1914–1922) and the Pursuit of Peace* (London: Geoffrey Chapman, 1999), xiii.

A. de Dreuzy (✉)
St. Mark's College at UBC, Vancouver, BC, Canada

© The Author(s) 2018
V. Latinovic et al. (Eds.), *Catholicism Opening to the World and Other Confessions*, Pathways for Ecumenical and Interreligious Dialogue, https://doi.org/10.1007/978-3-319-98581-7_3

25

and in a new understanding of the church's missionary activity. Benedict XV deserves a place among the architects of the Second Vatican Council, even though he may be among the most unexpected ones.

BENEDICT AND HIS SUCCESSORS

Benedict XV was born Giacomo Della Chiesa on November 21, 1854, into a noble Genoese family. He was ordained a priest in 1878, graduated doctor of theology *cum laude* in 1879, and received a doctorate in canon law in 1880. He later became a student at the Academy of Noble Ecclesiastics, "the training ground of Vatican diplomats."[2] Under the pontificate of Pius X (1903–1910) Della Chiesa held office at the Curia under the new Secretary of State Rafael Cardinal Merry del Val before being "exiled" to the see of Bologna in 1907. This move was interpreted as a covert dismissing of a prelate who had been held under suspicion of modernism. He was named cardinal in 1914, barely three months before his election to the throne of Peter on September 3, one month after the start of the First World War.

The responsibilities Pope Benedict gave to the men who would eventually hold his office demonstrate the bond of trust and confidence they shared. Benedict sent the future Pius XI as his personal representative, then as nuncio to Poland, making him a fine diplomat well aware of the struggle of the European continent. Once he was elected Pope Pius XI after the death of Pope Benedict, Pius XI kept Cardinal Gasparri as his Secretary of State, an important sign of continuity between their two reigns. Benedict's decision to appoint Eugenio Pacelli, the future Pius XII, as Secretary of the Department of Extraordinary Ecclesiastical Affairs in 1914 is even more important. Benedict sent Pacelli as nuncio to Munich in 1917 where he presented a *Peace Note*[3] to the Germans. These were crucial appointments as Vatican II would not have been possible without Pius XII's contribution.[4]

Benedict XV's reign was an overture to the reigns of Pius XI and Pius XII. Many of their achievements were made possible by Pope Benedict,

---

[2] Ibid., 7.

[3] Benedict XV, Apostolic Exhortation *Dès le début*, AAS 9 I (1917): 417–20 (French), 421–23 (Italian).

[4] The 16 documents of Vatican II make no less than 180 references to him and his teaching.

but among the popes who followed him, John XXIII arguably relied the most on Benedict and his modern understanding of the role of the church in the modern world. Benedict called Angelo Roncalli, the future John XXIII, to become Italian President of the Society for the Propagation of the Faith, a move that put Roncalli in regular contact with the pontiff. This appointment was the first major step on his path to the papacy. According to Peter Hebblethwaite, John XXIII's biographer, Benedict XV was John XXIII's favorite pope.[5] Roncalli had been the personal secretary of one of Benedict XV's best friends, Bishop Radini Tedeschi. His close friendship with and great admiration for the bishop of Bergamo were instrumental in the future pontiff's life and his calling the Second Vatican Council.

A REAPPRAISAL: BENEDICT XV AS AN UNEXPECTED ARCHITECT OF VATICAN II

The carnage of World War I forced Pope Benedict XV to develop new perspectives on the place of the church in the world. His vision was well ahead of his time, equipping the church for its future. His successors were all influenced by his understanding of the postwar world order and of the role of the church in this new context. The same new spirit of opening the church to a reshaped world permeates John XXIII's encyclical *Pacem in Terris*[6] and many of the documents of the Second Vatican Council. Key council documents largely vindicate Pope Benedict's vision, although they explicitly cite him and his teachings rarely. Close analysis of the constitutions *Lumen Gentium, Dei Verbum,* and *Gaudium et Spes,* and the decrees *Orientalium Ecclesiarum, Unitatis Redintegratio,* and *Ad Gentes* all show the meaningful degree to which Benedict's papacy shaped the Council's reflections on a diverse array of themes. At first glance, however, Benedict's influence seems comparatively minimal. These documents refer to him or his teachings seventeen times; by comparison, the texts cite Pius XII 101 times and mention Leo XIII and Pius XI thirty-three and thirty-six times, respectively. Only two of Benedict XV's writings are noticed more than once in the documents of Vatican II. His groundbreaking apostolic letter *Maximum Illud,* on

[5] Peter Hebblethwaite, *John XXIII: Pope of the Century* (London: Continuum, 2000).

[6] John XXIII, Encyclical Letter *Pacem in Terris,* AAS 55 (1963): 257–304.

the propagation of the faith throughout the world,[7] is mentioned twelve times—twice in *Lumen Gentium* and ten times in *Ad Gentes*, more than any other pontiff's writings. *Dei Verbum* cites his encyclical on St. Jerome, *Spiritus Paraclitus*,[8] three times. One would also expect to find mention of Benedict XV in the pastoral constitution *Gaudium et Spes*, due to the influence he exerted on his successors in his modern understanding of the role of the church in the modern world. While Pius XI and Pius XII are mentioned 41 times together, Benedict XV's name or writings appears nowhere in the document.

Looking exclusively at the direct mention of Benedict XV in the documents of Vatican II gives an incomplete picture of the role he effectively played during the Council. Popes Pius XI and Pius XII frequently mention Pope Benedict's writings in their encyclicals, as do other documents quoted in the official documents of Vatican II. The writings of popes Pius XI and Pius XII cited Benedict's *Maximum Illud* twenty times and his *Spiritus Paraclitus* five times. The motu proprio *Orientis Catholici*[9] that founded the Pontifical Oriental Institute and *Dei Providentis*,[10] which detached the Congregation for the Oriental Church from *Propaganda Fide*, is mentioned seven times by these two popes, and his inaugural encyclical *Ad Beatissimi*[11] and his brief *Quod Nobis*[12] are cited four times.

Therefore, Benedict XV had an influence on the documents of Vatican II through both the direct and indirect mention of his teaching, being mentioned fifty-three times.

Catholic Peacemaking: International Peace, Reconciliation, and Just War Doctrine

The received narrative on Catholic peacemaking is that the great shift in the Magisterium about war and peace came with Pope John XXIII, when "a moral theology concerned with defining and limiting war moved to a

---

[7] Benedict XV, Apostolic Letter *Maximum Illud*, AAS 11 (1919): 440–55.

[8] Benedict XV, Encyclical Letter *Spiritus Paraclitus*, AAS 12 (1920): 389–422.

[9] Benedict XV, Motu Proprio *Orientis Catholici*, AAS 9 I (1917): 531–33.

[10] Benedict XV, Motu Proprio *Dei Providentis*, AAS 9 I (1917): 529–31.

[11] Benedict XV, Encyclical Letter *Ad Beatissimi Apostolorum Principis*, AAS 6 (1914): 585–99.

[12] Benedict XV, Brief *Quod Nobis*, AAS 12 (1920): 440–41.

theology of peace aimed at implementing the Sermon on the Mount."[13] A closer look reveals that Pope Benedict's actions during the Great War began the transition that culminated with John XXIII's encyclical *Pacem in Terris* and Vatican II's *Gaudium et Spes*, a document that cannot be understood apart from the context of John's encyclical.

World War I changed the nature of warfare. We observed a move from classic war to total war bringing unprecedented threats to civilian populations. Benedict XV's main contribution in this domain is the new way he approached the problem of war, rejecting the dichotomy between just and unjust war[14] and maintaining active neutrality. In a context of total war, the pontiff challenged the just war theory as a guarantee for just peace. He addressed *jus post bellum* justice through the channel of reconciliation and forgiveness as political and theological principles, arguing that violations of the *jus ad bellum* and *jus in bello* principles of just war theory should not give either the victorious powers or the international community the right to impose justice, even softened by mercy. In his *Peace Note* of 1917 to the leaders of the warring nations, he qualified the war of "useless slaughter" and "suicide of civilized Europe" and voluntarily avoided speaking about just or unjust war.[15] He was vilified for this choice by governments, lay people, and clergymen alike, but for Benedict "whether just or unjust, war is the supreme disaster, a disaster for which nothing can compensate."[16] Furthermore, the war meant a dangerous disruption of unity and loyalty to the Holy See.

After Pope Benedict's reign and until John XXIII's pontificate and the Second Vatican Council, commitment to peace was often conditional and evolved in steps. At the time of the Second World War, just war theory was the official doctrine, despite the tension between that very doctrine and Pope Benedict's previous position. Pope John XXIII's

[13] Ronald G. Musto, *The Catholic Peace Tradition* (Maryknoll: Orbis, 1986), 187.

[14] Ibid., 104: "The theory of just war is not Christian in any proper sense of the word: it has no biblical, theological, or canonical foundation." The just war doctrine was first articulated by St. Ambrose and later developed by St. Augustine and St. Thomas Aquinas. According to it, all governments have an obligation to avoid war, but in some specific circumstances, can wage war in order to obtain justice. The act must be morally justifiable, be a last resort, be done with the right intention, and be proportional to the offense.

[15] Benedict XV, *Dès le début*, 420, 423.

[16] D. A. Binchy, "The Vatican and International Diplomacy," *International Affairs* 22 (January 1946): 50.

landmark encyclical *Pacem in Terris* rehabilitated Benedict XV's teaching on war and peace by promoting humanitarian assistance, nonviolence, and the defense of human rights as foundational to attain peace. Although John offered a wider and more complex teaching on war and peace, his understanding of the relation between the two goes back to Benedict's own rejection of violence, his call to respect human dignity, and the use he made of the Vatican's humanitarian intervention as a mean to restore peace.[17] Early in his diplomatic career, Roncalli realized that mercy and charity were key in time of war and that "this will have to be the whole world's task tomorrow if we want the future to belong to Christendom and not to become a prey to barbarism and chaos."[18]

The Second Vatican Council adopted a slightly different and subtler position. While discussing the issue of war and peace during the drafting of Chapter 5 of *Gaudium et Spes*, the Council Fathers made clear that the church was not renouncing just war theory in cases of legitimate defense. *Gaudium et Spes* declared that "As long as the danger of war remains and there is no competent and sufficiently powerful authority at the international level, governments cannot be denied the right to legitimate defense once every means of peaceful settlement has been exhausted" (GS 79). Still, the council rejected the idea of preventive war and stressed the rejection of total war. Conflict, if absolutely necessary, must be limited in scope. This crucial aspect of Pope Benedict's magisterium was reiterated at Vatican II in the new context of potential atomic war. *Gaudium et Spes* is very clear on this point, stating that "any act of war aimed indiscriminately at the destruction of entire cities of extensive areas along with their population is a crime against God and man himself. It merits unequivocal and unhesitating condemnation."[19] Following in Benedict XV's footsteps, the Council Fathers asserted that there is no room for just or unjust war discussions in this specific context. *Gaudium et Spes* thus represents a move toward a pacifist spirit but does not go to the point of completely rejecting war, an important nuance in comparison with Benedict XV's more absolute position.

---

[17] During the Great War, the Vatican was dubbed the "Second Red Cross." It tracked and secured the exchanges of thousands of prisoners of war, rescued civil populations from complete destitution, from starvation, and tried to prevent massacres in Armenia.

[18] John XXIII, *Letters to His Family* (New York: McGraw-Hill, 1970), 437, cited in Giancarlo Zizola, *The Utopia of Pope John XXIII* (Maryknoll: Orbis, 1978), 35.

[19] Ibid., 80.

Christian Reconciliation

In his inaugural encyclical *Ad Beatissimi* Pope Benedict wrote: "Who would imagine as we see them thus filled with hatred of one another, that they are... all members of the same human society? Who would recognize brothers, whose Father is in Heaven?"[20] To the pontiff, peace is not the result of a balance of power, but instead answers a requirement of nature that asks us to embrace a brotherhood of man because we all have God as Father.[21]

The same language is used in *Gaudium et Spes*. The Council Fathers reiterate Benedict XV's idea that "God, who has fatherly concern for everyone, has willed that all men should constitute one family and treat one another in a spirit of brotherhood" (GS 24), declaring later that "He has chosen men not just as individuals but as members of a certain community... This communitarian character is developed and consummated in the work of Jesus Christ" (GS 32). Because men are meant to be brothers united in love, Benedict XV and the Council Fathers came to the same conclusion that "peace results from that order structured into human society by its divine Founder" (GS 78). Therefore, one could conclude that, for a majority of the Council Fathers, this entailed that the greatest duty of the church is thus to develop a spirit of love, unity, and concord in order to maintain that order.

In his encyclical on peace, *Pacem Dei Munus*,[22] Benedict XV already insisted on the necessity to develop this spirit of love, the "love of others," and implored the bishops to "urge the faithful entrusted to [their] care to abandon hatred and to pardon offences."[23] In a most concrete way, Pope Benedict XV fought for a postwar settlement that would guarantee a just peace for the future. He argued that excessive and unreasonable demands for reparations as imposed by the Treaty of Versailles against Germany and its allies would destroy trust between states and individuals. Both the victorious powers and the international community, as represented by the new League of Nations, should, therefore, consider forgiveness and reconciliation as foundational principles to establish a just peace in the long term and avoid resentment and future violence.

[20] Benedict XV, *Ad Beatissimi*, 3.

[21] Joseph Joblin, "Le Saint Siège face à la guerre," *Gregorianum* 80 (1999): 306.

[22] Benedict XV, Encyclical Letter *Pacem Dei Munus*, AAS 12 (1920): 209–18.

[23] Benedict XV, *Pacem Dei Munus*, 7, 10, 13.

In *Pacem Dei Munus* Pope Benedict warned that "there can be no stable peace or lasting treaties, though made after long and difficult negotiations and duly signed, unless there be a return of mutual charity to appease hate and banish enmity."[24] *Gaudium et Spes* concurs with this insight, stating that "the teaching of Christ requires that we forgive injuries, and extends the law of love to include every enemy" (GS 28) and that "insofar as men vanquish sin by a union of love, they will vanquish violence as well" (GS 78).

The concept of the union of love and the unity of the human family, originally proposed by Benedict XV as foundational to ensure just and lasting peace, is clearly articulated in both *Lumen Gentium* and *Gaudium et Spes* as belonging to the nature of the church. In *Lumen Gentium* the Council defined the church as a "sacrament – a sign and instrument, that is, of communion with God and of unity among all men" (LG 1), and affirms in *Gaudium et Spes* that "the promotion of unity belongs to the innermost nature of the Church, for she is, 'thanks to her relationship with Christ, a sacramental sign and an instrument of intimate union with God, and of the unity of the whole human race'" (GS 42). That Benedict's encyclical *Pacem Dei Munus* finds no mention in the Council documents is striking, given the Council's obvious vindication of Benedict's approach to the issue of Christian reconciliation.

COMMUNITY OF NATIONS WITH PEACEMAKING FUNCTIONS

In the *Peace Note* of August 1917, Benedict XV had alluded to the creation of a community of nations stating that "instead of armies [he was calling for] the institution of arbitration with its lofty peacemaking function."[25] His thoughts on this topic evolved and matured. In *Pacem Dei Munus*, he calls for an "association of nations," a "sort of family of peoples"[26] and mentioned a Christian league inspired by principles of morality, integrity, and forgiveness. When Pope John XXIII speaks of a "universal common good"[27] in *Pacem in Terris*, he does not explicitly refer to Benedict XV but is clearly inspired by him. Both popes insist on

---

[24] Ibid., 1.
[25] Benedict XV, *Dès le début*, 417–20.
[26] Benedict XV, *Pacem Dei Munus*, 17.
[27] John XXIII, *Pacem in Terris*, 132–34, 137–38.

the "moral force of law"[28] and collective sanctions against the aggressor. While Benedict's *Peace Note* asks for "the institution of arbitration, with its lofty peacemaking function, according to the standards to be agreed upon and with sanctions to be decided against the State which might refuse to submit international questions to arbitration or to accept its decisions,"[29] Pope John develops his predecessor's thought in *Pacem in Terris*, stating that "the universal common good presents us with problems which are worldwide in their dimensions; problems, therefore, which cannot be solved except by a public authority with power, organization and means coextensive with these problems, and with a worldwide sphere of activity. Consequently, the moral order itself demands the establishment of some such general form of public authority."[30]

The Council documents, especially *Gaudium et Spes*, also affirm that the establishment of a world authority is a prerequisite to outlawing war. "It is our clear duty," states *Gaudium et Spes*, "to strain every muscle in working for the time when all war can be completely outlawed by international consent. This goal undoubtedly requires the establishment of some universal public authority acknowledged as such by all and endowed with the power to safeguard on the behalf of all, security, regard for justice, and respect for rights" (GS 81). A strong, just, and merciful international organization undergirds both Pope Benedict and the Council Fathers' vision of the peaceful development of the international community.

The Church's Role in the New World Order

Benedict XV's pontificate was a turning point regarding the role of the church in the new, postwar, world order. His diplomatic initiatives manifested the will of the church to participate in the transformation of the world not as a political force but as a moral authority. Benedict, in *Pacem Dei Munus*, was the first modern pope to sketch a Christian doctrine of international relations. He argues that the church, now "delivered" from

---

[28] Benedict XV, *Dès le début*, 418, 421.
[29] Ibid., 418–19, 422.
[30] John XXIII, *Pacem in Terris*, 137.

the Papal States, was not above the world but actively guiding it through the "precept of mutual charity."[31]

Two main guidelines structured his thought. He anticipated the movement of decolonization and the geo-political revolution that took place after the war. He prepared the global church for the future, liberating it from its identification to the Eurocentric model and guaranteeing its independence from imperial powers. The papacy became the center of the post-war world and acquired a renewed spiritual and political prestige worldwide, reinforcing its universal appeal.[32] In their relationship with the Holy See, most European powers were looking for political and social support in the wake of the militantly atheist Bolshevik Revolution and were keen to reconnect with their European Christian cultural heritage. Pope Benedict set an example of how to build the new world of international relations, guaranteeing long-term peaceful results.

In this context, Benedict developed in *Pacem Dei Munus* a Christian internationalism based on a just and fraternal international society following the Gospel's precepts.[33] In *Pacem Dei Munus* he declares that "the Church will certainly not refuse her zealous aid to States united under the Christian law in any of their undertakings inspired by justice and charity."[34] The barbarism of the war had undermined European confidence in its superiority, allowing the church to be proactive. This new positive interaction of the church with the world was rediscovered and embraced at Vatican II. It permeates most conciliar documents, but especially *Gaudium et Spes*, which insists that the church "exists in the world, living and acting with it" (GS 40). One must also note the pragmatic character of Benedict's approach here. He chose to intervene in the life of the international community with the specific goal of bringing a terrible world conflict to an end and ensuring a long and just peace. One could say that Vatican II and especially Paul VI developed his approach and supplemented it with added dimensions—particularly through

[31] Benedict XV, *Pacem Dei Munus*, 5: "Nothing was so often and so carefully inculcated on His disciple by Jesus Christ as this precept of mutual charity as the one which contains all others... 'Let us love one another for charity is God.'"

[32] Sisley Huddleston, "The Revival of the Vatican," *The Fortnightly Review*, July 1920, 67–77; Alexis François, *Semaine littéraire de Genève*, 29 October 1921.

[33] See Philippe Chenaux, "Les regards du Vatican sur la construction européenne," *Journal de Genève*, 8 October 1988.

[34] Benedict XV, *Pacem Dei Munus*, 18.

renewed establishment of and support for bilateral and international relations between the church and external states and institutions—especially with the subsequent more direct engagement by the church in such ventures and on the international stage.

The Church's Civilizing and Evangelizing Mission

Pope Benedict's apostolic letter *Maximum Illud*, promulgated on November 30, 1919, is the Magna Carta of foreign missions. It paved the way for *Lumen Gentium, Gaudium et Spes* and the decree *Ad Gentes* on missions.

In *Maximum Illud*'s chapter on "Those in Charge of the Missions," Benedict XV calls the bishops to be on the forefront declaring that "We want to address those who are in charge of the missions, whether as Bishops or as Vicars or Prefects Apostolic. All the responsibility for the propagation of the Faith rests immediately upon them, and it is to them especially that the church has entrusted her prospects of expansion."[35] Later in the encyclical, he sounds the alarm, appealing to the superior of missions and bishops "for a particularly vigorous approach to this problem [of scarcity of missionaries due to the war]. You will be performing a service eminently worthy of your love of the Faith," he wrote, "if you take pains to foster any signs of a missionary vocation that appear among your priests and seminarians."[36] *Lumen Gentium* references Benedict's teaching here when it asserts that although "each disciple of Christ has the obligation of spreading the faith to the best of his ability" (LG 17) it is the task of the episcopal College to announce the Gospel in the world through the help of their pastors.[37]

In this groundbreaking encyclical on missions, Benedict indicates three priorities: the formation of a native clergy, the recognition of the human dignity of all men and cultures, and missionaries' renunciation of nationalistic attitudes. Each of these priorities is developed in

---

[35] Benedict XV, *Maximum Illud*, 8.

[36] Ibid., 34.

[37] See also *Lumen Gentium* 23: "The task of announcing the Gospel in the whole world belongs to the body of pastors... Consequently, the bishops, each for his own part, in so far as the due performance of their own duty permits, are obliged to enter into collaboration with one another... Thus, they should come to the aid of the missions by every means in their power, supplying both harvest workers and also spiritual and material aids."

the documents of the Second Vatican Council. Regarding the formation of the native clergy, the pontiff wrote that it was crucial to "secure and train local candidates for the sacred ministry. In this policy lies the greatest hope of the new churches."[38] He introduced a new understanding of the goal of missions from saving souls to planting new churches. *Ad Gentes* (Vatican II Decree on the Mission Activity of the Church) develops this point, stating that "the proper purpose of this missionary activity is evangelization, and the planting of the church among those peoples and groups where it has not yet taken root. Thus from the seed which is the word of God, particular autochthonous churches should be sufficiently established and should grow up all over the world, endowed with their own maturity and vital forces. Under a hierarchy of their own, together with the faithful people... they should make their contribution to the good of the whole Church" (AG 6). From this local clergy eventually emerged the first local bishops whose successors represented the universal Catholic Church and its different cultures at Vatican II.

Pope Benedict was also very attentive to cultural sensitivity asserting that "the local priest... is remarkably effective in appealing to [the faithful's] mentality and thus attracting them to the Faith."[39] Benedict's understanding of the priest's role includes the pope's commitment to the equality of all peoples, clearly expressed in *Maximum Illud*: "He [the priest] represents a Faith in which 'there is no Gentile, no Jew... no slave, no free man, but Christ is everything in each of us' (Col 3:12)."[40] A paradigm shift occurred under Benedict's pontificate that was reinforced at Vatican II. The church engaged in new interaction with non-European cultures, recognizing the richness of local cultures and what they can offer to Christianity. *Lumen Gentium* tells us that "the Church... fosters and takes to itself, insofar as they are good, the ability, riches and customs in which the genius of each people expresses itself" (LG 13). *Gaudium et Spes* reinforces this idea, stating that the church is at the service of the world and "is not bound exclusively and indissolubly to any particular way of life or any customary way of life recent or ancient" (GS 58).

---

[38] Benedict XV, *Maximum Illud*, 14.
[39] Ibid.
[40] Ibid., 20.

Pope Benedict was the first pontiff to think in terms of globalization[41] and pave the way for the teaching of *Gaudium et Spes* on the human equality of men and women. This regard for equality supposes the renunciation by Catholic missionaries to impose their own national identity on local populations. Benedict XV drew a line between mission and imperialism. The international missionary network gradually moved away from a nationalistic spirit, eventually becoming the cornerstone on which Pope Benedict anchored the church in the modern world and prepared it for a universal mission embraced at the Second Vatican Council.

John XXIII was greatly influenced by *Maximum Illud* and the encyclicals on mission penned by Benedict's two successors on the papal throne.[42] Roncalli's appointment as President for Italy of the Central Council of the Papal Missions[43] in 1921 put him at the center of Benedict XV's missionary effort and helped him understand and apply the pontiff's revolutionary vision. Decades later, in a new world order built around the dynamic of the Cold War and the tensions between North and South, Pope John and the Council Fathers started to disengage the church from a Eurocentrism that had already been condemned and attacked by Pope Benedict and shifted its evangelizing efforts to the South.

Christian Unity

According to the new 1917 Code of Canon Law, published during Benedict XV's pontificate, non-Catholics were forbidden from joining Catholic associations. This severely limited the spiritual contact between Catholics and perceived "dissidents," but one could perceive other actions of the pontiff to have indirectly helped prepare the way for a future Catholic embrace of ecumenism. Benedict's main interest was the Oriental

[41] See Francesca Aran Murphy, "Globalization from Benedict XV to Benedict XVI: The 'Astonishing Optimism' of *Gaudium et Spes* in a Missionary Context," *Nova et Vetera*, English Edition, 8 (Spring 2010): 395–424.

[42] See Pius XI, Encyclical Letter *Rerum Ecclesiae*, AAS 18 (1926): 65–83; Pius XII, Encyclical Letter *Evangelii Praecones*, AAS 43 (1951): 497–528; and Pius XII, Encyclical Letter *Fidei Donum*, AAS 49 (1957): 225–48.

[43] Propaganda Fide regrouped three lay missionary societies (Society of St. Peter the Apostle for Native Clergy, Society of the Holy Childhood, and Society for the Propagation of the Faith) and transferred their headquarters from France to Rome in order to reorganize their fund-raising activities.

churches. He completed and institutionalized Leo XIII's ecclesiological approach in favor of an "intelligent unionism." Like Leo, he wanted to revive the Orient by the Orient. In the Motu Proprio *Dei Providentis* of May 1917, he detached the Congregation for the Oriental Church from *Propaganda Fide* "to forestall the fear that the Orientals might not be held in proper consideration by the Roman pontiffs."[44] Its role was to strengthen the position of the Eastern Catholic churches and make them "centres of contact"[45] with the Orthodox churches in order to facilitate their ultimate conversion.

Building on Leo XIII and Benedict XV's ecclesiology, the Council Fathers also looked at the Eastern Catholic churches primarily as a bridge with the Orthodox. Their role in ecumenical efforts was reasserted in *Lumen Gentium, Orientalium Ecclesiarum,* and *Unitatis Redintegratio*. In its conclusion, *Orientalium Ecclesiarum* stipulates that "The Sacred Council feels great joy in the fruitful zealous collaboration of the Eastern and the Western Catholic churches and at the same time declares: All these directives of law are laid down in view of the present situation until such time as the Catholic Church and the separated Eastern churches come together into complete unity" (OE 30).

Orientalium Ecclesiarum explicitly reminds readers that the decree should be understood in association with Vatican II's teaching on ecumenism developed in the earlier decree *Unitatis Redintegratio*. The later decree states that "the Eastern churches in communion with the Apostolic See of Rome have a special duty of promoting the unity of all Christians, especially Eastern Christians, in accordance with the principles of the decree, 'About Ecumenism,' of this Sacred Council... by religious fidelity to the ancient Eastern traditions, by a greater knowledge of each other, by collaboration and a brotherly regard for objects and feelings" (OE 24). In *Lumen Gentium* the Council reiterates its desire to see the Eastern churches retaining their distinctive traditions, declaring that "there are also particular Churches that retain their own traditions, without prejudice to the Chair of Peter which presides over the whole assembly of charity, and protects their legitimate variety while at the same time taking care that these differences do not hinder unity, but rather contribute to it" (LG 13). These documents on the preservation and the

---

[44] Benedict XV, *Dei Providentis*, 530.

[45] George Tavard, *Ecumenism: Two Centuries of Ecumenism* (Notre Dame, IN: Fides, 1978), 117.

integrity of the spiritual heritage of the Eastern Catholic churches confirm Pope Benedict's teaching that "the Eastern Churches in communion with the Apostolic See of Rome have a special duty of promoting the unity of all Christians... by the example of their lives, by religious fidelity to the ancient Eastern traditions, [and] by a greater knowledge of each other" (OE 24).

The Council Fathers encouraged the Eastern rite churches to maintain and fully embrace their specific Eastern traditions. While Vatican II put the burden on the Eastern churches themselves, Pope Benedict preferred to address the Latin clergy and warned them in *Dei Providentis* against the Latinization of the Eastern rites. "The Church of Jesus Christ," he wrote, "since she is neither Latin nor Greek nor Slav, but Catholic, makes no distinction between her children, and those, whether they are Greeks, Latins, Slavs or members of other national groups, all occupy the same rank in the eyes of the apostolic see."[46] At that time, in the heat of the world conflict, the Eastern churches were weak and needed Rome's support.

The main difference between Benedict XV's ecclesiology and the one developed at Vatican II is that Pope Benedict's thinking was not ecumenical. His decisions were the mark of an "intelligent unionism," as it is clearly stated in his encyclical *Principi Apostolorum* of October 1920 that conferred the title of Doctor of the Church to St. Ephrem, a Syrian monk. The pontiff sought to reach out to all Eastern Christians, pleading that he "humbly entreated God to return the Eastern Church at long last to the bosom and embrace of Rome," adding that "their long separation, contrary to the teachings of their ancient Fathers, keeps them miserably from this See of Peter."[47] In this encyclical, Pope Benedict is more assertive in his recognizing the Eastern churches as churches.[48] When three years earlier, he had detached the *Congregation for the Oriental Church* from *Propaganda Fide*, he did not change its name to the *Congregation for the Oriental Churches*. That step was taken after Vatican II, by Paul VI in 1967.

In the Motu Proprio *Orientis Catholici* of October 1917, the pope founded the Pontifical Oriental Institute as a center dedicated to supporting the Congregation for the Oriental Church and to promote

---

[46] Benedict XV, *Dei Providentis*, 530.

[47] Benedict XV, Encyclical Letter *Principi Apostolorum Petro*, AAS 12 (1920): 457.

[48] Leo XIII's Apostolic Letter *Orientalium Dignitas* of 1894 had already identified the Eastern rite churches as churches.

advanced studies on Eastern Christianity. It was conceived to serve an ecumenical and educational purpose. The ecumenical goal was to provide the Latin Church with a better understanding of the traditions of the Oriental churches and build a genuine interest in them. To this aim, the Pontifical Oriental Institute was to function as an educational center for the studies of the dogmatic, liturgical, spiritual, and canonical traditions of the churches of the East.

A concept of "exchange of gifts" developed by Vatican II and later embraced by Pope John Paul II emerged. The conciliar decree *Unitatis Redintegratio* stresses that "Catholics must... acknowledge and esteem the truly Christian endowments from our common heritage which are to be found among our separated brethren... which can be a help to our own edification" (UR 4). The same idea appears in *Lumen Gentium* (8, 13). This concept of "exchange of gifts" between churches goes back to Benedict XV when he writes in *Orientis Catholici* that "We would like indeed that this Institute pursue, at the same time, the explanation of both Catholic and Orthodox Doctrine, so that each of them, according to its own understanding, may clearly reveal... whether they come from the Apostolic Tradition passed down to us through the perennial Magisterium of the church, or from any other [source]."[49]

Benedict XV and the Catholic Church of his time were not ready for an interactive ecumenism of the kind developed at Vatican II, but the pontiff cannot be described as closed-minded. On the contrary, one could say that he engaged in different forms of ecumenism through prayers and education. It is highly significant, after all, that during his pontificate, the groundbreaking Malines Conversations were launched, initiated, in 1921, by the Belgian Cardinal Désiré-Joseph Mercier with the support of the Holy See. And although Pope Benedict never gave formal consent, he certainly supported the unofficial meetings between Catholics and Anglicans, therefore being at odds with Leo XIII's bull *Apostolicae Curae*,[50] which had denied validity to Anglican orders. In 1928, Pius XI's encyclical *Mortalium Animos*[51] cautiously shut the door on this monumental step from anti-Modernist tendencies toward the Second Vatican Council and John XXIII's *aggiornamiento*.

---

[49] Benedict XV, *Orientis Catholici*, 531.
[50] Leo XIII, Apostolic Bull *Apostolicae Curae*, ASS 29 (1896): 193–203.
[51] Pius XI, Encyclical Letter *Mortalium Animos*, AAS 20 (1928): 5–16.

From Benedict XV to Pope Francis

Benedict XV and the Second Vatican Council continue to challenge the church today, a challenge picked up by Pope Francis who describes peace as an art, loving your neighbor as foundational, and protecting Eastern Catholics and their heritage as a vital issue. In his 2014 address to the Diplomatic Corps Pope Francis stressed that "everywhere the way to resolve open questions must be that of diplomacy and dialogue. This is the royal road already indicated with utter clarity by Benedict XV when he urged the leaders of the European nations to make 'the moral force of law' prevail over the 'material force of arms'."[52] On July 27, 2014, the pontiff marked the 100th anniversary of World War I hoping that the world will not repeat "the mistakes of the past."[53] Like Benedict XV, he talked of "useless massacre" around the world. Building on Pope Benedict and John XXIII's teachings, as well as Vatican II's legacy, Pope Francis asked the leaders in the Middle East, Iraq, and Ukraine to "continue to join (me) [him] in praying that… the Leaders of those regions [be granted] the wisdom and strength needed to move forward with determination on the path toward peace."[54] Walking in the steps of Pope Benedict XV, the current pontiff reasserted Benedict's principle that "the common good and respect for every person, rather than specific interests, be at the centre of every decision," adding that "in war all is lost and in peace nothing."[55] When asking leaders to stop persecution in the Middle East, Pope Francis also made reference to Benedict XV who asked the Sultan to bring an end to the massacre of the Armenians in 1915. He spoke of "ecumenism of blood" through their martyrdom and persecution.

Finally, in his January 1, 2015 message for the Celebration of the World Day of Peace, Pope Francis reiterated Pope Benedict and his successors' teaching, reminding all that "fraternity constitutes the network of relations essential for the building of the human family created by God,"[56]

---

[52] Pope Francis, "Address of His Holiness Pope Francis to the Members of the Diplomatic Corps Accredited to the Holy See (January 13, 2014)," AAS 106, no. 2 (2014): 79–85.

[53] Pope Francis, "Angelus," July 27, 2014, http://w2.vatican.va/content/francesco/en/angelus/2014/documents/papa-francesco_angelus_20140727.html.

[54] Ibid.

[55] Ibid.

[56] Francis, "Message for World Day of Peace 2015," AAS 107, no. 1 (2015): 66–75, no. 2.

the only pathway to peace. The current pontiff's teaching on peace and unity highlights Pope Benedict's understanding of the church and its relation with the world, his teaching on peace and war, and his longing for unity, a task started by Pope Benedict XVI, who had chosen his name after Pope Benedict XV, the Pope of peace.[57]

CONCLUSION

This analysis, although far from exhaustive, of the documents of the Second Vatican Council, confirms that Pope Benedict XV's pontificate was foundational in developing a new spirit of opening to the world. His defense of international peace serves as a benchmark in the post-Vatican II era in his articulation of the doctrines of just war and nonviolence, as ensuring a long and just peace. His actions in favor of Christian unity, although not ecumenical per se, were a first step in the direction embraced by Vatican II. As for his understanding of the church's missionary activity in the world after World War One, Benedict XV was a pioneer and opened the path for later landmark developments in magisterial teaching, from Pius XI's *Rerum Ecclesiae* to the Second Vatican Council's *Ad Gentes*.

In a letter to a friend, written in 1936, Angelo Roncalli wrote that "an old world disappears... another one is being formed and within this I am trying to conceal some good seed or other that will have its springtime, even if it is somewhat delayed, when I am dead."[58] These could have been words uttered by Benedict XV.

---

[57] In his first message for the celebration of the World Day of Peace in 2006, then newly elected Benedict XVI declared: "The very name Benedict, which I chose on the day of my election to the Chair of Peter, is a sign of my personal commitment to peace. In taking this name, I wanted to evoke both the Patron Saint of Europe, who inspired a civilization of peace on the whole continent, and Pope Benedict XV, who condemned the First World War as a "useless slaughter" and worked for a universal acknowledgment of the lofty demands of peace." Benedict XVI, "Message for World Day of Peace 2006," AAS 98, no. 1 (2006): 56–64, no. 2.

[58] Angelo Roncalli to Msgr. Pezzoli, Prevost of St. Allessandro in Colonna, Bergamo, May 1936, in Zizola, *The Utopia of Pope John XXIII*, 17.

CHAPTER 4

Gaudium et Spes and the Opening to the World

Charles E. Curran

This chapter will discuss the church's opening to the world found in the Vatican II document *Gaudium et Spes*, the Pastoral Constitution on the Church in the Modern World, contrasting the Vatican II approach with what occurred before and discussing subsequent changes and developments. The essay will treat three significant methodological issues—a more theological approach to life in the world, a more personalist approach, and a more inductive approach—and briefly indicate important ramifications of these methodologies.

A More Theological Approach

Gaudium et Spes insists that "the split between the faith which many profess and their daily lives deserves to be counted among the more serious errors of our age" (GS 43). This statement constitutes a critique of the approach existing in Catholicism prior to the Council. According to the pre-Vatican II approach, life in this world was governed by reason and the natural law. There was a distinction and even separation between the realm of the natural and the realm of the supernatural. Those who

C. E. Curran (✉)
Southern Methodist University, Dallas, TX, USA
e-mail: ccurran@smu.edu

© The Author(s) 2018
V. Latinovic et al. (eds.), *Catholicism Opening to the World and Other Confessions*, Pathways for Ecumenical and Interreligious Dialogue,
https://doi.org/10.1007/978-3-319-98581-7_4

wanted to follow fully the Gospel left the world and followed the evangelical counsels in religious life.

The famous 1963 encyclical *Pacem in Terris* of John XXIII still followed the natural law approach. Today one would expect the bishop of Rome writing on peace to pose a very Christological and theological understanding of peace as the gift of God, which will be established in this world through the conversion of heart and the work of trying to overcome the sinful divisions that separate individuals, races, and countries. *Pacem in Terris*, however, starts out at the very beginning by noting that peace on earth can be firmly established only if the order laid down by God be dutifully observed. But where do we find this order? The laws governing the relationship between people and states are to be found where the Father of all things wrote them, that is, in the nature of human beings.[1]

Gaudium et Spes consists of two parts. The first part considers the church and human vocation and well exemplifies the more theological approach to the questions of Christians living and working in the world. The first chapter discusses the dignity of the human person, beginning with creation by God in God's own likeness. The chapter then discusses sin and its effects on human living. A long final section of the chapter deals with Christ as the new human being and discusses the need to see the human person and human existence in this world in light of the redeeming love of Jesus. The Christian person, through the gift of the Holy Spirit, becomes capable of living the new law of love (GS 12–22).

In terms of carrying out this more theological approach in practice, *Gaudium et Spes* itself does not really follow its own proposed method. The second part purportedly considers five questions of special urgency—marriage and family, culture, socioeconomic life, political life, and peace—"in the light of the gospel and human experience" (GS 46). But in reality there is very little mention of the distinctively theological and Christian aspects, such as faith, grace, and the message of Jesus Christ as affecting these five considerations. What happened here? Originally the second part was intended as an appendix, not an integral part of the document. Consequently, it never went through much discussion or revision. The second part became an integral part of the total document only at the

---

[1] John XXIII, Encyclical Letter *Pacem in Terris*, AAS 55 (1963): 257–304, no. 1–7. This encyclical, along with most of the key magisterial documents related to social ethics cited in this essay, is reprinted in *Catholic Social Thought: The Documentary Heritage*, expanded ed., ed. David J. O'Brien and Thomas A. Shannon (Maryknoll: Orbis, 2010).

fourth and last session of the council, but there was no time to fully integrate it into the method of the first part.[2]

The more theological approach of *Gaudium et Spes* opened the door to a changed understanding of the social mission of the church and the role of Christians working for a more just and peaceful human society. In the pre-Vatican II period, the mission of the church was twofold: divinization and humanization. Divinization was the work of sanctifying God's people, which was carried out above all by the hierarchical and priestly offices in the church. Humanization was the mission of working for the betterment of the world that was carried out by laypeople living in the world.[3] As a result of the more theological approach of *Gaudium et Spes* that overcame the distinction and even separation between the supernatural and the natural, the door was opened to understanding that there is only one mission of the church. "Justice in the World," the document of the 1971 International Synod of Bishops, made this point very succinctly: "Action on behalf of justice and participation in the transformation of the world fully appear to us as a constitutive dimension of the preaching of the gospel or, in other words, of the church's mission for the redemption of the human race and its liberation from every oppressive situation."[4] Working for justice and the transformation of the world thus is a constitutive dimension of the church and its mission. One can have the best preaching, the best liturgy, and even the best Eucharistic participation, but without a social mission there is not church.

Gaudium et Spes, however, did not explicitly recognize or deal with the tension inherent in the Catholic approach to working for a free, just, peaceful, and participative society. One advantage of the natural law approach was that the Catholic approach appealed to all people of good will to work together for the common good of society. John XXIII with *Pacem in Terris*, in 1963, began the policy of addressing social encyclicals not only to the people of the Catholic Church but to all people of good will.[5] However, this raises the problem of papal documents and other

---

[2] M. G. McGrath, "Note storiche sulla Costituzione," in *La Chiesa nel Mondo di Oggi*, ed. Guilherme Baraúna (Florence: Ballecchi, 1966), 155–56.

[3] John Courtney Murray, S.J., "Toward a Theology for the Layman I," *Theological Studies* 5 (1944): 71–5.

[4] International Synod of Bishops, "Justice in the World," in O'Brien and Shannon, *Catholic Social Thought*, 306.

[5] John XXIII, *Pacem in Terris*, 1.

teachings addressing two different audiences: the members of the church and all people of good will. There has been significant discussion of this issue since *Gaudium et Spes*, but all recognize that it is necessary to use approaches that are not specifically Christian in trying to convince people of good will to work for a better human society. The tension of trying to address these two different audiences can be found in official papal documents even to the present day.

I have criticized the more theological and faith-based approach of *Gaudium et Spes* with being too optimistic about what is happening and what can happen in the world.[6] *Gaudium et Spes* overcame the separation between the supernatural and the natural. Faith, grace, and the message of Jesus must affect this world, but there is a tendency to forget human sinfulness and that the fullness of the reign of God will only come at the end of time. This eschatological dimension—the tension between the now and the fullness of the reign of God at the end of time is not present in the first two chapters of part one, dealing with human activity and human community. Both of these chapters end with what Christ has brought to bear—"Christ as the new man" (GS 22) and "the Incarnate Word and human solidarity" (GS 32). There is no realization that the fullness of the reign of God and the final coming of Christ will only occur at the end of time. Since Vatican II many Catholic theologians have recognized that the approach of *Gaudium et Spes* is too optimistic. Today we are much more aware of the reality of conflict in our world.

After Vatican II, official Catholic documents, theologians, and ethicists began to recognize the importance of social sin or structural sin.[7] The Latin American bishops accepted the reality of social sin in their Medellín (1986) and Puebla (1979) documents. In Mexico before the Puebla meeting, John Paul II for the first time referred to sinful structures. John Paul II further developed the notion of social or structural sin in his 1984 apostolic exhortation *Reconciliatio et Paenitentia*[8] and

---

[6] See, e.g., Charles E. Curran, *Directions in Catholic Social Ethics* (Notre Dame, IN: University of Notre Dame Press, 1985), 49.

[7] Marciano Vidal, "Structural Sin: A New Category in Moral Theology," in *History and Conscience: Studies in Honor of Sean O'Riordan*, ed. Raphael Gallagher and Brendan McConvery (Dublin: Gill & Macmillan, 1989), 181–98; Margaret Pfeil, "Doctrinal Implications of the Use of the Language of Social Sin," *Louvain Studies* 27 (2002): 132–53.

[8] John Paul II, Apostolic Exhortation *Reconciliatio et Paenitentia*, AAS 77 (1985): 185–275.

in his 1987 encyclical *Sollicitudo Rei Socialis*.[9] For example, in the latter document he blames the two blocs of the East and West for some of the problems in the developing world. Social or structural sin comes from the accumulation and concentration of personal sins, but John Paul II also indicates the unconscious and unaware influence of sinful structures on individuals. Thus as the Canadian theologian Gregory Baum insists, there is a two-way relationship. Individuals' sins contribute to the existence of structural or social sin in the world, but structural or social sin also has a strong influence on how individuals act.[10]

The overly optimistic approach of *Gaudium et Spes* also comes through in its failure to give strong emphasis to the reality of poverty and the poor. *The New Dictionary of Catholic Social Thought* maintains that Vatican II did not deal in any depth with the issue of poverty.[11] However, there was a group of council fathers that had attempted to give a greater importance to the poor and the fact that the church must not only be for the poor but also one with the poor. A leading figure in this group was Paul M. Gauthier, a French-born worker priest in both France and Israel, who issued a challenge to the council with regard to the role of being for and with the poor.[12] Another figure insisting on the importance of dealing with poverty and the poor was the Cardinal Archbishop of Bologna Giacomo Lercaro.[13] Although these initiatives did not have any great effect on Vatican II, there can be no doubt that they were prophetic in the light of subsequent developments.

Liberation theology in South America strongly insisted on beginning with the experience of the poor and the oppressed. God has a special love and preference for the poor. Official Catholic teaching as illustrated by Pope John Paul II adopted this understanding of the preferential

---

[9] John Paul II, Encyclical Letter *Sollicitudo Rei Socialis*, AAS 80 (1988): 513–86.

[10] Gregory Baum, "Structures of Sin," in *The Logic of Solidarity: Commentaries on John Paul II's Encyclical on "Social Concern,"* ed. Gregory Baum and Robert Ellsberg (Maryknoll: Orbis, 1989), 110–26.

[11] John O'Brien, "Poverty," in *New Dictionary of Catholic Social Thought*, ed. Judith Dwyer (Collegeville, MN: Liturgical Press, 1994), 772.

[12] Paul M. Gauthier, *Christ, the Church, and the Poor* (Westminster, MD: Newman, 1965).

[13] Rohan Curnow, "Stirrings of the Preferential Option for the Poor at Vatican II: The Work of the 'Group of the Church of the Poor,'" *Australian Catholic Record* 89 (2012): 420–32.

option for the poor.[14] At the present time, Pope Francis has made the liberation of the poor a central and perhaps even primary aspect of his understanding of the social mission of the church. But in addition, Francis has strongly insisted on the fact that the church itself must be poor and one with the poor.[15]

CENTRALITY OF THE PERSON

The Declaration on Religious Freedom of Vatican II (*Dignitatis Humanae*) begins with a recognition that a sense of the dignity of the human person has been impressing itself more and more deeply on the consciousness of contemporary people (DH 1). The document then goes on to develop the right of all people to religious freedom—a right that had previously been strongly denied in the Catholic tradition. The older approach did not recognize the importance of the person or subject but rather gave priority to the objective aspect. Error has no rights; therefore, there cannot be religious freedom. The change at Vatican II was dramatic not only in the content of the teaching on religious liberty but also in the recognition of the important turn to the person and the emphasis on the freedom of the person.

Gaudium et Spes reinforced this turn to the subject and the person. The first chapter of the pastoral constitution develops the dignity of the human person who is created in God's image. In my judgment, the most startling change in the first chapter is the understanding of conscience and its dignity. The human person has in her heart a law written by God. Conscience is the most secret core and sanctuary of the human person where one is alone with God whose voice echoes in the depths of the heart. In fidelity to conscience Christians join others in the search for truth and for adequate solutions to the many problems facing the world today. One must strive for a correct conscience, but conscience frequently errs from invincible ignorance without losing its dignity (GS 16).

The pre-Vatican II approach saw law as the objective norm of morality and the conscience as the subjective norm that had to conform itself to the objective norm. But in this paragraph of *Gaudium et Spes* there

---

[14] Pope John Paul II, Encyclical Letter *Centesimus Annus*, AAS 83 (1991): 793–867, no. 57, in O'Brien and Shannon, *Catholic Social Thought*, 516.

[15] Robert W. McElroy, "The Church for the Poor: Pope Francis Makes Addressing Poverty Essential," *America* (October 21, 2013), 13–16.

is no mention of the objective norm existing out there. Instead there is the repeated recognition of the law written in the depths of the heart and the role of conscience to discern this law in its depths. The emphasis here has shifted from the objective moral norm existing outside the person to the law discovered by conscience. Elsewhere, however, this document does recognize the objective moral order and objective moral standards.[16]

There can be no doubt that Vatican II emphasizes the subject and centrality of the person, but it still strongly opposes individualism. *Gaudium et Spes* continues in its own way to recognize the accepted Catholic understanding that the human person is both sacred and social. In part one of the document, chapter one discusses the dignity of the human person, which lays the groundwork for chapter two's discussion of the community of humankind, stressing the interdependence of the person and society (GS 23–32). In my judgment, perhaps the biggest difference between the Catholic approach and the American ethos at the present time is the acceptance of individualism in the American ethos and the Catholic criticism of it because it fails to recognize the social dimension of the human person.

This anthropology recognizing the human person as both sacred and social is in keeping with the Catholic tradition and has served as the basis for its relationship to capitalism and communism or Marxism.[17] The traditional Catholic understanding before Vatican II recognized abuses in capitalism but condemned Marxism and communism as intrinsically evil. *Gaudium et Spes* continues this attitude to capitalism, but in keeping with the approach of John XXIII insisting on dialogue and no condemnations Vatican II made no condemnation of communism.[18] John XXIII had already moved away from the total opposition of the Cold War by opening up dialogue with Marxism and communism. Paul VI went further by recognizing different aspects in Marxism and

---

[16] Josef Fuchs, S.J., "A Harmonization of the Conciliar Statements on Christian Moral Theology," in *Vatican II: Assessments and Pespectives: 25 Years After (1962–1987)*, vol. 2, ed. René Latourelle, S.J. (New York: Paulist Press, 1989), 489–93.

[17] For my development of the papal attitudes to capitalism and communism, see Charles E. Curran, *Catholic Social Teaching 1891–Present: A Historical, Theological, and Ethical Analysis* (Washington, DC: Georgetown University Press, 2002), 198–209.

[18] Charles Moeller, "History of the Constitution," in *Commentary on the Documents of Vatican II, Volume Five: Pastoral Constitution on the Church in the Modern World*, ed. Herbert Vorgrimler (New York: Herder & Herder, 1969), 64.

indicating that some Christians while not accepting its atheistic and material approaches accept Marxism as a helpful tool of social analysis. Liberation theology in some of its approaches also accepted aspects of Marxism.[19] The collapse of the Soviet Union later resulted in an entirely new social situation.

As mentioned in the first section, poverty and the poor became even more significant in Catholic understanding in general and papal teaching as time went on. As will be discussed in the following section, Vatican II had a universal perspective that still tended to be heavily Eurocentric. Pope Paul VI recognized the needs of the third world and with it the acute problem of poverty. This recognition brought to the fore the negative aspects of capitalism.[20] John Paul II in light of his opposition to communism in Poland was more fearful and negative about Marxism as also illustrated in his problems with liberation theology.[21] On the other hand, Pope Benedict XVI in his encyclical *Caritas in Veritate* pointed out the scandal of glaring inequality between rich and poor nations and strongly criticized unregulated financial capitalism, which maximizes profits and consumption. The growing gap between rich and poor in the first world also pointed out problems with existing capitalism.[22] Pope Francis has been a strong opponent of unregulated capitalism and in the process has upset some conservative Catholics.[23]

This emphasis on the person has made the Catholic Church in the last fifty years a strong defender of human rights. *Gaudium et Spes* continues the emphasis on human rights, which had been developed in depth for the first time by Pope John XXIII in his 1963 encyclical *Pacem in Terris*. In the nineteenth and early twentieth century, Catholicism strongly opposed human rights as based on an individualistic liberalism, which failed to recognize the social dimension of

[19] Donal Dorr, *Option for the Poor and for the Earth: Catholic Social Teaching* (Maryknoll: Orbis, 2012), 106–21 and 155–99.

[20] The *Wall Street Journal* referred to Paul VI's encyclical *Populorum Progressio* as "warmed over Marxism." "Review and Outlook," *Wall Street Journal*, March 30, 1967, 14.

[21] Jonathan Luxmoore and Jolanta Babiuch, *The Vatican and the Red Flag: The Struggle for the Soul of Eastern Europe* (New York: Cassell, 1999).

[22] Benedict XVI, Encyclical Letter *Caritas in Veritate*, AAS 101, no. 8 (2009): 641–709, no. 21–22, in O'Brien and Shannon, *Catholic Social Thought*, 537–39.

[23] David Gibson, "Pope Francis' US Approval Rates Slump Sharply Led by Conservative Dismay" (July 22, 2015), https://www.ncronline.org/news/parish/pope-francis-us-approval-rates-slump-sharply-led-conservative-dismay.

the human person. The best illustration of this opposition to human rights was the opposition to the right to religious freedom, which was accepted by the Catholic Church only at Vatican II. However, as the twentieth century developed, the Catholic ethos recognized the existence of a newer problem with the totalitarianism of the right and especially of the left. As a result, even papal teaching began to recognize the rights of the human person, which were violated by these totalitarian regimes. Thus the stage was set for a newer approach to human rights. Pope John Paul II made human rights the central reality of his political and social teaching. Based on anthropology, however, the Catholic approach to human rights was distinctive. Based on the dignity of the human person, the Catholic approach recognizes political and civil rights in the sense of rights as "freedom from." Based on its understanding of the social nature of human beings, it also recognizes social and economic rights such as the right to food, clothing, shelter, education, and health care. Such an approach thus challenges both the theory of individualistic liberalism that recognized only political and civil rights and socialistic approaches which recognized only economic rights. In addition the Catholic understanding also saw an important place for duties and obligations as well as rights.[24]

The second part of *Gaudium et Spes* has one chapter on marriage and the family. In a sense, contraception was the elephant in the room in this discussion, but after much discussion and maneuvering it was decided to leave the morality of contraception to the pope and the papal commission that was studying it.[25] However, *Gaudium et Spes* did insist that the criterion for harmonizing conjugal love and the responsible transmission of life is the nature of the moral person and his acts (GS 51). Here again there is a significant shift. The older approach to sexual norms was based on human nature and the God-given purpose of the sexual faculty.

The condemnation of artificial contraception for spouses was based on the nature and purpose of the sexual power or as it was called the sexual

---

[24]Mary Elsbernd, "Rights Statements: A Hermeneutical Key to Continuing Development in Magisterial Teaching," *Ephemerides Theologicae Lovanienses* 62, no. 4 (1986): 308–32.

[25]William H. Shannon, *The Lively Debate: Response to Humanae Vitae* (New York: Sheed & Ward, 1970), 84–87.

faculty.[26] The sexual faculty has a twofold purpose: procreation and love union. Consequently, every single act of sexual actuation must be open to procreation and love union. Many criticize the Catholic position for being pro-natalist at any cost. But that is not the real problem with the Catholic teaching. The problem is that physicalism (or biologicalism) which, as I have said elsewhere, identifies the moral and human act with the act's physical or biological elements, ignoring that the human or moral aspect would also address other elements such as the sociological, psychological, physiological, eugenic, hygienic, etc.[27] In ignoring such other elements, the emphasis in such physicalism makes the physical act something normative which cannot be interfered with—whereas in so many other places, Catholic teaching recognizes such interference can be a moral good (e.g., removing a cancerous part of the body).

Those Catholics who dissent from the teaching on artificial contraception invoke the criterion not of the nature and purpose of the sexual faculty but the good of the person and the good of the person's relationships. Thus, one can justify interference in the sexual act if this is for the good of the person or the good of the marital relationship. Such a criterion logically also leads to a change in other Catholic teachings on sexuality such as homosexuality. Homosexual acts can be morally good based on the good of the person and the person's relationship.

As a matter of empirical fact, Catholic spouses practice artificial contraception to the same degree as non-Catholics.[28] Artificial contraception is no longer a major controversial issue since the vast majority of Catholic spouses have decided in their own conscience that they can and should practice artificial contraception. The question then naturally arises: why has the papal teaching continued to condemn artificial contraception in the light of the fact that this teaching has not been received by the vast majority of Catholic spouses? There are many reasons for such a position which lie beyond the parameters of this essay, but one is

---

[26] For an in-depth discussion of the older Catholic approach to sexuality and contraception and the revisionist approach, see Todd A. Salzman and Michael G. Lawler, *The Sexual Person: Toward a Revised Catholic Anthropology* (Washington, DC: Georgetown University Press, 2008), 48–191.

[27] Charles E. Curran, *The Development of Moral Theology: Five Strands* (Washington, DC: Georgetown University Press, 2013), 98.

[28] "Guttmacher Statistics on Catholic Women's Contraceptive Use," February 15, 2012 at www.guttmacher.org.

the fear that if the papal teaching on artificial contraception changes it will necessarily follow that other sexual teachings such as that on homosexuality will also change.

As a result, at the present time sexuality remains an ever bigger elephant in the room for hierarchical Catholic teaching. Unfortunately there seems to be no indication of any immediate change in the teaching even on artificial contraception. In the synods on the family of 2014 and 2015, there was little mention of contraception. In the discussion of communion for the divorced and remarriage, there was no discussion whatsoever about changing the teaching on divorce and remarriage, but the focus was solely on the pastoral practice of allowing some divorced and remarried people to frequent the Eucharist. Even those supporting such a pastoral approach went out of their way to say they were not advocating changing the teaching on divorce and remarriage. Pope Francis himself has pointed out he is a loyal son of the church and consequently accepts church teaching on issues such as gay marriage and contraception.[29] In the meantime, a good number of Roman Catholics have been leaving the church precisely because of its sexual teachings. The issue of sexuality is not going to go away. Pope Francis' 2016 post-synodal Apostolic Exhortation, *Amoris Laetitia*, has opened the door to creative and positive reinterpretations of Catholic teaching in these areas, but the debates that are vitally necessary here have some considerable distance to run yet.

The major criticism of Vatican II's emphasis on the centrality of the human person in subsequent years is that such an understanding is too anthropocentric. This criticism comes to the fore in the recognition of the importance of ecology. An anthropocentric approach gave a one-sided importance to the dominion of the human over the ecological. Many of our ecological problems have been brought about by such human arrogance. The material and natural goods of God's creation are not simply means that human persons can use for their own benefit. God's creation has a meaning and purpose in itself and does not exist merely as a reality that humans can do with it whatever they want. Pope Francis's encyclical *Laudato Si'* recognizes the dangers of a one-sided anthropological approach. Pope Francis sees human technological and economic power as causing many of the ecological problems that exist in our world today.[30]

[29] Pope Francis with Antonio Spadaro, *My Door Is Always Open: A Conversation on Faith, Hope, and the Church in a Time of Change* (London: Bloomsbury, 2014), 57–58.

[30] Francis, Encyclical Letter *Laudato Si'*, AAS 107, no. 9 (2015): 847–945, "Chapter 3: The Human Roots of the Ecological Crisis," no. 101–36.

A MORE INDUCTIVE METHOD

Before Vatican II, Catholic social teaching had employed a deductive methodology in dealing with Catholic social teaching. From an idea of society or the natural law, it deduced what the good society should be. This was most explicit in Pius XI's encyclical *Quadragesimo Anno* with its call for what in this country were called industry-wide councils: an organic understanding of society in which capital, labor, and consumers worked together to determine how that particular industry should function.[31] *Pacem in Terris* in 1963 still employed a basically deductive method based on the laws governing how individuals and states should act. According to John XXIII these laws are to be found in human nature where the Father of all things wrote them. Each of the four chapters in *Pacem in Terris*, however, ends with a section on the signs of the times—the characteristics of the present day.[32] *Gaudium et Spes* adopts a more inductive approach beginning with the signs of the times. To carry out its task of striving for a better society, the church has the duty of scrutinizing the signs of the times and of interpreting them in the light of the gospel. The second part of *Gaudium et Spes* deals with five urgent issues. Its concern is to consider these issues in the light of the gospel and experience (GS 46). Note here the use of the word "experience" and not the word "reason," recalling that the second part of *Gaudium et Spes* does not carry the emphasis on the Gospel found in part one. The discussion of these five particular issues begins with an analysis of the signs of the times, not with natural law (GS 47).

This more inductive method is intimately connected with the reality of historical consciousness. Pope Paul VI's apostolic letter *Octogesima Adveniens* in 1971 reflects the more inductive method with its recognition of historical consciousness. Paul insists it is neither his mission nor his intention in the midst of such widely differing situations to put forth solutions that have universal validity. Rather it is up to the particular Christian communities to analyze the situation proper to their own region in the light of the gospel and to draw principles of reflection,

---

[31] Pius XI, Encyclical Letter *Quadragesimo Anno*, AAS 23 (1931): 177–228, no. 76–98, in O'Brien and Shannon, *Catholic Social Thought*, 61–66.

[32] John XXIII, *Pacem in Terris*, no. 39–45, 75–79, 126–29, 142–45, in O'Brien and Shannon, *Catholic Social Thought*, 143–44; 150–51; 158–59; 161–62.

norms of judgment, and directives for action from the social teaching of the church.[33]

Bernard Lonergan, S.J., the acclaimed Canadian theologian, claimed that the ultimate reason for the changes at Vatican II came from the shift from classicism to historical consciousness. Whereas classicism sees the world in terms of the immutable, the eternal, and the unchanging, historical consciousness gives greater significance to the particular, the contingent, and the historical. Historical consciousness recognizes that the human subject, who is knower and actor, is also embedded in a history and culture that affect the ways in which the individual thinks and acts. However, historical consciousness opposes the sheer existentialism that sees the particular human person today with no real connection to past and future and no binding relationships with others in the present.[34]

Historical consciousness and a more inductive method have led to two significant developments after Vatican II. The first development concerns the need to start with the particular and not the universal. Vatican II as a document from the universal church claimed to have a universal perspective that proposed what is true in all places and circumstances. Such a claim to a universal perspective, however, risks seeing things through a somewhat narrow vision determined by one's own background and experiences. The emphasis on a particular perspective has led to theologies that begin with the experience of particular people, especially the oppressed and people on the margins. Liberation theology is a good example of such an approach, which begins with the situation of the poor and the oppressed. Feminism also illustrates this beginning with the particular by its insistence on beginning with the experience of women who have suffered from patriarchy. This emphasis on beginning with the particular and not the universal has had a lasting impact on Catholic thought after Vatican II.

Even if one begins with a particular perspective, there is still need for some universality. The Catholic tradition by its very emphasis on catholicity recognizes a universal dimension. The understanding today of the

---

[33] Paul VI, Apostolic Letter *Octogesima Adveniens*, AAS 63 (1971): 401–41, no. 4, in O'Brien and Shannon, *Catholic Social Thought*, 281.

[34] Bernard Lonergan, S.J., "The Transition from a Classicist World-View to Historical-Mindedness," in *Law for Liberty: The Role of Law in the Church Today*, ed. James E. Biechler (Baltimore: Helicon, 1967), 126–33; see also Thomas J. McPartland, *Lonergan and Historiography* (Columbia: University of Missouri Press, 2010).

importance of globalization also argues for some universality even in the midst of the emphasis on particularity. This need for some universality can be seen in the approach of liberation theology, which insists on God's preferential option for the poor. God loves all people and no one can be excluded from God's love, but there is a preferential option for the poor.[35] Catholic feminists also point out that the justice and equality they want for women must also be present for all other human beings.[36]

The second development based on historical consciousness and a more inductive methodology in the post-Vatican II church has been the emphasis on inculturation. The basic Christian message must become inculturated in all the various cultures of the world. What was previously thought to be the understanding of the universal church too easily turned out to be the experience of a Eurocentric church. Now theology recognizes that the church must be inculturated in all these different cultures. Thus, much more emphasis has been given to the church in Africa, Latin America, and Asia.[37]

The very existence of a more inductive methodology implies the recognition of the openness to the world and the possibility of learning from the world. *Gaudium et Spes* itself explicitly addresses in some detail this opening to the world. The first words of the pastoral constitution clearly set the tone for what follows: "The joys and the hopes, the griefs and the anxieties of the people of this age... are the joys and hopes, the griefs and anxieties of the followers of Christ" (GS 1). The next sentence has been traditional in Catholic thought: "Indeed, nothing genuinely human fails to raise an echo in their hearts" (GS 1). Chapter 4 of part one deals with the role of the church in the modern world. This section recognizes there is a two-way street between the church and the world—the church and Christians have something to teach the world, and the world has something to teach to the church and Christians (GS 40–45). The explicit recognition of the latter aspect is something new for the Catholic Church, but the reality itself is not that new. Think, for

---

[35] Daniel G. Groody, C.S.C., and Gustavo Gutiérrez, O.P., eds., *The Preferential Option for the Poor Beyond Theology* (Notre Dame, IN: University of Notre Dame Press, 2013).

[36] Margaret A. Farley, *Changing the Questions: Explorations in Christian Ethics* (Maryknoll: Orbis, 2015), esp. 88–111.

[37] Peter C. Phan, *Christianity with an Asian Face: Asian American Theology in the Making* (Maryknoll: Orbis, 2003). Phan is also the general editor of a multi-volume series entitled Theology in Global Perspective for Orbis Books.

example, of the fact that the church learned from the world even before Vatican II the dignity of the human person and human rights. Since Vatican II, the church has learned from the world the equal dignity and role of women in society and the recognition of an ecological awareness as illustrated in Pope Francis's encyclical. However, the church has rightly challenged the world for its individualism, materialism, and technological imperative, the misguided notion that if we can do it, we will do it.

This two-way relationship between the church and the world reminds us that the church does not have all the answers but can and should learn from others. In many other ways, the Second Vatican Council recog nized the same reality with its insistence on the importance of dialogue— dialogue with Protestants, with non-Christians, with science, and with the world.[38] Dialogue of course does not mean that one cannot criticize and challenge others.

The reality of the church open to learn from others corresponds with the explicit teaching of Vatican II on a pilgrim church always in need of reform.[39] Only in 1974 did the International Synod of Bishops point out that if the church is to call for the world to be just, she, too, must be just in her in own structures and operations. The church needs to have an examination of conscience about its modes of acting, possessions, and lifestyle.[40]

The appalling scandal of child sex abuse by priests and the cover-up by bishops and authorities has been a huge scandal in the church. Civil law, to its credit, recognized this problem before the church. Even now at times, leaders in the church have been unwilling to adhere to the just demands of civil law in the matter of reporting child abuse.[41]

On a more personal note, in the last few years I have learned that I have benefited greatly from white privilege and middle class privilege in

---

[38] Gregory Baum, "Grateful Remembrances of Vatican Council II," *Journal of Ecumenical Studies* 49, no. 1 (Winter 2014): 21–24.

[39] Yves M. J. Congar, O.P., "Moving Toward a Pilgrim Church," in *Vatican II Revisited: By Those Who Were There*, ed. Alberic Stacpolle (Minneapolis, MN: Winston, 1986), 129–52.

[40] International Synod of Bishops, "Justice in the World," Chapter 3, in O'Brien and Shannon, *Catholic Social Thought*, 312.

[41] Marie Keenan, *Child Sex Abuse in the Catholic Church: Gender, Power, and Organizational Culture* (New York: Oxford University Press, 2011).

our society. What is true for me as an individual is also true for the vast majority of Catholic theologians in the United States and for the church itself. There can be no doubt that such privilege has distorted the perspectives of all of us who have benefited from such privilege.[42]

A more inductive methodology has made a significant contribution to the theology and teaching of the Catholic Church after Vatican II. This methodology is connected with a number of other practical issues involving the church's relationship with the modern world and also has influenced the church to be more conscious of its own failings and shortcomings.

It is impossible in a short essay to discuss in detail the church's opening to the world at Vatican II in relationship to what occurred before the council and what came after the council. This paper has focused on three theological issues found in *Gaudium et Spes*—a more theological approach, the centrality of the person, and a more inductive methodology—to discuss significant aspects of the broader topic of the church's opening to the world at Vatican II and afterward.

---

[42] Laurie M. Cassidy and Alex Mikulich, *Interrupting White Privilege: Catholic Theologians Break the Silence* (Maryknoll: Orbis, 2007).

CHAPTER 5

Economic Activity in *Gaudium et Spes*: Opening to the World or Theological Vocation?

Matthew A. Shadle

Although not usually thought of in this way, the Catholic social tradition's teaching on work and other types of economic activity is an attempt to make sense of and respond to those changes in society we refer to as "secularization," an integral part of the broader process known as "modernization." Central fields of human activity, such as political life and economic life, were disembedded from the local, tradition-based ways of life of premodern society, in which religion played a unifying role. The development of capitalism represented the culmination of this process in the economic field, with the emergence of an autonomous sphere of market exchange, allegedly free from the particular, moral concerns of traditional, premodern culture. Catholic social teaching, beginning with Pope Leo XIII's consideration of the "worker question" in *Rerum Novarum* (1891) and the Catholic social movements that preceded it, is an attempt to both challenge and adapt to

M. A. Shadle (✉)
Marymount University, Arlington, VA, USA
e-mail: mshadle@marymount.edu

© The Author(s) 2018
V. Latinovic et al. (eds.), *Catholicism Opening to the World and Other Confessions*, Pathways for Ecumenical and Interreligious Dialogue,
https://doi.org/10.1007/978-3-319-98581-7_5

these sweeping changes, reexamining the role of religion and traditional morality in the modern economy. The Second Vatican Council represented a pivotal moment in the Catholic Church's engagement with modernity, and, as its title suggests, *Gaudium et Spes*, the Pastoral Constitution on the Church in the Modern World, is a key text. In *Gaudium et Spes* we find a dramatic tension between the document's recognition of the secularity of the economy, as one important dimension of "the world," and its proclamation of the deeply theological vocation of humankind to transform the world through labor.

In trying to make sense of this tension in *Gaudium et Spes*, in this paper, I will consider two things. First, drawing on recent work in sociology, I will explain what the process of secularization is and what it means for economic life. Second, I will turn to the text of *Gaudium et Spes* and analyze how it both embraces the secularity of the economy and provides a theological vision of the economic vocation.

SECULARISM AND THE ECONOMY

What do we mean by secularism and the process of secularization? In popular discourse, secularization often refers to the decrease of personal religious belief and the resulting diminishment of the presence of religious faith in public life, sometimes associated with a decline in traditional morality. Sociologists have long proposed this process of secularization as an inevitable outcome of modernity, echoing Émile Durkheim's claim that "the old gods are growing old or are already dead."[1] This understanding of secularization has certainly played a role in the Catholic social tradition's engagement with the world of work. In his 1891 encyclical *Rerum Novarum*, Leo XIII recognized that urban industrial workers uprooted from agricultural life in the countryside experienced both economic and religious dislocation, and that therefore both religious guidance and advocacy for their economic rights were needed.[2] The publication in 1943 of Yvan Daniel and Henri Godin's sociological work *La France, pays de mission?*, which demonstrated the alienation of the French working class from the Church, spurred a whole

---

[1] Émile Durkheim, *The Elementary Forms of the Religious Life*, trans. Joseph Ward Swain (New York: Free Press, 1965), 475.

[2] Leo XIII, Encyclical Letter *Rerum Novarum*, ASS 23 (1891): 641–670, nos. 41, 57.

wave of apostolates aimed at workers, both at the spiritual and economic levels.[3] Yet most sociologists now agree that understanding secularization in terms of the loss of religious belief is neither the most adequate way of defining the term, nor is it the most pertinent for understanding Catholic engagement with economic life.

As the sociologist José Casanova argues, secularization is better understood as the process by which "the secular" was differentiated or disembedded from "the sacred," and distinct secular systems—politics, the economy, law, education, etc.—were differentiated from each other, first in the West and later elsewhere through the growth of a more global society.[4] Secularization was a profound process of reimagining practically every area of life, not simply a change in beliefs or attitude regarding a single "religious" sphere. Casanova's point is not that the decline of religious faith and the privatization of religion often associated with secularization have not happened or are not important transformations, but rather that these do not appear to be universal phenomena of modernity the way the disembedding process does, and therefore do not provide the most satisfactory explanation of the secularization process.

DISEMBEDDING THE SECULAR FROM THE SACRED

The philosopher Charles Taylor has provided perhaps the most comprehensive account of the disembedding of the secular, immanent order from traditional ways of life. For Taylor, secularization is a process set in motion by transformations of Western Christian culture begun in the Middle Ages and extending to our own day. Taylor strongly resists what he calls "subtraction stories" of secularization, in which secularity "is to be understood in terms of underlying features of human nature which were there all along, but had been impeded by what is now set aside,"[5]

---

[3] Yvan Daniel and Henri Godin, *La France, pays de mission?* (Paris: Cerf, 1943). For a discussion of how the book influenced the apostolate to workers, see Oscar L. Arnal, *Priests in Working-Class Blue: The History of the Worker Priests (1943–1954)* (New York: Paulist Press, 1986), 53–56.

[4] José Casanova, *Public Religions in the Modern World* (Chicago: University of Chicago Press, 1994), 20–21, 212; see also Casanova, "The Secular, Secularizations, Secularisms," in *Rethinking Secularism*, ed. Craig Calhoun, Mark Juergensmeyer, and Jonathan VanAntwerpen (New York: Oxford University Press, 2011), 55.

[5] Charles Taylor, *A Secular Age* (Cambridge, MA: Belknap Press, 2007), 22.

that is, the superstitious, magical beliefs of the past. Instead, he proposes that secularization involved a radical transformation in "social imaginary," the way we imagine social life. It is the difference between wiping the dust from your glasses to see more clearly, and switching from reading glasses to sunglasses; in the latter case, some things become clearer and others less clear, without one pair being an obvious improvement over the other, or providing an obviously "truer" picture of reality.

Taylor's use of the terms "embedding" and "disembedding" helps communicate the radicalness of the change in social imaginary he associates with secularization. Something is embedded when it has been integrated into a larger whole, and its removal would disrupt or even destroy the functioning of the whole. Taylor argues that premodern religious life involved three types of embedding. First, religious life was embedded in society, meaning that religion primarily took the form of collective ritual action by the local community. Second, everyday life was embedded in the cosmos. There was a permeable boundary between the mundane world and the spiritual world; people could interact with gods, spirits, and ancestors through prayers and sacrifices, and particular places, objects, and people could be set apart as sacred or used by spiritual beings. And finally, human flourishing was largely understood to be in harmony with the purposes of the cosmos, and therefore religious ritual was primarily focused on ensuring forms of human flourishing such as health, fertility, and prosperity. A process set in motion in the Middle Ages by religious reform seeking greater devotion among the masses,[6] increased government discipline,[7] and an emerging instrumental view of nature[8] then served to dissolve this social imaginary, disembedding the mundane world from the world of the sacred. These processes had the effect of disenchanting the world, of severing the intercourse between the mundane and spiritual worlds.[9]

In Taylor's view, this transformation in the Western social imaginary involved, to a great extent, the working out of intrinsic elements of Christianity, but at the same time, it paradoxically created the possibility for the widespread abandonment of Christianity seen in the West

---

[6] Ibid., 61–89.
[7] Ibid., 99–112.
[8] Ibid., 90–99.
[9] Ibid., 146–58.

since the eighteenth century. The disembedding of the secular from the sacred in part reflected Christianity's insistence on the distinction of the Creator and Creation, on the transcendence of God. Christianity's positing of an extramundane source of human fulfillment contributed to the instrumentalization of the self, society, and the natural world in the pursuit of moral perfection. These transformations have been so thorough that we all now, at least in the West, take for granted that the world in which we live is autonomous and self-regulating and not suffused with spirits; that is, we live in "the immanent frame." Although the immanent frame emerged from Christian belief and some of us continue to believe that this immanent frame is open to something beyond it, its emergence has created the possibility for others to consider it closed: "It is something which permits closure, without demanding it."[10] This gets to the heart of Taylor's understanding of secularization, "a move from a society where belief in God is unchallenged and indeed, unproblematic, to one in which it is understood to be one option among others, and frequently not the easiest to embrace."[11] Religious faith in a secular age lacks the "givenness" of premodern religion. It is always a choice, requiring personal commitment.

DISEMBEDDING ABSTRACT SYSTEMS

We have been looking at the disembedding of the secular from the religious, but now we must turn to the process through which the different spheres of secular social life became differentiated or disembedded from each other. And this process was closely linked with the first. As the theologian Lieven Boeve points out, the distinct social spheres were disembedded from the very local customs and traditions that had served to embed the mundane in the sacred.[12]

According to the sociologist Anthony Giddens, a key component of the disembedding process was what he calls the "emptying out" of time and space. In traditional societies, time and space were closely connected with the local, with a sense of place, but gradually they came to be understood more as abstractions, voids in which people could be

---

[10] Ibid., 544.

[11] Ibid., 3.

[12] Lieven Boeve, *Interrupting Tradition* (Grand Rapids: Eerdmans, 2003), 37–39.

placed in relation to one another as on a timeline or in a spatial grid. These processes developed as awareness of absent others increasingly intruded into people's everyday activities.[13] What Giddens means is that people's everyday activities more and more implied an awareness of one's interconnectedness with others across space and time: a distant king regulating the production of textiles, farmers in Chile affecting the price of wheat with their exports, etc. The emptying out of time and space gradually made possible such significant shifts in social life as the transformation of politics from allegiance to a personal ruler to loyalty to an abstract "state," and the evolution of money from merely an object of exchange to a medium of finance and speculation.

The emptying out of time and space, according to Giddens, facilitated the disembedding of what he calls "abstract systems," the distinct secular social systems, from locally based ways of life. Just as Taylor opposes "subtraction stories" of secularization, Giddens prefers to speak of the "disembedding" of abstract systems rather than their "differentiation" to capture how these systems were transformed by being lifted out of their local context.[14] No longer based on the immediate relationships with those with whom one is physically present, social relations were reimagined through the lens of universal time and space. Political authorities were able to use empty time and space as conceptual tools to reconfigure political and economic life through the coordination and control of resources across time and space, diminishing the power of more locally based customs and authorities.[15]

Giddens proposes two basic types of abstract systems: symbolic tokens and expert systems. Symbolic tokens are "media of interchange which can be 'passed around' without regard to the specific characteristics of individuals or groups that handle them at any particular juncture."[16] Giddens provides the example of money, which enables investment against future risk and transactions with distant strangers. Other abstract systems, expert systems, are characterized by technical knowledge possessed by experts of different types: economists, engineers, doctors,

---

[13] Anthony Giddens, *The Consequences of Modernity* (Stanford, CA: Stanford University Press, 1990), 17–19.

[14] Ibid., 21–22; Giddens, *Modernity and Self-Identity: Self and Society in the Late Modern Age* (Stanford, CA: Stanford University Press, 1991), 17–18.

[15] Giddens, *Consequences of Modernity*, 20.

[16] Ibid., 22.

scientists, etc. We rely on these experts for much of our daily lives, and because expertise is highly specialized, an expert in one area is most likely unskilled in others.[17] Experts study their particular field in abstraction from others, making them both highly knowledgeable but incomplete in their knowledge or less capable of dealing with situations where multiple systems intersect, like the skilled doctor with poor bedside manner. This analytic chopping up of human experience has greatly increased humanity's scientific knowledge of the world, but contributes to the fragmentation experienced by modern people.

Trust is fundamental to both types of abstract systems. This is not a personal trust based on our expectations of a particular individual, however, but rather an impersonal trust. We put our trust first of all in the symbolic tokens and expert systems, and only secondarily in the people who participate in them.[18] What expert systems and symbolic tokens have in common is that they depend on and make possible relationships with people who are not immediately present to us. Although we sometimes consult experts like doctors and lawyers on a face-to-face basis, more commonly we rely on their expertise simply by carrying on with our daily lives, for example by trusting those experts who assure us that the food we eat is safe. And money makes it possible to purchase something from or invest money with total strangers. Each of these impersonal relations comes with certain expectations based on trust.[19]

To illustrate some of these ideas, let's compare the process of buying a horse-drawn cart in a premodern society to that of buying a car today. In a pre-modern village, to buy a cart I would approach one of my neighbors who is skilled in making carts. While in some times and places I might have engaged him in barter, perhaps giving him crops or livestock in exchange for the cart, more likely I am able to buy the cart with money. Even so, the money I provide him would certainly be metal coins, whose exchange value is based on their value as commodities. As my horses pull the cart away, I know that I can depend on its quality because the seller's livelihood depends on maintaining good relationships with his neighbors.

Today, buying a car still involves a face-to-face encounter at a local dealership, and in some cases, people develop ongoing relationships

[17] Ibid., 27–28; Giddens, *Modernity and Self-Identity*, 18.

[18] Giddens, *Consequences of Modernity*, 29–36.

[19] Ibid., 28.

with their dealer. So the point here is not that modern life has become completely impersonal. Rather, this example shows how even face-to-face encounters are penetrated by relations with absent others. Although like my premodern self I buy my new car with money, I do not actually exchange anything with the dealer; I just sign a few papers. My car is financed by anonymous bankers who, by analyzing a few numbers based on my past behavior, conclude that the chances are good that they can make money by loaning me the money to buy the car. And as I drive my car off the dealer's lot, although I have never met the people who made my new car, I trust that it will not fall apart as I drive it; that trust is not based on my own understanding of how the car works, which is minimal, but rather on the expertise of automotive engineers I will never know.

Giddens discusses one last characteristic of modern social life connected with the disembedding of abstract systems: reflexivity. Reflexivity refers to self-awareness, consciousness of not only what one is doing, but why one is doing it. Human beings have always monitored their own behavior, making sure they are doing the appropriate thing. What is characteristic of modern reflexivity is that it is applied at the social level; modern social norms, institutions, and knowledge are open to constant revision in the light of new information.[20] It is not that traditional societies never changed, but rather that the process of revision in modern societies is systematic. Tradition has little value of its own, but requires pragmatic justification.[21] This process of reflexivity is particularly linked to expert systems. Experts continuously provide analysis and commentary on social life—on what foods are healthy, on raising children, on successful relationships, on economic policy, etc.—that in turn shapes people's behavior, which again becomes grist for expert analysis and commentary.

THE CHANGING STATUS OF RELIGION

Returning to religion, most sociologists would agree that as a result of this dual disembedding process—the disembedding of the secular from the religious and the disembedding of abstract systems from one another—religion has become one of the "systems" of social life. While in the past it could be said that religion in a sense embraced all of social

---

[20] Giddens, *Modernity and Self-Identity*, 20.
[21] Giddens, *Consequences of Modernity*, 38–39.

life, that it served as a "totalizing narrative" to use Boeve's phrase,[22] in modern society religion inhabits its own distinct sphere of social life.[23] In this new position, religion takes on the characteristics of an expert system, and religious leaders no longer function as traditional authorities, but rather as experts, perhaps in spiritual matters, whom people can consult for guidance in making their individual choices.[24] It is worth noting that the leaders of the Catholic Church have to an extent embraced this new role, evident in the repeated claim that the Church is an "expert in humanity,"[25] offering its services to the world.

Although the process of secularization cannot simply be equated with diminishing religious belief, it has transformed the practice of religion in the West. We have already seen Taylor's claim that, in the secular age, religious faith must be a conscious choice. Indeed, the fact is many people choose not to practice religion, leading to a decrease in religious practice in the West. But religious practice persists in the West, and in some populations even thrives, although not in the same form as in premodern times. Taylor argues that in the age of secularism, religion puts far more emphasis on personal devotion, on faith as an inner conviction, than it did in previous times, where greater emphasis was placed on communal ritual.[26]

---

[22] Boeve, *Interrupting Tradition*, 40–42.

[23] Casanova notes the irony that whereas "the secular" was originally a theological concept that took on a life of its own, the concept of "religion" as something distinct from the rest of social life is in turn a product of secular modernity. Casanova, "Secular, Secularizations, Secularisms," 61.

[24] Giddens, *Modernity and Self-Identity*, 195.

[25] This phrase was first used by Pope Paul VI in his 1965 "Address to the United Nations Organization," AAS 57 (1965): 877–85. It is then repeated by Pope John Paul II in two encyclicals. Encyclical Letter *Sollicitudo Rei Socialis*, AAS 79 (1987): 513–86, no. 7; Encyclical Letter *Veritatis Splendor*, AAS (1993): 1133–1228, no. 3. It is cited in the Pontifical Council for Justice and Peace's *Compendium of the Social Doctrine of the Church*, no. 61. It was used on occasion by Pope Benedict XVI, most notably in his "Message for World Day of Peace 2010," AAS 102, no. 1 (2010): 41–51, no. 4. More recently, it has been used by Pope Francis, in his 2014 "Address to the Council of Europe," AAS 106, no. 12 (2014): 1005–13. Benedict XVI offered a variation on the theme elsewhere, telling Polish clergy that they should be "specialists in promoting the encounter between man [*sic*] and God." The faithful do not expect their priest to be an expert in secular disciplines, but "an expert in the spiritual life." "Meeting with the Clergy," http://w2.vatican.va/content/benedict-xvi/en/speeches/2006/may/documents/hf_ben-xvi_spe_20060525_poland-clergy.html.

[26] Taylor, "Western Secularity," in *Rethinking Secularism*, 38.

Although becoming more personal, religion in the secular age has not, at least in all cases, become private, defying the expectations of secularization theorists. With the creation of a distinct religious sphere separate from the political and economic spheres, it was expected that religion would become a largely private affair. As Casanova shows, however, in the secular age Western religions have not willingly accepted their marginalization, but have contested the very boundaries of the public and private.[27] At times this contestation has taken the form of traditionalist or fundamentalist resistance to secularism and modernity itself, but in other cases religions have worked within the basic framework of modernity while contesting its terms, for example by challenging the pretentions of the state or market to overwhelm communal life, or by resisting the trend toward individualism endemic to modernity.[28] He notes, in particular, that the Catholic Church has reached a kind of rapprochement with modernity, recognizing the autonomy of secular reality and reevaluating the Church's role in society, while also contesting the precise shape that secular society takes.[29] It is precisely this last form of contestation that characterizes *Gaudium et Spes*'s vision of economic life.

In summary, I think four key points are central to analyzing the secular/theological paradox in *Gaudium et Spes*:

1. The economy is an "abstract system," autonomous from both religious considerations and other social systems;
2. The economy is an "expert system," a system governed by its own laws that require expert knowledge for proper understanding and management;
3. Religious engagement with the economy no longer takes the form of integrating communal religious life with labor, but rather of an inner conviction brought to economic activity;
4. The public expression of this inner conviction is no longer to contest the autonomy of economic life, but rather the relative weight of economic values in relation to other public values such as human dignity and the common good.

---

[27] Casanova, *Public Religions*, 6.
[28] Ibid., 43, 228–29.
[29] Ibid., 62.

SECULARISM AND THE THEOLOGICAL VOCATION
OF ECONOMIC ACTIVITY IN *GAUDIUM ET SPES*

The Second Vatican Council was a watershed in the history of modern Catholicism. The council was, to use Pope John XXIII's phrase, an *aggiornamento*, an updating of the Church's thinking and practice to better respond to the modern world in which it found itself. Socially, the council represented a decisive repudiation of integralism. Although the term is most closely linked to the Church's intellectual and ecclesiastical response to the Modernist crisis beginning in the first decades of the twentieth century,[30] integralism also refers to the earlier and broader movement of Catholic resistance to modernity and the pursuit of the "reconquest" of Western society for the Church. In the social field, a key characteristic of integralism was the establishment of a wide variety of associations, including "women's groups, youth and educational movements, co-operatives, peasant leagues, sporting associations, workers' guilds, and trade unions," creating a distinct Catholic subculture within secular Western society.[31] It sought to recapture the harmonization of religious faith and social life characteristic of premodern times through this Catholic subculture.

The Catholic subculture central to the integralist phenomenon was at the same time a defense against modernity and an alternative form of modernity.[32] Integralism was a direct counter to secularization and modernization, seeing "the vast process by which vast areas of social life achieved a differentiated life of their own, beyond the control of the churches, as a departure from a sacred ideal."[33] Yet, "This anti-modern Roman Catholicism was very modern indeed."[34] Integralism implicitly acknowledged that Catholic faith was increasingly something that had to be chosen. It was dependent on Catholic participation in voluntary social organizations like Catholic Action, and was supported by voluntary

---

[30] Gabriel Daly, O.S.A., *Transcendence and Immanence: A Study in Catholic Modernism and Integralism* (Oxford: Clarendon, 1980).

[31] Martin Conway, "Introduction," in *Political Catholicism in Europe, 1918–1965*, ed. Tom Buchanan and Martin Conway (Oxford: Clarendon, 1996), 19.

[32] Paul Luykx, "The Netherlands," in *Political Catholicism in Europe*, 224–25.

[33] Joseph A. Komonchak, "Modernity and the Construction of Roman Catholicism," in *Christianesimo nella storia* 18 (1997): 358.

[34] Ibid., 383.

religious practices such as frequent communion, devotions to Mary and the Sacred Heart, and pilgrimages.[35] Integralism was clearly an instance of modern personalized religion and a movement of what Taylor calls the "age of mobilization."[36] The construction of the Catholic subculture was a recognition that, despite the church's pretentions to restoring its integrative role in society, it now was "a sub-culture forced to compete in a marketplace of meaning and value."[37]

Gaudium et Spes sought to move beyond this tension by embracing, rather than resisting, the secularity of economic life, but introduced its own tension by continuing to affirm that economic activity is an explicitly spiritual vocation. The document accepts the basic modern disembedding of the secular from the sacred. It also accepts the differentiation of the distinct spheres of social life from one another, including the differentiation of the religious sphere from the others. This recognition of a distinct religious sphere, however, should not be confused with accepting the privatization of religion. *Gaudium et Spes* maintains a public role for the Church and Christian witness by insisting that Christians (and in particular the laity) live out their vocations in the secular spheres. Through their personal commitment to the Christian narrative, Christians are tasked with transforming economic life to more fully embody human values. Let us look at these claims in greater detail.

The Secularity of Economic Activity

One way that *Gaudium et Spes* affirms the secularity of economic activity is in its recognition of the intrinsic value of human work. This affirmation represents a shift away from a spirituality that saw work having value primarily as a means of personal growth through performing the work with spiritual intentions. One sign of this shift can be seen in the document's claim that people "can justly consider that by their labor they are unfolding the Creator's work..." (GS 34, 57). Grounding itself in the divine call in Genesis for humankind to subdue the earth, this passage recognizes work's intrinsic significance. The human transformation

---

[35] Martin Conway, *Catholic Politics in Europe, 1918–1945* (New York: Routledge, 1997), 16–18.

[36] Taylor, *Secular Age*, 466–67.

[37] Komonchak, "Modernity," 378.

of the world through work is itself part of God's plan, not something incidental to God's ultimate plan of redemption.

To reinforce the point, *Gaudium et Spes* praises work precisely for its material benefits. It asserts that the value of human labor is not simply that it provides an opportunity for interior, spiritual growth, but rather that labor provides the material abundance necessary for the full development of the human person. Indeed, the council praises modern technology for the qualitative difference it makes toward human progress (GS 64). Material abundance is not the only end of human labor. Work is a collective effort that can potentially help generate a sense of communal solidarity (GS 33). *Gaudium et Spes* does not neglect the interior development that takes place through work, asserting that work transforms both the world and the person working: "Human activity, to be sure, takes its significance from its relationship to man [*sic*]. Just as it proceeds from man, so it is ordered toward man. For when a man works he not only alters things and society, he develops himself as well" (GS 35). Still, it is in and through work that the person is developed, not through giving the work a spiritual intentionality accidental to the work itself.

The autonomous, intrinsic value of work is just one manifestation of *Gaudium et Spes*'s affirmation of the autonomy or secularity of the world and its distinct systems (including the economic system). I will cite the key passage in full:

> If by the autonomy of earthly affairs we mean that created things and societies themselves enjoy their own laws and values which must be gradually deciphered, put to use, and regulated by men [*sic*], then it is entirely right to demand that autonomy. Such is not merely required by modern man, but harmonizes also with the will of the Creator. For by the very circumstance of their having been created, all things are endowed with their own stability, truth, goodness, proper laws and order. Man must respect these as he isolates them by the appropriate methods of the individual sciences or arts. Therefore if methodical investigation within every branch of learning is carried out in a genuinely scientific manner and in accord with moral norms, it never truly conflicts with faith, for earthly matters and the concerns of faith derive from the same God. (GS 36)

Here, we see a recognition and acceptance of the key transformations of modernity, both the disembedding of the secular from the sacred and the disembedding of distinct social systems. Both the natural and human worlds ("things and societies") consist in multiple systems that are subject to their own laws, discoverable through distinct scientific disciplines. All of these systems should also be autonomous from illegitimate religious interference or clerical control. It is also noteworthy that the council interprets this modern disembedding process as an outgrowth of Christianity itself, as "the will of the Creator," and not something alien imposed on Christian society. The council warns, however, that the secular world must remain "open" to God: "[I]f the expression, the independence of temporal affairs, is taken to mean that created things do not depend on God, and that man can use them without any reference to their Creator, anyone who acknowledges God will see how false such a meaning is" (GS 36). Here, we see an example of how modern religion insists on openness to the transcendent within an "immanent frame" shared with those who perceive it as closed. We also see a tension between secularity and the deeper theological significance of worldly activity that would shape all subsequent Catholic thinking on the economy.

Gaudium et Spes's recognition of the autonomy of the world goes hand in hand with the more prominent role for lay people affirmed in many of the council documents. The council's Decree on the Apostolate of the Laity, *Apostolicam Actuositatem*, states that the vocation of the laity is "the penetrating and perfecting of the temporal order through the spirit of the Gospel" (AA 2), and indeed the Dogmatic Constitution on the Church, *Lumen Gentium*, claims that "What specifically characterizes the laity is their secular nature" (LG 31). There is a clear link then between the mission of lay people and the secularity of the world.

We can also see that *Gaudium et Spes*'s acceptance of the autonomy of the world is linked to the recognition that the world is made up of distinct "expert systems," to use Giddens' term. For example, in paragraph 36 cited above, respect for the autonomy of the natural and human worlds entails mastery of the scientific disciplines relevant to each. *Gaudium et Spes*, in fact, recognizes the challenge that lay secular expertise poses to traditional forms of clerical authority precisely because clerics are not experts in the secular domains (GS 43). The document also notes the increased reflexivity of modern society, the human race's mastery over both the natural world and social life. It notes the "profound and rapid changes" characteristic of our "new stage of history," "triggered by the intelligence and creative energies of man [*sic*]." It then goes on to recognize the important role that the natural and human sciences play in exercising this mastery (GS 4–5).

The Christian Narrative

Now the secular vocation of the layperson is also a *Christian* vocation, according to *Gaudium et Spes*, returning us to the tension that is the focus of this paper. We have already seen this idea of the Christian vocation in the document's claim that work is carrying out the divine plan. But this sense of vocation is deepened by the document's insistence that human labor takes place in the midst of a spiritual struggle of historical proportions. The council makes the point quite starkly that human history is subject to both sin and grace: "all of human life, whether individual or collective, shows itself to be a dramatic struggle between good and evil, between light and darkness" (GS 13). The council is at pains to emphasize that this struggle does not simply take place in the recesses of the individual soul, but in everyday experience and the collective endeavors of humankind, as well. Speaking in broad terms, the council affirms the goodness of "human progress," the efforts of humankind across the centuries to improve its lot through collective effort. It warns, however, that "a monumental struggle against the powers of darkness pervades the whole history of man [*sic*]," insisting that all human accomplishments risk misuse and corruption (GS 37).

Gaudium et Spes also emphasizes the dynamic character of human history, its trajectory toward fulfillment in the Kingdom of God. Earthly well-being and eternal life are deeply linked. "[W]hile earthly progress must be carefully distinguished from the growth of Christ's kingdom, to the extent that the former can contribute to the better ordering of human society, it is of vital concern to the Kingdom of God" (GS 39). The document further elaborates: "On this earth that Kingdom is already present in mystery. When the Lord returns it will be brought into full flower" (GS 39). God's transformative presence is active in our concrete existence, but will become fully manifest only through a future purification of the world. The Kingdom is a lure drawing us toward that future but also as a judgment on the present reality of sin.

A beautiful passage from the section just cited encapsulates the document's theology of history. It states: "For after we have obeyed the Lord, and in His Spirit nurtured on earth the values of human dignity, brotherhood and freedom, and indeed all the good fruits of our nature and enterprise, we will find them again, but freed of stain, burnished and transfigured, when Christ hands over to the Father" His Kingdom (GS 39). In this life, we work toward the "good fruits of our nature," but these fruits will be "burnished and transfigured" through our final union with Christ.

Clearly, then, *Gaudium et Spes* presents a comprehensively theological vision of economic life. Yet this vision is presented in the form of a narrative—the narrative of salvation history—that the individual Christian believer adopts as a form of personal commitment. This narrative is not *simply* a personal one; it is the communally shared narrative of the Church, nurtured through catechesis and lived out through communal practice and reflection. But it nevertheless must by necessity be personal, adopted by the individual as a personal choice. This conclusion distinguishes *Gaudium et Spes*'s vision from any idea of a "Christian economy," in which Christian faith is woven into the fabric of everyday life. The council decisively rejects such a vision in its embrace of the autonomy and secularity of the world. Instead, here we see a vision in which faith is nurtured within the distinctive sphere of the Church but in some sense spills over into the others, including the economic sphere.

Therefore, it is fair to say that while the commitment called for in *Gaudium et Spes* is personal, it is by no means private; the Christian vocation of economic life demands contesting the shape of economic life, avoiding the evils of individualism, collectivism, materialism, and the exploitation of the poor and vulnerable. Here, we see the sort of public contestation described by Casanova as characteristic of a modern, public church. An analysis of how *Gaudium et Spes* contests the shape of the modern economy, which is beyond the scope of our reflections here, depends upon how the third chapter of Part II of the document discusses the dignity of the human person, the common good, and the reflection of these principles in economic life. It is worth pointing out, however, that although this chapter quite self-consciously builds on earlier documents, in particular, Pope Leo XIII's *Rerum Novarum* and Pope Pius XI's *Quadragesimo Anno*, in terms of what it has to say about the economy, there is also a significant shift in the theological framework. It is often forgotten that Leo lays out the mutual rights and responsibilities of owners and workers as part of a call for the "return to Christian life and Christian institutions,"[38] and even more explicitly Pius advocates for "the Christian reconstruction of human society."[39] They both express a longing for the time when Christianity was woven into the fabric of daily life, whereas *Gaudium et Spes* does not. Rather, the

---

[38] Pope Leo XIII, Encyclical Letter *Rerum Novarum*, no. 27.
[39] Pope Pius XI, Encyclical Letter *Quadragesimo Anno*, AAS 23 (1931): 177–228, no. 147.

latter document calls those who share a common personal commitment to the Christian narrative to advocate for a more truly human economy.

CONCLUSION

In conclusion, the Second Vatican Council embraced the secularity of the economy while at the same time claiming that participation in and the transformation of economic life is a Christian vocation. An analysis of what recent sociology has said about the secularization process helps us see that *Gaudium et Spes* embraced the secularity of the economy by recognizing it as an autonomous, "abstract system" and an "expert system" requiring expert knowledge independent of traditional clerical influence. Looking closely at the text of *Gaudium et Spes* shows how this embrace of secularity is reconciled with the document's highly theological account of economic life. The focus of Christian life shifts from communal practice to personal commitment, and the public role of the Church shifts from contesting secularity as such to contesting its shape, on behalf of human dignity and the common good.

PART III

Women and Vatican II

CHAPTER 6

Women During and After Vatican II

Patricia Madigan, O.P.

INTRODUCTION

The Second Vatican Council was a product of its times. Around the same time that John XXIII was preparing to call Vatican II Betty Friedan published *The Feminine Mystique*. Concerning her life during the 1950s she recorded: "I was experiencing a profound discontent, becoming increasingly conscious of the limitations of my narrow domestic world." Through her research she discovered that many women shared her experience and she named the false image to which they were unhappily trying to conform themselves "the feminine mystique." Among many other key insights, she declared: "The early feminists knew that marriage and motherhood are an essential part of life but not the whole of it."[1]

In the 1960s, the world experienced a rise in the societal status of women due to the actions of second-wave feminism and the lingering effects of first wave feminism. Whether it was self-consciously aware of

---

[1] Betty Friedan, *The Feminine Mystique* (New York: W.W. Norton, 1963).

P. Madigan, O.P. (✉)
Dominican Centre for Interfaith Ministry, Education and Research, Sydney, NSW, Australia
e-mail: pmm@accsoft.com.au

© The Author(s) 2018
V. Latinovic et al. (eds.), *Catholicism Opening to the World and Other Confessions*, Pathways for Ecumenical and Interreligious Dialogue,
https://doi.org/10.1007/978-3-319-98581-7_6

79

it or not, the Roman Catholic Church began to enlarge its understanding of women, their role in the family, and their rising social, political, and economic status. In the early years of the Council, under the leadership of John XXIII and Paul VI, the Church began to genuinely struggle with the issues related to women's participation in Church and society. However, these struggles were largely subverted during the long papacy of John Paul II during which ideologically motivated forces effectively promoted the "feminine genius" over the "feminine mystique" with devastating results for both women and the Church. Pope Francis seems not to have bought into this "culture war" so far and set about changing the conversation about women early into his pontificate, even if concrete changes were slower in following.

WOMEN AT THE COUNCIL

An important but perhaps less known aspect of the history of the Second Vatican Council was the experience of the lay auditors/guests. Although lay people had sometimes participated in previous church councils, it was usually as representatives of civic power, or indeed as those civic leaders themselves in convening councils.[2]

Belgian Cardinal Suenens made history when, in the first session, he declared from the Council floor, "Women too should be invited as auditors: unless I am mistaken, they make up half the human race." The topic was also raised by Melkite Archbishop George Hakim of Galilee.[3] These two speeches brought the matter into the open and paved the way for Paul VI's decisive action to invite lay auditors to the second session.

In the initial stages, there were twelve auditors, all male. Pope Paul VI was now welcoming of women. When the first list of lay auditors was brought to Paul VI he expressed surprise that there were no women on it, but someone else had control of the list. When Catholic women eventually arrived at the Council in the third session, they were greeted by the wives of the Protestant and Anglican observers who were

---

[2] See John W. O'Malley, S.J., *What Happened at Vatican II* (Cambridge, MA: Belknap Press of Harvard University Press, 2008), 26–27.

[3] Carmel E. McEnroy, *Guests in Their Own House: The Women of Vatican II* (Eugene: Oregon: Wipf and Stock, 2011), 41. Most of the information about the women at Vatican II comes from this source as there are few other records available. The women at the council are also discussed in detail in Chapter 9 of this volume by Gerard Mannion.

present in Rome with their clergy husbands. The twenty-four Catholic women who participated during the remaining sessions of the Council were a minority among the 500 experts (*periti*) and the 2500 Catholic bishops who attended from around the world. A complete list of these women is at the end of this chapter.

The women came as Paul VI's invited guests. They were, as Carmel McEnroy reported, "guests in their own house."[4] The women themselves saw their inclusion as a privilege rather than a natural baptismal birthright. Ten were women belonging to Religious Institutes, of whom eight were major superiors. Fourteen were lay women, most of whom were leaders of national and international women's organisations such as the World Union of Catholic Women's Organisations (WUCWO). Many were already well known in Rome to the pope, or to some of the cardinals or bishops. The marital status of these women was, almost without exception, either single or widowed and they tended to be in their senior years. The one outstanding exception was Luz-Marie Alvarez-Icaza from Mexico.

Luz-Marie and her husband José were the only married couple to attend and were an example of the different treatment of men and women. They were not invited as a married couple and it was José who insisted that his wife should also be invited since they were co-Presidents of the Latin American Christian Family Movement. Their entry to the Council, arm in arm through the main door, caused quite a stir. The bishops thought they were tourists. They also went to communion arm in arm, infuriating the Swiss Guards who were watching over Council protocol. There were also two coffee bars—Bar-None for women and Bar-Jonah for the men: male auditors could mix with bishops freely, but this was not so for the women. José Alvarez always went to the women's bar as a form of protest against the segregation.[5]

There were four women non-auditors who attended part of the Council: Dorothy Day of the Worker's Movement; Eileen Egan of the Peace Movement, who hoped the Council would ban nuclear weapons just as the Second Lateran Council in 1139 had banned the crossbow; world renowned economist Barbara Ward; and Patricia Crowley of Chicago, an authority on birth control.

---

[4] Ibid., 52.
[5] Ibid., 108–10.

The women who attended were well prepared for the Council. They were well read and had travelled widely, more widely than many bishops. Unlike some bishops who attended the Council without any experts and had difficulty in following the proceedings which were in Latin, the lay auditors sat in St. Andrew's Tribune with the theologians of the Council (*periti*) on one side, who did the translations for them, and cardinals on the other. The women's seats were also more comfortable—plush red seats and well upholstered.[6]

Attendance at the Council was a mixed experience for many of the women. Carmel McEnroy comments: When Paul VI let it be known that women would attend the Council, "little did they realise the traumatic effect their presence had on many bishops. Not knowing and not identifying with such seminary textbook definitions of themselves as temptress, the devil's gateway, etc., little did the women realise the iconoclastic alarms set off even by their silent, self-conscious presence."[7]

Forms of discrimination were suffered by the women. In an incident that became well publicised at the time, when a young journalist member of the Grail, Eva Fleischner, followed her male colleagues down the main isle to receive communion during a Mass at St. Peters she was "pushed back" by a Swiss Guard and physically prevented from going to communion. Instead of an apology being given, it was decided that no more journalists would be invited to the conciliar Mass.[8]

The women acted as equal partners with the male auditors except in one regard. The women auditors were never allowed to speak at the Council. In contrast Pat Keegan, a leading layman, presented the *Decree on the Laity* in English on the Council floor during the third session, even though Marie-Louise Monnet, a French auditor, was responsible for a large input into that document with her emphasis on the "independent milieux" of the laity.[9] The topic of the mission of the laity in the modern world was delivered in Spanish by another layman, while a paper on world poverty and hunger by the famous economist Barbara Ward had to be presented by auditor James Norris who read it in Latin.

[6] Ibid., 119–20.
[7] Ibid., 50.
[8] Ibid., 105.
[9] Ibid., 136.

When initially they were addressed with appellatives as *pulcherrimae auditrices* ("most beautiful female auditors") and referred to as "flowers" in the Church, the women made it clear that they wanted to be treated as ordinary human beings on an equal basis. As Rosemary Goldie stated:

> You can omit all those gratuitous flowery adjectives, the pedestals and incense, from your sentence. All women ask for is that they be recognized as the full human persons they are, and treated accordingly.[10]

During a meeting of the Mixed Commission on *Gaudium et Spes*, in which lay experts were able to ask for the floor and to speak, Pilar Bellosillo warned of the dangers involved in employing a different, romantic language to speak of women:

> This kind of language detached from life, puts women on a pedestal instead of on the same level as man. By doing so you demonstrate that that in reality you consider *man* the human being, but not woman. This does woman a disservice because it does not take seriously her equal dignity and humanity.[11]

Soon many of the bishops realised what a valuable resource they now had. The women were treated as experts (*peritae*) by many participants and by invitation attended meetings of subcommittees working on Council documents, especially texts that dealt with the laity. Some of the women, Marie-Louise Monnet (France), Rosemary Goldie (Australia), Pilar Bellosillo, José and Luz Alvarey-Icaza spoke at meetings with bishops outside the Council and to journalists. The women also met together on a weekly basis, reading draft documents and commenting on them.

Hospitality was a particular way that these women gained influence over the Council. All had open houses for bishops and seminarians. The Council Fathers and seminarians were invited to come freely and relax, and by the end of the Council over 1000 bishops had shared their hospitality. In this relaxed atmosphere, all got to know each other better and conversation flowed freely.

---

[10]Mary Luke Tobin, "Women in the Church since Vatican II," *America*, November 1, 1986.

[11]McEnroy, *Guests in Their Own House*, 145.

In this way the women, although excluded from speaking from the Council floor, had significant input into some of the Council's later documents. On the initiative of theologian Bernard Häring, C.Ss.R. (who earned the title "Häring the Daring"), Pilar Bellosillo, Rosemary Goldie, Suzanne Guillemin, Mary Luke Tobin, Marie-Louise Monnet and Maria Vendrik and others joined sub-commissions working on *Gaudium et Spes* which, along with *Apostolicam Actuositatem*, became the two key documents of the Council based on the theology of induction—experience.[12]

IMPACT OF THE COUNCIL ON CHURCH TEACHING ABOUT WOMEN

In October 1964, as the Council began its discussion on Schema 13, bishops increasingly acknowledged the need to address the issue of the growing public role of women in the world. The African and Canadian bishops were the first to plea for the recognition of the dignity of women. Bishop Gerard Coderre (Canada) and Bishop Augustin Frotz (Germany) both dedicated their entire intervention to the position of women in society.[13]

Bishop Coderre was among the first who stated that the growing recognition of the dignity of women was among the "signs of the times" that must be studied and included in the schema on the Church in the Modern World. He emphasised that men should not only give women their proper place in the world but recognize that they are necessary for the completion of the divine plan for human perfection, for the perfection of the family and of society in general. Bishop Frotz said that the Church has not yet become aware of the worldwide implications of the changed position of women in modern society. Women should be accepted as the Church's grown-up daughters, not just children. In the liturgy, they should be addressed directly as "sisters" and not just submerged in the term "brothers."

Some of the strongest comments made about women came from Archbishop Paul Hallinan of Atlanta, Georgia when he asked whether the Church "has given the leadership that Christ, by word and example,

---

[12] Ibid., 133–35.

[13] O'Malley, *What Happened at Vatican II*, 235; Aloysius J. Wycislo, *Vatican II Revisited: Reflections by One Who Was There* (New York: Alba House, 1987), 157.

clearly showed he expected of her." In proclaiming the equality of man and woman, he said, "the Church must act as well as speak by fraternal testimony, not only in abstract doctrine."

Quoting from a statement made in 1961 by Paul VI when he was Archbishop of Milan that "Women must come closer to the altar, to souls and to the Church in order to gather together the people of God," Hallinan continued:

> In our society women in many places and in many respects still bear the marks of inequality. This is evident in working conditions, wages and hours of work, in marriage and property laws. Above all it is present in that gradualism, bordering on inaction, which limits their presence in the tremendous forces now working for universal education, for peace, for the rehabilitation of the deprived, the just and compassionate care of the young, the aged and the needy, the dispossessed and the victims of human injustice and weakness.[14]

"The Church has been slow in denouncing the degradation of women in slavery, and in claiming for them the right of suffrage and economic equality,"[15] he said. "Particularly, the Church has been slow to offer women, in the selection of their vocations, any choice but that of mother or nun." Therefore, "we must not continue to perpetuate the secondary place accorded to women in the Church of the 20th century. We must not continue to be latecomers in the social, political and economic development that has today reached climactic conditions."[16]

At a press conference during the fourth session Cardinal Suenens called on the Church to abandon its masculine superiority complex—to learn to respect woman's true dignity and to appreciate her part in the plan of God.[17]

In the documents which flowed out of Vatican II evidence of the women's input is found, as one would expect, most notably in the later documents *Apostolicam Actuositatem* and *Gaudium et Spes*.[18]

---

[14] Placid Jordan, "U.S. Prelate Asks Women Be Given Roles in the Mass," *The Voice* (Archdiocese of Miami, Florida) 7, no. 31 (October 15, 1965): 4.

[15] Ibid.

[16] Ibid.

[17] Wycislo, *Vatican II Revisited*, 158–60.

[18] McEnroy, *Guests in Their Own House*, 155ff.

A sentence crafted by Rosemary Goldie was inserted with the support of two bishops into the decree on the Apostolate on the Laity.[19] "Since in our days women are taking an increasingly active share in the whole life of society, it is important that their participation in the various fields of the Church's apostolate should likewise develop" (AA 9). Another almost hidden reference to women occurs later in the same decree.

> Furthermore, centres of documentation and study not only in theology but also in anthropology, psychology, sociology, and methodology should be established for all fields of the apostolate, for the better development of the natural capacities of the laity – men and women, young persons and adults. (AA 32)

The influence of the women who participated in the discussions and amendments of *Gaudium et Spes* can also be clearly seen in texts like this:

> With respect to the fundamental rights of the person, every type of discrimination, whether social or cultural, whether based on sex, race, colour, social condition, language or religion, is to be overcome and eradicated as contrary to God's intent. For in truth it must still be regretted that fundamental personal rights are still not being universally honoured. Such is the case of a woman who is denied the right to choose a husband freely, to embrace a state of life or to acquire an education or cultural benefits equal to those recognized for men. (GS 29)

However, Aloysius Wycislo comments on the sparse mention of the role of women in Church and society in *Gaudium et Spes* despite Pope Paul's declared intention of bringing women into the Council's deliberations and some sixteen interventions similar to the ones mentioned above.[20] Gladys Parentelli had kept a copy of the original Schema 13 that fed into parts of *Gaudium et Spes*. She had analysed it and underlined parts of it that seemed to be an advance on the Church's doctrine but discovered that all those passages had been taken out of its final form.[21]

---

[19] Guiseppe Alberigo, and Joseph A. Komonchak, eds., *History of Vatican II*, vol. 5 (Maryknoll: Orbis/Leuven: Peeters, 2006), 268.

[20] Wycislo, *Vatican II Revisited*, 161.

[21] McEnroy, *Guests in Their Own House*, 157.

Catherine Clifford[22] interestingly points out that the silences of the Council regarding women should not necessarily be understood as the exclusion of women's perspectives. She draws attention to the fact that all the women at the Council wanted was to be recognised as full human persons and so they understood themselves to be included each time the Council referred to members of the baptised faithful. Rosemary Goldie was in favour of the Council speaking about women "on condition that women were not isolated as a problem apart, as it were on the fringe of society and the modern world, or as if the real problems that women experience were their exclusive concern." Clifford sees the approach of the Council as "inclusive" to the extent that it refrained from adopting a theology of "complementarity," and instead chose to define women not by gender roles but rather as equal participants sharing in the mystery of Christ through baptism.

Church Teaching on Women Following the Council

There have been a limited number of incremental changes in Church teaching about women since the era of first wave feminism in the 1880s. However, all too many such official Church teachings until relatively recently continued to bear the imprint of those influenced by certain writings of Augustine of Hippo and Thomas Aquinas (and interpretations of the same) using broadly the same categories of thought—particularly with regard to the "complementarity" of the roles of men and women, whereby what has often been entailed or at least implied thanks to such teachings, is that women are "naturally" subordinate to men in the "order of creation," while at the same time professing women to be equal in the "order of salvation."

Therefore, although John XXIII and the Second Vatican Council acknowledged the changing role of women in the secular world, too often, both the ecclesial discourse of that time and subsequent discourse continued to feature an emphasis upon the biological functions for women, primarily as mothers and wives. So in too many places we frequently see what beneath the surface can appear to be only a grudging acknowledgement to the advancement of women in society, stating that these advances must not be made at the expense of women's maternal role.

---

[22]Catherine E. Clifford, *Decoding Vatican II: Interpretation and Ongoing Reception* (Mahwah, NJ: Paulist Press, 2014), 73–74.

Equality for women continued to be qualified by an "equal but different" clause, without spelling out what might be entailed by such a qualification.

By the end of the pontificate of Paul VI, despite its promising beginnings, a patriarchal politics of identity given a religious justification can be seen to be taking hold at multiple levels in the Catholic Church. A chasm has continued to open up between the "social teaching" of the Church and its teachings on the role of women. Instead of developing a theology and anthropology which would promote a full vocational "flourishing" for each and every Christian, the focus has been on defining a positive and idealised role for women in the Church and world which at the same time will protect the Church's hierarchical and patriarchal power structures from the challenges posed by giving equal status to women.

A watershed was reached in the 1976 declaration of the Congregation for the Doctrine of the Faith, *Inter Insigniores* (On the Admission of Women to the Ministerial Priesthood)[23] which ruled out ordination of women, by introducing the novel idea that maleness was essential to image Christ, despite a more open verdict given by the Pontifical Biblical Commission. Already the Church at its hierarchical level was pulling back from the experiential-inductive theological methods it had begun to put into practice at Vatican II. What was especially significant here was that the document justified the exclusion of women from the priesthood not on anthropological but on theological and, especially, *christological* grounds. Although the CDF claimed to have consulted a large number of women in the preparatory stage of the document, one of the largest Catholic Women's organizations, the WUCWO representing 36 million women, was not part of that consultation.[24]

During the long papacy of John Paul II (1978–2005) the theology of womanhood expressed by the Catholic Church was greatly developed regarding their changing role, status, and place in the family, in society and in the Church in such documents as 1988's On the Dignity of

---

[23] Congregation for the Doctrine of the Faith, Declaration *Inter Insigniores* (On the Admission of Women to the Ministerial Priesthood), AAS 69 (1977): 98–116.

[24] McEnroy, *Guests in Their Own House*, 284.

Women (*Mulieris Dignitatem*).[25] The challenge for a Church leadership that many were now perceiving to be protecting a hierarchical and patriarchal power structure, first and foremost, was to seek to define a positive role for women in the Church while at the same time providing a theological justification for the exclusion of women from the sacramental priesthood. The problem here is that this entails that governing and teaching authority should be reserved, in the main, to men only, as well.

A whole new vocabulary and imagery were constructed for the purpose. It consisted of

- an essentialist understanding of the nature of sexual difference;
- a narrow choice of scriptural texts and images related to Christ's relationship with the Church (for example, why not accentuate vine and branches, instead of a concentration on nuptial imagery?);
- a continuing dependence on medieval understandings of anthropology and human biology (men as active agents, women as passive and receptive—therefore implicitly deficient by comparison to men); and
- the assertion that these roles have been ordained by God since the very beginning of creation.

Terms such as "a new feminism," "feminine genius," the "Petrine" and "Marian" aspects of the Church, and the "Theology of the Body" with its particular application of the term "complementary," became the new *lingua franca* of many Catholic forums attended by young adults. They seemed aimed to obscure the continuing subordination of women in the Church.

John Paul II's teachings as they affect women are problematic. He continued the papal tendency to idealise women and spoke constantly of the "dignity" of a woman. But issues such as rape and violence against women were not addressed. Neither did he address the contextual issues of women's social and economic disadvantage, including women's lack of voice and agency within the Church.

Benedict XVI (2005–2013) has said that although there are "limitations" on women, he expects that women themselves will know how

---

[25] John Paul II, Apostolic Letter Mulieris Dignitatem, AAS 80 (1988): 1653–1729.

to "make their own space" and achieve their fully effective place in the Church best suited to them.[26] This is a position that contains many contradictions.

POPE FRANCIS

In the early years of his pontificate, Francis appeared to display the same tendency as his predecessors towards romanticism when speaking about motherhood and women and he began his papacy badly with some ill-judged remarks concerning women:

> The fact is, woman was taken from a rib... I am kidding, that was a joke.[27]

> Women theologians "are the strawberries on the cake!"[28]

One commentator has suggested that the message of Francis can sometimes be lost in translation as his language and metaphors are tied to his cultural and linguistic background as an Italo-Argentine male.[29] And it does appear that Francis seems reluctant to allow his words to become part of "identity politics" or the "culture wars". He has not, for instance, blamed girl altar servers for the decline in vocations.[30] And he has not blamed women's emancipation as responsible for the decline in the institution of marriage. Francis called that "an insult," saying "No, it is not

[26] John Thavis, "Women Chip Vatican's Glass Ceiling with Increased Numbers, Influence," *Catholic News Service*, March 2, 2007 (this article is no longer available online).

[27] John Hooper, "Pope Francis Jokes 'Woman Was from a Rib' as He Avoids Vow to Reform Church," *The Guardian*, June 30, 2014, http://www.theguardian.com/world/2014/jun/29/pope-francis-woman-from-rib-avoids-pledge-reform-catholic-church.

[28] Diane Montagna, "Pope Calls Women the 'Strawberries on the Cake' of New International Theological Commission," *Aleteia*, December 5, 2014, http://www.aleteia.org/en/religion/article/pope-calls-women-the-strawberries-on-the-cake-of-new-international-theological-commission-6445408456802304.

[29] Massimo Faggioli, "Pope's Message Is Often Lost in Translation," *Global Pulse*, January 8, 2015, https://international.la-croix.com/news/popes-message-is-often-lost-in-translation/585.

[30] Matthew James Christoff, "Cardinal Raymond Leo Burke on the Catholic 'Man-Crisis' and What to Do about It," http://www.newemangelization.com/uncategorized/cardinal-raymond-leo-burke-on-the-catholic-man-crisis-and-what-to-do-about-it.

true!" Blaming the problem on efforts for women's rights "is a form of chauvinism that always wants to control the woman."[31]

> He recognizes that today's contemporary culture has opened new spaces, new freedoms and new depths for the enrichment of the understanding of the differences between men and women and regards the way Jesus considered women as shedding a powerful light on a road "along which we have only travelled a short distance... It is a road to be travelled with greater creativity and boldness."[32]

But neither has he as yet appointed women to any significant senior positions in the Church or made any concrete suggestions for greater participation by women in Church leadership and decision-making.

Pope Francis seems to be experimenting with some new concepts and language regarding women. He has blended the language of John Paul II (reinforcing the subordination of women in the Church under the guise of complementarity) with a fresh vocabulary of reciprocity and mutuality. Interestingly, he has used language aligned to that of Betty Friedan, saying "I would like to explain a bit about what I said about the participation of women in the Church. You cannot be limited to the fact of being an altar server or the president of Caritas... No! It must be more, but profoundly more, also mystically more, with this that I said about the theology of the woman."[33] He has gone on record as an advocate of equal pay for men and women and called the present disparity "a pure scandal."[34]

Repudiating his earlier "joke," Francis has emphasised that "the image of the rib does not at all express inferiority or subordination, but the opposite—that man and woman are the same substance and are

---

[31] Joshua J. McElwee, "Francis Firmly Backs Equal Pay for Women, Citing Christian 'Radical Equality'," *National Catholic Reporter*, April 29, 2015.

[32] "Pope Francis's Catechesis on the Family," *AsiaNews*, April 15, 2015, http://www.asianews.it/news-en/Pope:-no-opposition-or-subordination-between-men-and-women,-gender-theory-is-a-step-backwards-33982.html.

[33] Press Conference of Pope Francis during Return Flight from Rio de Janeiro, July 28, 2013, http://w2.vatican.va/content/francesco/en/speeches/2013/july/documents/papa-francesco_20130728_gmg-conferenza-stampa.html.

[34] Tierney McAfee, "Pope Francis Calls Pay Disparities between Women and Men a 'Pure Scandal,'" *People*, April 29, 2015, http://www.people.com/article/pope-francis-equal-pay-women-disparity-pure-scandal.

complementary, and also have this reciprocity." He pointed to ways that the rapport between men and women has been undermined by "the extreme negatives of patriarchal cultures."[35]

Seeming to address McEnroy's description of women at Vatican II as guests in their own house, Francis has said that "new criteria and ways" need to be found "so that women feel not as guests, but as full participants in the various areas of social and ecclesial life."[36] Although he has expressed the view that only men can be priests,[37] it has been offered as a personal viewpoint and not as unchangeable Church teaching. It needs to be understood in the context of the pope's immediate urgent and mammoth tasks of cleaning up the scandal-ridden Vatican finances and restoring a *synodal* structure of governance to the Church. These latter reforms will no doubt contribute to other changes needed in the future.

"Experience teaches us," Pope Francis says, that "to attain self-knowledge and grow harmoniously the human being needs the reciprocity between man and woman. When this does not happen, we see the consequences. We are made to listen to each other and help each other. We can say that without the mutual enrichment inherent in this relationship—in thought and action, in the affections and work, also in faith the two cannot even fully understand what it means to be a man and woman." The Pope also added: "God created man, male and female, in His image, giving them both the same dignity and equality: we must work in the Church and in society, to ensure that this equality is respected, rejecting all forms of abuse or injustice, particularly against women."[38]

Focusing his 2015 Easter Vigil reflection on the women who, going out early Sunday morning to anoint the Body of the Lord, were the first to see the empty tomb, he explained that entering into the mystery of

---

[35] Joshua J. McElwee, "Francis Calls for Renewal of 'Alliance' between Men and Women," *National Catholic Reporter*, April 22, 2015, http://ncronline.org/blogs/ncr-today/francis-calls-renewal-alliance-between-men-and-women.

[36] Francis, "Address to the Pontifical Council for Culture in Plenary Assembly on the Theme 'Women's Cultures: Equality and Difference,'" AAS 107, no. 3 (2015): 264–66.

[37] Cindy Wooden, "Pope Says Only Men Can Be Priests, But Women Must Have Voice in Church," *Catholic News Service*, November 26, 2013, http://www.catholicnews.com/services/englishnews/2013/pope-says-only-men-can-be-priests-but-women-must-have-voice-in-church.cfm. See also Anne E. Patrick's suggested understanding of Francis's intentions here (vis-à-vis the 'papal silence' to allow the church time to discern such issues with greater freedom) at the close of Chapter 9 of this volume.

[38] "Pope Francis's Catechesis on the Family," *AsiaNews*, April 15, 2015.

Easter "means the ability... to hear the tiny whisper amid great silence by which God speaks to us...," it "demands that we not be afraid of reality: that we not be locked into ourselves, that we not flee from what we fail to understand, that we not close our eyes to problems or deny them, that we not dismiss our questions..." and "to enter into the mystery means going beyond our own comfort zone, beyond the laziness and indifference which hold us back, and going out in search of truth, beauty and love." "We cannot live Easter," he said, "without entering into this mystery."[39]

WOMEN WHO PARTICIPATED IN THE SECOND VATICAN COUNCIL[40]

Auditors

Constantina Baldinucci, S.C. (Italy), Superior of the Milan-based Sisters of Maria Bambina (the Child Mary) and President of the Italian Sisters' Union. She was a personal friend of Paul VI (3rd and 4th sessions, 1964–1965).

Pilar Bellosillo (Spain), President of World Union of Catholic Women's Organisations (WUCWO) for thirteen years (3rd and 4th sessions, 1964–1965).

Jerome Maria Chimy, S.S.M.I. (Canada), Superior General of the Sister Servants of Mary Immaculate, a Ukrainian Byzantine rite (4th session, 1965).

Gertrude Ehrle (Germany), President of the German Catholic Women's League and a member of WUCWO, came from a very respected family in Ravensburg and was related to many bishops and priests including Jesuit curial Cardinal Franz Ehrle (d. 1934). She was known to the Jesuits and to Cardinal Bea (4th session, 1965).

Cristina Estrada, A.C.J. (Spain), Cuban born Superior General of the Sisters of the Handmaids of the Sacred Heart in Spain. She was well known to the Roman Curia and to Pius XII as well as John XXIII (3rd and 4th sessions, 1964–1965).

---

[39] Francis, "Homily at the Easter Vigil," AAS 107, no. 5 (2015): 442–43.

[40] Compiled Largely from Information Given in McEnroy, *Guests in Their Own House*.

Claudia Feddish, O.S.B.M. (United States), American-born Ukrainian rite Superior General of the Sisters of St. Basil the Great of Mount Saint Macrina. She took her appointment as a recognition of the Eastern rites. She was well-known to Cardinal Slipyi of the Ukrainian Greek-Catholic Church (3rd and 4th sessions, 1964–1965).

Marie-Henriette Ghanem, S.S.C.C. of the Sisters of the Sacred Hearts of Jesus and Mary was invited to the Council as the chair of the Assembly of Major Superiors of Lebanon, Coptic rite (3rd and 4th sessions, 1964–1965).

Rosemary Goldie (Australia), Executive Secretary of the Permanent Committee for International Congresses of the Lay Apostolate (COPECIAL) in Rome became the only "curial woman" when she was appointed as one of two Undersecretaries to the new Pontifical Council of the Laity created by Paul VI on 6 January 1967, a position she held for nine years (3rd and 4th sessions, 1964–1965).

Ida Marenco Grillo (Italy), was a war widow who, as secretary of a local branch of Italian Catholic Action, had spent many years in post-war relief work and was invited to the Council as an "expert in life" (3rd and 4th sessions, 1964–1965).

Suzanne Guillemin, D.C. (France), Superior General of more than 45,000 Daughters of Charity of St. Vincent de Paul (3rd and 4th sessions, 1964–1965).

Marie de la Croix Khouzam, R.E.S.C. (Egypt), Coptic rite Superior General of the Sisters of the Sacred Heart in Egypt was invited as the chair of the Union of Teaching Sisters in Egypt (3rd and 4th sessions, 1964–1965).

Margarita Moyana Llerena (Argentina), 38-year-old President of The World Federation of Catholic Young Women and Girls (WFCYWG) (4th session, 1965).

Catherine McCarthy (USA), a Bostonian widow and Dominican Tertiary, President of the National Council of Catholic Women (NCCW), a federation of fourteen thousand Catholic women's organizations, representing ten million women (3rd and 4th sessions, 1964–1965).

Alda Miceli (Italy), with many years involvement in Catholic Action and President of the *Centro Italiano Feminile* (Italian Women's Centre), was invited to the Council as President General of the Secular Institute, the Missionaries of Christ the King. She was known to Pius XII, and Paul VI knew her family well (3rd and 4th sessions, 1964–1965).

Marie-Louise Monnet (France), was a member of the renowned family of Cognac Brandy makers. She was well known to the French bishops from her founding of a number of Catholic Action groups for youth and adults and also to Paul VI for her role as President in the development of the International Movement for the Apostolate in the "Independent Milieux" (MIAMSI) (3rd and 4th sessions, 1964–1965).

Amalia di Montezemolo (Italy) was a war widow whose husband had suffered arrest and torture while resisting the German occupation of Italy in 1944. She became President of The Society for Spiritual Assistance to the Armed Forces of Italy, dedicated to offering every form of spiritual and material assistance to all branches and ranks of the military, and founded new branches in many Italian cities while at the same time bringing up five children on her own. Paul VI knew the story of the family. Her priest–son, Andrea di Montezmolo, became a cardinal in 2006 (3rd and 4th sessions, 1964–1965).

Gladys Parentelli (Uruguay), Vice-President of the female branch of the International Movement of Catholic Agricultural and Rural Youth (MIJARC) based in Louvain. The names of three auditors, two male and one female, were submitted to Paul VI who chose 30-year-old Parentelli. Until then, the Latin American presence of women was totally lacking (4th session, 1965).

Anne-Marie Roeloffzen (Netherlands), a 32-year-old Dutch lawyer, was one of the youngest auditors at the Council. She was General Secretary of the World Federation of Catholic Young Women and Girls (WFCYWG) (3rd and 4th sessions, 1964–1965).

Hedwig Skoda (Czechoslovakia)—founder and President of *Nouvelles équipes internationales de Rennaissance chrétienne* (International Teams of Christian Renaissance) based in Switzerland (4th session, 1965).

Juliana Thomas, A.D.J. (Germany), a sister of the Poor Handmaids of Jesus Christ and teacher of children with disabilities. She was the first general secretary of the Union of Major Superiors in Germany (1957–1968) and it was in this capacity that she was invited to the Council. She was known to several among the powerful minds of the German bishops and theologians (3rd and 4th sessions, 1964–1965).

Mary Luke Tobin, S.L. (United States), Superior General of the Sisters of Loretto at the Foot of the Cross and newly elected President of the Conference of Major Religious Superiors of Women in the United States (3rd and 4th sessions, 1964–1965).

Sabine de Valon, R.S.C.J. (France), Superior General of the Religious of the Sacred Heart and President of the Superior Generals in Italy, the forerunner of the International Union of Superiors General (UISG). She was well known in the Sacred Congregation for Religious (3rd and 4rd sessions, 1964–1965).

Luz-Marie Alvarez-Icaza (Mexico), Luz-Marie and her husband José Alvarez-Icaza were co-Presidents of the Latin-American groupings of the Christian Family Movement, and were the only married couple to attend (4th session, 1965).

Maria Vendrik (Netherlands), founder and national President for ten years of the Catholic Young Women's Organisation, a federation of all the Catholic young women's movements in the Netherlands, former President of WFCYWG and board member of WUCWO. She had made studies of women in many situations in life, and was invited to the third session because of her wealth of experience and expertise and as a careful follower of the work of the Commission on *Gaudium et Spes*—"The Pastoral Constitution on the Church in the Modern World".

Women Non-auditors Who Attended Part of the Council

Dorothy Day of the Worker's Movement.

Eileen Egan of the Peace Movement, who hoped the council would ban nuclear weapons just as the Second Lateran Council in 1139 had banned the crossbow.

Patricia Crowley of Chicago, an authority on birth control.

Barbara Ward whose paper on world hunger and poverty had to be read by a male, James Norris (in Latin).

Influential Women Beyond the Council

It is also worth mentioning here another group who sought to influence the council via a variety of approaches. St. Joan's Alliance, formed in 1911 and the first Catholic organisation to support the vote for women and women's ordination throughout the twentieth century, hovered in the background recommending changes to women's status and urging the auditors on. Dr. Gertrude Heizellman (a German lawyer) sent a cautious and respectful resolution to the Pope on the admission of women to the priesthood after writing a pamphlet entitled "We shall no longer be silent." The same group also asked for women's admission to the Diaconate and a revision of Canon Law.

CHAPTER 7

Opening to the World: A Reformed Feminist Posture of Openness

Mary McClintock Fulkerson

INTRODUCTION

As so many contributions to these two volumes make clear, Vatican II constituted a concerted effort on the part of the Roman Catholic Church to throw its doors open to the contemporary world in a manner that would have been unthinkable in the decades prior to the election of John XXIII, for whom such an opening up of the church was a foremost priority. "Opening to the world"—What a compelling theme! Theologically "opening to the world" is compelling if you believe that God, a God of creation, is everywhere. The theme is compelling if you believe that the world in all its particularity—creative, fallible, and broken—expresses itself through very different cultures, worldviews, and modes of communication. A believer must take each of these seriously, i.e., "be open to" them. The character of this openness is further specified when we think of our Creator God as Redeemer and as present through the Holy Spirit. This God calls us to an openness shaped by radical love, most simply expressed as the call to "love your neighbor as yourself" (Mark 12:31).

M. M. Fulkerson (✉)
Duke University, Durham, NC, USA
e-mail: mfulkerson@div.duke.edu

© The Author(s) 2018
V. Latinovic et al. (eds.), *Catholicism Opening to the World and Other Confessions*, Pathways for Ecumenical and Interreligious Dialogue, https://doi.org/10.1007/978-3-319-98581-7_7

This love is not referring just to a neighbor who lives near us, or looks pretty much like us, or someone we approve of, but to a neighbor who is everyone and everywhere. We are called to be open to and loving of the "neighbors" who are very different from us, people who come out of diverse locations, cultures, and worldviews.

But many would argue that such still sounds too vague. What if that neighbor is doing harm? What if a woman is experiencing domestic abuse-patterns of violence and control by a spouse? Is she supposed to just love this abusive husband as her "neighbor"? Being open to the world, as in loving it all no matter *what*, sounds like having no standards. Furthermore, this kind of openness sounds like capitulation or being completely passive. Specifying what complicates this love is a huge challenge, of course. As a step toward defining such openness, I will draw upon my own tradition, the defining commitments of the Reformed Presbyterian Church, to further elucidate this claim about love. The mantra "*ecclesia reformata, semper reformanda, secundum verbum dei*"[1] further specifies the call for openness to the world as grounded in the radical love of neighbor understood through the lenses of Biblical and Reformed traditions of idolatry and iconoclasm.[2] These themes are the basis for a theocentric or God-centered understanding of human beings in all of our particularity.

Such an understanding of human beings, or theological anthropology, comes with the assumption that human beings are finite creatures and that finitude is a good thing, not a sin. As created in the image of God,

---

[1] This phrase is originally attributed to St. Augustine (cf. Theodor Mahlmann, "'*Ecclesia semper reformanda*'. Eine historische Aufarbeitung. Neue Bearbeitung," in *Hermeneutica Sacra. Studien zur Auslegung der Heiligen Schrift im 16. und 17. Jahrhundert*, ed. Torbjörn Johansson, Robert Kolb, and Johann Anselm Steiger (Berlin: De Gruyter, 2010), 382–441) and in its longer form to Jodocus van Lodenstein, minister in Reformed Church from the United Provinces (Netherlands).

[2] This Latin mantra emerged in the 16th century with the Reformation and is found in the Presbyterian Book of Order in Chapter II, "The Church and its Confessions," F-2.02. While not employing this exact phrase, at Vatican II, itself *Unitatis Redintegratio*, §6 indicates that the church is always in need of "continual reformation" *(ad hanc perennem reformationem)*, while *Lumen Gentium* §8 states the church is "at one and the same time holy and always in need of purification" *(sancta simul et semper purificanda)*. See Peter De Mey, "Church Renewal and Reform in the Documents of Vatican II: History, Theology, Terminology," *The Jurist* 71, no. 2 (2011): 369–400; Gerard Bekes and Vilmos Vajita, eds., *Unitatis Redintegratio, 1964–1974: The Impact of the Decree on Ecumenism* (Rome: Anselmiana, 1977), passim.

we are thus created to be in relation to that which is truly God. As finite, our being created in the image of God does not mean that we are God-like, but rather that we find our true grounding or stability in relation to God. Identifying finitude as characterizing good and fallible creatures who are created in the image of God, thus *imago dei*, indicates that flesh and bones, bodies, desire and eros—all the features of living beings—are to be honored, but cannot be absolutized. Our characteristics will not be rescued from the fallibility of finitude. Pleasure and sexuality, for example, can be honored and enjoyed, but their limitations must be accepted; thus, sometimes these features must be criticized or rejected. Recognition of our need to accept human finitude and fallibility is crucial to understanding idolatry, which is rooted in our refusal to do so. Rather than its typical association with the worship of non-Christian gods, idolatry is about more subtle practices which refuse to accept finitude as finite goods we hope will secure us are idolized, as in, treated as our absolute security.

Key to this idolatrous absolutizing is that it fails, since the true good, or end of human beings is to be grounded in God, our only true security. Any worldly good is inevitably challenged or threatened *because it is finite*. Such challenges are fine, if we *accept* the fallibility of our worldly goods. An example: money is good, we need some to survive, but it cannot secure us absolutely. If we make it our ultimate security, it fails, because it can never be enough. Nothing finite lasts forever or will not be fragile and inevitably broken. We lock our doors, we built fences around our property, and can go on an endless process of wanting more securities. Because we have idolized money, we find ourselves in a never-ending downward spiral, because there will always be something perceived as a threat, and we will always think we need more. We will thus feel compelled to resist and reject any realities that appear to threaten our money, which can mean stereotyping and vilifying all sorts of particularities in order to justify rejection. And since our money will never secure us absolutely, and since idolatry is inherently linked to a broken relation to the neighbor, this endless anxiety will alienate us from many neighbors by creating all sorts of negatively stereotyped "others."

Iconoclasm, then, refers to the persistent need to discern and critique our idolizing practices, from the most blatant to the most subtle. And even discernment is quite a challenge, given that such practices are typically construed as "normal" and are sustained and reproduced by social structures and social imaginaries that support many of our practices of absolutizing. To be wealthy and want to enhance our income status is not typically vilified by the American work ethic. While critiqued by some, especially racially marginalized groups, white privilege and the structures that maintain and reproduce it are considered quite "normal" by most whites. The common practice of whites avoiding black male teenagers on the street, or the well-known expression, "driving while black"[3] both indicate the deeply embedded racist stereotypes in the white social imagination. So, idolizing can occur simply by virtue of our participation in and failure to resist what is perceived to be the dominant social world.

When it comes to the neighbor, then, love is neither simple acceptance nor is it the other extreme where we valorize a particular group, typically our own, and its unique features. An example of the latter would be the "love" of the Caucasian race because of its whiteness and its privilege—where, for example, police would never automatically assume that a white driver was doing anything bad. The love invoked by the gospel is minimally about honoring the finite goodness of all creatures—their worth as created in the image of God *and* their finitude. However, no feature of the human can be absolutized. That is not to say that love does not include the valorization of features of the other. The particularity of human beings, indeed of creation itself, is crucial to our value, and there would be no attraction without particularity. However, to recognize this is to recognize that particularities of other groups may well be unrecognized by our own group or falsely stereotyped. Even though stereotypes may well be rooted in some reality, we must recognize that valorizing all as *imago dei* may be a challenge, but it is our calling as creatures of God. In short, gospel love is not simply a call to a kind of blind generalized acceptance or rejection of all persons, but an opening to the honoring of particularity wherever and in whatever form we encounter it.

As I explore this theological frame as a constructive Presbyterian Reformed approach to feminist theology, I will thereby complicate "love" not reject it. I will complicate love with further examples of idolatry and iconoclasm; loving the neighbor must be "reformed and always reforming." I then wish to pose this exploration as a request.

---

[3] "Driving While Black" is a term used to share incidents of racial profiling by police officers while driving. It refers to the notion that a driver can be pulled over by a police officer simply because he or she is black.

Given my admittedly more limited knowledge of Vatican II and the Roman Catholicism, this article will end with an inquiry as to how the two themes (love of neighbor and "reformed and always reforming") are also part of Catholic traditions.

Feminist theology itself can be interpreted as a *reformation of our love of neighbor*. Its focus has been to respond critically to patriarchal structures, practices, and the symbols and stereotypes that support these practices. Laws going back for centuries that prohibited women from voting, owning property, or access to equal pay are examples of such practices and structures that grant dominant power to males and diminish the *imago dei* of females. Now, this is not a simplistic phenomenon where all men idolized maleness and vilified women, creating diminished definitions of what it meant to be females. Rather, patriarchy is a particular *form* of "loving and defining the neighbor" that itself needs reforming. The structural stereotypes and practices of patriarchy are complicated and can never be viewed as monolithic. The ways in which the particularity of being female are defined and treated may include what appears to be "honoring." However, the minimal shared feature of patriarchies everywhere is that women's agency and power have been controlled and diminished. Such minimization is framed in many ways. It can be direct and insulting, but patriarchy is quite frequently framed "positively," as a form of patriarchal love.

With race, the framework of idolatry is a bit more blatant. White power structures in the United States not only enslaved persons of color but dehumanized them to justify treating them as property. This was clearly not an honoring of particularity. And if this is not a version of the idolizing of "whiteness," I do not know what is—as in, saying that the full human, created in the image of God, is a white person—male. Of course, slavery meant white women had more power than black men or women. Yet as dominant and powerful as white racism has been, both masculinity and whiteness failed to provide the real grounding, or divine and ultimate security for white males that radical dependence upon God would. And that failure was no cure; it intensified male (and white) insecurity and the continued need to justify the stereotypes and mistreatment of blacks. Such social brokenness and its justification have not ended in the US.

Of course, only grounding in that which is truly God, not our racial or gender identity, can provide us with the courage to live with the inevitable insecurity and loss that come with life and to bravely care for and respect those neighbors who are very different—to honor particularities of all sorts. Such grounding allows us to live *without* idols.

The emergence of feminist theology, then, is *the response of faith to the social sin of patriarchy and its wounds*, a response that resists the sinful diminishing of women, as it pushes for recognition of women's full agency as *imago dei*. Like any faithful response to idolatry, it cannot push for a new idol, matriarchy, i.e., to make women the new group in control. It must work for discernment, confession and change in gender relations and new forms of sociality that honor all genders. Of course, feminist theology is not pure or perfect. Womanist and black feminist theologies challenge the unacknowledged whiteness of feminist theology, and further illustrate the way subtle forms of idolizing occur, typically formulated as a judgment about which group counts as the *real and full* human beings. Posing challenges to the white colorblindness of feminist theology, as well as the patriarchal habits of African American male theologies, Womanist theology exposes the "false universal" of "women's experience" as defined by white women, and the long-overlooked racist/sexist function of cultural stereotypes.[4] It also offers creative and ground-breaking new forms of the *imago dei* and understandings of God.

I have offered a quick review of the emergence of feminist and Womanist theologies as examples of theological discernment of what needs reforming. So, openness to the world in this view is a radical generosity in a posture of loving the world in its entirety in a way that honors particularity. Such openness also entails a willingness to critique existent cultural practices, symbols, structures, both secular and ecclesiological that diminish this radical love by subtle forms of "othering." I turn now to Vatican II as an opening to the world, offer my outsider observations, and conclude with questions.

Vatican II is relevant to the topic of "opening to the world" because, as feminist theologian Natalie Watson says, the Second Vatican Council can be understood as the most significant and revolutionary event in the history of the Roman Catholic Church in this present century. She quotes John Mahoney's *The Making of Moral Theology: A Study of The Roman Catholic Tradition*: "The council itself was the major event of this century in the Church's life and the most momentous exercise to

---

[4] For example, Warner Sallman's Caucasian Jesus, "Head of Christ" in 1941.

date of the Church's hierarchical *magisterium* in all its history."[5] Pope John XXIII "called for a worldwide council... with the goal of '*aggiornamento*'" whereby the church would open itself to the modern world, and "let fresh air into Catholicism." This is clearly a vision of the church opening to the world, to welcome the other. And a valuing of the *people* as church: one of the crucial insights of Vatican II was the promotion of the image of the church as a servant, rather than "judge and monarch,"—church as the "People of God."[6] And many Catholic feminists in the 1960s and 1970s were supportive of Vatican II insofar as its ideal was "that the people do indeed constitute the church, and as such, they have helped define what it is to be 'Catholic.'"[7]

However, what I do not find is an alteration of the patriarchal posture toward women. It is important that Pope Paul VI allowed women to come to the 3rd session of Vatican II. The previous two had been confined to males.[8] But if women cannot be ordained and those with the power to make this decision are male, is that not a social *stratification* of what is called the "people of God"? More bluntly put, Watson says that one of the crucial things for a feminist re-reading of *Lumen Gentium* requires recognition that some of its ecclesiological discourses "must be classified as to their essence: male self-reflections of a men's church."[9] This identifies conventional ecclesiology as "a male discipline."[10] Even if there are many ways that Catholic women can and do participate and influence the church, there appears to be a deeply embedded structural hierarchy, where males have dominant power and refuse to authorize full access to ministry to the female gender.

There are, of course, human particularities which have their own distinctive importance and function. Particularity, again, cannot always

---

[5] John Mahoney, *The Making of Moral Theology: A Study of The Roman Catholic Tradition* (New York: Oxford University Press, 1987), 302.

[6] Ibid.

[7] Mary J. Henold, *Catholic and Feminist: The Surprising History of the American Catholic Feminist Movement* (Chapel Hill, NC: University of North Carolina Press, 2008), 21–22.

[8] As discussed in this volume by Patricia Madigan, Chapter 6, and Gerard Mannion, Chapter 9.

[9] Natalie Watson, "A Feminist Critical Reading of the Ecclesiology of '*Lumen Gentium*'," in *Is There a Future for Feminist Theology?*, ed. Deborah Sawyer and Diane M. Collins (Sheffield: Sheffield Academic Press, 1999), 75.

[10] Henold, *Catholic and Feminist*, 243.

simply function as a universal. However, I am not aware of anything specific to ministry, such as presiding over the sacraments, preaching, or pastoral care that requires particular male bodily skills—in an analogous fashion to how, for example, pregnancy requires particular female bodily skills. Nor is it the case that there are no Catholic women who want to offer these ministries. One can here, for example, point to *Women's Ordination Worldwide*, a Catholic activist group started in 1996 to lobby for women's ordination.[11] It, therefore, seems to this observer that the requirement that one be male to be a priest indicates the employment and valorization of a human particularity that has strong resonance with idolizing maleness.

The questions we should all ask ourselves are: what are traditions of self-criticism and change in the Roman Catholic tradition that are analogous to the Reformed "reformed and always reforming"? Gaillardetz and Clifford stress "the far-reaching consequences of *the reform* undertaken at Vatican II," namely, that "the process of reform in the life of the church is an ongoing one. The orientations provided for the life of the Catholic Church by the Second Vatican Council continue to provide an impetus for the ongoing renewal of the Catholic community in our time."[12] They argue that the teaching of Vatican II "represents an important shift in the stance of the Catholic Church from one of isolation, fear, and condemnation to one of humble openness and willingness to learn through dialogue with other Christians, with other religions, and with the wider world."[13] As one of three features of the "present age" in his 1963 encyclical, *Pacem in Terris*, John XXIII said "Women are gaining an increasing awareness of their natural dignity. Far from being content with a purely passive role or allowing themselves to be regarded as a kind of instrument, they are demanding, both in domestic and in public life, the rights and duties which belong to them as human persons."[14] While *Gaudium et Spes* echoed these sentiments, the later *Inter Insigniores* ('The Declaration on the Question of the Admission of Women to the Ministerial Priesthood', 1976) quoted it, but went on to conclude that the "Church, in fidelity to the example of the Lord,

---

[11] https://womensordinationworldwide.squarespace.com.

[12] Richard R. Gaillardetz and Catherine E. Clifford, *Keys to the Council: Unlocking the Teaching of Vatican II* (Collegeville, MN: Liturgical Press, 2002), 188.

[13] Ibid., 189.

[14] John XXIII, Encyclical Letter *Pacem in Terris*, AAS 55 (1963): 257–304, no. 41.

does not consider herself authorized to admit women to priestly ordination."[15] Particularity is clearly recognized here, but as a marker that supposedly justifies confinement of certain creatures rather than the full honoring of their status as created in the image of God.

There is, however, some kind of redemptive logic nascent in Vatican II's teachings and demonstrated through the conciliar interactions themselves. Willingness to learn through dialogue with others signals the recognition that one's position may be faulty, e.g., diminishing the full humanity of another, and that one needs to learn from that other.[16] Would that include recognition of idolatries such as patriarchy? I also wonder what are the views of female particularity in the Catholic tradition that indicate and inevitably are used to justify the diminishing or constraint of their full humanity—subtle forms of "othering," that help justify the hierarchy? Women are not as smart as men? Women's bodies are overly sexual and will serve as temptations, so they cannot be in positions of authority?

In closing, I return to the theme of openness to the world. The primary focus here has been on loving the neighbor as a radical generosity toward human beings of all kinds. I confess that "world" should also include environmental reality, which requires so much more than I have been able to say here. But a "church reformed and always reforming" is a good start toward radical generosity, which includes the willingness to risk, repent, and learn something new as we enhance our posture toward the world. Gender is not the only identity marker that has been constructed in a hierarchical, problematic way; it is, however, and has long been constructed as a worldly wound that needs more healing.

---

[15] Congregation for the Doctrine of the Faith, Declaration *Inter Insigniores*, AAS 69 (1977): 98–116.

[16] "What impressed me about the Catholic church – and differentiated it from my conception of Protestantism – was the Church's emphasis on forgiveness. As an outsider, I saw this element as symbolized by the confessional." Sally Barr Ebest, "Evolving Feminisms," in *Reconciling Catholicism and Feminism? Personal Reflections on Tradition and Change*, ed. Sally Barr Ebest and Ron Ebest (Notre Dame, IN: University of Notre Dame Press, 2003), 263.

CHAPTER 8

Tensions Over "Feminism," US Women Religious, and the Contested Reception of Vatican II

Anne E. Patrick, S.N.J.M.

BACKGROUND: VATICAN II AND RECENT TENSIONS

The Easter alleluias were still sounding on April 18, 2012, when the Vatican's Congregation for the Doctrine of the Faith (CDF) made public its displeasure with an important group of US Sisters, the Leadership

---

Editors' Note: Sr. Anne E. Patrick passed away in 2016, just over a year after the conference that gave rise to the present volume. To honor the memory of her presence at that gathering, we produce here the text she sent us afterwards without significant editorial adjustments. An extended version of this essay, which added an important series of questions for today's church toward the end, was posthumously published as "The Vatican, Feminism and U.S. Women Religious," in *On Being Unfinished*, ed. Susan Perry (Maryknoll, NY: Orbis, 2017). We are most grateful to Sr. Maureen Delaney, Provincial of the Sisters of the Holy Names, for the Order's permission to include Anne's essay, as well as to Sr. Pat Parachini, S.N.J.M., Mary Patrick and Jane Malhotra, as well as the rest of the family of this late and much lamented theologian. Our sincere gratitude, also to Orbis Press.

A. E. Patrick S.N.J.M. (Deceased)
Silver Spring, MD, USA

© The Author(s) 2018
V. Latinovic et al. (eds.), *Catholicism Opening to the World and Other Confessions*, Pathways for Ecumenical and Interreligious Dialogue,
https://doi.org/10.1007/978-3-319-98581-7_8

Conference of Women Religious (LCWR). Tensions had been simmering for decades between Rome and this organization of some 1500 elected leaders of communities comprising 80% of the 54,000 sisters in this country, but the official reprimand stunned the group's officers and much of the American public. The CDF's Doctrinal Assessment judged LCWR as deficient in both doctrine and practice and said that its operations should be reformed within five years, under the supervision of Archbishop Peter Sartain of Seattle.[1] The assessment accused LCWR of fostering dissent on women's ordination and ministry to homosexuals, failing to speak out against abortion and euthanasia, and promoting "radical feminist" distortions of doctrine. This Doctrinal Assessment had coincided with a much larger investigation of nearly 400 non-cloistered US women's communities during 2009–2011, by a committee appointed by Cardinal Franc Rodé, head of the Vatican's Congregation for Institutes of Consecrated Life and Societies of Apostolic Life (CICLSAL). Known canonically as an Apostolic Visitation, the investigation was unprecedented in size and scope. Its stated purpose was to examine the "quality of life" of apostolic women's communities, although the very launching of such a visitation presumes the findings will turn up problems.[2]

On December 16, 2014, this Apostolic Visitation of non-cloistered US women's congregations that began in 2009 came officially to a close with gracious statements from representatives of the Vatican's Congregation for Religious, the Leadership Conference of Women Religious, the Council of Major Superiors of Women Religious, and the American sister who had been the official Visitator, Mother Mary Clare Millea, A.S.C.J.[3] And on April 15, 2015, in a report issued jointly by officers of LCWR and the three American bishops who had been mandated to investigate the group's doctrinal orthodoxy, both sides agreed that the *mandate* had been accomplished and their conversations had "borne much fruit." The report adds:

---

[1] Congregation for the Doctrine of the Faith, "Doctrinal Assessment of the Leadership Conference of Women Religious," http://www.vatican.va/roman_curia/congregations/cfaith/documents/rc_con_cfaith_doc_20120418_assessment-lcwr_en.html.

[2] The tensions during this period are discussed more fully in Anne E. Patrick, S.N.J.M., *Conscience and Calling: Ethical Reflections on Catholic Women's Church Vocations* (New York: Bloomsbury/T & T Clark, 2013), 1–2.

[3] Dan Stockman, Joshua J. McElwee, and Dawn Cherie Araujo, "Visitation ends with praise for US sisters," *National Catholic Reporter*, January 2–15, 2015.

The very fact of such substantive dialogue between bishops and religious has been a blessing to be appreciated and further encouraged. The commitment of LCWR leadership to its crucial role in service to the mission and membership of the Conference will continue to guide and strengthen LCWR's witness to the great vocation of Religious Life, to its sure foundation in Christ, and to ecclesial communion.[4]

These words were affirmed by Archbishop Peter Sartain and Bishops Leonard Blair and Thomas Paprocki, and by LCWR officers Sharon Holland, I.H.M., Marcia Allen, C.S.J., Carol Zinn, S.S.J., and Joan Marie Steadman, C.S.C.

In an essay for the volume *Power of Sisterhood: Women Religious Tell the Story of the Apostolic Visitation*, Dominican sister Patricia Walter aptly describes the Apostolic Visitation as part of "the contentious process of receiving the Second Vatican Council" and this is true of the Doctrinal Investigation of LCWR as well.[5] In *Conscience and Calling*, I observed that the two groups of officers of non-cloistered US women's communities, the LCWR and the Conference of Major Superiors of Women Religious (CMSWR) give evidence of being influenced by different conciliar documents. The larger group, representing about 80% of US sisters, has been especially influenced by *Gaudium et Spes*, with its emphasis on mission to eradicate injustice, including that toward women. This document helped to encourage feminism among these sisters and contributed to the development of feminist theology. Meanwhile, the CMSWR communities have instead stressed the Decree on the Adaptation and Renewal of Religious Life (*Perfectae Caritatis*) and undertaken their renewal with greater concern for preserving some monastic aspects of religious life, including a distinctive habit, and with following an agenda set by the hierarchy.[6] In distinguishing these two groups of sisters, it is important to recognize that there is diversity within both organizations, and that sisters from both sorts of communities have much in common, although their visions for "radical discipleship" may

---

[4] https://press.vatican.va/content/salastampa/it/bollettino/pubblico/2015/04/16/0278.pdf.

[5] Patricia Walter, "Situating the Apostolic Visitation in Historical and Theological Context," in *Power of Sisterhood: Women Religious Tell the Story of the Apostolic Visitation*, ed. Margaret Cain McCarthy and Mary Ann Zollmann (Lanham, MD: University Press of America, 2014), 24.

[6] Patrick, *Conscience and Calling*, 4–5.

differ. Theologian Christine Firer Hinze noted this in an (online) article for *America* in 2012:

> [B]oth LCWR and CMSWR communities serve the gospel at contemporary frontiers, living lives of passionate love in and from the heart of the church. Both articulate and practice the basic elements of consecrated life (vows of poverty, chastity and obedience; life in community, and mission) in light of prayerful discernment of the needs of the church and the signs of the times.[7]

That said, Hinze notes that the CMSWR communities tend to understand gender, sexual difference, and men and women's vocations in a way that is much closer to Pope John Paul II's emphasis on gender complementarity than do LCWR communities. Indeed, it seems clear that those responsible for initiating the Apostolic Visitation and the Doctrinal Investigation were more comfortable with understanding women's nature and role as special and limited, and with concerns that feminism, at least in the form they described as "radical" (without, however, defining its meaning), was having a harmful effect on women's religious life in the United States.

FEMINISM AND *GAUDIUM ET SPES*

There are many definitions and types of feminism, not to mention controversy over the meanings and normative implications of the various types. Moreover, feminists differ widely in their analyses of injustice, levels of commitment to liberating action, degrees of explicitness of commitment, and opinions regarding specific problems and their solutions. I have defined the term "feminist" broadly to indicate a position that involves a solid conviction of the equality of women and men, and a commitment to reform society so that the full equality of women is respected, which also requires reforming the thought systems that legitimate the present unjust social order.[8] Both aspects of this definition are important. Certainly, affirmations of women's equality show progress in

---

[7] Christine Firer Hinze, "At Cross Currents? The Vatican, U.S. sisters and the LCWR," *America*, June 18, 2012, online edition, http://americamagazine.org/content/article. cjm?article_id=134567.

[8] Anne E. Patrick, *Liberating Conscience: Feminist Explorations in Catholic Moral Theology* (New York: Continuum, 1996), 7–8.

a tradition that taught for centuries, thanks among others to Aristotle,[9] that females were a lesser form of humanity than males. Affirmations of women's equal human dignity achieve little, however, if they are not accompanied by efforts to remedy the twin injustices of sexism, namely patriarchy and androcentrism. Patriarchy literally means "father rule." As an ethical term, it designates social patterns of domination and subordination, especially (but not exclusively) those flowing from attitudes that do not respect the full humanity of females. Such attitudes, which revolve around the experiences of males, are termed androcentric.

Androcentric attitudes include not only viewing women as inferior to men, but also seeing them as so essentially different from men that their roles must be circumscribed, or "special." Often those who think this way are not so blatantly sexist as to say that women are deficient in reason or are less fully human than men, which once was the position of churchmen, but to my mind there is sexism in insisting that the essence of womanhood is to be complementary to men in ways that have historically been defined by men in power. It should not surprise us that popes educated in patriarchal cultures should think this way. Certainly, this was the case with Pope John Paul II, and many of Pope Francis's statements about women are tinged by this "essentialist" understanding of human nature, which sees women as complementary to men in a way that effectively limits women's contributions.[10] There are of course women who share such an understanding of women's nature, but the problems in this position quickly become evident if we imagine a situation in which all sacramental and decision-making power in the church were in the hands of women. If such an imaginary female prelate were to call for an infusion of "the masculine genius" into this woman-dominated structure, would that not seem condescending?

In 2007, Marin Alsop became Music Director of the Baltimore Symphony Orchestra, the first woman ever to head a major US orchestra. Was she recruited in order to bring a "feminine genius" to the symphony, or because of her outstanding musicianship? Alsop is known

[9] Cf. e.g. *Politics* (1254b13-14).

[10] See Anne E. Patrick, "Women in the Church in the Age of Francis," *A Matter of Spirit* (Summer 2015), www.ipjc.org/journal/AMOSSummer15.pdf. Michael G. Lawler and Todd A. Salzman provide a valuable comparison of these two popes' positions in "Pope Francis brings nuance to notion of complementarity," *National Catholic Reporter*, June 5, 2015.

for being highly effective in reaching out to audiences. Is this because of special "womanly gifts," or because she was influenced by a mentor, Leonard Bernstein, who made educating audiences, including children, a priority? To raise these questions is not to deny that there are differences between the sexes, but it is to suggest that there are many more differences among human beings than a rigid system of opposing gender roles tends to recognize, and to claim that both church and society will be all the richer when our institutions respect the gifts of everyone more fully. The Roman Catholic Church today is like all symphony orchestras were a century ago. Girls in the audience saw no role models on stage to encourage them to bring their musical gifts to the public. They were destined to entertain at home, or teach young pupils.

There is no doubt that the Second Vatican Council helped to encourage feminist thinking in many women religious, especially through *Gaudium et Spes*, which declared emphatically that "with respect to the fundamental rights of the person, every type of discrimination, whether social or cultural, whether based on sex, race, color, social condition, language or religion, is to be overcome and eradicated as contrary to God's intent" (GS 29). Although the status of women worldwide was by no means central to the concerns of the bishops at Vatican II, this statement and a few others gave strong religious support for moral convictions that were also gaining force from secular movements for justice for women. In the United States, a "first wave" of feminism had been associated with efforts in the nineteenth and early twentieth centuries to obtain woman suffrage, achieved in 1920 with the passage of a constitutional amendment. Then, after World War II came a "second wave" of feminism inspired by the writings of Simone de Beauvoir, Betty Friedan, and others, which gained impetus from the Civil Rights movement in the 1960s. In the years since then women's studies programs have been developed in colleges and universities, feminist journals have been established, and feminist theory has grown quite complex. Some have identified a "third wave" of US feminism that has gained influence since the 1980s, which emphasizes the diversity of women's experiences of injustice due to factors such as race, ethnicity, class, and nationality.

Although *Gaudium et Spes* is the product of an androcentric culture, it encouraged feminism among Catholics. It did this in the first place by affirming that God wills for society to reflect the essential equality of the sexes, and that history is the locus of the activity of God's Spirit. Those already influenced by secular movements for women's educational and political rights found in this document a powerful rebuttal to the old arguments against women's advancement in society, and an invitation to contribute to solving problems of social injustice, indeed a duty to "build a better world based upon truth and justice" (GS 55). To read *Gaudium et Spes* was also to be invited to make connections, to move by a logic implicit in the text from affirmation of women's rights in society to affirmation of women's rights in the church. And, in the second place, by expressing the hope that "more of the laity [*plures laici*] will receive adequate theological formation and that some among them will dedicate themselves professionally to these studies and contribute to their advancement" (GS 62), *Gaudium et Spes* opened up the possibility that women would enter a field that had previously been dominated by males. Furthermore, by affirming intellectual freedom in theology, the highly significant final sentence of the section on culture (GS 62) states a principle that contributed both to male support of women's involvement in the discipline and also to the development of feminist positions by both male and female theologians:

> But for the proper exercise of this role [of theologian], the faithful, both clerical and lay, should be accorded a lawful freedom of inquiry, of thought, and of expression, tempered by humility and courage in whatever branch of study they have specialized.

Women's participation in theological education and research has increased dramatically since the Council, and the influence of *Gaudium et Spes* in this historical development is significant.[11] During a 2013 flight from Brazil, Pope Francis declared that "we don't yet have a truly deep theology of women in the church. We talk about whether they can do this or that... but we don't have a deep theology of women in the church."[12] In declaring this, Pope Francis spoke rightly of official church literature, which has yet to incorporate the excellent

---

[11] For a full discussion of the influence of *Gaudium et Spes* on Catholic feminism, see Anne E. Patrick, "Toward Renewing 'The Life and Culture of Fallen Man': *Gaudium et Spes* as Catalyst for Catholic Feminist Theology," in *The Church in the Modern World Two Decades after Vatican II*, ed. Judith A. Dwyer (Washington, DC: Georgetown University Press, 1986), 55–74.

[12] Quoted by John L. Allen, Jr., "Pope on Homosexuals: 'Who Am I to Judge?'" (July 29, 2013), http://ncronline.org/blogs/ncr-today/pope-homosexuals-who-am-i-judge.

theology that women have published for decades. The People of God, however, already have access to such theology in the writings of Elizabeth Johnson, Margaret Farley, Rosemary Radford Ruether, Sandra M. Schneiders, and many others.[13] Women religious studied all the major documents of Vatican II more avidly than most Catholics, and those who were especially inspired by *Gaudium et Spes* have tended to be the ones more greatly influenced by feminist theology.

SOME ISSUES AND QUESTIONS THAT REMAIN

While a deep love of God and the church, together with considerable patience and charity on the part of churchmen and women religious, have allowed for relations between the Vatican and US women religious to reach a new level of respectful dialogue following the difficulties of 2009–2014, there remain a number of issues and questions still to be addressed. There is the sociological fact of the great diminishment in younger Catholics' involvement in the church, and the decline in women's interest in religious vocations. There are questions about what changes are truly for the advancement of women, and how much change is optimal in a culturally diverse global church, as well as about how changes that are desirable can best be introduced. There is also the question of how to maintain charity and unity in a church whose members have different perspectives on feminism and other topics. And, to my mind, there is a need for feminists who are critical of hierarchical social structures to recognize that hierarchy does not necessarily entail claims of ontological superiority and unjust power relationships but can simply be an effective way of administering a large and complex institution, with clear lines of accountability.

It is impossible to probe all these matters further here, but in conclusion, I will discuss in some detail the fundamental theological issue I believe to be at the heart of the tensions that were so pronounced during 2009–2014. This is the question of whether the gender-based imbalance of power in Catholicism that made the Apostolic Visitation and Doctrinal Investigation possible in the first place is a human construct subject to reform, or a divinely established order to be maintained despite the cultural change.

---

[13]For an overview, see Anne E. Patrick, "Feminist Theology," *New Catholic Encyclopedia*, Second Edition (Detroit: Thompson/Gayle, 2003) 5: 675–81.

In approaching this question, I have found the distinction between classicism and historical consciousness, originally drawn by the late Canadian theologian Bernard Lonergan, S.J., to be very helpful. Using Lonergan's categories, the idea that gender roles in the church are divinely established represents a "classicist" position, one emphasizing the stability of truth and tradition, without regard for historical evidence of change and development. Modernity, however, has opened up the possibility of a "historically conscious" position, which recognizes that formulations of truth and social arrangements are culturally conditioned and limited by the historical circumstances in which they were developed.[14]

The gender-based imbalance of power that contributed to tensions between the Vatican and US women religious is clearly evident in the fact that according to canon law all females are excluded from the sacrament of orders, which has long been a prerequisite for holding church office, that is, for exercising the power of authority in the church. Women have always exercised moral and spiritual power, but in Roman Catholicism, they lack the juridical power of office. Thus, it would have been theoretically possible, although a pastoral disaster, for Roman officials to decree harsh punishments for women religious with whom they disagreed. Is this arrangement God's will forever, as a classicist might say, or is God free to endorse other sorts of arrangements in the community of believers?

Theologically, it seems to me that posing the question in these terms yields the conclusion that God, who transcends all our images and ideas of Divinity, is surely free to draw human beings along new paths. The Bible is replete with narratives in which people are called to leave past assurances behind and venture in a new direction. As the prophet Isaiah expresses it, there are times when God declares, "Remember not the events of the past, the things of long ago consider not; See, I am doing something new! Now it springs forth, do you not perceive it? (Is 43:18–19a)" On the other hand, remembering God's gracious deeds, and acting deliberately in memory of Jesus, is also both necessary and salvific. How then can we discern what we should "remember," and what we should "forget" of past attitudes and practices, especially where gender roles are concerned?

[14]See Bernard J. F. Lonergan, S.J., "The Transition from a Classicist World-View to Historical-Mindedness," in *A Second Collection*, ed. William, F. J. Ryan, S.J., and Bernard J. Tyrrell, S.J. (Philadelphia: The Westminster Press, 1974), 1–9.

One approach is to look at the effects of these practices, on whether they are helpful or harmful to individuals and the church community. Here, given the cultural diversity in global Catholicism, there will likely be some evidence on both sides of gender role questions, but in many societies, the psychological, moral, and social harms caused by excluding females from leadership roles in the church are increasingly being recognized. As I note in my book on Catholic women's church vocations, sociologist Andrew Greeley estimated in 1984 that more than a million Catholic women of all ages did not attend church regularly because of a "complex of imagery" regarding God, Woman, Mother, and Church. He also found emphasis on gender roles to be a significant factor in the non-attendance of some 200,000 young Catholic men.[15] Another sociologist, Patricia Wittberg, S.C., observed in 2012 that for the first time in history young Catholic women ("millennials," or those born during 1981–1995) were more likely than their male counterparts to say they do not go to mass, and have never considered a religious vocation. Wittberg concluded that failing to address this changed social situation would likely result in fewer young women, and eventually their families, remaining Catholic, which will greatly diminish the church's influence in society.[16]

Another approach is to examine the reasons used to maintain the status quo. One of the reasons often given for excluding women from sacred orders and church leadership is based on an interpretation of the gospel narrative about Jesus' celebration of Passover with his apostles before his death, and especially the words now so central to the Christian Eucharist: "This is my body, which will be given for you; do this in memory of me" (Luke 22:19). Here Lonergan's categories of classicism and historical consciousness can be very helpful. A classicist interpretation of this text, and of the similar words in 1 Cor. 11:24 ("Do this in remembrance of me"), assumes that these words amount to Jesus ordaining his twelve male apostles to the priesthood, and limiting his church to male leadership forever. By contrast, the historically conscious approach, held by most biblical and theological scholars today, understands such texts very differently. As Raymond E. Brown wrote in 1975, "[Jesus] chose the Twelve (Luke 22:30), but they were to sit on thrones judging the twelve tribes of Israel. There is no biblical evidence that he

---

[15] Patrick, *Conscience and Calling*, 62.

[16] Patricia A. Wittberg, S.C., "A Lost Generation?" *America* 206, no. 5 (February 20, 2012): 13–16.

thought about any of his followers, male or female, as priests, since there were already priests in Israel."[17]

Historians recognize that ministries were quite fluid in the early years of Christianity, and approaches to church governance and understandings of sacraments evolved over time. Kevin Madigan and Carolyn Osiek provide convincing evidence of this in their volume *Ordained Women in the Early Church: A Documentary History*, and Gary Macy explains how understandings of ordination changed dramatically in the eleventh and twelfth centuries in his study *The Hidden History of Women's Ordination: Female Clergy in the Medieval West*.[18] As a committee of the Catholic Theological Society of America observed in 1997, "St. Paul had a number of women as his co-workers in ministry," but by the time 1 Timothy 2:12–14 was written "women were being excluded from roles that involved teaching and authority over men," not with reference to the example of Jesus, but because of an alleged unsuitability due to beliefs about the role of Eve in the Fall. The CTSA committee acknowledged that historical studies turn up some "references to the fact that Jesus chose only men among the Twelve," but found it "undeniable that a consistent argument for the exclusion of women from the priesthood was rooted in the conviction that women were not apt subjects for such ministry because of the inferiority of their sex and/or their state of subjection in the social order."[19] The implication is that the modern recognition of women's equal human dignity, which has been strongly asserted in Catholic teaching since the time of Pope John XXIII, weakens the prohibition against ordaining women, and opens up the matter for reexamination today.

In the forty years since 1975, which the United Nations designated the first "International Women's Year," the momentum of Catholic feminism has grown significantly, and yet there remains the "stained glass ceiling" of sacramental sexism. Women serve in many pastoral, educational, and administrative capacities today, but the canonical ban on women's ordination continues to undermine claims of the hierarchy

---

[17] Raymond E. Brown, S.S., *Biblical Reflections on Crises Facing the Church* (New York: Paulist Press, 1975), 54.

[18] Kevin Madigan and Carolyn Osiek, *Ordained Women in the Early Church: A Documentary History* (Baltimore: Johns Hopkins University Press, 2005); and Gary Macy, *The Hidden History of Women's Ordination: Female Clergy in the Medieval West* (New York: Oxford University Press, 2008).

[19] "Tradition and the Ordination of Women," *CTSA Proceedings* 52 (1997): 199–200.

to respect women's equal human dignity. Although Pope Francis is unwilling to open up this topic for consideration, his position strikes me as significantly different from that of his immediate predecessors, who argued vehemently against the possibility of ordaining women priests and bishops. Instead of making unconvincing arguments and forbidding a discussion, Pope Francis has simply said that the "door is closed" on the subject of women's ordination and gone on to devote his energies to many genuinely transformative reforms in the church and the global struggle for environmental and social justice, as well as working to promote dialogue and peace in general. Meanwhile, I have interpreted his remark about the closed door as "the gift of papal silence" that is buying some time for the universal church to prepare for a momentous change in the canonical status of baptized females.[20]

Francis's 2015 papal encyclical, *Laudato Si'*, invited everyone to historical consciousness, especially concerning humanity's role in what has happened to the earth and our environment since the rise of modern technology. It also invited us to an awakened sense of responsibility for changing unsustainable practices. My hope is that Catholics will increasingly see the connections between traditional attitudes toward "nature" and toward women, and will through prayer, study, and discussion be inspired to adapt our structures and activities so as to give appropriate respect to all of creation, and especially to female humanity.

[20] Anne E. Patrick, "The Gift of Papal Silence," April 14, 2015, http://globalsistersreport.org/column/speaking-god/gift-papal-silence-23291.

CHAPTER 9

Women and the Art of Magisterium: Reflections on Vatican II and the Postconciliar Church

Gerard Mannion

Introductory Remarks

This essay explores transformations in the understanding of teaching authority and also considers an often neglected group of subjects who have exercised such in the period during and since the Second Vatican Council. In particular, it explores both topics *vis-à-vis* the role of women in the church, especially their contributions to the church's exercise of magisterium.

Women in the church have helped transform the understanding and living out of subjectivity in many profound ways in the period since the council. Indeed, there were many contributions by women around the world before and during the council which impacted a number of the final conciliar texts. The contributions of those few women who actually *attended* the council would prove especially significant here. Of course, during the conciliar period and in the years which immediately followed

G. Mannion (✉)
Department of Theology, Georgetown University, Washington, DC, USA
e-mail: gm751@georgetown.edu

119
V. Latinovic et al. (eds.), *Catholicism Opening to the World and Other Confessions*, Pathways for Ecumenical and Interreligious Dialogue, https://doi.org/10.1007/978-3-319-98581-7_9

the council, feminist theology (and the subdisciplines of discourse by and for women which would branch off from what became known as feminist theology per se) was something still in formation. But, nonetheless, such currents of thought and concern would impact the council and postconciliar church considerably.

By and large, the motivation behind such contributions would be driven, first and foremost, by a moral concern, particularly a concern for justice. This fact sharpens our critical and hermeneutical focus. That is to say, there is a moral dimension that particularly comes into play when one considers the role and contribution of women in the church. In this chapter, I explore some questions and considerations pertaining to the role of women, primarily (although not exclusively) as theologians, in contributing to the church's exercising of magisterium. Much needs to be done to increase awareness, acknowledgment and appreciation of the contribution of women to church teaching authority and, most importantly of all, to increase their participation in the same.

First of all, I will consider the role which those few women played at the Council and consider the question 'what were they *doing* there?' It is, of course, a rhetorical question and my answer shall be that they were teaching with authority, i.e. exercising magisterium. I will then explore some of the confusions and controversies surrounding the notion of what magisterium actually is and who should exercise it, before surveying some brief examples of how women have exercised magisterium throughout the history of the church. The paper next considers how events in the church have developed from a stance of confrontation toward the more positive steps that have been taken in relation to the role of women in the church under Pope Francis. It concludes with reflections on the future and why attention to *aggiornamento* for magisterium is essential in order that the church becomes a body of greater and wider co-responsibility, including the indispensable collaboration of women practicing the art of magisterium.

Women at Vatican II: What Were They Doing There?

The Second Vatican Council contains a number of statements about the role of women in the church and it contains even more statements about the role of the laity in the church in general. It should go without saying that all references to the laity and its apostolate in the conciliar texts, except where explicitly intended to refer to one or other gender, refer both to men and women. Then there are numerous texts that address religious congregations and so, because the vast majority of religious were (and remain) women, once again these texts would be of direct relevance in not just addressing but also reflecting the ecclesial reality of women in the church.[1]

We should not presume that somehow the council fathers magically came to these insights alone. Nor should we underestimate the campaigning that was taking place not only to encourage the council to address specific questions of particular importance for women in the church and beyond, but also in order that women should be involved in and represented at the council and impacting conciliar work in general.

Those recounting the story of the women of Vatican II often display differing perspectives, which, in more recent times, frequently reflect the ecclesial perspectives, issues and questions of later years.[2] These range from the hopeful retelling, with admiration, of the arrival of the women auditors to the council and the contributions they made—suggesting that at last the glass ecclesiastical ceiling was beginning to show cracks— to those who pessimistically say that the whole business of inviting some

---

[1] On the conciliar documents and their eventual impact and reception from the perspective of women, see Margit Eckholt, 'Eine Relektüre großer Leitlinien des Konzils in Frauenperspektive,' in *Ohne die Frauen ist keine Kirche zu machen: Der Aufbruch des Konzils und die Zeichen der Zeit*, Margit Eckholt (Ostfildern: Matthias Grünewald Verlag, 2012): 43–61. In the same study, see, also, 'Das "Aggiornamento" und die Frauenfrage als "Zeichen der Zeit",' 25–33, which considers the question and place of women in the church with reference to the Vatican II watchwords of ecclesial renewal and discerning the signs of the times.

[2] The key and groundbreaking study of women at the council remains Carmel Elizabeth McEnroy's, *Guests in Their Own House: The Women of Vatican II* (New York: Crossroad, 1996, revised edn. Wipf & Stock, 2011). This study also charts many such contributions prior to the council (especially Chapter 1, 19–51). Three other especially informative texts are Eckholt, *Ohne die Frauen ist keine Kirche zu machen*, Adriana Valerio, *Madri del Concilio. Ventitré donne al Vaticano II* (Rome: Carocci editore, 2012); Marinella Perroni and Hervé Legrand, eds., *Avendo qualcosa da dire. Teologhe e teologi rileggono il Vaticano II* (Rome: Edizioni Paoline, 2014). The latter also explores further issues pertaining to the role of women in the post-conciliar church. The women at the council are also discussed in detail in Chapter 6 of this volume by Patricia Madigan, O.P., which offers additional and specific details concerning the experiences of the women at the council, including a list of the women who participated in the council in an appendix to her chapter.

women to the council was both 'too little and too late' and by and large a monumental exercise in tokenism.

As is so often the case, the truth lies somewhere in-between—although both poles of the hermeneutical perspective concerning the women of the council do communicate significant truths about the church of that time.[3] Women were not officially involved in the formal preparatory work, nor were they present as *official* consultors or *periti* in name. However, as we shall see, in terms of function the reality became very different. They did not play any *formal* role at all in the first two sessions of the council.[4] Nonetheless, the perspectives of many women were already influencing what was going on at the council and had been for some considerable time.

The credit for women being brought to the conciliar table in any form at all, particularly given that, for the first two sessions of the council,

[3] A sample of other discussions include the dissertation, Giuliana Bragantini, 'Le Donne nel Concilio Vaticano II' (Rome: Pontificia Università Lateranense, 1984); Mary Luke Tobin, 'Women in the Church since Vatican II', *America* (November 1, 1986), available online at http://www.americamagazine.org/content/article.cfm?article_id=11898 (Nov. 1, 1986; accessed 1 May 2017); Ida Raming and Iris Müller, *Contra Legem—A Matter of Conscience: Our Lifelong Struggle for Human Rights for Women in the Roman-Catholic Church; Autobiographies, Background Papers, Documents, Future Prospects* (Münster: LIT Verlag, 2011), esp. Ida Raming, 'Women in the Council', 192–200; Joseph A. Komonchak, 'Toward an Ecclesiology of Communion', in *History of Vatican II*, vol. IV, ed. Alberigo and Komonchak, *Church as Communion: Third Period and Intersession Sept. 1964–September 1965*, 19–24, 26–28; María Salas, *De la promoción de la mujer a la teología feminist: cuarenta años de historia* (Santander, Editorial Sal Terrae, 1993): 85–93. Some further incisive reflections can be found in George H. Tavard, *Woman in Christian Tradition* (Notre Dame, IN: University of Notre Dame Press, 1973) 125–50, with a treatment of the council's approach to women, as reflected in representative samples of the conciliar debates at 126–30. See, also, his discussion of Paul VI's closing words at the council on women, 135–36, Tavard's anthropological reflections at 193–94 and, finally, his treatment of 'Controverted Questions' at 212ff. and 225.

[4] See Komanchak, 'Toward an Ecclesiology of Communion', 20. But, there is one partial and qualified exception here. It appears that Blanche Shaffer, General Secretary of the Friends' World Consultative Council, was permitted to be present in the aula for around one week during the first session, thereby being the first woman permitted to remain in the aula for a working session. However, she was neither an 'official' observer nor an officially invited guest. I am most grateful to John Borelli for bringing this lesser-known fact to my attention.

women could neither enter the council's hall (at least not officially) nor receive communion at the conciliar sacred liturgies,[5] is frequently bestowed upon the Belgian Cardinal Leo Joseph Suenens (1904–1996).[6] His speech at the close of the council's second session concerning the validity of discussing the reality and future of the church when half of it was not represented at the council, along with his suggestion of inviting more auditors, including women,[7] 'prodded council members to invite a few "token" women to the ensuing sessions', as one of these 'token' women, Mary Luke Tobin, later reflected.[8]

The reality was that the men who were the most influential church teachers and leaders at the time did, indeed, hold the key to whether or not women might be brought into participate in some form or other at the council. To borrow from Mary McClintock Fulkerson's groundbreaking study, they retained 'the institutional capacity to host the discussion and provide chairs at the table'.[9] However, as Margit Eckholt states, while this was not a council *of* women, it was now to be a council *with* women.[10] Adriana Valerio places the involvement of women in the council

---

[5] Not until September 16, 1964, the Third Session's second day. See Komanchak, 'Toward an Ecclesiology of Communion', 20. One female journalist, Eva Fleischsner, 'was physically restrained from receiving communion with her male colleagues.' Ibid., 21; see also, McEnroy, *Guests in Their Own House*, 105, Valerio, *Madri del Concilio*, 34–35 and n5. McEnroy notes that 'Not a single mention was made of women in the first conciliar session', only two were made in the second session and, once women were actually present at the council, the third session saw fifteen and the fourth session ten. However, 'Not all were positive or contributed to women's advancement...', McEnroy, *Guests in Their Own House*, 36.

[6] As also discussed in Chapter 6 by Patricia Madigan, above, 79–96.

[7] See Komanchak, 'Toward an Ecclesiology of Communion', 21.

[8] Tobin, 'Women in the Church since Vatican II'.

[9] Mary McClintock Fulkerson, *Changing the Subject: Women's Discourses and Feminist Theology* (Eugene, OR: Wipf and Stock Publishers, 2001, original edn., Fortress Press, 1994), 16.

[10] Margit Eckholt, 'Kein Konzil der Frauen, aber eines mit Frauen', in *Ohne die Frauen ist keine Kirche zu machen*, 34–43.

in the context of the overall conciliar atmosphere of a 'new Pentecost',[11] and McEnroy describes the eventual admission of women to the council as a 'new springtime'.[12]

Despite the ecclesiastics retaining the exclusive right to a chair at the table, it was equally the case that what was often stated on the council floor was the direct result of and a reflection upon much wider debates going on elsewhere—be these in the conversations among council fathers behind closed doors, with or without their *periti* present, the petitions and supplications of groups, organizations and individuals from the four corners of the ecclesial world, down to the wider questions and issues that were catching the attention of the global media who were watching the council carefully throughout.

Indeed, while Suenens may often receive the greater portion of the credit, many others had been canvassing for such change long before him.[13] For example, the executive committee of the World Federation of Female Catholic Youth and the International Union of Catholic Women wrote to the Pope, during the second intersession, to request that women auditors be appointed.[14] Also during that second intersession,

[11] Valerio, 'Un Nuova Pentecoste', in *Madri del Concilio*, 33–38. Monika Hellwig, who was in Rome during the Council, would later write of 'Vatican II: The Glorious Years,' in *Vatican II: Fifty Personal Stories*, ed. William Madges and Michael J. Daley (Maryknoll: Orbis, 2012), 14–20. She recounts the great energy and excitement generated by the council and how the debates on the council floor were mirrored in the universities, Vatican district streets and even the bars and restaurants of Rome at that time, with much ecclesial strategizing taking place in the various *pensioni* and religious houses (ibid., 15). Hellwig speaks of the great hope for a renewed church that the council sessions were generating (ibid., 17–18), in particular the great sense that the laity is the church, which was especially welcome news for women in the 1960s (ibid., 18).

[12] McEnroy, *Guests in Their Own House*, 101. McEnroy does not, however, perceive the development through rose-tinted spectacles in any sense.

[13] Indeed the progress of the ecumenical movement, particularly in the 1950s also helped lay much of the groundwork for opening up debates about the role of women within Catholicism, too.

[14] Komanchak, 'Toward an Ecclesiology of Communion', 21. A further snapshot of the feelings being expressed at the time around the world is illustrated by the fact that, in May 1962, a Swiss lawyer, Gertrud Heinzelmann wrote to the council's preparatory commission demanding that the council affirm equality for women and that women be ordained to the priesthood (see her *Frau und Konzil; Hoffnung und Erwartung: Eingabe an die hohe vorbereitende Kommission des Vatikanischen Konzils über Wertung und Stellung der Frau in der Römisch-katholischen Kirche* (Zürich: Verlag der "Staatsbürgerin", 1962), and *Wir schweigen nicht länger! Frauen äußern sich zum II. Vatikanischen Konzil* (Zürich: Interfeminas, 1964).

a lay auditor, Vittorino Veronese[15] wrote on behalf of the auditors to ask for an increase in their number, especially as the third council session would be concerned with many questions of direct interest to the laity. He also asked that differing regions, professions and social classes be represented, as well as 'the irreplaceable cooperation of women'.[16] Other council fathers, aside from Suenens, expressed similar sentiments at the close of the Second Session.[17] Then one must take into account the extraordinary influence upon Suenens of the woman he liked to refer to as his 'brains', Veronica O'Brien, whom he first met in 1947 and who advised him on so many of the areas in which his greatest ecclesial accomplishments would be forthcoming.[18] In fact, there were influential women in and around Vatican II long before their formal appearance at the council. As one of the auditors, Pilar Bellosillo said long after, 'We were already living the council for two years *from the outside*'.[19]

On September 8, 1963, Paul VI announced in an address to women from the diocese of Albano, that 'some qualified and devout women' would be present, as auditors, at the third session and be able to be present at some of the 'solemn rites' and 'general congregations' that would be 'discussing questions of particular interest to women'.[20]

Yet there seem to have been some continuing communication difficulties around the Vatican, confirming Komonchak's judgment that 'This has all the appearances of a last-minute decision'. In fact, the letters inviting women were not sent out until September 21—some six days

[15] Who served as the first general secretary of the Permanent Committee for International Congresses of the Lay Apostolate (COPECIAL) from 1952 to 1958 (Rosemary Goldie also joined the organization in 1952). He also served as Director Genera of UNESCO between 1958 and 1961, having previously served as president of Azione Cattolica Italiana from 1946 to 1952 (and president of the Bank of Rome from 1961 to 1976).

[16] See Komanchak, 'Toward an Ecclesiology of Communion', 20 (*AS* VI/3, 37–38).

[17] See, for example, Valerio, *Madri del Concilio*, 35–38.

[18] In a very real sense, then, O'Brien might be considered another important 'woman of the council'. See Léon Josef Suenens, *The Hidden Hand of God: The Life of Veronica O'Brien* (Dublin: Veritas, 1994). I am most grateful to John Haughey, S.J., for bringing the extent of O'Brien's influence upon Suenens's conciliar contributions to my attention.

[19] McEnroy, *Guests in Their Own House*, 40 and see 41–50 which recounts further the reflections and aspirations of women with regard to the council prior to 1964.

[20] Komanchak, 'Toward an Ecclesiology of Communion', 22, citing *Insegnamenti*, II, 529.

after the Pope's speech which formally opened the Third Session and in which he welcomed the new women auditors! Marie-Louise Monnet, the founder and President of the International Movement for the Apostolate in Independent Social Milieux, was the first woman to attend a council congregation on September 25.[21]

Looking back over twenty years after the council's conclusion, Mary Luke Tobin reflected, 'That women auditors were at the council—only 15 of us were [initially] invited from as many countries—was at least an important first step'.[22] It appeared that the initial batch of invitations to women (eventually twenty-three women auditors would take part in the council) was an attempt to bring in representation from Catholic women's organizations and from religious congregations from the differing continents. When the qualification concerning which particular conciliar congregations these auditors would be permitted to attend was explained to Tobin, i.e. that her pass admitted her to council sessions of interest to women, her reply was 'Good, then I can attend them all'.[23]

Although women were not formally permitted to speak during the official sessions in the council hall[24] (again reflecting the exclusionary ecclesial atmosphere of the time), their impact upon the debates in those halls, despite their small number, would prove to be highly significant.[25] Indeed, conciliar documents offer a validation of the role of

---

[21] Komanchak, 'Toward an Ecclesiology of Communion', 22.

[22] Tobin, 'Women in the Church since Vatican II'.

[23] Komanchak, 'Toward an Ecclesiology of Communion', 23. Even attempts to segregate the women by setting up their own coffee bar, dubbed Bar-Nun, would eventually fail as mingling took places across the differing bars. Ibid., 23–24. Although, perhaps with more poignant evocations pertaining to the exclusionary context, it is termed 'Bar None' (reflecting the Italian feminine plural for ninth) in McEnroy, *Guests in Their Own House*, 108, and also in Valerio, *Madri del Concilio*, 52 – this joke most likely emerged from the English-speaking contingent, the wordplay requiring some explanation in Italian from Valerio to ensure the humor carries.

[24] Komonchak, 'Toward an Ecclesiology of Communion', 24, McEnroy, *Guests in Their Own House*, 136.

[25] Additional work stills needs to be done on the other women who were influential in various ways in and around both the council and the Vatican in general at that time, including, for example, not simply those such as the economist Barbara Ward who had a great deal of input into *Gaudium et Spes* (yet whose speech to the council was read by a man), but also those working, teaching and studying in and around Rome. This includes those in the houses and institutions connected to female religious congregations, especially in leadership roles and the other 'hidden influences', for example, Monika Hellwig, who worked as a research assistant to a Vatican official during the council and I have already noted the deep influence of Veronica O'Brien upon Cardinal Suenens.

women in contributing to and exercising magisterium in some surprising places. It is less well remembered in some histories that women auditors of the council were eventually included in the subcommissions that prepared the conciliar documents. And while women would never formally be appointed as conciliar *periti*, the Australian council auditor, Rosemary Goldie did state that, 'both for *Apostolicam Actuositatem* and schema XIII [part of what would eventually become *Gaudium et Spes*], the auditors were [effectively] treated as "periti", participating in subcommissions and attending plenary meetings'.[26]

Mary Luke Tobin locates the credit for such an inclusive move in one particular place, praising

> the further valuable insight of a council theologian, Bernard Häring, C.Ss.R. (1912–1998), that if women were invited, they should have a place in the commissions formulating the documents.[27] As a result, some were invited to attend commission meetings. There we were allowed to speak as freely as we wished, and each of us did speak. Although we did not create a countervailing current turning around the attitude toward women, our presence was noticed immediately by the press, and at least a few bishops began to see the problems more clearly.[28]

The importance of the participation of these women in the *commissions* in relation to questions of magisterium was enormous—and its full historical significance has yet to be fully appreciated, as we shall see.[29]

[26] In correspondence with Joseph Komanchak, 'Toward an Ecclesiology of Communion', 20n.58. Note that it would take some time and struggles, still, before women were permitted to *address* the council session itself, see Komonchak, 'Toward an Ecclesiology of Communion', 24–27.

[27] On Häring's role here see, also, McEnroy, *Guests in Their Own House*, 131–34.

[28] Tobin, 'Women in the Church since Vatican II'; see also, McEnroy, *Guests in Their Own House*, 99–100.

[29] Some sources, such as McEnroy, point to Maria Vendrik as having served as a *perita* (*Guests in Their Own House*, 94). Rosemary Goldie describes her as having been invited as a lay 'expert' to the council, although she does not specifically describe her as a *perita*, as such: '... Maria Vendrik, une des experts laïcs invités au Concile', Rosemary Goldie, 'La participation des laïcs aux travaux du concile Vatican II', *Revue des Sciences Religieuses* tome 62, fascicule 1 (1988) 54–73 at 72n.47. Part of the problem here is that, technically, only priests were officially listed as serving as *periti*—despite many others, including laypeople and among them women, as we shall see, serving in the same function without necessarily enjoying that official title (others were listed as *auditores*—including priests—or *auditrices*). See, also, n.24, above, on Monica Hellwig who also seems to have served as a *perita* in all but name and n.32, below, referencing Pilar Bellosillo describing how Paul VI viewed the auditors.

To take but a few brief examples of the precise influence the women at the council had upon the conciliar documents (and therefore also teachings), it is beyond question that *Apostolicam Actuositatem*, the Decree on the Lay Apostolate, received considerable input from Marie-Louise Monnet.[30] Further examples of the impact women auditors impact had can be seen in places such as *Gaudium et Spes* §29, alongside *Lumen Gentium*, chapter four, and especially §32. Furthermore, there is a clear endorsement of the wider role of all lay persons in the church, therefore including women, *inclusive of teaching roles*, in *Lumen Gentium* §31–33, 37–38.[31]

These and other texts[32] point toward a logical conclusion which follows from many of the documents of Vatican II: women bear witness

[30] See McEnroy, *Guests in Their Own House*, 134–37; also Valerio, *Madri del Concilio*, 113–15.

[31] See, for example, §32. None of this is to deny the presence of more hierarchical ecclesiological perceptions throughout these and most other council documents (in fact in this very passage we are provided with an example of such), alongside the more participatory ecclesiological vision that would come to dominate the council. See also, McEnroy, *Guests in their Own House*, 33–34. Among other council texts, Mary Catherine Hilkert, O.P., also draws attention to *Lumen Gentium* §31, *Apostolicam Actuositatem* §2–3, on the sharing in the threefold ministry of Christ and *Ad Gentes* §35 on the entire faithful's responsibility to bear witness to the gospel and 'announce' the good news. See 'Anointed and Sent: the Charism of Preaching,' in *Retrieving Charisms for the Twenty-First Century*, ed. Doris Donnelly (Collegeville, MN: Liturgical Press, 1999), 47–64 at 54–62.

[32] Here see, also, McEnroy, *Guests in Their Own House*, especially 130–66 on the direct impact the women auditors had upon the conciliar documents and 156–57 on *Lumen Gentium* and *Gaudium et Spes*, in particular. Valerio, *Madri del Concilio*, 146–52 briefly discusses the impact of the women auditors, in particular on these same two monumental documents (respectively illustrated by §32 for the former and §§9, 29, 49, 52, 60, 90 for the latter and also on *Apostolicam Actuositatem* (e.g. §§9–10) and *Ad Gentes* (§§9, 32). Valerio also comments upon the general impact the women auditors had upon the council's renewal of religious life (53–56) and upon the lay life, the laity's responsibilities and the lay apostolate in general (56–60). In one sub-commission for *Gaudium et Spes*, Goldie later remarked how she had been a voting member whereas the Polish Archbishop Karol Wojtyla had no such voting rights. McEnroy, *Guests in Their Own House*, 133. One of the auditors, Pilar Bellosillo, particularly underlined the fact that Paul VI called the auditors, male and female alike, 'experts in life' with reference to the preparations of *Gaudium et Spes*, a document which marked an ecclesial sea-change as the conciliar fathers listened to and learned from the laity, '"This *inductive method* was new. It was both exciting and gratifying to be part of this magisterium of the laity in practice"', cited from an interview with McEnroy (January 27–29, 1989) in McEnroy, *Guests in Their Own House*, 134.

to and help to make sense of the faith: *ergo* they exercise magisterium.[33] The women at the council were religious and lay, with a wide range of differing expertise and of diverse life and cultural experiences. They were deliberately selected because of such. This was a conscious decision by the council to bring such life-experience and expertise to the council's deliberation.

If women playing such a significant role in the subcommissions which prepared the texts that would eventually constitute the teaching documents of a general council of the Roman Catholic Church is not one of the most clear and unambiguous examples of their exercising of magisterium and so therefore of their contribution to the teaching documents that ensued when the conciliar magisterium was exercised, it is difficult to think of any better example.

Furthermore, in addition to the increasing roles played by women of differing experiences, skills and background (both lay and religious) in the postconciliar church, one can also point toward a further encouraging fact. If theologians continue to exercise a particular charism of magisterium as they have done from the earliest times of the church, then the postconciliar explosion in numbers of ever-more gifted women theologians underlines the actuality of women teaching with authority on a wider scale still.

WOMEN AND MAGISTERIUM: BY WHAT AUTHORITY?

'Official teachers of the Church know that they too must exhibit the virtue which is basic for every good teacher; this virtue is the ability to learn from anyone'.[34] So stated the Jesuit biblical scholar, John McKenzie, writing in 1967, just two years after the council completed its formal work and the church began the arduous task, still very much incomplete to this day, of implementing the conciliar teaching. One of the questions that will serve as a backdrop to the reflections which follow is this: How willing have church leaders been to learn from the voices of teaching

---

[33] And this notwithstanding more outdated perceptions of the role of women in both church and society in some council and post-conciliar documents.

[34] John L. McKenzie, S.J., *Authority in the Church* (New York: Sheed & Ward, 1966), 136.

authority exercised by and for women throughout history, during the council and subsequently?

One does not normally hear the words women and magisterium related in a participatory sense—i.e. that women contribute to and exercise magisterium. The employment of the term magisterium, itself, is a relatively recent phenomenon (from the later eighteenth century in particular), as a *common* term in ecclesial discourse (previously it was a term employed more rarely). And I would also suggest that the most helpful and effective understanding of the term magisterium[35] is to employ it not to refer to any group of persons or individuals,[36] but rather to signify a function, an act or, as I prefer to term it, an art: the art of teaching-with-authority—teaching, explicating, interpreting and making better understood, appreciated and affirmed the multiple aspects and wondrous gifts of the Christian faith. A faith that itself constitutes the diversely-refracted testimony to the wondrous gift of God's own very self-communication.

This, despite the emergence of what came to become a common (mis-)understanding of the term from the late nineteenth century and beyond, whereby the term became synonymous with one influential group of its practitioners.

---

[35] And what the term came to be employed to refer to.

[36] The numerous writings from Yves Congar are the most obvious examples of painstaking researches into the history of the church which demonstrate this fact. For example, 'Theologians and the Magisterium in the West: From the Gregorian Reform to the Council of Trent,' *Chicago Studies* 17, no. 2 (Summer 1978): 210–24; 'Magisterium, Theologians, the Faithful and the Faith,' *Doctrine and Life* 31 (1981): 548–64; 'A Semantic History of the Term "Magisterium",' and 'A Brief History of the Forms of the Magisterium and Its Relations with Scholars,' the latter two both available in *The Magisterium and Morality*, ed. Charles E. Curran and Richard A. McCormick, Readings in Moral Theology, No. 3, (Mahwah, NJ: Paulist Press, 1982), at 297–313 and 314–31. Although the term magisterium as it is often understood in recent times can be found in some eighteenth century texts, Congar is adamant that it is not until the nineteenth century that the term magisterium (as employed by and with reference to the life of) the church either acquires a sense in regular usage that, (in certain languages) involves a preceding definite article ('the magisterium') or is used by default to refer not to the function or activity of magisterium but rather to those in positions of church leadership and office who perform the function or activity. Congar underlines this point in explicit detail in his 'A Semantic History...', 298, 'A Brief History...', 324–26, and 'Magisterium, Theologians, the Faithful and the Faith', 552–55. All in all, Congar concludes, 'In the sense of "body of pastors" exercising authoritatively the function of teaching, *magisterium*, "*the* magisterium", seems to us to be of recent usage', 'A Semantic History...', 309–10.

Certainly, there have been particular groups of people and individuals across that ecclesiastical history who have been charged with and/or gifted enough to exercise this art in a special way that has brought much good to the church and has proved life-giving. There have been others who have tried to exercise it in ways which have been narrow, confined and rigid and which have proved the opposite of life-giving and have sucked the vitality out of the church's day to day life, whether in a local, national or indeed universal context.

There are, of course, many issues that pertain to discussions of women *in* the church *vis-à-vis* magisterium. They include various forms of ministry, religious life, ordination, sexuality and sexual and interpersonal ethics, reproductive ethics, education, the method and practice of theology, varieties of feminist theology, pastoral service and so on. But more frequently, and certainly in recent decades, when women and magisterium appeared in the same sentence or even wider discussion, the context was too often that of the subordinate position of women, be this individually or in terms of congregations of women religious and 'the' magisterium, that is to say in relation to certain church leaders and/or to 'Rome', by which was usually meant subordinate to the wills and diktats of certain offices of the Roman Curia and/or the authority of the papacy itself, alongside certain bishops' conferences or that of individual bishops. But this is not and cannot be the whole story. And thankfully, under the pontificate of Pope Francis, we have seen developments move in a much more positive and deliberately inclusive direction.

Magisterium—A Question of What, Not Whom

The pioneering work of the ecumenical Groupe des Dombres, *Un Seul Maitre*, reminds us of a fundamental ecumenical fact,

> Every *believer, in and through baptism*, receives the task of vigilance in doctrinal matters, according to his or her means, in particular, that of judging the preaching of the gospel. This is a direct consequence of the universal priesthood of believers. Obviously, the authority of each grows according to the quality of Christian living.[37]

---

[37] Le Groupe Des Dombres, '*Un Seul Maitre*': *L'autorité doctrinal dans L'Église*, (Bayard, 2005), translated by Catherine Clifford as *One Teacher: Doctrinal Authority in the Church* (Grand Rapids, MI and Cambridge, UK: Eerdmans, 2010), §339, p. 103. This echoes aspects of *Lumen Gentium*, in particular.

Here we see an ecumenical refraction of some of the insights reached at Vatican II itself (many of those, in turn, reached thanks to ecumenical dialogue and a willingness to learn). The Groupe des Dombres goes on to help further point towards that need for a greater participatory ecclesial vision of magisterium, one in which the 'corrective vision' offered to the church by many women has, can and indeed should continue to play a very significant role. Questions of ecclesial participation and exclusion have impacted women in the church at many stages of its history, and today, it seems, this remains the case. Of course, many improvements have been seen. But much work remains to be done.[38]

Indeed, the prevailing understanding of magisterium in the church in recent decades has also appeared to exhibit a further misunderstanding in relation to magisterium—it not only confuses the act of teaching with authority, magisterium, with a group of actors, to the exclusion of other actors alongside whom those actors are charged with carrying out such an action, but it also confuses the main product of such activity with the actual thing that the activity and its product are designed to serve and explicate, viz., the Catholic faith. As John McKenzie stated back in the 1960s, 'There must be a clear distinction between faith and doctrine. Faith is the response to revelation; doctrine, the product of theology, is an understanding and an application of the faith… theology and doctrine… are the means by which the Church evolves with the world and with history. Faith never becomes antiquated; doctrine very easily does'.[39] The prevailing understanding of the nature and reach of magisterium in much of the church today, as well as its accompanying implied understanding of the role of the Catholic theologian as being merely to explicate and justify the official teachings of the church at any given time, do not sit well with the reality of the church's history and its tradition.

Therefore, if magisterium, as key historical, etymological and ecclesiological discussions indicate, is more a *doing* word, concerned with a particular action, a function, (or, more accurately a collection of activities and functions towards particular ends), then the actors who carry out magisterium cannot be restricted to one narrow group. Those same sources confirm a plurality of actors of this art throughout the story of

---

[38] See the various contributions in Dennis M. Doyle, Timothy J. Furry, and Pascal D. Bazzell, eds., *Ecclesiology and Exclusion: Boundaries of Being and Belonging in Postmodern Times* (Maryknoll: Orbis, 2012).

[39] McKenzie, *Authority in the Church*, 126.

the church. *This also means that there also cannot be a restriction of who can exercise magisterium in terms of gender.* There exist no church traditions that convincingly reserve the exercise of magisterium either to men alone or even to one particular group of men.

Whatever stances one adopts in the debates about women's ministry in general and ordination, in particular, it is incontrovertible that women have exercised magisterium—understood in both pastoral leadership terms and in terms of teaching. And so it is equally incontrovertible that women have contributed in numerous ways to the stock of authoritative teaching that serves the church.

If human experience, both individual and collective is a proper source and norm for Christian theology and so for doctrine, and the evidence clearly suggests that it is—with Vatican II preeminent in underlining such throughout its documents and especially with the call to discern the signs of the times—then the experiences of women have been particularly influential on so much that has shaped the church and theology and increasingly so in the modern era and especially in the decades since the council formally closed.

Admittedly, the council, because of many divisions and the compromises forced upon it in order to have key documents approved, also sent out mixed and sometimes conflicting messages with regard to various aspects of the understanding and practice of magisterium. This remained one of the areas where the council's unfinished business led to many subsequent problems and further disagreements and divisions in the post-conciliar church.

These considerations help us further appreciate that what I term the 'subject-object' debate in assessing magisterium comes down to the fact that, particularly in the modern period and contemporary era, there is a frequent confusion evident in much discourse about magisterium. This is frequently due to a confusion being made between the *object* of magisterium, i.e. what its purpose, its function is, what it addresses and seeks to discern, make sense of and communicate (in short, the gospel, the gracious and loving self-communication of God and all the implications of this for our world or, if one prefers shorthand theological parlance, revelation, the Word of God) and the *subject* or subjects of magisterium—i.e. the actors, functionaries or practitioners, those who seek to fulfill this activity in the church.

Relatively recent convention has seen people continuously employ the term magisterium as an abbreviation for the 'Official Magisterium', i.e., the teaching authority of the college of the Bishops and of the Pope. But the church as a whole (*sensus fidelium*) clearly also has a part to play in the magisterial process.[40] And while this subject-object debate has always been with the church, keeping the focus on the latter as opposed to the former should always be the most important concern for the church as it strives to fulfill its mission as faithfully as it might. In sum, the *subject* of magisterium being the '*who*', the *object* of magisterium being the '*what*', and the *art* of magisterium the *how* and the *means* by which the *who* serve the *what*.

All this entails that magisterium requires many actors from different parts of the church in addition to those who presently hold formal episcopal office. Among those additional actors of specific important throughout the history of the church are those whose studies, researches, deliberations and discernments earned them the title of theologian—literally those who explore the word of God. The greatest of the church's theologians have included women in their number. It would be strange were it otherwise. It would imply the Spirit was somehow biased in bestowing particular charisms in a manner that the New Testament indicates is certainly not the case in terms of the beliefs about God that the earliest Christians held fast to. Needless to say, if the *sensus fidelium* continues to be of central importance to the understanding of Catholic magisterium, then the majority of faithful whose sense informs the shaping, interpretation and communication of doctrine are also women.

That the practice of magisterium requires many actors from different parts of the church in addition to those who presently hold formal episcopal office is further supported by the canon lawyer Ladislas Örsy, who also offers grounds to expand the definition of and right to practice magisterium: 'side by side with the hierarchical magisterium, there has been continually another kind of magisterium in the church',[41] the long-standing recognition of which he rightly roots in the fact that the deposit of revelation is, of course, entrusted to the church entire. Vatican I affirms such[42] as does Vatican II (again, cf. LG 12).[43] The church does

---

[40]Cf., for example, Richard A. Gaillardetz, *Teaching with Authority* (Collegeville, MN: Liturgical Press, 1997), 160.

[41]Ladislas Örsy, *The Church: Learning and Teaching: Magisterium, Assent, Dissent, Academic Freedom* (Wilmington, Del.: Michael Glazier, 1987), 63.

[42]DS 3074.

[43]Örsy, *The Church: Learning and Teaching*, 64–65.

not and should not be taken to be a shorthand for 'the hierarchy'.[44] Nor, then, we might add, should magisterium.

Rather, 'once it is clear and accepted that revelation is in the possession of the whole church, it becomes obvious that all believers have access to it; all can perceive it, witness the truth, have insights into its depths'.[45] He concludes, 'So, there has always been a genuine and recognized magisterium by others than popes and bishops: the magisterium of graced, learned and wise men and women to whom it was given to have new insights into the old truths'.[46]

The Role of the Magistra—Acknowledging a Long Line of Women Who Have Taught with Authority

To counter the long-standing anachronistic practice of projecting a narrower view of women's participation in certain offices and roles in the church backwards onto earlier historical periods (or forwards onto the present day), we state a simple and obvious fact: Women who taught with authority throughout the emergence and history of the church are so numerous as to warrant an entire collection of ongoing volumes in their own right. Women have borne witness to and discerned, interpreted and explicated the faith from its earliest times. They have also exercised pastoral leadership from the earliest times. We have ample contributions to patrology, less cohesive and comprehensive *collections* in terms of *matrology*.[47]

---

[44] Ibid., 64.

[45] Ibid., 65 and also 67.

[46] Ibid., 67. Örsy then cites a fascinating passage from Gratian's *Decretum Magistriani Gratiani*, ed. Aemilius Friedberg (Graz: Akademie Verlagsanstalt, 1959), col. 65 about the respective competencies of the 'interpreters of scripture' in contrast with the 'pontiffs', ibid., 67–69. And all of this despite Örsy concurring with Francis Sullivan (Magisterium, p29, contra Avery Dulles) that in contemporary times, confusion could result in speaking of 'two magisteria'. Effectively, Örsy in these pages provides all the evidence to the contrary of Sullivan's point himself. The real confusion enters in when the term magisterium is employed only to refer to a specific group of actors rather than to the act of exercising magisterium.

[47] There has been a continuously growing amount of literature that explores the role and functions of women in the church at various stages of its history (of course, among the many scholarly and theological learned studies, one can also find polemical perspectives that generalize to a degree that mirrors the very polemic that downplays the role and function of women in the church that such studies wish to critique). Among the vast body of literature available are the following examples. Andrew Kadle's, *Matrology: A Bibliography*

Jesus, himself, the Christian model par excellence of teaching with authority as the Gospels demonstrate, was brought to greater insight by the many women around him. At times, the Bible stories inform us, he even stood corrected by their authoritative wisdom. Some of what kenosis took out, one might say, a network of wise, grace-filled women helped put back in!

We know that, in the early church communities, women played very prominent roles and continued to do so. The evidence from the early church seems to indicate, then, that women were prophets and teachers, and even, in some cases, considered apostles,[48] from the earliest times of the Christian communities.

The emergence of patterns of what came to be called religious and consecrated life also involved women leaders with great teaching authority.[49] Women exercised leadership, oversight and authority over such communities from early times and some served as abbesses over communities of both men and women alike. We hear often of the desert fathers, but, of course, from the earliest times, there were also desert mothers, too (who

---

of Writings by Christian Women from the First to the Fifteenth Centuries (New York: Continuum, 1995); Ute E. Eisen, *Women Officeholders in Early Christianity: Epigraphical and Literary Studies* (Collegeville, MN: Liturgical Press, 2000); Eldon Jay Epp, *Junia: The First Woman Apostle* (New York: Fortress, 2005); Elisabeth Schussler Fiorenza, *In Memory of Her: A Feminist Theological Reconstruction of Christian Origins* (New York: Crossroad, 1983 and 1994); Ross Shepard Kraemer and Mary Rose D'Angelo, *Women & Christian Origins* (New York: Oxford University Press, 1999); Patricia M. Rumsey, *Women of the Church: The Religious Experience of Monastic Women* (Dublin: Columba Press, 2011); Laura Swan, *The Forgotten Desert Mothers: Sayings, Lives, and Stories of Early Christian Women* (New York: Paulist, 2001); J. N. M. Wijngaards, *Women Deacons in the Early Church: Historical Texts and Contemporary Debates* (New York: Crossroad, 2006); Ben Witherington and Ann Witherington, *Women and the Genesis of Christianity* (Cambridge: Cambridge University Press, 1990); Phyllis Zagano, *Women and Catholicism: Gender, Communion and Authority* (New York: Macmillan, 2011). The numerous works of Gary Macy are also of special relevance here. See also, Christine E. Joynes and Christopher C. Rowland, eds., *From the Margins 2: Women of the New Testament and Their Afterlives* (Sheffield: Sheffield Phoenix Press, 2009); and Eleni Kasselouri-Hatzivassiliadi, Fulata Mbano Moyo and Aikaterini Pekridou, *Many Women Were Also There: The Participation of Orthodox Women in the Ecumenical Movement* (Geneva: WCC Publications, 2010).

[48] Most significantly, Mary Magdalene was long honored with the title *apostolorum apostola*. A 2016 decree elevating her liturgical memorial to the rank of a feast enables her to be celebrated liturgically like the rest of the apostles, and the new preface for that feast states that Christ "honoured her with the task of being apostle to the apostles" (*eam apostolatus officio coram apostolis honoravit*), Congregation for Divine Worship and Discipline of the Sacraments, Decree *Resurrectionis dominicae primam*, AAS 108, no. 7 (2016): 798–99; see also the accompanying letter by Archbishop Arthur Roche, Secretary for the Congregation, and the official communiqué from the Vatican Press Office, 10 June 2016.

[49] See, for example, Rumsey, *Women of the Church*.

have consistently been more highly regarded in the Orthodox traditions than in the Latin 'west').[50]

As the church spread further afield, we see that the processes of inculturation (which are as unavoidable as they should be embraced and cherished) also brought into the heart of the Christian life, in multiple contexts, practices and customs (social, intellectual, political and interpersonal) originally distinctive to the places which the gospel was reaching for the first time. So, if we examine, for example, ancient Ireland, the traditions surrounding St. Brigid of Kildare (c. 453–525) offer one prominent instance of such, as do those pertaining to Hilda of Whitby (c. 614–680) and the later German, Hildegard von Bingen (1098–1179). Commenting on the situation in ancient Ireland, Maeve Callan observes that 'The number of Irish female saints and scholars will probably never be known, but a few of their stories are still told in their own Lives and those of their male teachers and students, stories which tell us that from the most renowned school of all Ireland to the most isolated cell in the wilds, women as well as men helped to earn Ireland the epithet, the Land of Saints and Scholars'.[51]

The constraints of space here mean we cannot go on and list in sufficient detail even a small sample of women who in subsequent periods of history taught with authority in the church—be these founders and members of religious orders—for example from Saint Clare of Assisi (1194–1253) to Mary Ward (1585–1545), or famous women dissenters who brought the church to greater insight through their dissent—from Catherine of Siena (1347–1380) who chastised a pope, to Australia's first saint, Mary MacKillop (1842–1909) to activists such as Dorothy Day (1897–1980). The modern era down to our present day offers countless further examples of the variety of differing ways in which women have exercised ecclesial authority, magisterium in the church. As we have noted earlier, increasingly during this period they have done so as theologians.

From Prophets Without Honor to the Papacy of Francis

Aside from the aforementioned fact that the notion of 'the' magisterium is demonstrated by history to be a category mistake, such a framing of the church's exercise of magisterium that confuses the practice with

---

[50] See, for example, the *Apophthegmata Patrum*.

[51] Maeve B. Callan, 'St Darerca and Her Sister Scholars: Women and Education in Medieval Ireland', *Gender and History* 15, no. 1 (April 2003): 32–49 at 45.

a group of its hierarchical practitioners is also in danger of leading to a still greater mistake: that of obscuring or even ignoring women's contributions to ecclesial magisterium throughout the church's long history and particularly their increasing contributions in the modern and contemporary eras. When such contributions are ignored, it poses the risk of serving further to *exclude* women's voices and subsequent contributions from the table of ecclesial magisterium.

The irony was captured by Sandra Schneiders at the height of tensions between the Vatican and women religious under the previous pontificate, i.e. the clash between women religious congregations in the United States—represented through the Leadership Conference of Women Religious (LCWR) and the church's hierarchical authorities, in the main the Congregation for the Doctrine of the Faith, the Congregation for Consecrated Life and Societies of Apostolic Life (and, in effect, the USCCB).[52]

Schneiders' study bore testimony to the negative experiences of women in the church, those of women religious in particular, being made to feel like 'Prophets in their own country'. Schneiders was convinced that the battle for the Second Vatican Council lay behind those tensions between the hierarchical authorities and women religious in recent times. Women religious were following the call of Vatican II to renew their ministry in and to the world.[53] She suggested that, at the heart of the conflict, lay two radically differing understandings of obedience. On the one hand, the hierarchical demand of submission to 'official teaching' and the rejection of all alternative perspectives as (sinful and disobedient) dissent, obedience to office and authority. On the other hand, religious obedience which is 'an exercise of a prophetic vocation calling its members to carefully discern the meaning of the Word of

---

[52] See Congregation for the Doctrine of the Faith, 'Doctrinal Assessment of the Leadership Conference of Women Religious', http://www.usccb.org/loader.cfm?csModule=security/getfile&pageid=55544. See, also, the preceding chapter in this present volume by the late Anne E. Patrick, S.N.J.M which details the tensions of this period and offers further analysis of the situation at length.

[53] Sandra M. Schneiders, *Prophets in Their Own Country: Women Religious Bearing Witness to the Gospel in a Troubled Church* (Maryknoll: Orbis, 2011), 119. Again, the preceding chapter by Anne E. Patrick also argues at length that the interpretation of Vatican II was the core factor at the heart of the divisions among US women religious during this period, as well as between the LCWR and the church authorities of the USCCB and in Rome.

God in and for a particular situation'. Such 'may at times involve dissent, not as defiance or disobedience but as creative contributions to a fuller discernment of and obedience to the will of God in the present situation'.[54] Such captures very well the wider tensions and conflicts that have beset the church as it grapples with trying to better understand, appreciate and facilitate the role of women in the church. Schneiders argued against any neutralizing of the prophetic role of religious in the church and warned that 'nothing constructive can be built on denial of what is actually going on. We can build a house for Wisdom only on the bedrock of truth'.[55]

Thankfully, in recent years, with the pontificate of Pope Francis, there have been concerted efforts to overcome these polarities and tensions through a renewed appreciation of the fact that magisterium is something which, ultimately, involves the whole people of God and must do so. Vatican II reaffirmed such an understanding very clearly. Across history, a more openly participatory sense of understanding and exercising magisterium has always proved to be that which has served the church best. In the conflict between women religious and the Vatican under Benedict XVI, the church witnessed a regression to a more restricted and exclusive sense of who can and should exercise magisterium in the Catholic Church. And yet, at the Second Vatican Council, many involved went to great lengths to encourage a much more open, collaborative and participatory understanding of the church and of magisterium in particular, despite several mixed messages and divisions on these very issues.

A further clear signal that the church was changing for the better under Francis came about directly in relation to the final outcomes of the conflict between the LCWR and the CDF/USCCB. In December 2014, the Final Report of the Apostolic Visitation which had been ordered by the Congregation for Consecrated Life and Societies of Apostolic Life—effectively an investigation of the LCWR—was released. It reflected the more positive and engaging tone sweeping through much of the Curia under Pope Francis yet also contained a number of criticisms.[56] At that stage, many awaited with foreboding the outcome of the additional *doctrinal* investigation the CDF had ordered back in 2009, when

[54] Ibid., 120.

[55] Ibid., 27.

[56] The report can be accessed at: http://www.apostolicvisitation.org/en/index.html, with reactions from the LCWR featured at: https://lcwr.org/media/report-vaticans-apostolic-visitation-us-women-religious.

Archbishop J. Peter Sartain of the Archdiocese of Seattle was appointed in 2012 to head that investigation and bring about major changes to the LCWR.

But then, to the surprise of many around the world, in April 2015, the CDF doctrinal investigation into the women religious was brought to an unexpected close. Pope Francis met with a delegation of the religious sisters for over an hour. And a *joint* final report was issued on behalf of both the LCSR and the CDF on April 16, 2015[57] by the officers of LCWR and the bishops involved in the investigation.

The report was striking in its affirmation of the work and witness of the American women's religious congregations. What had started out some years before as looking most likely to result in ecclesial rupture in fact resulted in a transcendence of divisions and no censure of the women's congregations was forthcoming in the end at all. As one sister remarked, after personally meeting with Pope Francis, both sides came to realize that what they shared in common was much more important than what they disagreed on.[58] This, of course is a common theme of Francis's own teaching and approach to dialogue. It was also a key to that of John XXIII. Other past and recent church leaders regrettably accentuated where divisions lay rather than unity.

Given the structures of organization and authority in the Vatican and Roman Curia it is beyond any shadow of a doubt that this harmonious end to the investigation of these tireless women servants of the church was brought about by Pope Francis himself. He recognized and affirmed the ministry of the many congregations affiliated to the LCWR. Whereas under his predecessor conflict in relation to these servants of the church appeared to be the default approach, Francis has sought to focus on unity, but unity in legitimate and healthy diversity.

This was far from an isolated intervention. Indeed, Pope Francis stated in the very first year of his pontificate 'It is necessary to broaden the opportunities for a stronger presence of women in the church'. He also made clear that 'We must therefore investigate further the role of women in the church.... We have to work harder to develop a profound

---

[57] Joint Final Report on the Doctrinal Assessment of the Leadership Conference of Women Religious (LCWR) by the Congregation for the Doctrine of the Faith (CDF), https://lcwr.org/sites/default/files/news/files/joint_final_report_of_conclusion_of_cdf_mandate.pdf (16 April 2015).

[58] Sister Sharon Holland.

theology of the woman. Only by making this step will it be possible to better reflect on their function within the church. The feminine genius is needed wherever we make important decisions. The challenge today is this: to think about the specific place of women also in those places where the authority of the church is exercised for various areas of the church'.[59] Here we have a pope inviting discussion on the role and authority of women in the church. It seems clear Francis intends such discussions to have practical outcomes. This introduces the possibility of embracing change not only in actual ecclesial structures but also in the operative conceptions of what magisterium is and who should practice it.

Pope Francis, in his second public audience, spoke of the special position of women in the church, including their particular gifts for sharing the faith.[60] He spoke of the fact that women were the first witnesses to the resurrection and said 'Women have had and still have a special role in opening doors to the Lord, in following him and communicating his face, because the eyes of faith always need the simple and profound look of love'. The 'eyes of faith' is an old form of referring to the *sensus*

---

[59] 'Intervista del Direttore a Papa Francesco', *La Civiltà Cattolica* Anno 164 (19 settembre 2013): 449–77 at 466–67. The interview took place on August 19th, 2013 with Father Antonio Spadaro, S.J., editor in chief of *La Civiltà Cattolica*. An English translation appeared as 'A Big Heart Open to God' in *America* (September 30, 2013): 13–38 at 28. The term 'feminine genius' has been the subject of much debate and criticism (e.g. see the preceding chapters by Patricia Madigan and Anne E. Patrick) and here, as with his other statements on women, translations of Pope Francis's exact words have proved more controversial perhaps than his own original intended meaning. There is no doubt this phrase has caused consternation and offense to some—being identified with the subordinationist tendencies of the 'complementarity' theology that emerged during the pontificate of John Paul II in particular. However, those issues of translation and the hermeneutics of Francis's own understanding here remain live and continue to be debated (as Madigan and Patrick, respectively, both acknowledge in differing ways) and, in reading the wider interview, along with his many subsequent statements on women, in addition to surveying his subsequent actions with regard to promoting a wider involvement for women in ecclesial roles—as evidenced here and in the further examples that follow—it is beyond doubt his intentions have been constructive and positive.

[60] http://www.vatican.va/holy_father/francesco/audiences/2013/documents/papa-francesco_20130403_udienza-generale_en.html (3 April 2013). See, also, http://ncronline.org/news/vatican/francis-women-have-special-role-church (3 April 2013) and, coverage in more depth, at http://www.indcatholicnews.com/news.php?view-Story=22276 (6 April 2013).

fidelium.[61] It is clear Pope Francis was directly speaking about women bearing witness to, communicating and making sense of the faith.[62] I believe magisterium is a shorthand word for such activities. The pope's further reflections in the interview of August 2013 reinforce such an interpretation as do many of his subsequent statements and actions, some misunderstood terms of expression aspects perhaps 'lost in translation' notwithstanding.

Preaching in the Cathedral of Saints Peter and Paul in Philadelphia on September 26, 2015, Francis recalled the story of the American Saint Katharine Drexel, who implored Pope Leo XIII to do something about the light of the missions. Francis recalled that Leo had responded to her by asking what she was going to do about it. And he went on,

> Those words changed Katharine's life, because they reminded her that, in the end, every Christian man and woman, by virtue of baptism, has received a mission. ... [T]hose words – "What about you?" – were addressed to a young person, a young woman with high ideals, and they changed her life. They made her think of the immense work that had to be done, and to realize that she was being called to do her part. ... One of the great challenges facing the Church in this generation is to foster in all the faithful a sense of personal responsibility for the Church's mission, and to

---

[61] See Ormond Rush, *The Eyes of Faith: The Sense of the Faithful and the Church's Reception of Revelation* (Washington, DC: The Catholic University of America Press, 2009).

[62] Lest there be any doubt, when the pope preached at Vespers in St. Patrick's Cathedral on September 24th during his visit to the United States he stated that 'In a special way I would like to express my esteem and gratitude to the religious women of the United States. What would the Church be without you? Women of strength, fighters, with that spirit of courage which puts you in the front lines in the proclamation of the Gospel. To you, religious women, sisters and mothers of this people, I wish to say "thank you", a big thank you... and to tell you that I love you very much.' In words that almost replicate the sentiments of Schneiders above, Francis continued, saying, 'I know that many of you are in the front lines in meeting the challenges of adapting to an evolving pastoral landscape. Whatever difficulties and trials you face, I ask you, like Saint Peter, to be at peace and to respond to them as Christ did: he thanked the Father, took up his cross and looked forward!', 'Vespers with Priests and Religious, Homily of His Holiness Pope Francis', St Patrick's Cathedral, New York, http://w2.vatican.va/content/francesco/en/homilies/2015/documents/papa-francesco_20150924_usa-omelia-vespri-nyc.html (24 September 2015).

enable them to fulfill that responsibility as missionary disciples, as a leaven of the Gospel in our world. This will require creativity in adapting to changed situations, carrying forward the legacy of the past not primarily by maintaining our structures and institutions, which have served us well, but above all by being open to the possibilities which the Spirit opens up to us and communicating the joy of the Gospel, daily and in every season of our life. "What about you?" It is significant that these words of the elderly Pope were also addressed to a lay woman. We know that the future of the Church in a rapidly changing society will call, and even now calls, for a much more active engagement on the part of the laity. ... Our challenge today is to foster a sense of collaboration and shared responsibility in planning for the future of our parishes and institutions. This does not mean relinquishing the spiritual authority with which we have been entrusted; rather, it means discerning and employing wisely the manifold gifts which the Spirit pours out upon the Church. In a particular way, it means valuing the immense contribution which women, lay and religious, have made and continue to make, in the life of our communities.[63]

Pope Francis has backed up his words with actions, ensuring women have, indeed, been appointed to a number of the arenas where the church discerns its most important decisions. And their presence continues to grow in such places. Many call for still further appointments, but the direction in which this pontificate is moving the church on this issue is clearly a positive and welcome one. Perhaps somewhat slowly but nonetheless surely, the understanding, appreciation and facilitation of the role of women in the church are being transformed. On August 2, 2016, Pope Francis established a 'Commission of Study on the Diaconate of Women' to explore both the historical and contemporary issues pertaining to this aspect of women's ministry. Six of its twelve members were women and it was widely taken as a first step toward the church reexamining the status of the long-standing closed door to ordained ministry for women. On May 8, 2018, Pope Francis approved revised statues for the recently formed Dicastery on Integral Human Development. Among the additions to the previous version of the statutes was an explicit mandate to promote reflection on the role of women in the church and society alike, with Article 9 citing Pope Francis's 2014 interview in stating 'The Dicastery works to deepen the reflection on the relationship

[63] https://w2.vatican.va/content/francesco/en/homilies/2015/documents/papa-francesco_20150926_usa-omelia-philadelphia.html (27 September 2015).

between men and women in their respective specificity, reciprocity, complementarity and equal dignity. Valuing the feminine "genius", it offers a contribution to ecclesial reflection on the identity and mission of women in the Church and in society, promoting their participation'.[64]

Yet Schneiders' study continues to stand as testimony to the continued negative experiences of women in the church being made to feel like 'Prophets in their own country'. This refers directly to Jesus's sadly ironic statement—prophets are only without honor in their own country. The women of the church have been honored far and wide beyond the church. In seeking to find ways to ensure that positive and life-giving energy more uniformly surrounds their experiences of church in the future, perhaps the legacy of the women of the council and those who took up the torch after them is a good place to find ongoing inspiration.

No magic wand would remove all of the organizational fault-lines of the church simply by placing women would in key positions of authority instead of men—human beings are human beings with all their failings regardless of gender. Some women's voices that might be brought to the table from which they have been excluded could no doubt prove as harsh and uncompromising (from whatever ecclesial standpoint they may come), as those of some male voices heard in the church today. And there will be little gained if an exclusive small group of privileged women's voices are added to those privileged groups of male voices in the church. Nonetheless, the legacy of the women of Vatican II demonstrates that so much could also be added to the thinking, leadership and reform of the church if still more women's voices are heard at differing levels of where the church does its thinking and decision-making.

CONCLUSION: WOMEN AND THE ART OF MAGISTERIUM

As I have sought to suggest elsewhere, magisterium deserves *aggiornamento* as much as any other part of the church and its theological enquiries. The 'what', the deposit of faith itself remains the core focus of magisterium. The 'who', if narrowed to a small group of male and ordained church leaders is a limiting of magisterial subjectivity that history demonstrates has no traditional justification. Retrieving a wider subjectivity and participatory understanding of magisterium is the key

---

[64] Statutes of the Dicastery for the Laity, Family and Life (May 7, 2018), at http://www.laityfamilylife.va/content/laityfamilylife/en/il-dicastero/lo-statuto.html.

to 'authentic' magisterium for our times. Therefore, renewed attention to the 'how', the art of magisterium itself, is perhaps one of the most urgent and important undertakings for the church today. The latter is essential in order that the wider co-responsibility of an expanded 'who' once more comes to pass.[65]

As the 'battle for the council' was beginning to develop into an increasingly polarized conflict in the immediate decades subsequent to Vatican II, Bernard Häring, C.Ss.R., remarked that, 'The few women who were present in the council have spread the message and done much to keep the conciliar spirit alive. What would have happened if hundreds of women of the same calibre had been actively engaged in the council?' Even so, women in the church, sisters and laywomen, are guarantors that the spirit of Vatican II will be kept alive with all its dynamics'. He then makes a plea 'let the spirit of the council not be aborted by men more concerned for law and order than for growing life'.[66]

The contribution of women theologians to taking the church forward in the light of the debates that emerged from the council has been greatly significant. They have been influenced by those ecclesial winds of empowering change from Vatican II, indeed have often led the efforts to implement the spirit and letter of the council's teaching across a wide expanse of ecclesial life, including, perhaps in a preeminent fashion with regard to the theological sciences, in the field of moral theology.

In particular, they have offered much inspiration and helped to retrieve and develop old and new resources alike for more dialogical, participatory, liberating, empowering and ecumenical forms of ecclesial discernment and therefore of church teaching, also, i.e. magisterium.[67] Often they have done so by example.

These contributions have helped the church appreciate anew, alongside many other significant scholars, that when it comes to magisterium

---

[65]Some of the material here helped form the basis of a considerably shorter essay published in Italian as 'Donne E Magistero Teologico', in *Avendo qualcosa da dire*, ed. Perroni and Legrand, 95–106. I examined these and related themes in still further detail in 'Changing the (Magisterial) Subject: Women Teaching-with-Authority—From Vatican II To Tomorrow', *Irish Theological Quarterly* 81, no. 1 (Spring 2016): 3–33. I am most grateful to all editors concerned for permission to draw upon those articles here.

[66]McEnroy, *Guests in Their Own House*, x.

[67]For example, consider the themes discussed in Letty M. Russell, *Household of Freedom—Authority in Feminist Theology* (London: Westminster Press, 1987).

the *what* and not the *who* is the important question. As in the ancient church, the *regula fidei*, the faith itself, its building up and passing on are the most important things to focus on. Not who is deemed to be 'in charge' of such. So many women theologians, activists and religious have demonstrated such by example over the Christian centuries. Too often their contributions are overlooked, forgotten or given in-depth treatment mostly in minority sub-disciplinary studies.

Again echoing the sentiments of Vatican II, as James Coriden so rightly notes, through ecclesial communion as our common context 'We are all in this together: theologians, bishops and baptized believers. This is our theological conviction, but it also finds strong canonical expression. The Church's canons remind us that we are all members of the Christian faithful, sharers in Christ's own prophetic function, and that we are all called to exercise the Church's mission, including its teaching mission, in the world (c. 204)'.[68]

The contributions of the many women theologians involved in taking forward the challenging ecclesial task of living out the vision of Vatican II and helping to facilitate its reception through the *sensus fidelium*, should be acknowledged for what they are: contributions to the church's ability to teach with authority—to its magisterium. Therefore, these contributions should be listened to. When, on November 20, 1964, Pope Paul VI held an audience with the council auditors (along with parish priests invited for the third session), it seems clear he recognized and acknowledged the role that women auditors were performing on the church's behalf during the council. Spotting the Australian, Rosemary Goldie, he smiled at her and said 'Ah, *nostra collaboratrice*'—'our co-worker'.[69]

So many women, before, during and after the council have been and continue to be valued collaborators in the church's magisterium. The many particular and grace-filled ways in which women have contributed

---

[68] James A. Coriden, 'Theologians and Bishops: Good Procedures Promotes Collaboration,' in *Theology and Magisterium* (*Concilium* 2012/2), ed. Felix Wilfred and Susan A. Ross (London: SCM Press, 2012), 64–74 at 65. Coriden's reflections were in the context of an essay about the case of Elizabeth Johnson.

[69] Rosemary Goldie, 'Una donna nella Concilio', *Review of Religious Sciences* (*Pontifical Regional Seminary*, Pius IX, Maufetta), (January 1989), 376, translation by Rosemary Goldie as 'A Woman at the Council: Memories of an Auditor', cited in McEnroy, *Guests in Their Own House*, 129.

through their practice of magisterium to the church's overall teaching, continue to be of lasting value for the church and have accentuated the authoritativeness of church teaching precisely *because* these were contributions from women. They exercise the magisterium that they are called to make real—that is to say magisterium that is genuinely (in an existential sense) authentic. Theology in particular and the church in general are so much the better for their ministry in so doing. They have taught the church much and will continue to do so.

PART IV

Inculturation: The Contextual Reception of the Council

CHAPTER 10

We Are the Church: Church in Dialogue in Papua

Jan Nielen

Historical Context

The period of time during the Second Vatican Council and the first years afterward was full of turmoil and radical transformation in Indonesia, in Papua, and in the church. Dutch colonial rule came to an end in Papua, the former Dutch colony New Guinea, in 1962, and Papua "integrated" into the Indonesian state in 1963. A military coup in 1965 inaugurated the authoritarian rule of the Suharto regime, which lasted for a period of almost thirty years. The much disputed "Act of Free Choice" took place in 1969. After losing its status as a Dutch colony in 1962, Papua became a part of the Indonesian Republic through international political manipulations, dramatically infringing Papua's desire to become an independent country. Although an "Act of Free Choice" was staged under the United Nations' supervision in 1969, this Act left the population with no choice at all. The referendum should have been conducted with the highest respect for the choice of each individual of the Papuan nation, under the principle that one person is entitled to one vote.

J. Nielen (✉)
Oegstgeest, The Netherlands
e-mail: jnielen@xs4all.nl

© The Author(s) 2018
V. Latinovic et al. (eds.), *Catholicism Opening to the World and Other Confessions*, Pathways for Ecumenical and Interreligious Dialogue,
https://doi.org/10.1007/978-3-319-98581-7_10

151

Instead, what happened was a consensus process in which 1026 people selected by Indonesia were allowed to represent the Papuan population of approximately 800,000. This occurred under heavy pressure from the Indonesian military so that Papua would become part of Indonesia. This experience of international treachery has left deep, if not traumatic, marks in the hearts of the Papuan population.

Conflicts in Papua ran and still run along vertical as well as horizontal lines. The most important conflict was and is the vertical one between Papua on the one hand and government and army of Indonesia on the other. This basically was about the right of self-determination and cultural (Papuan) identity and dignity. At the same time, a system of structural violence created and is still creating conditions of economic, political, social and cultural injustice for the Papuan population. In the case of Freeport's Grasberg gold and copper mine in Mimika, not only the larger part of economic benefits were channeled straight to Jakarta and abroad, but also massive environmental and social damage was done. Conflicts along horizontal lines were and are still running in the case of the conflicts between the Papuan population and the increasing number of immigrants coming to Papua, as well as the conflicts linked with the significant cultural and sub-ethnic differences between the more than 250 Papuan sub-ethnic groups themselves.

The Second Vatican Council occurred during this period of upheaval in Papua, and the church in and of Asia awakened through the establishment of the Federation of Asian Bishops' Conferences (FABC) in 1970. The church was opening to the world. Theologically speaking, the bishops followed the mandate of the Council as they sought to articulate, for their contexts, how the Church is continuously called to be sent to the world, just as the Son was sent to the world and his disciples sent out into the world. *Gaudium et Spes* gives the rationale for openness to the world: the dignity of the human person (GS 3). The Church is called to serve and not to be served. This is an important characteristic of original Franciscan spirituality. In a Franciscan way, the Church is called to open to the world not from a position of power, but in an attitude of service to the forgotten world and with a preferential option for the poor. Saint Francis and his brothers wanted to place themselves at the service of others and to be subject to them,[1] especially to the people who had

---

[1] See, among other places, Francis of Assisi, "Earlier Rule (1221)," in *Francis of Assisi: Early Documents*, vol. 1, ed. Regis J. Armstrong, O.F.M.Cap., J. A. Wayne Hellmann,

no prospect in life and were excluded from mainstream society. They did not want to be *maiores* and *domini*, but *minores* and *subditi*.[2] Their "being-subject" was not a passive acceptance and endurance of a situation of oppression imposed on them by the rich and the powerful. It was a free choice of certain forms of work that were not much appreciated in Assisi in those days, as a protest against the emerging system of Assisi and as a realization of an alternative society which is not built on obtaining ever more possessions and power, but on service which leads to true sister- and brotherhood and to true peace.[3]

Gaudium et Spes is imbued with a strong spirit of dialogue and learning from other disciplines, faiths and movements. It moved away from triumphalism when it admitted that the Church does not possess the solution to all problems of humanity. Following the spirit of *Gaudium et Spes*, the Church must be open to learn from the findings of other disciplines in understanding the "signs of the times." Christianity must be studied from a historical, sociological and phenomenological perspective, in intense conversation with the broader society as well as peoples of other faiths. Christians can learn from the way that peoples of other faiths interpret our Scripture and theologies, a multi-faith hermeneutics.

It is the fruit of Vatican II to call the Church to be in dialogue with other religions and cultures. In *Nostra Aetate* it is stated that the Church rejects nothing that is true and holy in the religions (NA 2). Likewise, in his encyclical *Ecclesiam Suam*, Paul VI attends to dialogue as a path to carry out the Church's mission in the contemporary world. Paul VI refers to four categories or levels of dialogue: dialogue with all humankind, dialogue with other religions, dialogue with other Christians and dialogue within the Catholic Church.[4] I shall elaborate below on dialogue as a path to carry out the Church's mission in the context of Asia in general and Papua in particular.

The Church must also tap the treasures of Asian popular religiosity and of its great religious traditions in order to form a church with an Asian face. But how open are we, really, to a critique of our traditions and to a

O.F.M.Conv., and William J. Short, O.F.M. (Hyde Park, NY: New City Press, 1999), 74; hereafter, these volumes will be cited as FA:ED.

[2] Jan Hoeberichts, *Francis and Islam* (Quincy: Franciscan Press, 1997), 78.

[3] Ibid., 79.

[4] Paul VI, Encyclical Letter *Ecclesiam Suam*, AAS 56 (1964): 609–59, no. 96ff.

reformulation of the language of development, theology and rituals that draws from Asian spiritual resources? A mature understanding of inculturation does not understand inculturation as a one-way process, but the danger of an antiquated understanding of the relationship between the Gospel and non-European cultures remains strong in many circles in the Church. Through the establishment of the Federation of Asian Bishops' Conferences, the Asian churches gradually developed their own vision of the mission of the Church in light of their specific context. Opening to the world for the Church in Asia meant a Church in dialogue with Asia's poor, with its local cultures, and with other religions. Dialogue and inculturation became important and necessary for the transformation of a Church *in* Asia toward a Church *of* Asia, borrowing from the customs and traditions of their people, from their wisdom and their learning, from their arts and disciplines.[5] It is in this connection that servanthood and service became constitutive elements of the Asian Church itself: The Church does not exist for itself but for the Kingdom (or reign) of God. This emphasis on the Kingdom of God and the servant role of the Church created a new image of the Church. The Church was called upon to truly become the Church of the poor and to commit itself to the establishment of a just and peaceful society and to the defense of human rights. It was in this connection that the Federation of Asian Bishops' Conferences spoke about servanthood and service.[6] The emerging Asian Church commits itself in a spirit of service to the realization of the Kingdom of God. This means being with the people, especially the poor, and responding to their needs with sensitiveness to the presence of God in other cultures and religious traditions. In other words, can the presence of a glimpse of God be caught in the other rather than bringing God to the other?

In this context, it is interesting to refer to the advice Saint Francis gave to his brothers how to live and work among the Muslims, namely by being subject to them and waiting patiently for a sign from God, meanwhile delaying their preaching and baptizing activity until they saw it pleased the Lord.[7] The particular method of Franciscan missionary work, with special reference to mission in Muslim societies, was a way of life being subject to all in which preaching and baptizing activity come

---

[5] *Ad Gentes* (Degree on the Mission Activity of the Church), 1965: 22.

[6] Hoeberichts, *Francis and Islam*, 171.

[7] Francis of Assisi, "Earlier Rule," 74; Hoeberichts, *Francis and Islam*, 103.

second. This method will be discussed in greater detail below in the context of Franciscan accompaniment in Papua.

In a statement of the Asian bishops' meeting in 1970, the importance of dialogue with fellow Asians committed to other faiths was already mentioned. The Asian bishops urged a deep respect for the culture and traditions of their peoples, and expressed the hope that the catholicity of the Church, the root of their diversity in the oneness of faith, may serve to help Asia remain truly Asian, and yet become fully part of the modern world and the one family of humankind. At the first FABC Plenary Assembly in 1974 the Asian bishops defined the task of evangelization in Asia as follows: "In Asia especially this involves a dialogue with the great religious traditions of our peoples. In this dialogue we accept them as significant and positive elements in the economy of God's design of salvation."[8]

At the Asian Synod (1998) in Rome, the issue of the "threefold dialogue," that is, a dialogue with the poor, a dialogue with other religions of Asia, and a dialogue with Asian cultures, was a key issue for the Asian bishops. I like to mention here the role of our good friend late bishop Bunluen Mansap of Ubon Ratchathani, Thailand, and the role of Fr. Aloysius Pieris, S.J., reflecting upon the process of developing from the Church *in* Asia to the Church *of* Asia. According to Pieris, the baptism of Jesus at the river Jordan was a baptism into the religiousness of the culture of his time. Following in the footsteps of Jesus, the Church in Asia also has to take this step, which is to submit itself to a baptism in the river of Asia's religiousness. This means that the Church must be extensively immersed and involved with Asia's other religions. It also means that the Church takes seriously the people who make up the cultures and religions of Asia.[9] There also is a need to develop an Asian theology of religions that is critical of any theological position based on a dogma of intolerance. The Church should adopt a principled position against fundamentalist or extremist thinking within any religion.[10] The Vietnamese bishops suggested at the Asian Synod that "Western, and especially Scholastic theology, is not adapted to the religions of Asia, because it

---

[8] Edmund Chia, *Towards a Theology of Dialogue: Schillebeeckx's Method as Bridge between Vatican's Dominus Iesus and Asia's FABC Theology* (Ph.D. Dissertation, University of Nijmegen, 2003), 39.

[9] Ibid., 241.

[10] As we see, in the process, the Church should demonstrate its firm commitment to social justice. Bishop Mansap stood for a firm commitment to social justice.

is too rational... [whereas,] for the Asians, one cannot analyze the truth nor explain the mystery. [Instead,] there is a preference for silence over words."[11] A preference for silence over words is something I learned from my Asian partners. In Asia, there is a tradition to generate communion through wordless exchange.[12]

In a relatively short span of time both within Papuan society and within the Church, drastic changes took place. The Dutch Franciscan friars were both observers of and participants in these processes of transformation. Living together a visionary experience in particularly constraining situations and amidst many contradictions, the Dutch Franciscan friars found themselves in a dialectical process: They saw continuous tension between being idealistic (what we "are") on the one hand, and being flexible and pragmatic (what we can "do"), on the other hand. Particularly challenging was the firm intention to let the Papuan people fully participate in the Church, whereas the forced political integration in the Indonesian Republic prevented the Papuans from full participation in the governance of their own society.

FRANCISCAN ACCOMPANIMENT[13]

The missionary approach chosen by the Dutch Franciscan friars and sisters was characterized by respect for what already was present in Papua: the ways of thinking, the cultural and spiritual values, and the patterns of leadership within the Papuan communities. Basic human values in the cultures of the Papuans were recognized and were built upon to create a community of people living their faith and togetherness. As a result of this, Franciscan friars in Papua strove to learn and understand local cultures from the very beginning of their missionary work in Papua in 1937. Much later, this same attitude was reflected in making anthropological study one of the key components in the curriculum of the School of Theology for the formation of pastoral workers and priests in Papua. Anthropology and scripture were at the heart of the school's curriculum. The Franciscans encouraged their students to consider how

---

[11] Ibid., 84.

[12] Aloysius Pieris S.J., *Give Vatican II a Chance* (Ragama: Pubudu Press, 2010), 207.

[13] For a more detailed summary of the approach I sketch here, see Budi Tjahjono and Ruth Kilcullen, *Franciscans in Papua: The Journey of Dutch OFM Friars with the Papuans in the Struggle for Their Dignity* (Geneva: Franciscans International, 2014).

best to integrate the Gospel into their specific local contexts. What was the best way to live out their faith in the contexts in which they found themselves?

Pastoral care was a crucial part of the work of the Franciscans during times of conflict and uncertainty. Sacraments and celebrations with the Papuans gave communities the opportunity to come together and grow in faith. Reading the Bible together and interpreting the Good News in the context of their difficult situation gave the people courage to deal with the difficulties they faced as individuals and as communities. The people read the Bible and talked in groups together, discussing the readings, their views, and their problems. For the Franciscans, pastoral care was aimed at giving people strength through their faith. This complemented the importance of ancestors in local traditions: God and their ancestors were accompanying believers in the great caravan of life, giving them strength. One of the challenges that Papuan people faced was succeeding in building a positive future without breaking with their past.

The Dutch Franciscan friars observed the enormous impact that the Indonesian regime had on local Papuan culture. The new administration brought unprecedented modernization to the region, the nature and delivery of which often clashed irreconcilably with indigenous ways of life. For the Franciscans, so deeply concerned with the anthropology of Papua, this manifested itself most clearly in the diminution of local languages. Young students moved away from home to go to school where they would learn Indonesian and gradually, from lack of practice, lose their maternal language. By the time they finished school, they could no longer talk to their families in their traditional tongue; in this way, the oral tradition of passing songs, prayers and rituals from generation to generation diminished. The result was that, in losing touch with their traditions, young people became more and more Indonesian. This process continues to pose a particularly grave threat to the smaller tribes, many of which have as few as one hundred members; with ever-dwindling numbers, the unique languages spoken by these tribes are on the brink of extinction. With greater numbers to sustain the traditional language, the larger tribes have a better chance of preserving their languages for a longer period. This is also aided by the fact that most of the linguistic research conducted in Papua focused on the larger tribes.

The Franciscans played a significant role in recording and preserving several Papuan languages, particularly in the Wissel Lakes region and in the Star Mountains. Many of the linguistic studies, dictionaries and teaching workbooks researched and written by the friars are now housed in a library in the Netherlands. The friars also undertook a lot of translation work, for instance, with the Bible. When people went to a Sunday celebration and the readings were written in the local language, they were sometimes unable to read it because they had never seen their language written down. The bulk of the translation occurred during the Dutch administration before the Indonesian government took charge. A number of evangelical Christian churches also established linguistic centers in Papua, in keeping with their ideological goal to translate the Bible into every language of the world. There is a dire need to reinvigorate many of these minor tribal languages because, since so little has been written down, when the last of the members of a tribe dies, their unique language dies with them.

In the view of the Franciscan friars, participation and contextualization became more and more important in the course of the 1960s and 1970s. In the beginning, these concepts were discussed and developed amongst the more "intellectual" layers of the Franciscan community. More generally, the mission of the Franciscan friars was characterized by simply being and living with the Papuans, and living the Gospel meant helping people in whatever way they could to improve their daily lives. For both Franciscans and Papuans, pastoral and developmental work went hand in hand.

Another important aspect of the missionary work of the Franciscans was inculturation. They placed a great emphasis on the need to be culturally sensitive. Anthropologists among the Franciscan friars had a significant impact on the Franciscan approach to working within the context of the local cultures of Papua. Being aware of the importance of listening to the Papuans, their approach was to immerse themselves in the local cultures and to let change happen in an organic way. This did not mean that they had not come with a mission to bring the Good News. Neither did it mean that there were no tensions between this approach focused on immersion and a more pragmatic approach characterized by the "straight-forward" mentality of the Dutch Franciscan friars. Some aspects of local culture, including the regular warfare between tribes, were clearly challenges for the proclamation and acceptance of the Gospel alike, and stood in the way of full immersion and acceptance.

Inculturation sometimes brought the friars into conflict with the policy of the Indonesian government and its active attempts at "Indonesianization." In the early 1970s the government introduced

"Operation Koteka" to bring the Papuans to a "higher" level of civilization. Koteka is the name for the traditional clothing used by men to cover their genitals. Papuan men were requested to shave their beards, to abandon their Koteka, to wear clothes, to give way their sacred objects, and to stop organizing their big traditional feasts where they slaughter their pigs.

In many cases, the Franciscan friars had a different view of how development should be brought and introduced in Papua. The Pastoral Council of the Baliem region in the highlands of Papua for example protested against this policy. Development and mission should be done with the people (*missio cum gentibus*). The approach was to let people themselves make the choice. Even until today this remains an issue in the sensitive relationship between the center (Jakarta) and Papua.

There was a closeness of the Franciscan friars with the Papuans. There was a strong urge among them to be with the people, to live with them, to defend them in any situation, and to ask that the Papuans be respected and acknowledged as human beings and children of God. That was the bottom line for the vast majority of missionaries in Papua, not only Franciscans, but also the Sacred Heart fathers, the Crosier fathers and the Augustinians. To be with the Papuans turned the bitterness of their experience of being looked down upon as "primitives" by outsiders into the sweetness of experiencing being fully acknowledged and respected as human beings.[14] Franciscan friars had come to Papua to serve and to bring justice and peace.

After Papua's integration in Indonesia in 1963 it became increasingly difficult for foreign missionaries to live and work in Papua. It became clear that the establishment of a self-sustaining church was necessary for the continuation of the work of the Franciscans. This was achieved through "We are the Church" movement that intended to facilitate the transfer of running the Church to the Papuan communities themselves. It emphasized that everyone has a role to play. It started with catechism programs in the mountainous villages. While schooling during the Dutch period was only provided until grade three, during the Indonesian period this was extended until grade six. In towns, secondary schools were opened, but it was increasingly difficult for the Dutch Franciscans to be

---

[14] Francis of Assisi described his conversion in these terms, when he came to perceive lepers, whom he had once found bitter, as sweet. See Francis of Assisi, "The Testament (1226)," in FA:ED, I: 124.

employed as teachers in these schools. In 1980 they started to send local candidates for these jobs: Papuan priests, catechists and pastoral workers. There were new seminaries opened in 1986, not only for the education of priests, but also for pastoral workers. The Franciscans tried to have in each parish a team with one priest, one catechist and one pastoral worker. This expanded their capacity to minister to the more remote, inaccessible regions. The objective was, step by step, to transfer the work of the Dutch Franciscan friars to the Papuans themselves.

"WE ARE THE CHURCH" MOVEMENT[15]

The bishop of Jayapura of that time, Mgr. Rudolph Staverman, O.F.M., attended the sessions of the Second Vatican Council. Vatican II famously defined the Church as the "People of God," helping to promote an ecclesiology that was not rigidly hierarchical in nature. Staverman was very much inspired by the new visions developed and formulated during these sessions and brought them home to Papua. After his return from Rome, Staverman publicly mentioned that he was fully supporting the *aggiornamento* of the Church and the Franciscan Order. He saw this not only as a task for himself but for all people in the Church and the Franciscan Order. These visions were very much in line with developments that already were going on in Papua and strengthened the conviction of the Dutch Franciscan friars to continue to work along those lines. As far as Staverman was concerned, it was not only about introducing new ideas, but also about finding ways to operationalize these ideas. It was about a new way of working.

Obviously, the process of *aggiornamento* was not undisputed. For example, the issue of using the local language in the liturgy became a delicate problem. There were quite a lot of discussions about which (local) language(s) should be used in the liturgy. In Papua there are many local languages and the use of Indonesian language rather than local tribal languages was the trickiest issue. Staverman and some of his Dutch Franciscan friars had different opinions about this.

Staverman's successor, Mgr. Herman Münninghoff, O.F.M., took this new approach toward the relationship between the Church and the Papuans further. Instead of bringing the Papuans to the Church, he

---

[15] Tjahjono and Kilcullen, *Franciscans in Padua*.

brought the Church to the Papuans. In doing so, he made the Papuans feel that not only the Catholic Church was there for them, but that they themselves—the Papuans—were the Church! As manifestations of this, Münninghoff gave more space to involvement of lay pastors in the life and work of the Church and to efforts of the Church to improve the quality of the life of the Papuan communities. He explained that the work of liturgy and catechism should constitute only fifty percent of the labor of parish priests in his diocese, including the bishop himself. Priests should focus the remainder of their time on improving the quality of life for the Papuan people. Therefore they employed a wider understanding of the role of the Church. Although often instructed by the Vatican to give full attention to the liturgy of the Church, Münninghoff believed that improving the quality of life for people should be the key priority for the Church, and this not just in Indonesia or Papua but globally. Justice and peace became important aspects of the Church's activities. He called upon people to actually practice what they prayed for and to assist those in need.

This new spirit also motivated the Dutch Franciscan friars in the early 1970s to put their full weight behind the initiative of Münninghoff to organize a diocesen-wide pastoral consultation. The pastoral consultation was held under an interesting banner: "We are the Church". This slogan covered various aspects, among others, the recognition that the indigenous community had its own very important values that should be kept alive and recognized as Christian values as well; it covered also the very attitude of the church leaders/missionaries that they have to listen to the people; and it covers also the conviction by the Franciscan missionaries that a church is made up by its members, and not just by the hierarchy. So, however the future of the Christian community/church might unfold, it should be based on local tradition, values and insights and based on participation of all. All the members of the community are responsible for what kind of community/church will be built up. The creation of a sense of belonging and "owning" the church was very central in this diocese-wide pastoral consultation that continued for two years. To promote this substantial participatory approach special cadre trainings have been set up and a very honest effort was made to make room for lay pastoral workers as rightful leaders of the local communities alongside the priests. This was an emerging Papuan-style of church-building.

The Franciscan friars organized groups of people to come together and to discuss issues related to the church and their daily life. Men and women walked for days to take part in these meetings. These meetings sometimes lasted for a couple of days and during that time the people of that specific location opened up their homes to host those who had come from far away to take part in the discussions. Despite speaking different languages and coming from various tribes, people shared their stories, songs, and dances. When the meeting was ended, the host people accompanied their visitors for the first day of their journey home. These meetings brought people together beyond territorial, cultural, and linguistic barriers. In this way church-building was community-building. The idea of togetherness was a new element in a highly divided and fragmented tribal society.

The "We are the Church" movement had a positive impact on the Papuans. It empowered them to play an active role in the Church and instilled in them the confidence and belief that they could make an important contribution to their community. Vatican II had made it possible to open up space for lay people to get involved in the mission of the Church. The Franciscan friars saw this as an opportunity to ensure that lay people got pastoral functions and left them in charge of these. Considering the importance of having children and passing on the family name to the next generation in many Papuan cultures, it was not very likely that Papuan men and women would opt for a religious life.

The Franciscan friars capitalized on the opportunity that emerged out of Vatican II to shape the local church with the support of local lay people in Papua. They had been called upon to make the church more local both in terms of its expression and administration. The idea was that everybody has a responsibility for the Church. The Church is not something from outside. We are the Church. We own the Church. We make the Church. The Church's mission does not consist in building churches and prayer houses, but in building communities responsive to the needs of the time. The message to the Papuans was: don't depend upon the priests, upon the foreigners. The process started with educating people to prepare them for leadership roles within their parishes. After graduating from school male and female students started this leadership training in the Theological High School. There was a steady influx of students in the 1980s, but this slowed down in the 1990s.

The work at the theological school was very much a continuation of "We are the Church" movement. Münninghoff's goal with this movement was to empower people and to elaborate a distinctly Papuan identity for the local church. The theological school played its part in educating pastoral workers to be self-supporting and self-reliant in the communities they served. People were happy with the slogan "We are the Church." Under the Indonesian administration they did not feel responsibility or control over so much in their communities. With this movement, it was recognized that they were respected by the church as Papuans. Not only did they feel that the Indonesian government did not acknowledge their culture as distinct from wider Indonesian culture, they also felt that the military and government were actively suppressing it. For the Catholic population of Papua the Church came to be a place where they were free and respected, while the Indonesian administration was seen as a tyrannical institution. One of the Dutch Franciscan friars recalled Münninghoff's role in Papua with great fondness and admiration: "The Bishop was great, he was always on the side of the Papuans. He would visit the highlands, the remote areas, and he was always one of the people. It was his style of being a bishop, very informal, and always with the people. He was also very tolerant and flexible; he didn't pay too much attention to the rules of the Church because in that situation you just can't follow all the rules."[16]

However, within the Dutch Franciscan community in Papua the "We are the Church" movement was not without opposition. One particular criticism was that the protagonists of the movement were moving ahead too fast. Changes in attitude and behavior often take a long time. The Dutch Franciscan friars had often to remind themselves that change takes time. They had to learn over time that they had to walk and work with the people at their own ideal pace and take their lead from the local communities. Other criticisms were that the momentum of the movement was largely limited to the upper layers of the church community in Papua.

As Franciscan friars from Flores and other parts of Indonesia arrived, the dynamics between the lay workers and the clergy changed. The friars from other parts of Indonesia often took a more conventional approach with the focus on the clergy leading the Church in all key aspects. Furthermore, tensions emerged due to the discrepancy between magisterial teaching on the role and appropriate responsibilities of the laity and the actual responsibilities that the laity in Papua took on.

A further comlication came about when Indonesian Franciscan friars expressed some difficulties with the ways in which the Dutch Franciscan friars interpreted the "We are the Church" movement. This was seen by

[16] Ibid., 32.

the Indonesian friars as a Dutch construction, a perspective that was not completely surprising in view of the post-Vatican II developments that took place in the Netherlands and similarities with how developments were emerging in Papua.

Finally, while the Dutch missionaries had gradually learned through their collective experience in Papua that this new approach could be both workable and effective, as well as being in line with the theology of Vatican II, the Catholic Bishops' Conference of Indonesia saw it differently. The Conference felt that there was too much emphasis on the role of the lay people in the church in Papua. The then head of the Conference was appointed as bishop in Papua to bring the "lay church of Papua" back to the mainstream church in Indonesia.

CONCLUSION

The essence of being Church in Papua basically meant for the Dutch Franciscan friars just 'being with', accompanying, the Papuans. Their mere presence has been often experienced as the very heart of their mission. While being with the Papuans was the main base and source of their missionary endeavors, it equally invited the Dutch Franciscan friars and sisters to serve the Papuan community and to be sensitive to the daily and basic needs of the Papuans in terms of food, education and health. Within a changing context of increasing oppression and marginalization the basic option for the Papuans remained unchanged, but it underwent transformation as it became more and more an option for the marginalized and oppressed Papuans. In doing so, the friars felt very much supported by the new spirit of Vatican II. It supported their conviction that the Church is constituted by its members and based on local tradition, values, wisdom and the participation of all. To promote this participatory approach efforts were made in terms of special cadre trainings and the appointment of lay pastoral workers as leaders of the local Papuan communities alongside the ordained priests. Vatican II had made it possible to open up space for lay people to get involved in the mission of the church in Papua.

The Dutch Franciscan friars practiced the triple dialogue with the Papuans through development, inculturation, and interreligious dialogue. Dialogue requires an open mind that appreciates differences and pluralism. This was not always easy, but during the process the emphasis became more focused on learning *from* the other rather than on converting the other. Efforts were made to learn and understand the local culture and make it a part of building a community of people living their faith and togetherness. The Dutch Franciscan friars made anthropological study one of the cornerstones of the curriculum of the study of pastoral workers and priests in Papua. In other words, their mission was not simply seen as mission *to* the Papuans (*missio ad gentes*), but as work for the reign of God *among* the Papuans (*missio inter gentes*) and *with* the Papuans (*missio cum gentibus*) through the "We are the Church" movement. Mission was not only seen as bringing the Good News to other cultures, but also as discovering the Good News in other cultures.

The "We Are the Church" movement in Papua was the expression of the intimate relationship between the Church and the world. It included the notion that the Papuan community had its own important values that should be kept alive. It also included the notion that the attitude of the clergy must be to listen to the people and that all members of the community are responsible for building and being church in Papua. This sense of belonging and owning the Church was very central to the "We Are the Church" movement. Whereas the Papuans were being marginalized in the very midst of their own society, they were placed at the very center of the movement.

Finally, for me personally and, as a professional development worker with 30 years of experience of working in Asia, the quotation "The joys and hopes, the griefs and the anxieties of the men of this age, especially those who are poor or in any way afflicted, these are the joys and hopes, the griefs and anxieties of the followers of Christ" (GS 1) remains a driving force to walk that extra mile.

CHAPTER 11

Mary as Type and Model of Church in *Lumen Gentium*: Reception in Asia

Agnes M. Brazal

VATICAN II: FROM CHRISTOTYPICAL TO ECCLESIOTYPICAL MARIOLOGY

As is well known, the immediate years preceding Vatican II (1950–1958)—under Pius XII—were witness to an intensification in Marian devotion, and yet this devotion somehow was also combined with an isolation of such Mariology from important developments in biblical scholarship and in other forms of theology. Throughout the council, the intended and proposed schema on Mary was one of the most vividly debated themes. The discussion centered on whether there should be a separate document or whether this schema should be integrated into *Lumen Gentium*.

Those in favor of a separate schema advocated "Christotypical Mariology" that stressed the integral link between Christ and Mary

This work was supported by a grant from the University Research Coordinating Office, De la Salle University.

A. M. Brazal (✉)
Theology and Religious Education Department, De La Salle University,
Manila, Philippines

© The Author(s) 2018
V. Latinovic et al. (eds.), *Catholicism Opening to the World and Other Confessions*, Pathways for Ecumenical and Interreligious Dialogue,
https://doi.org/10.1007/978-3-319-98581-7_11

167

in the act of redemption, from which emerged the coredemption and mediating role of Mary. Those in favor of an integrated document preferred an "Ecclesiotypical Mariology" that regarded Mary as a type of church[1]—an embodiment of the Church's spiritual reality—and model of virtues for the Church to imitate. It was clear that the issue was not so much one of doctrine and devotion but rather, the manner of presenting Mary's role.

Cardinal Rufino Santos of Manila, spokesperson for the Christotypical Mariology, defined the historical, theological, and practical arguments in favor of a separate schema.[2] Concerning historical arguments, he feared that the faithful would see an integrated document as a sort of diminution of the status of Mary. On the theological level he thought that Mary, although a part of the Church, could assume a soteriological role because of her intimate association with Jesus. On the practical level, integrating Mary in *Lumen Gentium* would necessitate reworking the whole draft. He instead suggested that a document on Mary might come after that of the Church so as to make the link between ecclesiology and Mariology.

Cardinal Franz König of Vienna, spokesperson for the Ecclesiotypical Mariology presented, in turn, four types of arguments—theological, historical, pastoral, and ecumenical. Because of limited space, I will focus solely on his theological and ecumenical arguments. In his view theologically, the Second Vatican Council was concerned with the Church and therefore Mary should be part of the document on this central theme, to highlight her relation to Christ and the Church. Mary should indeed be recognized as "sublime cooperator with Christ" but not as

---

[1] *The History of Vatican II*, ed. Giuseppe Alberigo and Joseph A. Komonchak, vol. 4, *Church as Communion: Third Period and Intersession, September 1964–September 1965* (Maryknoll: Orbis, 2004), 53. Leading the maximalist experts in the council, who desired a new dogma declaring Mary the Mediatrix of all graces were Carlo Balić, President of the International Pontifical Marian Academy, and Gabriele Maria Roschini, Dean of the Marianum in Rome. Roberto de Mattei, *Il Concilio Vaticano II: una storia mai scritta*, 314–24, portions translated by Francesca Romana, "Our Lady Left Behind: The Marian Question in Vatican II," http://rorate-caeli.blogspot.com/2012/09/our-lady-left-behind-marian-question-in.html.

[2] Natalia Imperatori-Lee, "The Use of Marian Imagery in Catholic Ecclesiology since Vatican II" (PhD dissertation, University of Notre Dame, 2007), 18–20.

coredemptrix.[3] She is a type of Church since she conceived Jesus not only physically but also spiritually. He also argued that ecumenically, the integrated schema would be more acceptable both to the Eastern Church and Protestant traditions.[4]

The voting took place on October 29, 1963, with the integrated schema winning in a very tight race.[5] After numerous drafts and heated arguments, the final version was approved, dedicating the eighth chapter of *Lumen Gentium* to the Blessed Virgin Mary, Mother of God, in the Mystery of Christ and the Church. The text follows the ecclesiotypical Mariology in line with the teachings of St. Ambrose: "the Mother of God is a type of the Church in the order of faith, charity and perfect union with Christ" (LG 63). She is to serve as an example as a virgin (in her faith and obedience) and as a mother in her maternal love in the Church's mission "for the regeneration of men" (LG 65).

The Christotypical element is integrated only in some lines in LG 62, that recognize that through Mary's "constant intercession [she] continued to bring us the gifts of eternal salvation." Subsequently she is to be appealed to under the titles of "Advocate, Auxiliatrix, Adjutrix, and Mediatrix" (LG 62). A word of caution however immediately follows that there is only one mediator, that is Christ (LG 62).[6] John Paul II rightly referred to Chapter 8 of *Lumen Gentium* as the "Magna Carta of the Mariology of our era"[7] as it provides a synthesis of the doctrine on Mary within the history of salvation, that is relevant to and adapted to the modern times.

---

[3] The teachings of Pius X and Pius XI employed the term "*coredemptrix*" for Mary. Kathleen Coyle, *Mary in the Christian Tradition from a Contemporary Perspective*, rev. Asian ed. (Manila: Divine Word Publications, 1998), 67.

[4] Alberigo and Komonchak, *The History of Vatican II*, vol. 3, 97.

[5] Those in favor of an integrated document garnered 1114 votes versus 1074 for those who opposed; there were five spoiled ballots.

[6] It is significant to note that in the document itself, Mary is not addressed as "Mother of the Church." It was only at the closing of the Council's third session on November 21, 1964 when Paul VI declared her Mother of the Church. This means Mary is the spiritual mother who has given birth to all members of the Church as mystical body of Christ. Paul VI, "Speech at the Conclusion of the Third Session," AAS 56 (1964): 1007–18; for an English translation, see https://vaticaniiat50.wordpress.com/2014/11/22/pope-pauls-speech-at-closing-session/.

[7] John Paul II, Discourse at General Audience, May 2, 1979, https://w2.vatican.va/content/john-paul-ii/en/audiences/1979/documents/hf_jp-ii_aud_19790502.html.

RECEPTION IN ASIA

Throughout the years following the Second Vatican Council, churches in Europe and North America experienced something of a generational decline in Marian piety, though, according to several interpretations, this was not so much related to Vatican II as to numerous other cultural, theological, liturgical, and ecumenical trends, as well as abuses tending toward Marian devotions that were centered on private revelations isolated from the wider Church.[8] Stefano De Fiores notes though that the "crisis in Mariology" in the decade immediately following the Council was also partly due to the "dampening" effect of *Lumen Gentium* and a period of making sense of the Council's understanding of the relationship between Mary, Christ, and the Church. A process of "renewal, recovery and cultural encounter" occurred later, although not universally.[9]

The first decade after the Council was similarly a period of Asian magisterial and theological silence on Mary. This does not mean, however, that Marian devotion has significantly declined in Asia. The silence may as well be assigned to the fact that theologians were still trying to grasp the new perspectives in conciliar theology and were actively engaged in the renewal of liturgy.[10] But as the document *Ecclesia in Asia* has noted, "Throughout Asia there are hundreds of Marian sanctuaries and shrines where not only the Catholic faithful gather, but also believers of other religions too" (51).[11] Likewise, Asian Marian devotion continues vibrantly in the diaspora, as seen in the shrines which draw thousands of pilgrims dedicated to Our Lady in Asia in the National Shrine of the Immaculate Conception in Washington, DC.[12]

---

[8] Cf. Imperatori-Lee, "The Use of Marian Imagery in Catholic Ecclesiology since Vatican II." For an excellent review of the development of Mariology after Vatican II, see Stefano De Fiores, "Mary in Postconciliar Theology," in *Vatican II: Assessment and Perspectives*, vol. 1, ed. René Latourelle, S.J. (Mahwah, NJ: Paulist Press, 1988), 469–539; Avery Dulles, S.J., "Mary Since Vatican II: Decline and Recovery," *Marian Studies* 53, article 5 (2002): 9–22.

[9] De Fiores, "Mary in Postconciliar Theology," 477.

[10] Coyle, *Mary in the Christian Tradition*, 73.

[11] John Paul II, Post-Synodal Apostolic Exhortation *Ecclesia in Asia*, AAS 92 (2000): 449–528.

[12] These include Our Lady of Antipolo, Our Lady of Velankanni, Our Lady of China, Our Lady of La Vang, Our Lady of the Korean Martyrs, and Our Lady of Korea at Cana.

Noteworthy, however, is that despite the general theological and episcopal silence on Mary, certain pastoral shifts began to occur in the first years following the conclusion of the Council. Before the publication of Paul VI's *Marialis Cultus* in 1974 and the first pastoral letter on Mary by the Catholic Bishops' Conference of the Philippines the following year, the Redemptorists had already prepared their revision to the novena to Our Mother of Perpetual Help (OMPH) at the Baclaran Church in Manila. This 1973 revision sought to respond to the Council's call for renewal, as one can see in the significant shifts from the 1948 version to the postconciliar revision. First, in the 1948 pre-Vatican II novena, Mary is the main source of help. In contrast, the 1973 novena is more Christocentric. The revised novena broadens concerns from "my needs" to the "needs of others" including the societal need for justice and peace. Finally, the notion of Mary as the perfect Christian is represented in the prayers as model of faith, love, peacebuilding. The revised novena was positively received by the devotees, dissolving the apprehensions of some members of the revision committee. Around 120,000 devotees come to the Baclaran Church every Wednesday making OMPH the most popular Marian icon in the Philippines. This liturgical shift highlighted theological shifts that occurred in the second decade after Vatican II, and after the release of Paul VI's *Marialis Cultus*.[13] At that point, Mariology in Philippine magisterial and theological statements developed more strongly along ecclesiotypical lines, particularly focused on Mary as a model in the context of injustice and oppression.

Ang Mahal Na Birhen

In February 1975, the Catholic Bishops' Conference of the Philippines released a pastoral letter, *Ang Mahal na Birhen*.[14] Taking up from the spirit of *aggiornamento* of Vatican II and *Marialis Cultus*, this letter urges reflection on Marian devotion in order to attain the "golden

---

Jonathan Tan, "Asian-American Marian Devotions as Ritual Practice," *New Theology Review* (August 2010): 35–44.

[13] Paul VI, Apostolic Exhortation *Marialis Cultus*, AAS 66 (1974): 113–68.

[14] Catholic Bishops Conference of the Philippines, *Ang Mahal na Birhen*: Mary in Philippine Life Today, http://www.cbcponline.net/documents/1970s/1975-mahal_na_birhen.html.

mean" between the "deviations" of the popular devotion and the principles stated in the council (no. 3). It praises the Filipino devotion to Mary as mother but also emphasizes the need for a mature faith (nos. 53, 56). Quoting from St. Augustine, it adds that we too must be "brothers and sisters, parents and children to each other spiritually" (no. 57). It also underlines the meaning of Mary's virginity as an active response to God's initiative characterized by a relationship of mutuality (no. 54).

Affirming "the special place of Mary" in the hearts especially of Filipino Catholics and the value of Marian devotions and practices, it offers a carefully worded encouragement for reform and *aggiornamento*. The letter explicitly prohibits, for instance, the usage of multiple images of Mary in the church/chapel, the treatment of scapulars, medals and votive candles as possessing magical properties for material and bodily protection (no. 79). It condemns the transformation of the Santacruzan procession[15] into a fashion show (no. 81) and dissuades people from easily believing "visions" and "visionaries."

This pastoral letter came out in 1975, four years after late dictator Ferdinand Marcos placed the country under martial law. In this context of increasing poverty and oppression in the country (no. 96), *Ang Mahal na Birhen* identifies Mary of the Magnificat (Lk 1:46–55) with Mary of the Anawim (no. 38).[16] While cautioning that her words should not be seen as an endorsement of class struggle, it affirms that "they point to a reversal of the social order in the Kingdom of God" (no. 94). The bishops hope that devotion to Mary will mature into a commitment to social justice in line with "Mary's special role in... the development of humanity to a community of justice and peace" (no. 67).

As in *Marialis Cultus*, the document asserts that "[i]mitation of Mary does not mean keeping women within the cultural limitations which bound the women of Mary's time" (no. 91). It calls for the need, on the one hand, to integrate within Marian piety a new anthropology of women and their role in society. On the other hand, the pastoral letter suggests that the quality of Mary's life as spouse and mother "can imbue

---

[15] The Santacruzan, which dates back to the Spanish colonial period in the nineteenth century, is the most widely celebrated folk religious procession in the Philippines. It is held at the end of Flores de Mayo, a month-long celebration in May honoring the Virgin Mary.

[16] A Hebrew word from the Old Testament that describes the "poor ones."

the ordinary chores of women in the home with a deeper meaning and significance" (no. 91).

Regarding Marian ecumenism, the document recognizes the veneration of Mary among the members of the *Iglesia Filipiniana Independiente* (a national church) and in the Philippine Episcopal church as is manifest for instance in their liturgical celebrations of Marian feasts (no. 23).

THE MARIAN YEAR

To celebrate the Marian Year, the Filipino Bishops released another pastoral letter in 1985, a period of "crisis" and "bleak prospects" in the nation's history (nos. 4–5).[17] One year later, the People Power Revolution would oust Marcos and bring an end to his fourteen years of dictatorial rule.

"Groaning and weeping in this valley of tears, to turn her eyes of mercy upon us," the Bishops highlighted Mary as "*omnipotentia supplex*" whose intercession is "all powerful." They urged the faithful to pray for "conversion, toward renewal in private and public life, towards justice and reconciliation, brotherhood [sic] and peace in our troubled land" (no. 7). In contrast to the previous pastoral letter, this one entails much more Christotypical elements, framing Mary as an intercessor not just for individuals, but also for collective social concerns. The letter combines these Christotypical elements with an ecclesiotypical Mariology focused on Mary of the Magnificat, citing John Paul II, who speaks of Mary as model for: "those who do not passively accept the adverse circumstances of personal and social life, ... but who instead join with her in proclaiming that God is the 'avenger of the lowly' and will, if need be, depose 'the mighty from their thrones'..."[18] Affirming what has been said in *Ang Mahal na Birhen*, it advocates the integration in Marian piety of

---

[17] Catholic Bishops Conference of the Philippines, "The Marian Year 1985: A Pilgrimage of Hope with our Blessed Mother," http://www.cbcponline.net/documents/1980s/1985-pilgrimage_hope.html.

[18] John Paul II, Homily at Zapopan, Mexico, 30 January, AAS (1979): 227–31; reproduced in Third General Conference of Latin American Bishops (CELAM), *Puebla: Evangelization at Present and in the Future of Latin America* (Washington, DC: NCCB, 1979), 77.

"the preferential love for the poor which is an authentic sign of Christian commitment" (no. 22).

On the ecumenical level, the document invites Muslim sisters and brothers, who likewise respect Mary in a special way, to unite with Christians in prayer for "true reconciliation and peace" in the country (no. 22). It also encourages Filipino Christians of other confessions "to honor Mary in ways which are in keeping with their own understanding of her role in the history of salvation" (no. 2).

MARY AS MOTHER OF ALL CREATION

Partly because of the influence of John Paul II's Christotypical Mariology,[19] we witnessed in the third decade after Vatican II a strengthening of Christological elements, including the reemergence of the cosmological Mary, albeit with an ecological twist. In a pioneering pastoral letter on ecology in 1988, *What is Happening to our Beautiful Land*, the Philippine bishops linked motherhood to concern for life. It teaches that as Mother of Life, Mary "challenges us to abandon the pathway of death and to return to the way of life." Referring to Mary as Mother of Humanity and the New Eve, Sri Lankan theologian, Tissa Balasuriya likewise spoke of Mary as a model of one who is concerned with preserving the earth as a home for humans, rereading the Magnificat as a call for ecological justice.[20]

MARY AS A SYMBOL OF A NEW HUMANITY AGAINST PATRIARCHAL SOCIETY

In 1987, the ecumenical Consultation of Asian Women's Theology, held in Singapore, produced a "Summary Statement on Mariology."[21] It focuses on how Mary, like Jesus, has become a model for full humanity for Asian women. Here, "Mary as virgin" is a self-defining woman

---

[19] John Paul II, for instance, used the term coredemptrix for Mary in at least five occasions in homilies and talks. See Mark Miravalle, "The Pope of Mary Co-Redemptrix," http://www.fifthmariandogma.com/articles/881/.

[20] Tissa Balasuriya, *Mary and Human Liberation: The Story and the Text* (London: Mowbray, 1997), 56.

[21] Chung Hyun Kyung, *Struggle to Be the Sun Again: Introducing Asian Women's Theology* (Maryknoll: Orbis, 1990), 74–84.

who has no need for a man in her participation in the birth of a new humanity, symbolizing resistance to patriarchy. "Mary as mother" was Jesus's model for "compassionate justice" and resilience in faith. As a wise older woman who stayed on to give comfort and hope to the disciples, she became the "mother of the church." In the visitation, "Mary as sister," shows solidarity with Elizabeth, and in the Magnificat, expresses her unity with the struggles of oppressed women. Mary is the "model of true discipleship" not only in her motherhood, but in her hearing the word of God and putting it into practice; she demonstrates not passive obedience to the powerful but discernment and active risk-taking. While the Mariology in the Summary Statement is predominantly ecclesiotypical, some of the Filipino women theologians in the consultation held on to Christotypical perspectives supporting Mary's role as co redemptrix or as an equal "co-redeemer" with Jesus for the salvation of humans.

Mary and the Eucharist

As Asian theologians became more comfortable discussing the body, they began to link the other bodily aspects of Mary's mothering, such as breastfeeding, to the Eucharist. Indian theologian Samuel Rayan writes in 2003 of a "eucharistic mother-child bonding" between Mary and Jesus when she fed him his dinner, breastfed him as a baby and nourished him inside her womb: "Take, eat, this is my Body; and drink, this is my Blood..." (Mk 14:22–24).[22] Astrid Lobo Gajiwala, pushes the logical implications of Mary as Eucharistic person further as model for the Church, to challenge women's exclusion from being presiders of the Eucharist.[23]

---

[22] Samuel Rayan, "My Body for You," in *Body, Bread, Blood: Eucharistic Perspectives from the Indian Church*, ed. Francis Gonsalves, S.J. (Delhi: ISPCK, 2003), 196.

[23] "Did the woman say, when she held him for the last time in the dark rain on a hilltop, after the pain and the bleeding and the dying, 'This is my body, this is my blood?'... Well, that she said it to him then, for dry old men, brocaded robes belying barrenness, ordain that she not say it for him now." Frances Croake Frank, quoted by Astrid Lobo Gajiwala, "The Passion of the Womb: Women Re-living the Eucharist," in *Body and Sexuality: Theological Pastoral Perspectives of Women in Asia*, ed. Agnes M. Brazal and Andrea Lizares Si (Quezon City, AdMU Press, 2007), 193–94.

Korean Bishops on Proper Marian Devotion

Marian devotion in Korea started in the early nineteenth century. Like in the Philippines, it has emerged to become Catholics' most common form of spirituality. However, some Protestants have criticized them for fostering a "Marian religion" because of distortions in new Marian novenas.[24] In 2005, The Commission for the Doctrine of the Faith of the Korean Bishops' Conference (CBCK) published *Correct Devotion to the Blessed Virgin Mary* as guide toward a proper Marian devotion.[25] In 2009, the CBCK released this as a pastoral letter titled "Proper Marian Devotion."[26] Aiming to legitimize Marian devotional practices based on doctrinal and historical criteria (no. 10) it briefly narrates the history of Marian devotion in Korea (1811–1954), the doctrinal basis for Marian devotion, and the foundational and classical forms of Marian devotion. It then corrects mistaken views and practices, particularly in relation to four relatively new Korean Marian devotions: (1) the private revelation of Theresa Hwang of Sangju; (2) miracles and private revelations in Naju; (3) apparitions in Bayside New York; and (4) pseudo-spirituality (the "Family Tree" healing practice). On the positive side, among the images of Mary it emphasized her as a model and Mother of all Christians, a "dedicated companion" of Jesus in the plan of salvation, and a "preeminent intercessor."

Mary in the Documents of the FABC and Its Offices

On the level of the FABC and its offices, there was no reference to Mary until 2010, except for invocations for Mary's intercession,[27] or short

---

[24] "Proper Marian Devotion," CBCK Newsletter, http://www.cbck.or.kr/bbs/bbs_read. asp?board_id=e5100&bid=13001596.

[25] The Commission for the Doctrine of the Faith of the Korean Bishops' Conference (CBCK), "Correct Devotion to the Blessed Virgin Mary," 2005, http://koreajoongang-daily.joins.com/news/article/Article.aspx?aid=2993388.

[26] Catholic Bishops Conference of Korea (Commission for the Doctrine of the Faith), *Proper Marian Devotion*, February 11, 2009.

[27] Peter N. V. Hai, "Models of the Asian Church," *Australian eJournal of Theology* 18, no. 1 (2011): 61–73. See also James Thoppil's book-length study of Asian ecclesiology, which has no reference at all to Mary's role within the Church. *Towards an Asian Ecclesiology: The Understanding of the Church in the Documents of the FABC (1970–2000)* (Bangalore: Oriens Publications and Asian Trading Corporation, 2005).

statements on Mary and Marian devotion. For example, the 1998 Final Statement of Bishops Institute for Lay Apostolate on Women (BILA) on Women II exalts Mary as an example of one who listens to and acts on the Word of God, particularly "in the public sphere."[28] The statement "Women Living the Eucharist in South Asia" by the BILA South Asia Meeting on Women III in 2010 emphasized the need "[to] learn from Mary's Eucharistic life" (1.3) "to the extent of being bread broken."[29] The Consultation on Christian Presence among Muslims in Asia in 2010 recommended that "Mary ... could be promoted as the patroness of unity and fellowship which should exist between Christians and Muslims" (no. 41).[30]

"Mary Truly a Woman of our Times" (2010) was the first complete document on Mary on the level of the FABC. This document was the short Final Statement of the East Asia BILA on Women II.[31] It highlights Mary as one who lived through many challenges that women do today and holds her up as a model of femininity, virginity, and maternity. It links Mary's femininity to the "recovery of the femininity of God,"[32] her virginity to being "filled with the Spirit closely following God's Word," and her maternity to "nurturing life through work for peace and justice."[33] For Korean Hae-Young Choi, R.S.C.J. (who together with Cardinal Luis Antonio Tagle served as resource persons for the East Asia BILA on Women II), the ideal person is one who has integrated both his/her femininity and masculinity, and Mary embodies this. Through Mary, the "male dominated, rigid, and hierarchical" Church can express the maternal love and compassion of God. Furthermore, the

---

[28] The BILA meetings are composed of laywomen and men, priests and bishops. These meetings provided a venue for the articulation of developing images of Mary.

[29] Statement of the South Asia Meeting on Women III, "Women Living the Eucharist in South Asia," in *Discipleship of Asian Women at the Service of Life*, vol. 2, ed. Virginia Saldanha (Quezon City: Claretian Publications, 2011), 283.

[30] "Consultation on Christian Presence Among Muslims in Asia, Recommendations of the Participants of the Consultation," no. 6. FABC Papers no. 13, "A Glimpse at Dialogue in Asia," 30th anniversary, First Bishops' Institute for Interreligious Affairs, p. 19, http://www.fabc.org/fabc%20papers/FABC%20Paper%20131.pdf.

[31] East Asia Bishops' Institute on Lay Apostolate (BILA), "Mary Truly a Woman of out Times: Statement," in *Discipleship of Asian Women at the Service of Life*, vol. 2, ed. Saldanha, 301–4.

[32] Ibid., 303.

[33] Ibid., 301.

Church needs to recover its femininity through Mary to be filled with the Spirit.[34]

From a postcolonial perspective, the Final Statement refers to Mary as having herself witnessed women being battered, raped and marginalized during her time.[35] The paper presented by Cardinal Tagle spoke of Mary in the Bible as one who experienced many trying situations in Roman-ruled Palestine, like that of being an oppressed and refugee woman and a victim mother, among others. Mary's Magnificat today, the Final Statement stresses, would denounce "violence to women and to all the weak and wounded by society."[36]

REMEMBERING THE FUTURE: SOME CHALLENGES

Ecumenical and Interfaith Relations

Lumen Gentium's recognition of other churches that give honor to Mary (LG 69) has made bishops and theologians more conscious of other faith groups that practice Marian devotion. *Ang Mahal na Birhen* cites the similar devotion to Mary in the Philippine Episcopal Church and the Iglesia Filipiniana Independiente (IFI), a national church in full communion with the episcopal church (no. 23). It made no mention though of the IFI's central Marian image, the Virgin of Balintawak, an iconic symbol of nationalist resistance against Spanish and US American imperialism as well as of women's capacity to participate in the struggle for emancipation.[37]

---

[34] Hae Young Choi, R.S.C.J., "Mary Model of Discipleship in the Church," in *Discipleship of Asian Women at the Service of Life*, vol. 2, ed. Saldanha, 230–31.

[35] East Asia BILA, "Mary Truly a Woman of our Times: Statement," in *Discipleship of Asian Women at the Service of Life*, vol. 2, ed. Saldanha, 303.

[36] Ibid., 303.

[37] She is said to have appeared to one of the revolutionaries to warn them that their plan had been discovered. It was in Balintawak where the Philippine revolution against Spain started. In the dream, the Virgin is dressed in Filipiniana peasant garb together with a boy holding a bolo shouting "Freedom! Freedom!" Gregorio Aglipay, *Novenary of the Motherland—The Motherland is Symbolized in the Envisioned Mother of Balintawak* (Manila: n.p, 1926), i. The Virgin of Balintawak was regarded then as a symbol of the country while the child Jesus represented the Katipuneros or revolutionaries fighting against the colonizers. Today, the image revered is the Virgin with the boy holding a tablet saying, "Father, may our independence be born!"

Even before Mary of the Magnificat became a symbol for feminists of women resisting oppression, the IFI, which claimed to be the only church established by the working class, has been revering Mary as such since the early twentieth century.[38] In the Virgin of Balintawak, the Philippines has a Mariology born from the heart of people's resistance to oppression. It would certainly enrich the Catholic Church in the Philippines to engage more actively in dialogue with the IFI, which is known not only for their enculturated theology and liturgy but also their engagement in justice and peace issues.[39]

Shared devotions to Mary can be a fertile starting point not only for ecumenical but also for interfaith encounters. As *Ecclesia in Asia* (no. 51) noted, there are many Marian shrines in Asia that are visited by Christians from other confessions as well as believers from other religions. Examples include the Shrine of Our Lady of Health at Vailankanni in Tamil Nadu, India, that receives more than 1.5 million visitors each year, many of which are non-Christians. One may also consider the shrine of Our Lady of Madhu, that is often visited by Buddhists, Hindus and Protestants. Interestingly, this process is bidirectional. In the Philippines, Christians and Buddhists both revere Our Lady of Caysasay, which is actually the statue of Kuan-yin or Ma-cho, the classical Chinese Buddhist goddess of compassion and mercy. The statue which was found at either a river or a cave, was appropriated as that of Mary by the Christians. She is now revered by both Christians and Buddhists. According to Sabino A. Vengco, Jr., she "is one of the earliest 'local' images of Mary that helped facilitate the conversion of the Filipinos who

---

[38] It was the first labor union in the Philippines, the Union Obrera Democratica, that founded the IFI on August 3, 1902. At that time, almost a tenth of the country's population were members of the IFI.

[39] Isabelo de los Reyes, a founder of the IFI, is said to be the forerunner of Filipino theology. Feorillo Petronilo A. Demeterio III, "Don Isabelo de los Reyes (1864–1938): Forerunner of Filipino Theology," *Philippiniana Sacra* 68, no. 142 (September–December 2012): 883–916. In 2007, the IFI and the Catholic Church ceased hostility centered on a discussion as to which church owns the "original" Sto. Niño statue, meaning that which is worthy of veneration. For the first time both churches held a joint procession on the eve of the feast of Sto. Niño in a colorful Buling-Buling festival where the two icons meet. "'Hidden' Sto. Niño for 300 Years to Rise," http://newsinfo.inquirer.net/128099/hidden-sto-nino-for-300-years-to-rise#ixzz4JFcOepL7. We hope that in the future, a joint procession of the icons of Virgin Mary would also happen.

find in her a mother always needed."[40] Kuan-yin is revered not only by Buddhists but also the general populace in China, Vietnam (where she is known as Quan Âm Thi Kính), Korea, and Japan (where she is known as Kannon).[41] Peter Phan underlines the significance of Kuan-yin for interreligious dialogue in Vietnam with the words: "[b]ut it is beyond doubt that both of them [Mary and Kuan-yin] allow us to imagine God as a loving, merciful, compassionate, saving, protecting, liberating Father/ Mother for all the Vietnamese people, irrespective of their religious traditions, and that all Vietnamese are thereby called to promote a society of love, mercy, compassion, and freedom."[42]

With regard to the common shrines, in my opinion it is very important to maintain them as venues for ecumenical/interfaith encounters. The Church must be careful not to over-Christianize the place in a way that offends the sensibilities of the peoples of other faiths. Filipino church historian Antonio de Castro, for instance, criticized the over-Christianization of the formerly open space shrine of *La Virgen del Pilar* in Zamboanga visited by both Christians and Muslims. He cites the addition of other statues of saints, the stations of the cross, a blessed sacrament chapel, as offensive to the sensibilities of the Muslims, and the absence of an Islamic symbol in the shrine as exclusionary.[43]

From Maternal Image of God to Miriam of Nazareth, Mother and Sister

After the taming effect of the Vatican II council on Christotypical Mariology, the clamor to proclaim Mary as *coredemptrix* has experienced a resurgence leading to a worldwide petition for its proclamation, with the laity in the Philippines and Mexico as its most ardent supporters.[44] While Vatican II

---

[40]Sabino A. Vengco, Jr., "Mary among the Goddesses," *Landas* 19, no. 1 (2005): 119–40.

[41]Peter C. Phan, *In Our Own Tongues: Perspectives from Asia on Mission and Inculturation* (Maryknoll: Orbis, 2003), 104.

[42]Ibid., 108.

[43]Antonio de Castro, "La Virgen del Pilar: Defamiliarizing Mary and the Challenge of Interreligious Dialogue, *Landas* 19, no. 1 (2005): 88–89.

[44]"Cardinals Hoping for a 5th Marian Dogma: To Declare Mary as Mother of Humanity," February 11, 2008, http://zenit.org/articles/cardinals-hoping-for-a-5th-marian-dogma/.

had rightly stressed the importance of Mary in the Bible and as model of faith, this seems to be just one pole that needs to be considered in the problem of so-called Marian excesses. As Kilian McDonnell, O.S.B., has pointed out, the popular acclamation of Mary in history preceded the theological defects in the teachings about Mary, and is therefore not simply rooted in inadequate catechesis.[45]

The divinization of Mary, that is a strong tendency in Christotypical Mariology, was partly an outcome of a process of enculturation in the context of the mystery cults of goddesses in the Mediterranean world of the fourth century, as well as the goddess traditions in non-Western cultures.[46] Prominent feminists theologians like Kari Børresen, Marina Warner, and Elizabeth Johnson, C.S.J., have also shown in their studies how the divinization of Mary is a reaction to an excessively patriarchal view of God.[47] Johnson has pointed out that this development of Mary as our compassionate mother is "directly related to an over-emphasis on a masculinized image of God, and functions as a remedy for what is lacking in such an image."[48] It is thus part of a desire for a female principle in the divine. Jose de Mesa

---

[45] For instance, three catacomb frescoes exist in which Mary is enthroned; one dates as early as the first half of the second century. There are also three sarcophagi or sculptures of the enthroned Mary amidst the Adoration of the Magi. The title *Theotokos* had been employed by Hippolytus of Rome since 220 AD. Kilian McDonnell, O.S.B., "Feminist Mariologies: Heteronomy/Subordination and the Scandal of Christology," *Theological Studies* 66 (2005): 560.

[46] See, for instance, Ivone Gebara and Maria Clara Bingemer's discussion of the Virgin of Guadalupe as an Indian assimilation of the European Mary in the image of the mother goddess Tonantzin of the pre-Columbian Mesoamerica, a synthesis of a new Mother who provides maternal care and compassion in defense of the Indians. *Mary: Mother of God, Mother of the Poor* (Maryknoll: Orbis, 1989), 144–54. See also the comparative study of Hindu goddesses and Mary by Francis X. Clooney, S.J., which shows that "Mary functions analogously to a goddess, as a supreme female person who is not-God, but rather God's Mother." *Divine Mother, Blessed Mother. Hindu Goddesses and the Virgin Mary* (New York: Oxford University Press, 2005), 234.

[47] See Kari Børresen, "Mary in Catholic Theology," in *Mary in the Church*, ed. Hans Küng and Jürgen Moltmann, *Concilium* 168 (New York: Seabury, 1983), 48–56; Marina Warner, *Alone of All Her Sex: The Myth and the Cult of the Virgin Mary* (New York: Alfred A. Knopf, 1976); Elizabeth A. Johnson, C.S.J., "Mary and the Female Face of God," *Theological Studies* 50 (1989): 507–10; Johnson, "Mary, Friend of God and Prophet: A Critical Reading of the Marian Tradition," *Theology Digest* 47, no. 4 (2000): 317–25; and Johnson, *Truly Our Sister: A Theology of Mary in the Communion of Saints* (London: Continuum, 2006).

[48] Johnson, "Mary and the Female Face of God," 514.

further elaborated on this in the context of the Philippine culture where the mother is oftentimes more approachable than the usually stern and strict father.[49] Johnson has rightly argued however that to compromise and substitute Mary as feminine or motherly face of the divine in the Catholic Church (for example in Leonardo Boff's—*The Maternal Face of God*)[50] will always remain inadequate. Mary is not God. Nevertheless, it remains necessary to respond to people's attraction to a female principle/image of the divine, which she has noted is "arguably necessary for the full expression of the mystery of God."[51] Amirtham Metti, S.C.C., sees the need for the Church to include female images of God in order to enculturate Christianity especially in contexts like India where the goddess tradition is part of the living culture.[52] As for the Miriam of Nazareth, Johnson aptly expressed it, "Let God have her own maternal face. Let Miriam the Galilean woman rejoin the community of disciples."[53]

In pursuit of employing the metaphor of mother to refer to the God on the one hand, and of Mary as sister-disciple on the other, de Mesa proposes in the Philippine context the title of *ate* (eldest sister or in her absence the next sister in line) for Mary. The eldest sister plays a central role in Filipino families as role model, the parents' right hand, protector, tutor, caregiver of siblings, and in the death of the parents, takes charge of keeping the unity of the family. The *ate* intercedes as well for siblings. The title *ate* captures three qualities linked with Mary: familiarity (she is one of us as sister and fellow disciple); difference (she is distinct in her privilege of being the mother of Jesus and possesses primacy of honor among the disciples, therefore the "eldest sister"); inspiration and challenge (she is a model in the way she lived her life). *Marialis Cultus* speaks of "Mary as held up as an example for the way in which, in her own particular life, she fully and responsibly accepted God's will (see Lk

---

[49] Jose de Mesa, "Ate: Honoring Mary as Our Eldest Sister," *MST Review II*, no. 1 (1998): 1–12.

[50] Boff proposes that Mary is the incarnation of the Holy Spirit. Leonardo Boff, *The Maternal Face of God: The Feminine and Its Religious Expressions* (London: Collins, 1989).

[51] Johnson, "Mary and the Female Face of God," 500.

[52] Amirtham Metti, S.C.C., "Bodily Representations of Hindu Goddesses: A Feminist Perspective," in *Body and Sexuality: Theological Pastoral Perspectives of Women in Asia*, ed. Agnes M. Brazal and Andrea Lizares Si (Quezon City: Ateneo de Manila University, 2007), 266.

[53] Johnson, *Truly Our Sister*, 92.

2:38), because she heard the Word of God and acted on it, and because charity and a spirit of service are the driving force of her actions. She is worthy of imitation because she was the first and most perfect of Christ's disciples" (no. 5). To this we can add Pope Paul VI's homily on October 11, 1963 that stressed the intricate relationship between Mary and the Church when he called her "Mother and daughter, and elect *sister.*"[54]

The image of the eldest sister may understandably have different cultural connotations. In the Philippines where daughters are treated in a relatively equal position to sons, the image of Mary as eldest sister may be apt, but this may not be so in other Asian countries. Nevertheless, it may be inconceivable at the present time to many devotees to shift from calling Mary as mother to Mary as sister. Perhaps the most that may be achieved for the moment, especially among devotees, is a model which sees Mary as both mother and sister.

So long as our language for God excludes that of God as Mother, and church structures remain male dominated, the projection of divinity onto Mary will persist. The challenge for the Church at present is to allow for a multiplicity of metaphors, including female ones in our language for God, to be used most especially in our worship and liturgies. This should go hand-in-hand with de-patriarchalizing church structures as changing God language to include female metaphors does not automatically lead to structural changes toward greater participation of women. It remains to be seen though when Miriam of Nazareth can truly rejoin the community of disciples as our Mother/Sister.

Conclusion

Episcopal conferences, both national and regional (FABC), have received positively the emphasis of *Lumen Gentium* on ecclesiotypical Mariology, providing guidelines for the proper conduct of Marian devotions, including a focus not only on personal needs but also on societal intercessions and action for justice and peace. Both in the writings of the episcopate and Asian theologians, the motherhood and virginity of Mary have been reinterpreted in ways that aim to transform Mary as an empowering model for women, the poor, the oppressed. A renewed interest in the cosmological Mary (mother of life and of creation) emerged, albeit

---

[54] George Henry Tavard, *The Thousand Faces of the Virgin Mary* (Collegeville, MN: Liturgical Press, 1996), 205, emphasis added.

with an ecological twist. Integrating the bodily aspects of mothering, South Asian theologians have explored the Eucharistic mother bonding between Jesus and Mary and its implication for the church.

Based on readings of Mary in the Bible, other relevant images of Mary have also developed. Feminists (both Catholic and Protestant women) see Mary as model of new humanity for the liberation of Asian women, while the image of Mary as eldest sister has been proposed in the Philippine context. The FABC, for its part, invites us to see Mary as truly a model for the woman of our times.

Based on such an admittedly modest and limited survey, we might conclude that the conciliar teaching on Mary has been positively received by the churches in Asia, even if Christotypical Mariology (e.g. the cosmological Mary; clamor for the Church to declare Mary as *coredemptrix*) strengthened in and after the third postconciliar decade, the period coinciding with the pontificate of John Paul II.

In terms of the future of Mariology in Asia, one of the main challenges resulting from *Lumen Gentium* is how shared devotions to Mary with devotees of other faiths/religions can be maximized to promote ecumenical and interfaith dialogue. Another persisting challenge is how to address more deeply the distortions in Marian devotions. It is our contention that the ecclesiotypical orientation of *Lumen Gentium* is not adequate to check Marian excesses which are rooted in people's search for a maternal image of God. We therefore need to consider expanding our language for God to include female metaphors especially in our worship and liturgies, de-patriarchalize church structures, at the same time that we retrieve and continue to develop Miriam of Nazareth as the model mother and/or sister.

CHAPTER 12

From *The Cardinal* to *The Shoes of the Fisherman*: Hollywood's Curious Fascination with Vatican II

Paul G. Monson

Scholarship on Vatican II more or less confines the council's "ecumenical" import to ecclesial circles. However, the council's language of ecumenism also garnered the attention of broader secular culture, particularly in a curious if not perplexing mid-twentieth-century dialogue between the Catholic Church and Hollywood's influential film industry. This untold story remains absent from specialized studies of Hollywood's interaction with American Catholicism. Most historians instead focus on the National Legion of Decency (1933–1966) and its controversial influence on America's film rating system. For instance, Gregory Black has demurred the Legion's "crusade" against creative cinematic art in the name of morality, yet his study of Catholic interaction with Hollywood between 1940 and 1975 fails to mention Vatican

P. G. Monson (✉)
Sacred Heart Seminary and School of Theology, Milwaukee, WI, USA
e-mail: pmonson@shsst.edu

© The Author(s) 2018
V. Latinovic et al. (eds.), *Catholicism Opening to the World and Other Confessions*, Pathways for Ecumenical and Interreligious Dialogue,
https://doi.org/10.1007/978-3-319-98581-7_12

185

II at all.[1] Catholic historian Anthony Burke Smith has recently nuanced the conversation to show how Hollywood was anything but docile in its dealings with Catholics. On the contrary, producers consciously employed the communal dimension of Catholicism to instill a national sense of unity, solidarity, and assimilation in American culture during and after World War II.[2] As Smith adeptly concludes, this practical marriage between Hollywood and Catholicism distracted American Catholics from greater social and ecclesial exigencies. Nevertheless, Smith's enlightening work concludes with the 1950s. Like Black, Smith omits how Vatican II impacted and shifted American Catholic interaction with Hollywood elites.

In light of these lacunae, this study extends the trajectory of Smith's work into the 1960s to show how Hollywood employed Vatican II with its own "ecumenical" agenda. This nuanced story emerges both on the screen and in archives, including those of the Academy of Motion Picture Arts and Sciences in Beverly Hills, California. Through original archival work, this study focuses on two Academy Award nominees that intentionally brought conciliar themes to the screen: *The Cardinal* (1963), produced by Otto Preminger (1905–1986), a Jewish filmmaker, and *The Shoes of the Fisherman* (1968), based on the bestselling book by Morris West (1916–1999), a Catholic novelist. Both films took explicit note of the council and together provide bookends for Hollywood's "infatuation" with the council. A comparison of these films demonstrates how Hollywood embraced Vatican II as an opportune moment in ecumenism while simultaneously failing to grasp the dialogical dimension of authentic ecumenism. In other words, both films approached Vatican II's

---

[1] Gregory D. Black, *The Catholic Crusade against the Movies, 1940–1975* (New York: Cambridge University Press, 1997). See also Frank Walsh, *Sin and Censorship: The Catholic Church and the Motion Picture Industry* (New Haven: Yale University Press, 1996); Thomas Doherty, *Hollywood's Censor: Joseph I. Breen and the Production Code Association* (New York: Columbia University Press, 2007); and Alexander McGregor, *The Catholic Church and Hollywood: Censorship and Morality in 1930s Cinema* (New York: I.B. Tauris, 2013). On the Legion of Decency, see James M. Skinner, *The Cross and the Cinema: The Legion of Decency and the National Catholic Office for Motion Pictures, 1933–1970* (Westport, CT: Praeger, 1993); Una M. Cadegan, "Guardians of Democracy or Cultural Storm Troopers? American Catholics and the Control of Popular Media, 1934–1966," *The Catholic Historical Review* 87, no. 2 (April 2001): 252–82.

[2] Anthony Burke Smith, *The Look of Catholics: Portrayals in Popular Culture from the Great Depression to the Cold War* (Lawrence: University Press of Kansas, 2010), 8–15.

call for ecumenism as a grand international event rather than as an invitation for constructive theological dialogue. Moreover, a contextual and comparative study of each film's development and reception poses questions and lessons for postconciliar Catholicism's dialogue with secular culture today. After examining the Catholic Church's official engagement of the film industry before and after Vatican II, this study charts the historical and theological significance of each film, illuminating a complex chapter in secular culture's engagement of Vatican II.

ROME, HOLLYWOOD, AND THE LEGION

Inter Mirifica, the council's *Decree on the Means of Social Communications*, offers the best starting point for tracing a shift in the dialogue between Catholicism and Hollywood in the 1960s. As one observer poignantly noted on the decree's twentieth anniversary, *Inter Mirifica* is arguably the council's most forgotten (and forgettable) document. Some even deride it as "preconciliar" in its content.[3] Promulgated with *Sacrosanctum Concilium* on December 8, 1963, *Inter Mirifica* was the unhappy orphan of a fatigued compromise. Embarrassed with meager progress after a year of proceedings, council leadership introduced a schema on social communications mere weeks before the closing of the first session. Many thought it would provide an oasis from more controversial topics, yet several bishops recommended revisions in light of its verbosity. A shortened schema surfaced during the second session the following year. However, it quickly met a vociferous attack from American Catholic journalists and theologians, who derided it as abstract and unsophisticated.[4] In a move of desperation, the council trimmed the original schema and passed the document with a slim majority on November 25, 1963. Guiseppe Alberigo considers the final document a "wasted opportunity," noting that the majority

---

[3] Robert P. Waznak, "The Church's Response to the Media: Twenty-Five Years after *Inter Mirifica*," *America* 160, no. 2 (January 21, 1989): 36–40.

[4] Ibid., 37. The American prelate Martin John O'Connor, then rector of the North American College in Rome, had a key hand in drafting both documents as the head of various incarnations of the Vatican office for communications from 1948 to 1971. Records of O'Connor's leadership of this body can be found in The Archbishop Martin J. O'Connor Collection in The American Catholic History Research Center and University Archives at The Catholic University of America in Washington, DC (hereafter ACHRCUA).

of the bishops were simply apathetic about the topic.[5] A more robust reflection on media and film finally emerged in 1971 with *Communio et Progressio*, a product of the Pontifical Commission (now Council) for Social Communications and its collaboration with experts.[6] Walther Kampe contends that both documents should be read together as a whole, and their joint legacy more or less converges on the establishment of an annual World Communications Day for prayer and the financial support of the Church's media apostolates.[7] Even if read alongside *Inter Mirifica*, *Communio et Progressio* offers considerably more reflection on the Church's relationship with cinema.[8]

For the purposes of this study, the reception of these texts in America's secular film industry is more important than their content. For its part, Hollywood barely took notice. The major industry magazines—*Variety*, *The Hollywood Reporter*, and *Motion Picture Daily*—ignored *Inter Mirifica* altogether. The exception, perhaps, is an erudite summary of *Communio et Progressio* on the front page of *Variety* in 1971, yet interest in Catholic approaches to social communications practically ceased afterward.[9] Likewise, Hollywood's yawn extends to the copious records of the Academy's archives. What may seem at first glance trivial and expected is actually perplexing when compared to the industry's approach to Catholic commentary on film *before* Vatican II. Preceding *Inter Mirifica*, and indeed inspiring it, were Pope Pius XII's discourses on the potentials and problems of film and faith in the 1950s,

---

[5] Giuseppe Alberigo, *A Brief History of Vatican II*, trans. Matthew Sherry (Maryknoll: Orbis, 2006), 28, 39.

[6] Pontifical Council for Social Communications, Pastoral Instruction *Communio et Progressio*, AAS 63 (1971): 593–656.

[7] Walther Kampe, "Communicating with the World: The Decree *Inter Mirifica*," in *Vatican II Revisited: By Those Who Were There*, ed. Alberic Stacpoole (Minneapolis: Winston, 1986), 197; see *Inter Mirifica* 18; *Communio et Progressio* 100. In 1992 the same pontifical body commemorated *Communio et Progressio* with a new document, *Aetatis Novae*. Pontifical Council for Social Communications, Pastoral Instruction *Aetatis Novae*, AAS 84 (1992): 447–68.

[8] Compare, for instance, *Communio et Progressio* 142–147 to *Inter Mirifica* 14.

[9] "Catholic Church's Bright View of Communications covers Pix," *Daily Variety* 152, no. 11 (June 21, 1971): 1, 8. The report compares the tone of "extreme caution" and "suspicion" in *Inter Mirifica* with that of "positive, optimistic and constructive" language in *Communio et Progressio*.

including his 1957 encyclical, *Miranda Prorsus*.[10] Whereas one searches in vain for a mere reference to *Inter Mirifica*, the Academy's archives contain physical copies of *Miranda Prorsus*. The correspondence of the Association of Motion Picture and Television Producers Records contains one copy (with an attached memo), and the other copy lies hidden in the files of Hollywood's acclaimed Academy Award-winning director and producer, Fred Zinnemann (1907–1997).[11] Although the copies are not heavily annotated, they at least reflect the industry's acknowledgment of official Catholic approaches to film prior to the council.

What accounts for such a stark contrast between the industry's acknowledgment of *Miranda Prorsus* and *Inter Mirifica*? At the heart of this shift was the waning influence of the National Legion of Decency, an American Catholic organization that had partnered with the Motion Picture Association of America's (MPAA) Production Code to enforce strict moral standards in the industry. A more thorough history of the Legion's shadow over Hollywood, especially under the direction of the Irish-American Catholic Joseph Breen (1888–1965), remains beyond the purview of this particular study.[12] Nevertheless, the fracturing of the tortured alliance between the Legion, the Production Code, and the industry is essential for understanding the cultural shift between *The Cardinal* and *The Shoes of the Fisherman*. Although aggressive American film producers like Preminger played an integral role in this fracture, the Legion's own demise ultimately came from pressure abroad, especially from Pius's *Miranda Prorsus*.

The 1950s witnessed a gradual wedge splitting the censorship opinions of French and Italian Catholic film organizations and those of American Catholics. European films that had received Catholic endorsements in France and Italy (many made by Catholic producers and

---

[10] The other discourse on the subject is Pius XII's apostolic exhortation, "To the Representatives of the Italian Cinematograph Industry," June 21, 1955.

[11] See File 90 "Clark, Kenneth," Box 9, Association of Motion Picture and Television Producers (AMPTP) Records, and File 678 "THE NUN'S STORY—Censorship 1957," Box 50, the Fred Zinnemann Papers, both in Special Collections, Margaret Herrick Library, Academy of Motion Picture Arts and Sciences, Beverly Hills, California (hereafter SCMHL, AMPAS). The AMPTP copy contains a note from Kenneth Clark to Duke Wales (AMPTP spokesman), inviting Wales to use the encyclical in public relations; Zinnemann seems to have examined the encyclical while producing *The Nun's Story* (1959).

[12] See Thomas Patrick Doherty, *Hollywood's Censor: Joseph I. Breen and the Production Code Administration* (New York: Columbia University Press, 2007).

directors) remained banned in the United States through the advocacy of the Legion. By 1959 European Catholics had gained the upper hand, and *Miranda Prorsus* played no small role.[13] After initially demurring Pius's encyclical as yet another Catholic remonstration against a phantom culture of immorality in American films, Hollywood's dailies began to recognize how the document marked a significant shift in tone from Pius XI's *Vigilanti Cura* (1936), an encyclical that had been at the core of Legion's work for over two decades.[14] Some industry magazines shifted their own tone to use *Miranda Prorsus* against the Legion. One critic in *Motion Picture Exhibitor* provocatively challenged the Legion to adopt the more "balanced" view of censorship in the encyclical, rather than its own policy of "all 'knock' and no 'boost.'"[15] The Legion's archives reveal how this particular article created a stir within the organization, particularly in the work of Msgr. Thomas F. Little (1912–1986), the longtime director of the Legion.[16] After all, how could the Legion ignore the more benevolent advice of the pope himself, especially amid an ingrained American Catholic ultramontanism? Similar records demonstrate how *Miranda Prorsus* spurred two changes within the Legion. Just prior to the opening of Vatican II, the Legion had revised its pledge, recited annually in practically all Catholic parishes in the United States. This new pledge, initiated in 1959 and finished by 1963, substituted an earlier Catholic promise to "condemn absolutely those salacious motion pictures… corrupting public morals" to a new, more enlightened

[13] On this shift, see Black, *The Catholic Crusade*, 176–80.

[14] For example, compare *Variety's* headline, "Networks Fear Sponsor Scare in Vatican Edict to Supervise TV" (September 18, 1957) with a new headline one week later, "Catholic Church and Good Films, Italian Filmites Think Pope Put It Just Right" (September 25, 1957).

[15] Paul Greenhalgh, "All Knock and No Boost," *Motion Picture Exhibitor* 58, no. 26 (October 23, 1957). Greenhalgh, after contrasting *Miranda Prorsus* and the more positive resolutions of a recent international Catholic conference on film in Havana with the Legion's foot-dragging in the United States, concludes, "From where we sit, most of the influence of the Catholic Church [in the United States] seems to be directed at, and not with, the motion picture business…a policy of all 'knock' and no 'boost.'"

[16] A copy of Greenhalgh's article is attached to a memo by Msgr. Little, notifying episcopal leadership that he is in the midst of arranging a meeting with Greenhalgh about his criticism of the Legion. See Folder 1, "Information Media: Motion Pictures: Censorship, 1956–59," Box 31, Series 1.1, General Administration, Records of the Office of the General Secretary, ACHRCUA.

commitment to "promote by word and deed what is morally and artistically good in motion picture entertainment."[17] Moreover, just after the conclusion of the council, the Legion changed its name to the National Catholic Office for Motion Pictures (NCOMP). Little had encouraged a name revision to counter the perception of a "pre-Johannine anachronism," preferring a title that would foster "a communications climate in which Catholic artists may be developed and assisted."[18] Most important, he insisted on a new name that would more aptly correspond to those of the Pontifical Commission on Social Communications and numerous Catholic media agencies around the world. Nevertheless, the name change amounted to little more than a distraction. By 1968 *Variety* reported (with thinly-veiled glee) that most Catholic parishes in the United States now omitted the annual renewal of the pledge, and by 1980 NCOMP dissolved altogether.[19]

These changes in the Legion are essential for understanding Hollywood's complex dialogue with the council. The film industry had learned to appeal to transatlantic Catholic voices to counter the Legion's influence at home, and this strategy determined the industry's approach to the council itself. For Hollywood producers, the council and its language of "ecumenism" offered a timely international event that could definitively dismantle the Legion's hegemony in American cinema. In other words, the Legion's complicated legacy gave rise to Hollywood's interest in Vatican II in the 1960s. Rather than ignore this distant international gathering of the world's Catholic episcopacy, the American film industry relished an opportunity to exploit the spectacle as "ecumenical" leverage against an obscurantist lobby at home. A prime example of this trajectory is Preminger's 1963 film, *The Cardinal*.

[17] Skinner, *The Cross and the Cinema*, 37, 155.

[18] Thomas F. Little to Paul Tanner, May 17, 1965, in File 2, "Information Media: Motion Pictures: Censorship, 1960–1966," Box 31, Series 1.1, General Administration, Records of the Office of the General Secretary, ACHRCUA.

[19] "Many Catholic Churches Here Omit Legion of Decency Pledge," *Daily Variety*, 138, no. 4 (December 11, 1967): 1; Skinner, *The Cross and the Cinema*, 175–76.

THE CARDINAL AND HIS CRITICS

Mere days after the promulgation of *Inter Mirifica* and the closing of the council's second session, *The Cardinal* appeared in American theaters. News footage of the council was fresh in moviegoers' minds. Based on the 1950 bestselling novel by Henry Morton Robinson (1898–1961), *The Cardinal* tells the story of a newly minted Bostonian priest named Stephen Fermoyle who overcomes a variety of social and personal challenges before joining the august College of Cardinals. His tumultuous and eventful life includes an interfaith romance between a Catholic and a Jew, the moral dilemma of an abortion, a sudden crisis of priestly vocation, a dramatic conflict with the Klan and racism in the South, and an indefatigable triumph over Nazi anti-Catholic aggression in Europe.

The whirlwind movie opened to fair but more or less incredulous reviews, many noting the basic implausibility of the narrative. As one writer put it in *Variety*, "How many extraordinary experiences can one man have in a life-time?"[20] Nevertheless, the coinciding of the film with the council was not lost among the critics. Several reviews recognized that the film might interest general audiences given that the "Ecumenical Council is under way again in Rome and has stirred wide interest anew among persons of all faiths in the workings of the Roman Catholic Church."[21] Such an endorsement marked something of a vindication for Preminger, who had infamously locked horns with the Legion over *The Moon is Blue* in 1953.[22] For many Americans, Preminger's embrace of an indisputably Catholic theme was audacious, if not ironic. In the end, Preminger's most glowing review came from a real-life cardinal that he

---

[20] *Variety*, October 16, 1963, clipping in File, "The Cardinal (Gamma Prod., 1963)," Motion Picture Association of America, Production Code Administration Records, SCMHL, AMPAS.

[21] *Motion Picture Daily*, October 16, 1963, clipping in File, "The Cardinal (Gamma Prod., 1963)," Motion Picture Association of America, Production Code Administration Records, SCMHL, AMPAS. Despite its negative evaluation of the film's content, *Variety* (October 16, 1965) echoed *Motion Picture Daily* in recognizing the film's timeliness: "It might even enjoy what the trade calls blockbuster business in view of the fortuitous 'pre-sell', so to speak, coming out of Rome as a consequence of the Ecumenical Council and the curiosity it has engendered about the Catholic Church and its hierarchy among people of all faiths."

[22] Foster Hirsch, *Otto Preminger: The Man Who Would Be King* (New York: Alfred A. Knopf, 2007), 197–98.

craftily courted for the film's release: Boston's Richard Cardinal Cushing (1895–1970).

A living cardinal's endorsement of the film proved to be Preminger's greatest attack on the Legion. After a private showing, Cushing penned a glowing review of *The Cardinal* in Boston's *The Pilot*, stating that it was "among the best post war pictures concerned with themes and personalities specifically Catholic."[23] Cushing flattered Preminger's film as "both entertaining and informative, educational and inspiring." The prelate went so far to claim that the movie contained "something for everyone" and provided "excellent substance for parish and in-school discussion clubs." This latter endorsement alarmed the Legion, which had given *The Cardinal* its new A-III rating, "suitable for adults only," in light of its treatment of abortion and a crisis of vocation. Cushing's review embarrassed the Legion, which in turn had to revise its original statement to avoid contradicting a prominent member of the American Catholic hierarchy. Columbia Pictures quickly used Cushing's endorsement against the Legion, even sending Little a copy of the review with Cushing's lines above underlined.[24] The Legion quickly found itself on the defensive, having to explain to the leadership of the National Catholic Welfare Conference (later the USCCB) that Preminger was employing Cushing for "exploitational purposes."[25] Little contested that the film stressed "legalism" over the "supernatural character of the Church," such that "neither Christ nor charity play any significant role in this story of His Church."[26] He moreover insisted that the film contradicted the reform trajectory of Vatican II, claiming that some of the Legion's reviewers thought "strongly that the film sets the Ecumenical movement back fifty years." Church hierarchy, it seems, paid little notice to these protests. Instead Preminger's match with the

---

[23] "Cardinal on 'Cardinal': New Film is Superb," *The Pilot* 134, no. 37 (September 14, 1963).

[24] See note and copy of Cushing's review from J. Raymond Bell to Thomas Little, October 8, 1963, in Folder 3, "The Cardinal," Box 21, United States Conference of Catholic Bishops Communications Department/Office of Film and Broadcasting Records (hereafter OFB), ACHRCUA.

[25] Thomas Little to Archbishop John Krol, October 31, 1963, Folder 3, "The Cardinal," Box 21, OFB, ACHRCUA.

[26] Thomas Little to Archbishop John Krol, November 4, 1963, Folder 3, "The Cardinal," Box 21, OFB, ACHRCUA.

Legion ended in a threefold checkmate. A press release for *The Cardinal* announced to the world that the film was "screened four times at St. Peters Auditorium for members of the Curia, Bishops, and Fathers of the Ecumenical Council," that Preminger himself was presented with the Grand Cross of Merit by the Knights of the Holy Sepulcher at one of these screenings, and that the same producer was granted a private office with Pope Paul VI.[27] The real-life cardinal who arranged these honors was none other than Alfredo Ottaviani (1890–1979).

If Preminger's wooing worked on Catholic churchmen, it decidedly failed on a churchwoman. Moira Walsh (1919–1996), film critic for the Jesuit weekly *America*, rejected the film as a string of clichés. She compared its entertainment value to "thumb sucking," ridiculing the film's protagonist as "a secular, soap-opera version of Everyman, given to flabby emotional thinking" and "expressing no religious or ethical convictions except 'safe' and popular ones."[28] Preminger resented these remarks and publically chastised Walsh for not yielding to Cushing, who, he reminded Walsh, was her ecclesiastical superior. Walsh retorted that "great men... tend to be the worst possible judges of films."[29] She defended her criticism of the film from a "structured and nuanced ecumenical position" that insisted that Catholics must both "understand the limitations as well as the advantages of living in a pluralistic society" and "master the techniques of fair debate before they can expect to be taken seriously by their neighbors."[30] In the end, she reserved most of her ire for the Vatican's love affair with the film and the aloof conservatism of the council in its first two sessions:

> These Fathers obviously would not accept the proposition, "Let the truth be told in films." Instead they seem to harbor the unrealistic hope that there are such things as "safe," pious movies that will somehow pierce the hard hearts of their straying flocks and restore to the church the same

[27] Press Release from Raymond Bell, Folder 3, "The Cardinal," Box 21, OFB, ACHRCUA.

[28] Moira Walsh, "The Cardinal," *America* (January 4, 1964), clipping in File, "The Cardinal (Gamma Prod., 1963)," Motion Picture Association of America, Production Code Administration Records, SCMHL, AMPAS.

[29] Moira Walsh, "Otto Preminger Looks at the Catholic Church" *Catholic World* (March 1964): 365.

[30] Ibid., 370.

happy, ignorant, tractable, pious children they once were. This school of thought has many adherents in Italy.[31]

In the end, Walsh's assessment found support among other film critics who dismissed Preminger's work both as a "mass of sentiments" and as testimony that "Hollywood has failed to create a real person on the screen."[32] The film was financially successful but quickly forgotten.

Papal Shoes to Fill

Preminger was not alone in his perception of Vatican II as ripe material for Hollywood. A few days after the opening of the council in 1962, novelist Morris West wrote Fred Zinnemann, claiming that his new book, *The Shoes of the Fisherman*, provided ready material for a box office hit. The book tells the tale of a Ukrainian bishop named Kiril Lakota who, upon his release from a Siberian prison and swift election to the papacy, becomes the sole man who can bridge the East–West divide and avert an impending World War III. In his letter, West introduces the storyline to Zinnemann as depicting the "first six months of the pontificate of the *next* Pope."[33] In addition to this provocative claim, West provides a detailed and colorful portrayal of the plot, layered with inescapable allusions to Pope John XXIII's fresh, personal approach to the papacy. Pope Kiril is one who "understands the secret landscape of the human heart" in his quest to "break through the historic bureaucracy of Rome to meet the hearts of his people." Unlike his predecessors, this new pope "goes out... into the city to see the way his people live." A gripping drama unfolds that West describes as "concentric." At the core of the story, Pope Kiril wrestles with Vatican bureaucracy to make it more humane, only to witness the censure of his brilliant and theologically progressive Jesuit friend Jean Telemond. By making this priest also a scientist, West indisputably alludes to Teilhard de Chardin. On another level, the book hinges on a more fragile and complex relationship with the Russian Premier, Pope Kiril's former interrogator in Siberia.

---

[31] Ibid., 371.

[32] Bosley Crowther, *New York Times* (December 15, 1963); Courier *Journal* (January 10, 1964), clipping in Folder 3, "The Cardinal," Box 21, OFB, ACHRCUA.

[33] Morris L. West to Fred Zinneman, October 15, 1962, in File 1719 "W (1932–1990)," Box 110, Fred Zinnemann Papers, SCMHL, AMPAS, emphasis original.

The pope rises above the pain of his past to emerge as an emissary of peace in a world on the brink of nuclear apocalypse, guided by a "growing resolution to go out from Rome into the other countries of the world, to present himself as an apostolic missionary and not a Prince." Overall, West pitches the book's *ecumenical* outlook as its greatest cinematic opportunity: "I don't have to point out to you the current relevance of all this to the council which is now being held in Rome, and to the worldwide interest in the question of reunion for the Christian Churches." Worth noting is how West employs this final theological point for a Jewish producer, insisting that only someone with his "taste and vision" and "sense of history and the human dilemma" could translate the story for the screen.[34] This appeal is likely in recognition of Zinnemann's earlier success with Kathryn Hulme's novel, *The Nun's Story*, a work the author (a convert to Catholicism) defended as "ecumenical" from its inception.[35]

Ultimately *The Shoes of the Fisherman* made its way to the Hollywood screen, albeit without Zinnemann's direction. Instead Michael J. Anderson, Sr. (1920–) took on the project. In the film's climactic final scene, Pope Kiril addresses a crowd in St. Peter's Square from the basilica's iconic loggia, removes his papal tiara in a gesture of humility, and announces the emptying of Vatican coffers to alleviate the famine of Red China. For this scene, Anderson brought his crew to Rome to shoot footage of the closing ceremonies of Vatican II in St. Peter's Square.[36] In the final cut, this remarkable footage blends scenes of the real, historic event with the film's fictitious plot. However, this cinematic adaptation of the book did not appear in theaters until November 1968, six years

---

[34] Ibid.

[35] Kathryn Hulme to Harold C. Gardiner, June 2, 1959, File 708, "The Nun's Story: Correspondence, Religious 1958–1976," Box 52, Fred Zinnemann Papers, SCMHL, AMPAS. This letter was published with Hulme's permission in "'The Nun's Story' – A Symposium," *America* (June 27, 1959). Aside from West's explicit reference to the council as an ecumenical event, he curiously omits key scenes. For instance, he remains silent about how Kiril ventures out into the streets of Rome incognito and prays over a dying Jewish man in Hebrew, something the pope claims to have gleaned from a friendship in his Siberian prison. Was West concerned that Zinnemann, a Jewish producer and director, would judge such a scene as a superficial interfaith encounter? West's reason remains unclear.

[36] See James Wall's review in *The Christian Century*, clipping in File "The Shoes of the Fisherman (MGM 1962)," Motion Picture Association of America, Production Code Administration Records, SCMHL, AMPAS.

after West's letter to Zinnemann. Whereas Preminger's film enjoyed perfect timing with a climate of curiosity surrounding the council, Anderson's film suffered the worst timing, coming just on the heels of *Humanae Vitae* (July 25, 1968). Morris's "next" pope, Paul VI, whose popularity in America had surged after his historical apostolic visit to the United States in 1965, suddenly became an object of widespread scorn and distrust. Whereas the ceremonial splendor of the opening of the council complemented the release of *The Cardinal*, American Catholic division and controversy over the authority of the papacy engulfed the release of *The Shoes of the Fisherman*.

As with *The Cardinal*, West and Anderson's use of Vatican II's "ecumenical outlook" was not lost on the critics.[37] Nevertheless, the critics were merciless in their assessment of the film, particularly as a failed ecclesial opportunity. One *Newsweek* review compared the film to *Roman Holiday* (1953), "with Anthony Quinn [as Pope Kiril] playing the Audrey Hepburn part as a Pope instead of a princess."[38] The same critic described the film's plot as "couched" in "sci-fi (or theo-fi) terms," with a "basically silly script [that] suffers occasionally severe spams of intelligence." The critic reserved his harshest critique for Anderson's uses of the council's closing ceremonies: "The climax, truncated and tentative, was clearly as preposterous to the people behind the camera as it is to those in front of the screen." *Time* added insult to injury, ridiculing the film as a "saccharine Pope opera" that "would be hard to imagine a parochial-school sixth-grader taking seriously."[39] The same critic offered a stinging observation: "At a time when Roman Catholicism is rent by internal rebellion and dissent, the church could use some aid. *The Shoes of the Fisherman* makes a pompous offering and in the act of genuflecting, falls on its face." Other critics agreed that the film was a missed opportunity in ecumenism. What had once seemed an imminent

---

[37] Untitled review by John Mahoney, clipping in File "The Shoes of the Fisherman (MGM 1962)," Motion Picture Association of America, Production Code Administration Records, SCMHL, AMPAS.

[38] Joseph Morgenstern, "The Shoes of the Fisherman," *Newsweek* (November 25, 1968), clipping in File "The Shoes of the Fisherman (MGM 1962)," Motion Picture Association of America, Production Code Administration Records, SCMHL, AMPAS.

[39] Untitled review from *Time*, November 29, 1968, clipping in File "The Shoes of the Fisherman (MGM 1962)," Motion Picture Association of America, Production Code Administration Records, SCMHL, AMPAS.

possibility now appeared to be a dashed dream. Disillusionment with West's ecumenical agenda gave way to scorn in a Protestant review in *The Christian Century*. The author considered the plot a farce, jeering, "There are more than few moments when the shoes appear to pinch the papal bunions."[40] In particular, the critic claimed that the film was littered with contrived "*dei ex machinae*" in its attempt to speak to contemporary ecumenism. Dismissing the film as an "ecclesiolatrous mime" in its "ostentatious" display of Catholic pageantry, the reviewer ridiculed West's optimism and its translation to the screen: "If it is indeed a cinematographic paradigm of the ecclesiastical shape of things to come, God help us every one!" Nevertheless, Moira Walsh's review in *America* stood out in its sincerity and insight. Acknowledging that the film glossed over theological and social complexities, she identified some merit in the final scene on the loggia. Pope Kiril's gesture of benevolence toward starving China had the potential "to demonstrate the Church's new openness to the world. That gesture... has been robbed of its dramatic impact in five short years by the globe-trotting activities of our present Pontiff."[41] In observing something of Paul VI on the screen, Walsh thought that the overall demeanor of Pope Kiril symbolized the spirit of Vatican II. Nevertheless, even she had to admit that film failed to convince its audience of Kiril's plausibility, especially in the shadow of intra-Catholic controversies over contraception and the implementation of conciliar reforms.

CONCLUSION: LESSONS THAT "REMEMBER" THE FUTURE?

In light of the theme of the conference that gave birth to these volumes, what should one make of *The Cardinal* and *The Shoes of the Fisherman* as examples of "dialogue" between the council and Hollywood? Both films gained Academy Award nominations: *The Cardinal* for direction and cinematography (among other categories) and *The Shoes of the Fisherman* for musical score and art direction. However, neither film won an Oscar. Moreover, in the wake of the critics' reviews the films witnessed more

---

[40]Trevor Wyatt Moore, "Habemus Papam ex M-G-M," *The Christian Century*, clipping in File "The Shoes of the Fisherman (MGM 1962)," Motion Picture Association of America, Production Code Administration Records, SCMHL, AMPAS.

[41]Moira Walsh, "The Shoes of the Fisherman," *America* 119, no. 18 (November 30, 1968): 577.

hype around their release than their reception. What lessons in ecumenical dialogue does such meager success offer, if any?

A seminal answer to this question lies in the positive reception of the very film that Zinnemann produced in lieu of West's novel. In 1967, Zinnemann swept the Academy Awards with his widely acclaimed film, *A Man for All Seasons* (1966). At first glance, the story about Sir Thomas More's unyielding conscience and Henry VIII's split from Rome seems an unlikely candidate for ecumenical dialogue. On the contrary, *A Man for All Seasons* received the first ecumenical joint film award between the recently renamed Legion (NCOMP) and the National Council of Churches of Christ in America, the latter describing its opinion of the film as "positive and enthusiastic."[42] Reviews in Hollywood's magazines were euphoric, and the film garnered enough international attention that Paul VI asked Columbia Pictures to arrange a private (and confidential) viewing of the film.[43] The pope's secretary reported that the pontiff "thoroughly enjoyed" the film.[44]

Why did *A Man for All Seasons* succeed where *The Cardinal* and *The Shoes of the Fisherman* failed? Here Walsh's review in *America* is insightful. Likewise stunned by the film's quality, Walsh concluded that its success could be seen in how the film's "main cinematic tool... is the camera, artfully capturing the faces of superb actors speaking superb dialogue—dialogue that is the outward manifestation of electrifying confrontations and inner conflicts."[45] Walsh's description of the film's focus on "dialogue" captures Zinnemann's authentic communication of human

---

[42] David Poindexter to Raymond Bell, January 27, 1967, File 584, "A Man for All Seasons, Correspondence, 1967," Box 45, Fred Zinnemann Papers, SCMHL, AMPAS. See also the Catholic announcement in "A Man for All Seasons," "A Guide to Current Films," in *NCOMP Classifications*, March 9, 1967 (vol. 32, no. 12), copy in File 392, "National Catholic Office for Motion Pictures—Classifications, 1966–1968," Box 40, AMPTP Records, SCMHL, AMPAS.

[43] Jack Valenti (MPAA President) to Raymond Bell, February 6, 1967, File 584, "A Man for All Seasons, Correspondence, 1967," Box 45, Fred Zinnemann Papers, SCMHL, AMPAS.

[44] Paul C. Marcinkus to Emilio Panchadell (Columbia Pictures), August 2, 1967, File 584, "A Man for All Seasons, Correspondence, 1967," Box 45, Fred Zinnemann Papers, SCMHL, AMPAS.

[45] Moira Walsh review in *America*, clipping in File 662, "A Man for All Seasons—clippings and reviews (United States) 1967–1968," Box 44, Fred Zinnemann Papers, SCMHL, AMPAS.

inquiry and integrity in the film's portrayal of conflicts of conscience and the pursuit of truth. Rather than reducing the birth of Anglicanism to a king's lustful libido, the story offers dilemmatic dialogue to ponder, starkly different from the neat, triumphalistic conclusions of *The Cardinal* and *The Shoes of the Fisherman*. Zinnemann's film arguably delves into the deeper meaning of the council instead of falling prey to a superficial sense of ecumenism. Whereas Preminger and West approach the council as a historic event, ripe for a blockbuster hit, Zinnemann creates an interpersonal encounter that subtly echoes the assertion of *Gaudium et Spes* that "human dialogue" is not reducible to modern "progress" but rather resides at the "deeper level of interpersonal communion" (GS 23).[46] *The Cardinal* is the story of a priest climbing the ecclesiastical ranks for his own social progress. *The Shoes of the Fisherman* is the story of another priest using ecclesiastical rank for the social progress of the world. *A Man for All Seasons* is the story of a layman in actual dialogue with his interlocutors. The latter is a story of authentic listening and discernment rather than triumphalistic problem-solving.

A final voice worth adding to this reflection on the lessons for dialogue between Hollywood and the council is that of Walter Cardinal Kasper. In his recent work on mercy, Kasper speaks of the "new dialogical style" of Vatican II:

A dialogue that was not concerned with the truth would not deserve the name dialogue. Dialogue, rightly understood, presupposes a listening heart and reciprocal listening to each other. It means mutually vouching for the truth and coming to an exchange, ready to understand the truth, in order, as far as possible, to arrive at a common agreement in the truth, but there, where that is not possible to say honestly that we agree to disagree.[47]

This description of ecumenical and interreligious dialogue in relation to truth complements Walsh's earlier maxim, "Let the truth be told in films." Both Kasper and Walsh strike at the heart of authentic ecumenism, one searching for truth in all its complexity rather than in ready,

---

[46]The translation above is my own; the Latin reads, "Tamen fraternum hominum colloquium non in istis progressibus, sed profundius in personarum communitate perficitur, quae mutuam reverentiam erga plenam earum dignitatem spiritualem exigit."

[47]Walter Kasper, *Mercy: The Essence of the Gospel and the Key to Christian Life*, trans. William Madges (New York: Paulist Press, 2014), 162–63.

convenient answers. Ecumenism does not begin with a world event or (in the case of *The Cardinal* and *The Shoes of the Fisherman*) a series of events. Rather, ecumenism begins with dialogue rooted in listening and searching for the truth. The story of how other Hollywood films sought this more authentic and conciliar sense of ecumenism in the 1960s regrettably lies beyond this study. Nevertheless, the dialogical myopia of Preminger and West serves as an essential lesson for charting future dialogue between Vatican II and culture.

PART V

Ecumenical Readings of Vatican II

CHAPTER 13

Bridges and Doors: An Ecumenical Reading of Vatican II

Dale T. Irvin

In his 1909 essay titled "Bridge and Door," George Simmel noted that human beings conceptualize the world at a fundamental level by separating and connecting.[1] The world that we encounter always presents itself to us both as a unified whole and as discrete objects that are separated by

---

[1] George Simmel, "Brücke und Tür," *Der Tag: Moderne illustrierte Zeitung* 683 (September 15, 1909): 1–3. The English version used here is Mark Ritter, trans., "Bridge and Door," in *Simmel on Culture*, ed. David Frisby and Mike Featherstone (Thousand Oaks, CA: Sage, 1997), 170–74; see also Victoria Lee Erickson, "On the Town with Georg Simmel: A Socio-Religious Understanding of Urban Interaction," *Cross Currents* 51, no. 1 (2001): 21–44.

An extended version of the first part of this essay, on Simmel, has been published in *The Living Pulpit* in January 2015. I thank that journal for permission to use an abridged section of that essay to introduce this paper.

D. T. Irvin (✉)
New York Theological Seminary, New York City, NY, USA
e-mail: dirvin@nyts.edu

© The Author(s) 2018
V. Latinovic et al. (eds.), *Catholicism Opening to the World and Other Confessions*, Pathways for Ecumenical and Interreligious Dialogue, https://doi.org/10.1007/978-3-319-98581-7_13

both space and time, Simmel argued. In order to understand the world, our perception separates the unified whole into parts, and makes connections among the various parts to make them whole. Separating and connecting, said Simmel, are "two sides of precisely the same act."[2] They are two sides of the process by which we uncover meaning and construct identity.

This perception began when human beings first began building huts, Simmel speculated. In doing so, they divided the universe into an inner and an outer world. The door marked the passageway between these two, he noted. One knows when one is going in and when one is going out. The door marks the space of separation, which leads to an identity of one's self or one's people. It opens up to what is beyond, but only by first establishing the self. In this sense, the door separates in order to connect. Doors establish "us" and "them."

Doors in turn, however, open up upon pathways that lead eventually to other doors, said Simmel. They had to. Human beings could not survive without connections. It is the pathway that connects. Having separated themselves by building huts, those first hypothetical humans simultaneously connected themselves by building paths between and among their huts. The path connects things that would otherwise remain separated. The path itself does not move but it is the occasion for movement. It is dynamic precisely because it is static.

Simmel argued that the path reached the zenith of its achievement in the form of a bridge. Bridges are paths that connect in the most elegant manner. The bridge is an especially important form of connection for it embodies a level of intentionality and volition that is not so explicitly revealed in the making of a path or a road. Paths and roads can be built from one direction, but for a bridge to be built there must be intentionality and commitment from two directions, on both sides of the riverbank. Bridges do not demarcate a world of "us" and "them" in the manner that doors do. Instead they connect, joining "us" and "us." As Simmel noted, while the door displays a clear distinction between entering and exiting, "it makes no difference in meaning in which direction one crosses a bridge." For Simmel, the bridge is a moment in which the metaphysical or spiritual overcomes what appears to be a natural divide.

---

[2] Simmel, "Bridge and Door," 172.

In the following pages I intend to look at the documents of Vatican II though this Simmelian lens of doors and bridges to interpret the ecumenical spirit that is at work in Vatican II. One can find numerous examples of doors in Vatican II. The bridges are subtler, but they are also there. In true Simmelian fashion, I will argue that the term "ecumenical" itself names both a door and a bridge in the documents of Vatican II. That which is ecumenical is both separating and connecting. The question I have is which aspect of the "ecumenical"—the door or the bridge—is predominant. I will argue that Vatican II was more concerned about maintaining and reinforcing the ecumenical door, but that it nevertheless opened up an important ecumenical bridge that we are still trying to cross some fifty years later.

The word "ecumenical" (or "œcumenical" in its older form) is derived from the Greek word *oikoumenē*, meaning "the inhabited world." Originally the term was used by Greek writers to name that portion of the earth that human beings inhabited, or the totality of human civilization. Within the Roman Empire the term came to be more limited to naming that portion of the world that was under Roman imperial rule. Leaders of the dominant party of the Christian movement picked up the imperial implications of the term in the fourth century CE when they used it to describe the nature of the Council of Nicaea. Nicaea was the first council to be named "ecumenical." On an ideological level the term was used to project the appearance of universality of what was called the Great Church, but at a critical level it was closely bound to Roman imperial power and identity and thus marked a boundary.[3]

Eventually, the Great Church divided into separated communions that continued each to claim for itself the label of being "ecumenical." The bishop of Constantinople, for instance, became known at the Ecumenical Patriarch, while the bishop of Rome continued to convene what were self-consciously identified as ecumenical councils, but at which only the Latin-speaking churches were represented. In 1876, in the aftermath of Vatican I and in reaction to the manner in which the term "ecumenical" was appropriated by the Roman Catholic Church for a council of

[3] For a fuller critical appraisal of the meaning of "*oikoumenē*" and "ecumenical" in the first centuries of the Christian movement, see Dale T. Irvin, "Specters of a New Ecumenism: In Search of a Church 'Out of Joint'," in *Religion, Authority, and the State: From Constantine to the Contemporary World*, ed. Leo D. Lefebure (New York: Palgrave Macmillan, 2016), 3–32.

its own, the General Conference of the Methodist Episcopal Church in the United States issued a call for an "Ecumenical Conference of Methodism" that would bring together representatives from Methodist conferences around the world in a manner similar to the gathering that had taken place several years earlier in Rome.[4] The initiator of that call, A.C. George, envisioned not just Methodists, but eventually other Protestants joining in this new ecumenical effort. He wrote:

> When Anglican Episcopal Convention, Presbyterian Pan-Council, Methodist Ecumenical Conference, world-wide Baptist Association, and other bodies of similar import, can speak in the name and with the authority of the great Churches which they represent, there will soon come to be, not only a growing feeling of fraternity, but also more practical exhibitions of the common brotherhood of worship, work, and warfare for the common object of the world's evangelization. In a word, our children will see, if we do not, a *Parliament of Protestantism*, aiming not at uniformity, but rejoicing in spiritual unity, helping the coming, and heralding the advent of the millennial glory.[5]

The effort was clearly to construct a pan-Protestant house (*oikoumenē*) that would stand over against Rome's claims to be the sole claimant to the "ecumenical." The terminology took hold among the dominant Protestant communions, who eventually made a very shaky alliance with the Orthodox, and the modern Ecumenical Movement resulted.[6]

On January 25, 1959, after only three months in office, Pope John XXIII announced to a gathering of Cardinals in Rome his decision to convene "an ecumenical council for the Universal Church."[7] That council, formally known as *Concilium Oecumenicum Vaticanum Secundum* or "The Second Vatican Ecumenical Council," and officially recognized as

---

[4] See A. C. George, "Ecumenical Methodism," *Methodist Quarterly Review* 62, no. 4 (1880): 667–80. The first conference was eventually held in 1881. Referring to the planning meeting that took place in 1880 in Cincinnati, George wrote: "Everybody seemed to discern that 'Ecumenical' was not now the symbol of Roman power or of Papal pretension. The word οικουμενη ecumenical, the whole human race, the inhabitable world, is, indeed, a word having the sanction of frequent New Testament use" (671).

[5] George, "Ecumenical Methodism," 679, emphasis original.

[6] See also Dale T. Irvin, *Hearing Many Voices: Dialogue and Diversity in the Ecumenical Movement* (Lanham, MD: University Press of America, 1994), 13–34.

[7] John XXIII, alloc. *Questa Festiva*, AAS 51 (1959): 65–69 at 68.

the twenty-first such ecumenical council by the Roman Catholic Church, began its work in October 1962. As part of the preparation leading up to the council, John XXIII two years earlier had established a new commission called the Secretariat for Promoting Christian Unity (later renamed to The Pontifical Council for Promoting Christian Unity). Cardinal Augustin Bea, a Jesuit who had been serving for nearly two decades as the rector of the Pontifical Biblical Institute in Rome, was tapped to serve as the first president of the new Secretariat. One of the first tasks he undertook was to select delegates from other Christian communions and from the Jewish community who would be invited to attend the forthcoming council as "observers." At the council itself the Secretariat served as one of the commissions, preparing the documents on ecumenism (*Unitatis Redintegratio*), non-Christian religions (*Nostra Aetate*), and religious liberty (*Dignitatis Humanae*); and collaborating on the document on divine revelation (*Dei Verbum*). Cardinal Bea made it clear on several occasions that rather than calling upon other Christians to return to the one true Church, he preferred to walk together with them into a common future.[8]

This does not mean that Vatican II abandoned traditional Roman Catholic doctrine that identifies the Roman Catholic communion as being the one true universal church on earth. In paragraph 6 of *Lumen Gentium*, or the "Dogmatic Constitution on the Church," we read, "The Church is a sheepfold whose one and indispensable door is Christ." Further in the same paragraph the church is called the building of God whose foundations were set by the apostles, with Christ now the cornerstone. "This Church constituted and organized in the world as a society, subsists in the Catholic Church, which is governed by the successor of Peter and by the Bishops in communion with him..." The Church, the council asserts, "is necessary for salvation" (LG 14). Now the doorway to the church is baptism, for through baptism, "as through a door," the document states, human beings enter the church and thus attain salvation. Baptism marks the threshold that separates the church and the world. It is a line of demarcation between inside and outside, the ecclesiastical self and other.

The ecumenical implications of this position are made explicit a bit further on in *Lumen Gentium*.

---

[8] See Maureen Sullivan, O.P., *101 Questions and Answers on Vatican II* (New York: Paulist Press, 2002), 22.

The supreme power in the universal Church, which this college [of bishops] enjoys, is exercised in a solemn way in an ecumenical council. A council is never ecumenical unless it is confirmed or at least accepted as such by the successor of Peter; and it is prerogative of the Roman Pontiff to convoke these councils, to preside over them and to confirm them. (LG 22)

The same document in section 28 envisions not just the unity of the Christian churches, but the unity of the human race as the family of God being realized within the Catholic communion:

Because the human race today is joining more and more into a civic, economic and social unity, it is that much the more necessary that priests, by combined effort and aid, under the leadership of the bishops and the Supreme Pontiff, wipe out every kind of separateness, so that the whole human race may be brought into the unity of the family of God.[9]

The unity not just of the church but of humankind is envisioned as being achieved by those who are outside the Roman Catholic Church somehow being brought inside this particular household of faith. To be "ecumenical" means to come in through this door.

Bridges, as I noted above, are harder to see in the documents of Vatican II. The most obvious place to look for one is in *Unitatis Redintegratio*, the "Decree on Ecumenism." Adopted by an overwhelming vote of the bishops in 1964, *Unitatis Redintegratio* opens by stating: "The restoration of unity among all Christians is one of the principal concerns of the Second Vatican Council." Bridges need to be rebuilt, in other words. Christ only founded one Church. Yet various Christian communions today represent themselves as being the true followers of Christ, even though they "differ in mind and go their different ways." The result is that Christ himself is made to appear as if he were divided. "Such division openly contradicts the will of Christ, scandalizes

---

[9] See also the conciliar decree *Ad Gentes* ("On the Missionary Activity of the Church"), which referenced the argument set forth in *Lumen Gentium* that the Church is necessary for salvation for all humankind: "For Christ Himself 'by stressing in express language the necessity of faith and baptism (cf. Mk 16:16; Jn 3:5), at the same time confirmed the necessity of the Church, into which men enter by baptism, as by a door. Therefore those men cannot be saved, who though aware that God, through Jesus Christ founded the Church as something necessary, still do not wish to enter into it, or to persevere in it'" (AG 7, quoting LG 14).

the world, and damages the holy cause of preaching the Gospel to every creature." On the other hand, *Unitatis Redintegratio* states, God has already given us a plan of grace for salvation, which is another way of saying that God has given us a plan for a bridge, reconnecting communions that have become separated from one another.

> Everywhere large numbers have felt the impulse of this grace, and among our separated brethren also there increases from day to day the movement, fostered by the grace of the Holy Spirit, for the restoration of unity among all Christians. This movement toward unity is called "ecumenical."

The decree thus begins by recognizing the separation that exists among communions of the world that claim to be following Christ. It does so from a particular location, that of the Roman Catholic Church. What was especially groundbreaking at the Council, was how *Unitatis Redintegratio* recognizes that others also claim to be the one true universal Church, or part of that Church. Without explicitly acknowledging the validity of those claims made by other communions, the opening paragraph of the decree acknowledges that Christ is effectively divided. Furthermore, it asserts that a construction project intended to build a bridge is already underway, a movement "fostered" by the bridge-building grace of the Holy Spirit that is seeking to restore the connections, which is another way of saying to overcome separation, among Christians. This movement to build bridges is called "ecumenical." *Unitatis Redintegratio* cautiously called upon Roman Catholics at every level of life in the church to join it.

> Today, in many parts of the world, under the inspiring grace of the Holy Spirit, many efforts are being made in prayer, word and action to attain that fullness of unity which Jesus Christ desires. The Sacred Council exhorts all the Catholic faithful to recognize the signs of the times and to take an active and intelligent part in the work of ecumenism. (UR 4)

The same document continues to provide a brief overview of the life and work of the ecumenical movement up to the 1960s, and a brief description of what the authors of the decree understood to be the ecumenical methodology.

The term "ecumenical movement" indicates the initiatives and activities planned and undertaken, according to the various needs of the Church and as opportunities offer, to promote Christian unity. These are: first, every effort to avoid expressions, judgments and actions which do not represent the condition of our separated brethren with truth and fairness and so make mutual relations with them more difficult; then, "dialogue" between competent experts from different Churches and Communities. At these meetings, which are organized in a religious spirit, each explains the teaching of his Communion in greater depth and brings out clearly its distinctive features. In such dialogue, everyone gains a truer knowledge and more just appreciation of the teaching and religious life of both Communions. In addition, the way is prepared for cooperation between them in the duties for the common good of humanity which are demanded by every Christian conscience; and, wherever this is allowed, there is prayer in common. Finally, all are led to examine their own faithfulness to Christ's will for the Church and accordingly to undertake with vigor the task of renewal and reform. (UR 4)

The goal was the unity that the decree's authors believed already subsists in the Roman Catholic Church, and which it can never lose:

This is the way that, when the obstacles to perfect ecclesiastical communion have been gradually overcome, all Christians will at last, in a common celebration of the Eucharist, be gathered into the one and only Church in that unity which Christ bestowed on His Church from the beginning. We believe that this unity subsists in the Catholic Church as something she can never lose, and we hope that it will continue to increase until the end of time. (UR 4)

The bridge, one is tempted to say, leads back to the door of the one true Church. Nevertheless crossing the bridge entails the risk of change. Two passages of *Unitatis Redintegratio* later state this clearly:

There can be no ecumenism worthy of the name without a change of heart. For it is from renewal of the inner life of our minds, from self-denial and an unstinted love that desires of unity take their rise and develop in a mature way. (UR 7) ...

This change of heart and holiness of life, along with public and private prayer for the unity of Christians, should be regarded as the soul of the whole ecumenical movement, and merits the name, "spiritual ecumenism." (UR 8)

A new connection is called for in the end, one in which all parties involved experience a change of heart and a new kind of ecumenism that is spiritual, as opposed to simply natural.[10]

One can easily argue that what Vatican II called "spiritual ecumenism" is that spiritual element that Simmel perceived to be at work in bridges. Vatican II sees the spiritual meaning of baptism to be just such a bridge. *Lumen Gentium* says:

> The Church [meaning the Roman Catholic Church] recognizes that in many ways she is linked with those who, being baptized, are honored with the name of Christian, though they do not profess the faith in its entirety or do not preserve unity of communion with the successor of Peter. (LR 14)

"Linking" is what bridges do well. One perceives here the elegance that Simmel argued bridges tend to display. *Lumen Gentium* goes on to state that "in some real way [these other baptized Christians] are joined with us in the Holy Spirit" (LG 15). How precisely that bridge of baptism actually joined them inside the Christian movement was not explained by the Council Fathers. As with any bridge, however, both its foundations and its workings were visible. *Lumen Gentium* later calls upon the laity to work in the world for justice and virtue. "By so doing they will imbue culture and human activity with genuine moral values; they will better prepare the field of the world for the seed of the Word of God; and at the same time they will open wider the doors of the Church by which the message of peace may enter the world" (LG 36). Here the door itself takes on elements of the pathway or bridge, as Simmel described them.

The divine revelation found in sacred scriptures was also a bridge. *Dei Verbum* ("Dogmatic Constitution on Divine Revelation") encourages cooperation with "separated brethren" in translating sacred scriptures into different languages, "should the opportunity arise and the Church authorities approve" (DV 22).

This last encouragement toward bridge-building reappears in *Ad Gentes*, the decree "On the Missionary Activity of the Church." *Ad*

---

[10]For a fuller discussion of the background to the term "spiritual ecumenism" that appears in *Unitatis Redintegratio* 8, including the role of Paul Couturier ("Paul Couturier can be Considered the Father of Spiritual Ecumenism"), see Pontifical Council for Promoting Christian Unity, "Reflection by Card. Walter Kasper: Charting the Road of the Ecumenical Movement," 2008, http://www.vatican.va/roman_curia/pontifical_councils/chrstuni/card-kasper-docs/rc_pc_chrstuni_doc_20080117_kasper-ecumenismo_en.html.

Gentes spoke of the ministry of "presence" among other peoples. It connected missionary activity, pastoral practice among those already baptized, and the effort to restore unity among Christians. In doing so, it transformed the understanding of baptism from being a door to being a bridge. Baptism connects Christians who are otherwise separated and divided.

> Catholics should cooperate in a brotherly spirit with their separated brethren, [according to the] norms of the Decree on Ecumenism, making before the nations a common profession of faith, insofar as their beliefs are common, in God and in Jesus Christ, and cooperating in social and in technical projects as well as in cultural and religious ones. Let them cooperate especially for the sake of Christ, their common Lord: let His Name be the bond that unites them. (AG 15)

Clearly, the documents of Vatican II sought both to separate and to connect. One finds ample examples of doors that were reinforced as Roman Catholic identity was at stake. There are numerous examples of Vatican II thinking in terms of "us" and "them." But one also finds more subtle evidence of bridges being built, at least from the Roman Catholic side of the divide.[11] In these moments Vatican II envisions a deeper spiritual reality in which "us" and "them" gives way to "us" and "us," and eventually simply "we."

One of the most enduring metaphors that emerged from Vatican II that circulated throughout many of its conversations was that of walking together into the future. It is often identified with Cardinal Augustin Bea, whose influence at Vatican II was noted above. Bea was a Jesuit who had served as rector of the Institute of Superior Ecclesiastical Studies and a professor at the Pontifical Biblical Institute in Rome before becoming its rector in 1930. In 1959 Pope John XXIII elevated him to the rank of a Cardinal Deacon, and the following year appointed him to serve as the first head of the newly formed Secretariat for Promoting Christian Unity. Two years later in 1962 John XXIII consecrated him as a bishop, just six months before the first session of Vatican II opened. Pope Paul VI, who was elected by the conclave of cardinals in 1963 following the death of John XXIII, reconfirmed Cardinal Bea's appointment as president of the

---

[11] In his original essay, Simmel noted that for a bridge to be built there must be cooperation on both sides of the project. One cannot effectively build a bridge across a chasm or divide if those on the other side remains hostile to the project, and are capable of defeating it.

Secretariat (now the Pontifical Council for Promoting Christian Unity), a position Bea held until his own death in 1968.

Roman Catholic Church teaching had long asserted that the only way for the unity of the Church to be realized was for followers of Jesus Christ who were members of other churches and communions to "return" to Rome. As Pope Leo XIII wrote in his 1896 encyclical, *Satis cognitum* ("On the Unity of the Church"), "...no small share of Our thoughts and of Our care is devoted to Our endeavour to bring back to the fold, placed under the guardianship of Jesus Christ, the Chief Pastor of souls, sheep that have strayed."[12] At Vatican II, due in no small part to the influence of Cardinal Bea, the metaphor shifted substantially. No longer were other Christians told that they had strayed and that unity could only be achieved by their return to Rome. Rather, in the words of Bea, Roman Catholics and other Christians would begin to walk together toward a new future. Bea is quoted later in an interview as saying:

> We are not talking about *un ritorno*. ... Members of other Christian churches who are living today never 'left' the church. So they cannot 'return' can they? We are talking about going together, hand in hand, toward a new future.[13]

The image took hold quickly in the halls of the Vatican. In an audience with Pope Paul VI early in the second session of the council on 17 October, 1963, Kristen Skydsgaard of the Lutheran World Federation spoke on behalf of all the delegates when he said:

> We also rejoice wholeheartedly at the new ecumenical spirit which is becoming manifest in this council. We find ourselves meeting together at the beginning of a road whose end God alone knows. It is for us to walk together in hope because we believe that the crucified and risen Christ is with us on the way. ...
>
> In concluding, I find myself moved to say: Yes, we are walking together, but our path leads us also "out of ourselves" toward our fellow men [and women]. ... It is thus that we shall be truly disciples of the Christ who did not desire to exist for Himself but solely for the world.[14]

---

[12] Leo XIII, Encyclical Letter *Satis Cognitum*, ASS 28 (1896): 708–39, no. 1.

[13] Quoted by Sullivan, *101 Questions and Answers on Vatican II*, 22.

[14] Floyd Anderson, ed., *Council Daybook Sessions I–II* (Washington, DC: National Catholic Welfare Conference, 1966), 198.

Walking together is, in Simmel's terms, an act of connecting. As an ecumenical act it entails two distinct moments. The first is to walk toward one another, or others, and the second is then to journey on together. The first act is necessary for the second to ensue, but it is the second that can be deemed the moment in which the spiritual connection begins to overcome what appears to be a natural divide. The path between two huts, or two communions, can appear to emerge naturally. The act of building a bridge requires a greater amount of visible intentionality, so that crossing it together can be better deemed a spiritual act. The willingness to walk a road or cross a bridge whose end God alone knows is truly a spiritual act of faith. It is truly the moment when the spiritual overcomes historical divides. Cardinal Bea warned that it would take time for the followers of Jesus Christ on earth to learn to walk together across the ecumenical bridge to the future.[15] Cardinal Kasper alerts us that it is a perennial task.[16] Now, more than fifty years after Vatican II we are still trying to do so.[17]

[15] See Cardinal Augustin Bea, "The Catholic Attitude Towards the Problem," in *The Unity of Christians*, ed. Bernard Leeming (London: Geoffrey Chapman, 1963), 23–37; see also Bea, *The Way to Unity after the Council*, trans. Gerard Noel (London: Geoffrey Chapman, 1967).

[16] "In every age of history, the principal artisans of reconciliation and unity were persons of prayer and contemplation, inspiring divided Christians to recommit themselves to walk the path of unity." Cardinal Walter Kasper, *A Handbook of Spiritual Ecumenism* (Hyde Park, NY: New City Press, 2007), 11.

[17] See Catherine E. Clifford, "Journeying Together: Ecumenism in the 21st Century," *One in Christ* 48, no. 1 (2014), 2–25; John A. Radano, *Lutheran and Catholic Reconciliation on Justification: A Chronology of the Holy See's Contributions, 1961–1999, to a New Relationship between Lutherans and Catholics and to Steps Leading to the Joint Declaration on the Doctrine of Justification* (Grand Rapids: Eerdmans, 2009); and Thaddeus D. Horton, ed. *Walking Together: Roman Catholics and Ecumenism Twenty-Five Years after Vatican II* (Grand Rapids: Eerdmans, 1990). Most recently Pope Francis reiterated the point that "[religious life] shows us precisely that this unity is not the fruit of our efforts, but is a gift of the Holy Spirit, Who realises unity in diversity. It also shows us that this unity can be achieved only by journeying together, if we take the path of fraternity in love, in service, and in mutual acceptance," quoted in "Francis: 'Unity is Achieved by Walking Together,'" *Vatican Information Service*, Monday, January 26, 2015, http://visnews-en.blogspot.com/2015/01/francis-unity-is-achieved-by-walking.html.

CHAPTER 14

Vatican II: A Shift in the Attitude of the Roman Catholic Church Toward the Reformation Churches?—A Protestant Perspective

Dagmar Heller

INTRODUCTION

The Second Vatican Council is first of all an event of and within the Church of Rome. But it is at the same time "a milestone also from a Protestant perspective,"[1] as one of the leaders of the Evangelical Church in Germany (EKD) has pointed out in recent years. In this paper I explore the way in which this council is to be considered as such a milestone for Protestant churches, particularly in the German context. I thus use the

---

[1] Thies Gundlach, the Vice President of the Church House of the Evangelical Church in Germany, made this comment in one of the largest-circulating German daily newspapers. "Das Zweite Vatikanische Konzil ist auch in protestantischer Perspektive ein Meilenstein," *Frankfurter Allgemeine Zeitung*, October 30, 2012, http://www.faz.net/aktuell/politik/inland/fremde-federn-zweites-vatikanum-und-reformation-11943859.html, my translation.

D. Heller (✉)
Institute for Ecumenical Studies and Research, Bensheim, Germany
e-mail: dagmar.heller@ki-eb.de

© The Author(s) 2018   217
V. Latinovic et al. (eds.), *Catholicism Opening to the World and Other Confessions*, Pathways for Ecumenical and Interreligious Dialogue,
https://doi.org/10.1007/978-3-319-98581-7_14

term 'Protestant churches' here in the narrow sense of 'churches of the Reformation,' especially the Lutheran and Reformed churches. The German ecclesial landscape has a few specificities compared with other countries in Europe and the world. Germany is, of course, the land where the Reformation began. But more importantly, Germany is also a country, where Protestants—now existing as members of Lutheran, Reformed and United local churches, which are in full communion with each other—and Catholics live closely together. The two traditions are the majority among the Christian traditions in the country, and after the Second World War the distribution of the Catholic population and the Protestant population changed from a geographical separation to a nearly equal mixture in all the geographical regions of Germany. Therefore, among the Christian population in Germany there are very seldom families that are 'purely' Catholic or 'purely' Protestant.[2] This development has had an enormous influence on the cohabitation of the two churches. Because of this, the interest among Protestants in what happens in the Roman Catholic Church in general and in what happened in Vatican II in particular was significant at the time of the council and remains so today. For this reason, I focus my reflections on the Catholic Church's shift in attitude mainly on the German context, but at the same time I will take into consideration the perspective of the World Council of Churches (WCC) insofar as it was discussed in the German context.

First, I will give a brief overview of how the announcement of the Council was received by Protestants, before I will examine the significance of the Second Vatican Council in the view of Protestant commentators and observers. The third part of my essay will explore Protestant critique at the Council, before I provide a survey of how Protestants assess the Council fifty years after its conclusion. I will end with an evaluation of how the achievements of the Council could be taken forward in the future.

PROTESTANT REACTIONS TO THE ANNOUNCEMENT OF THE SECOND VATICAN COUNCIL

The announcement of the Second Vatican Council by Pope John XXIII came as a surprise for the Roman Catholic Church itself, but even more so for the non-Catholic world.[3] The simple idea that an ecumenical

---

[2] Exceptions to this rule can be found, of course, but mostly in rural areas.

[3] See Bernard Sesboüé, "Vatican II (Concile de)," in *Encyclopédie du protestantisme*, ed. Pierre Gisel, 2nd rev. ed. (Geneva: Labor et Fides, 2006), 1471–73, at 1471.

council should take place, i.e. a council which was to take decisions for the whole Roman Catholic Church, was unthinkable in the eyes of many, because after the definition of papal infallibility at the First Vatican Council another council seemed no longer necessary.[4] But even more surprising was the fact that the pope invited non-Catholic churches and individuals to send or to attend the council as observers. The Lutheran theologian André Birmélé at Strasbourg (France) writes that this "ecumenical openness which was announced in the convocation of the council provoked a certain skepticism on the side of the Reformation churches that were engaged in an ecumenical effort officially condemned by Rome in 1928 (Pius XI's Encyclical *Mortalium Animos*)."[5] But in addition to the skeptical voices there were also enthusiastic and very positive reactions. The German Protestant theologian Peter Meinhold, for example, encouraged Protestant Christians to await this council with certain hopes.[6] In brief, there were a variety of reactions on the Protestant side,[7] but one point was clear for almost everyone: this council would have an effect beyond the Roman Catholic Church. Therefore, its convocation produced many expectations among Protestants.

Meinhold pointed out that Protestant Christians felt directly addressed by the announcement of the Council in 1959, because this convocation was, according to Pope John XXIII's own words, also "a renewed invitation to the faithful of the separated communities that they also may follow us amiably in this search for unity and grace, to which so many souls aspire in all parts of the earth."[8] This announcement expressed that the Council's objective was the renewal of the church, which is the precondition of all efforts toward the unity of the

---

[4] See André Birmélé, "Vatican II (Concile de)," in *Encyclopédie du protestantisme*, 1473; see also Edmund Schlink, *After the Council: The Meaning of Vatican II for Protestantism and the Ecumenical Dialogue* (Philadelphia: Fortress, 1968), 21; and Paul Metzger, "'Eine Blume in einem unerwarteten Frühling': Das 2. Vatikanische Konzil aus evangelischer Sicht," in *Pfälzisches Pfarrerblatt*, http://www.pfarrerblatt.de/.

[5] Birmélé, "Vatican II (Concile de)."

[6] Peter Meinhold, "Was erwarten evangelische Christen vom angekündigten ökumenischen Konzil?," in *Der evangelische Christ und das Konzil* (Herder: Freiburg, 1961), 19–48, at 37.

[7] See Ernst Benz, "Das zweite Vatikanische Konzil in protestantischer Sicht," *Ökumenische Rundschau* 15 (1966): 137–61, at 137.

[8] John XXIII, alloc. *Questa festiva*, AAS 51 (1959): 65–69, at 69.

Christians.[9] Meinhold sees very clearly that 'unity' in this announcement neither means the proposal of a union nor the idea of a reunification, but that it is an invitation to the other churches to journey with the Roman Catholic Church in the search for Christian unity.[10] It is an invitation that does not ask for any conditions, i.e., it does not question a priori the dogmatic bases of the other churches. Based on this observation Meinhold articulates—already before the beginning of the Council— several expectations of the Protestant churches:

- that the Council would not declare new dogmas, as this would be an obstacle for the other churches;
- a development of the teaching on the church that takes into consideration the self-understanding of the separated churches;
- a search for unity in two directions: with the Christians of the East and the Christians of the Reformation.[11]

An interesting aspect of Meinhold's reflections is his clear recognition, as a Protestant, that the Orthodox churches and the Roman Catholic Church regard their ecclesiologies as closer to each other than the Roman Catholic Church does to the Reformation churches. But he reminds at the same time that culturally and intellectually the Protestant churches and the Roman Catholic Church are connected through a common history, which links the two deeply in service of, as he says, the "*salus animarum*," the salvation of the souls.[12]

THE SIGNIFICANCE OF VATICAN II IN PROTESTANT PERSPECTIVE

The Second Vatican Council was announced as an 'ecumenical' council. In other words, it was meant to give direction to the whole church and to deal with issues that are relevant for the whole world. In this sense it was clear from the beginning that this council was not merely intra-Roman Catholic business but would have repercussions in the other

[9] Peter Meinhold, "Was erwarten evangelische Christen vom angekündigten ökumenischen Konzil?," 22.

[10] Ibid., 23.

[11] See Meinhold, "Was erwarten evangelische Christen," 38–39.

[12] Ibid., 41–42.

churches. Protestants would have to relate in some way to the decisions of the Council.

One can identify two closely linked areas in which Vatican II is significant for Protestants. Firstly, the Council marks a general opening of the attitude of the Roman Catholic Church toward the other churches, including the Protestant churches. A comparison with official teaching from just three decades before Pope John called the council makes this clear: While Pius XI's *Mortalium Animus* wanted to bring about "the return to the one true Church of Christ of those who are separated from it,"[13] the Decree on Ecumenism of Vatican II, *Unitatis Redintegratio*, speaks about the Christians separated from the Catholic Church in a totally different way. "[T]he Catholic Church embraces upon them as brothers, with respect and affection" (UR 3). Secondly, and more specifically, the Council is, in relation to some divisive theological issues, the beginning of a movement toward convergences[14] with Protestant convictions. Let us examine these two areas in greater detail.

Opening Toward Other Churches

The Second Vatican Council has to be understood in the context of the changing world in the twentieth century. Two world wars, rapidly growing technical development, increasing means of communication, and at the same time the changing situation of Christianity with a significant growth in the global South and signs of secularization and stagnation in the North provided sufficient reasons for Christians to re-think their mutual relationships. The Protestant churches, together with their Orthodox brethren, had already in 1948 taken part in the creation of the World Council of Churches (WCC), putting the unity of the churches and the question of peace for the world in the center of its raison d'être.

---

[13] Pius XI, Encyclical Letter, *Mortalium Animos*, AAS 20 (1928): 5–16, no. 10.

[14] I use here the term 'convergence' in the meaning that was developed by the work of the Commission on Faith and Order of the WCC and especially through its first 'convergence document,' "Baptism, Eucharist and Ministry" (Geneva: WCC Publications, 1982). Convergence is not consensus, but a certain rapprochement of different positions. The rapprochement between the Roman Catholic and the Lutheran Church, that began with the Second Vatican Council, culminated in 1999 in the Joint Declaration on Justification, which used as method the 'differentiated consensus,' which is a variation of the convergence method.

It is probably not by chance[15] that Vatican II was being prepared for around the same time that the WCC was consolidated at its Assembly in New Delhi in 1961, an assembly marked by the expansion of the WCC membership to the global South and to the Orthodox East.

While in 1928 the Encyclical *Mortalium Animos* also stated that "it is clear that the Apostolic See cannot on any terms take part in their assemblies [i.e., those of "non-Catholics who loudly promote the brotherly fellowship in Jesus Christ"], nor is it anyway lawful for Catholics either to support or to work for such enterprises,"[16] Pope John XXIII in his announcement of the Council clearly addressed also the "separated communities" and his hopes that the Council would be "a gentle invitation to seek and find that unity for which Jesus Christ prayed so ardently to His Father in heaven."[17] This was a clear change in the Roman Catholic mind and an opening to the ecumenical movement, which resulted in the even more surprising decision of John XXIII to send Roman Catholic observers to the WCC assembly in New Delhi.

This new attitude is connected with a fundamental change of the Roman Catholic Church in its official ecclesiology as it found its expression at the Second Vatican Council. The Protestant theologian from Heidelberg, Edmund Schlink, who attended the Council as observer of the Evangelical Church in Germany (EKD), describes the ecclesiological approach beginning from salvation history which is found in the Dogmatic Constitution on the Church, *Lumen Gentium*, as "a significant advance from the *schema* on the church in the First Vatican Council [...] The concepts and lines of thought are now determined far more strongly by the Bible [...] it concentrates on the understanding of the church as the onward-moving, saving, all-inclusive activity of the triune God."[18] It is here, that Schlink finds the door for "new possibilities for ecumenical dialogue,"[19] because *Lumen Gentium* replaces "the

---

[15] Several commentators pointed to the mutual influence between Vatican II and the WCC Assembly at New Delhi; see Klaus Fitschen, "Das II. Vatikanische Konzil in der deutschsprachigen evangelischen Kirchengeschichtsschreibung," *Berliner Theologische Zeitschrift* 31 (2014): 244–55, at 244.

[16] Pius XI, *Mortalium Animos*, 8.

[17] The whole third part of John's encyclical manifests this tone of openness. John XXIII, Encyclical Letter, *Ad Petri Cathedram*, AAS 51 (1959): 479–531, no. 62.

[18] Schlink, *After the Council*, 68.

[19] Ibid., 69.

traditional ontological structure of nature and super-nature" of the church.

One of the most crucial issues that needs to be mentioned here from a Protestant point of view is the famous formula in *Lumen Gentium* 8: The "Church constituted and organized in the world as a society, subsists in the Catholic Church, which is governed by the successor of Peter and by the Bishops in communion with him..." Observers note that this formulation was a change to the original proposal in the schema, and is thus specifically important to understand the new thinking in the Roman Catholic Church. Schlink tells us that "[o]ccasionally...theologians of the Council were heard to say that this modification of the church's exclusiveness was merely taking into account the fact that the church is a reality not only on earth in the Roman church but also in the heavenly fellowship of the perfected saints."[20] But it is clear to him from the context and from the reasons which led to this formulation "that the exclusiveness of identifying the one, holy, catholic and apostolic church with the Roman church was to be relaxed within the realm of the church's earthly existence itself."[21] For Kristen E. Skydsgaard this formula "indicates clearly a change in the spiritual climate of the Roman Catholic Church of today."[22] Also the fact, that "[t]he fathers... changed the statement of the second draft [of *Lumen Gentium*] that elements of holiness and truth 'can be found' (*inveniri possint*) to 'are found' (*inveniantur*) in churches not in communion with Rome"[23] indicates a real change of attitude. Several decades later the late Friedrich Weber, bishop of the Lutheran Church of Braunschweig in Germany, characterized this formula as a "self-relativization" (*Selbstrelativierung*) which until today is actual, but at the same time constitutes one of the 'open questions' of the Council. Weber means that the text's failure to say 'the Church is (*est*) the Catholic Church'—as was originally proposed—opens the possibility that the church exists also outside the Catholic Church. This is something new. But Schlink already had noted that "the possibilities for openness toward others suggested by 'subsists in' are to be pursued only

---

[20] Ibid., 87–88.

[21] Ibid., 88.

[22] Kristen E. Skydsgaard, "The Church as Mystery and as People of God," in *Dialogue on the Way: Protestants Report from Rome on the Council*, ed. George A. Lindbeck (Minneapolis: Augsburg, 1965), 145–74, at 155.

[23] Ibid., correcting a typographical error in the Latin.

with extreme caution."[24] Skydsgaard also realized that "the text... will probably cause many and different interpretations in years to come."[25] Indeed, until today the Latin word *subsistit* in the quoted formula is open to different interpretations—but I will return to this matter later. It needs to be noted here that in any case this formula is the basis for the Council's ability—in the same text, *Lumen Gentium*—to recognize "elements" of ecclesiality also outside of its own borders. And further: the text can even speak about a 'connection' or link with those who are baptized outside the Catholic Church. "The Church recognizes that in many ways she is linked with those who, being baptized, are honored with the name of Christian, though they do not profess the faith in its entirety or do not preserve unity of communion with the successor of Peter" (LG 15).[26] This is definitely new in the Roman Catholic Church, where only decades before declarations were made that nobody outside the church could be saved.[27] This new perspective on the church finds even stronger expression in the Decree on Ecumenism *Unitatis Redintegratio*. Schlink shows that the decree "goes beyond the assertion in the [Dogmatic] Constitution on the Church"[28] in that *Unitatis Redintegratio* speaks about "churches" outside the Roman Catholic Church, while *Lumen Gentium* merely finds "elements" of the church outside the borders of the Roman Catholic Church.

But the Decree on Ecumenism is above all important—as Protestant theologians highlighted—because it said farewell to an ecumenism of return (*Rückkehrökumene*).[29]

> [...] it remains true that all who have been justified by faith in Baptism are members of Christ's body, and have a right to be called Christian, and so are correctly accepted as brothers by the children of the Catholic Church. [...] It follows that the separated Churches and Communities as

[24] Schlink, *After the Council*, 88.

[25] Skydsgaard, "The Church as Mystery," 155.

[26] The original Latin text uses the word *coniunctam*, "connected," for "linked" here. The text cites Gal 4:6 and Rom 8:15–16, 26 as support for this approach.

[27] See, for example, Pius IX's 1854 allocution *Singulari Quidem*, 1856, http://www.papalencyclicals.net/Pius09/p9singul.htm.

[28] Schlink, *After the Council*, 103.

[29] See, for example, Heinz-Dietrich Wendland, *Die ökumenische Bewegung und das II. Vatikanische Konzil* (Cologne: Westdeutscher Verlag, 1968), 17.

such, though we believe them to be deficient in some respects, have been by no means deprived of significance and importance in the mystery of salvation. For the Spirit of Christ has not refrained from using them as means of salvation which derive their efficacy from the very fullness of grace and truth entrusted to the Church. (UR 3)

This is definitely a new tone for Protestant ears, especially if one compares it with the condemnations of Protestants in decrees of the Council of Trent, for example, and Schlink is right in saying: "This decree... is without a doubt a significant change and correction of the traditional position of the Roman Catholic Church."[30] Ernst Benz and others showed that this newness, though, is not a change that would destroy the continuity of Roman Catholic doctrine. The Catholic Church preserved its basic attitude, but "the form and the method of the encounter with non-Catholic Christians was changed."[31]

Theological Convergences with Reformation Positions

Secondly, I will examine some of the main *theological issues* in the texts of Vatican II with which Protestants were able to identify convergences with Reformation thought.

Following Pope Paul VI,[32] Birmélé describes the systematic of the whole work of the Council as three concentric circles[33]: the first circle is dedicated to issues concerning the Roman Catholic Church itself; the second one deals with issues concerning the non-catholic churches; and the last one deals with other religions and humanity in general. But Birmélé sees clearly that "the ecumenical options and the opening toward the world [the second and third circles] are only the application of the new orientations which were stated in the first of the concentric circles."[34] This means that the openness of the Council consists in the consequences of its reflections on the *church*, on *revelation* and on the

---

[30] Edmund Schlink, "The Decree on Ecumenism," in Lindbeck, *Dialogue on the Way*, 186–230, at 188.

[31] Benz, "Das zweite Vatikanische Konzil in protestantischer Sicht."

[32] In his encyclical *Ecclesiam Suam*, AAS 56 (1964), 609–59; see Schlink, *After the Council*, 42.

[33] Birmélé, "Vatican II (Concile de)."

[34] Ibid.

liturgy, which are the three main areas of work related to the Roman Catholic Church itself, the first circle.[35] For this reason, one must examine closely the Council's teaching on these three themes and how Protestants commented upon it.

The Church

The importance of the Council's understanding of the church as a 'mystery' as well as the emphasis on the Eucharist and its significance for the life of the church was noted by Lukas Vischer, the official observer for the WCC, already in his report on the third session of the Council.[36] For Vischer the text of *Lumen Gentium* is—in an ecumenical perspective— "of highest significance" (*von höchster Bedeutung*).[37] He discovers in *Lumen Gentium* a conception of the church that differs from the traditional one in Catholic theology, in that the text emphasizes the church as people of God. Thus, the hierarchy is not located in a place above the people, but in the midst of the people. Vischer also observes that the idea of collegiality opens a new dimension in Roman Catholic ecclesiology, namely the possibility that in the future the responsibility for the direction of the church will lie with the bishops as a community more than in the past.[38] These are certainly rapprochements toward ideas that the churches of the Reformation emphasized and developed.

Revelation

Birmélé states that "The Constitution on Divine Revelation gives new importance to the study of the Word of God, of which Holy Scripture is the first witness."[39] The novel element is *Dei Verbum*'s teaching that "the study of the sacred page is, as it were, the soul of sacred theology" (DV 24). In another place this Constitution says "She [=the church]

---

[35] "Die Bedeutung des Konzils liegt ...in erster Linie darin, dass sich in ihm wie in einem Prisma Themen und Fragen der damaligen Gegenwart bündelten und so auf den Weg gebracht wurden, dass sie bis heute nachwirken." Metzger specifies this for the Protestant perspective in three ways: (1) the understanding of the church, (2) the understanding of revelation, and (3) the understanding of worship. Metzger, "'Eine Blume in einem unerwarteten Frühling.'"

[36] Lukas Vischer, "Nach der dritten Session des zweiten Vatikanischen Konzils," *Ökumenische Rundschau* 14 (1965): 97–116, at 99.

[37] Ibid.

[38] Ibid., 100.

[39] Birmélé, "Vatican II (Concile de)."

has always maintained them [=the Scriptures], and continues to do so, together with sacred tradition, as the supreme rule of faith" (DV 21). The Magisterium or "teaching office" of the church "is not above the word of God, but serves it" (DV 10). Oscar Cullmann, another Protestant observer and New Testament scholar, showed that practically in all texts of Vatican II "the biblical... ferment is trying to make its way."[40] This role given to Scripture is thus another point, where Protestants can identify a rapprochement toward them from the side of the Roman Catholic Church, although they criticize that Scripture is still not seen as critical norm of the tradition.[41] The Lutheran theologian Ulrich Kühn, therefore understands *Dei Verbum* as the ecumenically most important text of the Council.[42]

The Liturgy

The new accent on Scripture finds expression also in the Constitution on the Sacred Liturgy, *Sacrosanctum Concilium*. In this constitution several requests of the reformers were finally adopted, primarily that the "full and active participation by all the people is the aim to be considered before all else; for it is the primary and indispensable source from which the faithful are to derive the true Christian spirit..." (SC 14). Observers also considered the constitution's description of worship as the word of God and the response of the people (SC 33) in line with the insights of Martin Luther.[43] In addition, Protestant commentators highlight the possibility of the communion from the chalice for the people and

---

[40] Oscar Cullmann, "Was bedeutet das Zweite Vatikanische Konzil für uns Protestanten?," in *Was bedeutet das zweite Vatikanische Konzil für uns?*, ed. Werner Schatz (Basel: Reinhardt, 1967), 15–52; see also Cullmann, "The Bible in the Council," in Lindbeck, *Dialogue on the Way*, 129–44.

[41] See Friederike Nüssel, "Dei Verbum – die Offenbarungslehre des II. Vatikanischen Konzils in der evangelisch-theologischen Rezeption," *Berliner Theologische Zeitschrift* 31 (2014): 256–82, at 272. Also Karl Barth sees a progress in how the Council places the Bible, but at the same time he finds passages that obscure these new insights. See Karl Barth, *Ad Limina Apostolorum* (Zürich: EVZ-Verlag, 1967).

[42] See Nüssel, "Dei Verbum," who refers to Ulrich Kühn, *Die Ergebnisse des II. Vatikanischen Konzils* (Berlin: Evangelische Verlagsanstalt, 1967), 47.

[43] See Friedrich Weber, "Das II. Vatikanische Konzil und die Ökumene. Beobachtungen aus der Sicht eines Protestanten," Vortrag am 13. February 2012 im ökumenischen Forum Osnabrück, 3–4, http://www.landeskirche-braunschweig.de/uploads/tx_mitdownload/Vortrag_Vaticanum_II_Osnabrueck_2012.pdf.

the celebration of the liturgy in the vernacular as steps forward. Weber emphasizes that the celebration of mass in the local language has helped many Christians of different churches to know each other better.[44]

PROBLEMS OF THE SECOND VATICAN COUNCIL IN PROTESTANT PERSPECTIVE

It was clear for the Protestant observers of the Council that all new ideas and changes manifest in the texts of Vatican II, including the more open attitude toward other Christians, had their limits. Oscar Cullmann, for example, observes that while the new emphasis on the college of bishops the Roman Catholic Church comes closer to the structure of the church of the New Testament, it is also clear that the dogma of the primacy of the pope cannot be removed.[45]

Considering these limits Protestant theologians in general see the Second Vatican Council and its texts positively,[46] but they discern also some problems. Benz sees in the Council a fundamental tendency expressing a spiritual and theological attitude that is new and irrevocable, but nevertheless states that all the decisions of Vatican II pointing in a new direction are formulated in a way permitting their interpretation in a traditional sense.[47] This observation is confirmed, for example, for one detail in Vischer's report after the third session of the Council. He saw that the text of the *Lumen Gentium* contains two possibilities: the continuation of the monarchic structure, which comes from the First Vatican Council, or the substitution of that structure by a collegial structure.[48] In his final report Vischer on the one hand appreciates the ecumenical

---

[44] Ibid., 4.

[45] Cullmann, "Was bedeutet das Zweite Vatikanische Konzil für uns Protestanten?," 36; see also Schlink, *After the Council*, 75.

[46] For a survey on reactions from observers of Vatican II, see André Birmélé, "Le Concile Vatican II vu par les observateurs des autres traditions chrétiennes," in *Volti di fine concilio: Studi di storia e teologia sulla conclusione del Vaticano II*, ed. Joseph Doré and Alberto Meloni (Bologna: Mulino: 2000), 225–64, at 263.

[47] "Im II. Vatikanum sind zwar alle in eine neue Richtung weisenden Beschlüsse so sorgsam gefasst, dass sie im Notfall auch ganz traditionalistisch rückinterpretiert werden können…" Benz, "Das Zweite Vatikanische Konzil in protestantischer Sicht," 144.

[48] Vischer, "Nach der dritten Session…," 100.

progress of the Council, but also the limitations of the Council here, which he summarizes in three points[49]:

- The Catholic Church is able to open itself to other churches, but she has difficulties to integrate herself into a community of churches;
- When there is a conflict between the renewal of the church in its universality and ecumenical responsibility, a form of Roman Catholic universalism can take priority—one can describe the Catholic attitude toward ecumenism as: 'Yes, but not too much';
- Ecumenism has achieved support at official levels of the Catholic Church, but at the same time, this limits the spontaneity of the movement.

Concretely Vischer sees the Second Vatican Council as a major step forward for ecumenism in the Roman Catholic Church but also recognizes that this council did not solve the question of *how* the churches can live in communion.[50]

This becomes even clearer when one studies the question of the church in the texts of Vatican II more closely: Although the Council recognizes also in the other churches elements which lead to salvation—as shown above—it seems that the only way toward unity is conversion. For example, *Unitatis Redintegratio* begins very positively and admits mistakes on both sides.

> Even in the beginnings of this one and only Church of God there arose certain rifts, which the Apostle strongly condemned. But in subsequent centuries much more serious dissensions made their appearance and quite large communities came to be separated from full communion with the Catholic Church – for which, often enough, men of both sides were to blame. (UR 3)

But, a little later in the same section, Protestants often have the impression that the text moves ecumenically backward.

---

[49] Vischer, "Nach der vierten Session des Zweiten Vatikanischen Konzils," *Ökumenische Rundschau* 15 (1966): 81–120, at 118.

[50] Ibid., 119.

Nevertheless, our separated brethren, whether considered as individuals or as Communities and Churches, are not blessed with that unity which Jesus Christ wished to bestow on all those who through Him were born again into one body, and with Him quickened to newness of life - that unity which the Holy Scriptures and the ancient Tradition of the Church proclaim. *For it is only through Christ's Catholic Church, which is "the all-embracing means of salvation," that they can benefit fully from the means of salvation.* We believe that Our Lord entrusted all the blessings of the New Covenant to the apostolic college alone, of which Peter is the head, in order to establish the one Body of Christ on earth to which all should be fully incorporated who belong in any way to the people of God. (UR 3)[51]

Weber describes this paragraph as the most disappointing text of *Unitatis Redintegratio*, because it expresses clearly that in order to achieve unity, others must 'incorporate' themselves into the church over which Peter presides.[52] This is also the reason why some Protestants, including Dietz Lange, concluded that the Second Vatican Council did not ultimately change anything in the Roman Catholic understanding of ecumenism as the attempt to bring the other churches back to Rome.[53]

Another point of Protestant critique relates to the role of Holy Scripture: Metzger and Weber[54] highlight the tension between the idea of Scripture as the highest rule of faith, and a continuing emphasis on the role of the ecclesial teaching office. The first, as I showed above, draws near to Luther's idea of Scripture as the highest judge. The second, including texts like this, troubles Protestants: "But the task of authentically interpreting the word of God, whether written or handed on, has been entrusted exclusively to the living teaching office of the Church, whose authority is exercised in the name of Jesus Christ" (DV 10).

These are not the only points that Protestant commentators found problematic in the texts of Vatican II. Schlink talks about a "dialectic" and offers a whole list of tensions in the texts of the Council.[55]

---

[51] Italics mine.

[52] Weber, "Das II. Vatikanische Konzil," 11.

[53] Bernd Oberdorfer gives an overview on different German Protestant theologians interpreting Vatican II; see "Ein anderes Gegenüber? Protestantische Dogmatik nach dem II. Vatikanum," *Berliner Theologische Zeitschrift* 31 (2014): 359–82, at 374.

[54] Metzger, "'Eine Blume in einem unerwarteten Frühling,'" Chapter 2; see also Weber, "Das II. Vatikanische Konzil," 7.

[55] Schlink, *After the Council*, 187–88.

Here I mention only the most important for the ecumenical quest. Tensions lie:

- between a strong and new accentuation of Holy Scripture on the one hand, and on the other the placement of Scripture in the Tradition and its subordination under the magisterium;
- between a strong accentuation of the structure of communion and a new understanding of ecclesial unity as communion of particular churches on the one hand, and on the other a doctrinal and juridical guarantee of papal primacy in the line of Vatican I;
- between the positive declarations on the non-Catholic churches and communities in the Decree on Ecumenism on the one hand, and on the other a recognition of only "elements of sanctification" and truth outside of the borders of the church of Rome;
- between the idea of unity of the churches as mutual reconciliation on the one hand, and on the other elements of the concept of others' return and submission;
- between the recognition that grace is effective beyond the baptized on the one hand, and on the other the attachment to the phrase 'there is no salvation outside the church'.

While many Protestant commentators believe that these tensions result from the nature of the conciliar documents as compromises, Schlink thinks that these tensions manifest not only tactical or political necessities. The Council affirmed them "as an appropriate expression of the catholicity of the Roman church."[56]

THE SECOND VATICAN COUNCIL AND THE FOLLOWING 50 YEARS

After the Second Vatican Council, Benz said that the change of attitude of the Roman Catholic Church toward the other churches would need to be tested through the practical consequences that would follow the Council.[57] Thus, if one wants to say something about the Second Vatican Council from a Protestant perspective, one must also look at the reception of the decisions of the Council. In other words, one must

---

[56] Ibid., 189.
[57] Benz, "Das zweite Vatikanische Konzil in protestantischer Sicht," 156.

examine how the Council was received by the Catholic Church and how its decisions were put into practice. In this regard two developments have to be mentioned.

First, there have been many ecumenical initiatives on the part of the Catholic Church. For example, after the Council the Catholic Church began to participate in the Commission on Faith and Order of the WCC and established a Joint Working Group with the World Council of Churches. In addition, a wide range of bilateral dialogues with different churches was established and sincere ecumenical work was promoted in different ways. For Benz one of the expected consequences, which would serve as a test, would be the withdrawal of the condemnations, which were expressed by the Council of Trent in the sixteenth century. The Lutheran churches and Rome during the years following Vatican II worked on this question, resulting in the *Joint Declaration on the Doctrine of Justification (JDDJ)*, in which it states:

> 41. Thus the doctrinal condemnations of the 16th century, in so far as they relate to the doctrine of justification, appear in a new light: The teaching of the Lutheran churches presented in this Declaration does not fall under the condemnations from the Council of Trent. The condemnations in the Lutheran Confessions do not apply to the teaching of the Roman Catholic Church presented in this Declaration.
>
> 42. Nothing is thereby taken away from the seriousness of the condemnations related to the doctrine of justification. Some were not simply pointless. They remain for us 'salutary warnings' to which we must attend in our teaching and practice.[58]

Have Benz's expectations been accomplished? The answer in my view is: yes and no. The *Joint Declaration* does not withdraw the condemnations, but declares that the condemnations no longer concern the other side. This is, in a certain way, the same tension that we saw in the texts of Vatican II. On the one hand, they raise hopes and express a sincere respect for the Protestant side; on the other, they contain formulas that are difficult for Protestants to understand and to accept, especially if they have no further consequences concerning a common Eucharistic table.

---

[58] The Lutheran World Federation and the Roman Catholic Church, *Joint Declaration on the Doctrine of Justification* (Grand Rapids: Eerdmans, 2000), nos. 41–42.

Second, during recent decades Protestants have also observed a tendency among *some* Catholics to interpret the texts of Vatican II in a conservative way regarding the Council's attitude toward Protestants.[59] I mention here only the discussion about how to understand the phrase *subsistit in* (LG 8). The 2000 Declaration *Dominus Iesus*, issued by the Congregation for the Doctrine of the Faith, clearly states that there is only one single true church. The declaration interprets *Lumen Gentium* in the following way:

> With the expression *subsistit in*, the Second Vatican Council sought to harmonize two doctrinal statements: on the one hand, that the Church of Christ, despite the divisions which exist among Christians, continues to exist fully only in the Catholic Church, and on the other hand, that 'outside of her structure, many elements can be found of sanctification and truth,' that is, in those Churches and ecclesial communities which are not yet in full communion with the Catholic Church. But with respect to these, it needs to be stated that 'they derive their efficacy from the very fullness of grace and truth entrusted to the Catholic Church.' ... Therefore, there exists a single Church of Christ, which subsists in the Catholic Church, governed by the Successor of Peter and by the Bishops in communion with him.[60]

As Birmélé puts it: "Although the Council did not emphasize it expressis verbis, it was now [in *Lumen Gentium*] thinkable that the Church of Jesus Christ could be realized also in other traditions. But *Dominus Iesus* puts paid to this idea."[61] Birmélé shows the hermeneutical problem of this passage, which tries to combine two statements of the Council that were originally not connected with each other.

---

[59] Some Protestant theologians, however, are of the opinion that *Dominus Iesus* simply repeats the positions of *Lumen Gentium* and *Unitatis Redintegratio* and does not show a 'conservative' turn; see Eilert Herms, "Das Ökumenismusdekret. Sein Ort in der Lehre des Zweiten Vatikanums und seine heutige Bedeutung," *Berliner Theologische Zeitschrift* 31 (2014): 283–306, at 298. Some Catholic theologians hold to a similar position, too.

[60] Congregation for the Doctrine of the Faith, Declaration *Dominus Iesus*, AAS 92 (2000): 742–65, no. 16–17.

[61] André Birmélé, "Die Rezeption des zweiten Vatikanischen Konzils in der Ökumene: ein evangelischer Beitrag," Gastvorlesung an der Katholischen Fakultät der Universität Tübingen, 13–14. http://www.strasbourginstitute.org/wp-content/uploads/2012/11/DialogLuthRCReceptionVatikanII.pdf; translation mine.

In 2007 a clarification on the matter came from the Congregation for the Doctrine of the Faith under the title "Responses to Some Questions Regarding Certain Aspects of the Doctrine on the Church." It stated:

> It is possible, according to Catholic doctrine, to affirm correctly that the Church of Christ is present and operative in the churches and ecclesial Communities not yet fully in communion with the Catholic Church, on account of the elements of sanctification and truth that are present in them. Nevertheless, the word 'subsists' can only be attributed to the Catholic Church alone precisely because it refers to the mark of unity that we profess in the symbols of the faith (I believe... in the 'one' Church); and this 'one' Church subsists in the Catholic Church.[62]

The fact that the word *subsistit* is reserved for the Roman Catholic Church raised—and still raises—questions on the Protestant side.[63] This one example illustrates that the danger commentators like Vischer already saw during their presence at the Council is real. They noticed that the texts of Vatican II had a certain openness to several interpretations, including a conservative one.

CONCLUSION

In summary, this survey shows clearly that most Protestant commentators agree that the Second Vatican Council was an "event of extraordinary dimensions."[64] It meant an opening of the Roman Catholic Church toward the other churches and toward the world, and a change in the church's sense of self at the center of that shift. In relation to the Protestant churches clear convergences with ideas of the Reformers of the sixteenth century can be identified. At the same time, the main critique on the Protestant side is the observation of a certain ambiguity or lack of clarity in the texts of the Council.

---

[62] Congregation for the Doctrine of the Faith, "Responses to Some Questions Regarding Certain Aspects of the Doctrine on the Church," AAS 99, no. 7 (2007): 604–8, Response to the Second Question.

[63] See Michael Plathow, "Unerledigt und verheissungsvoll: Zum 50. Jubiläum des Ii. Vatikanischen Konzils aus evangelischer Sicht," *Deutsches Pfarrerblatt* 112 (2012): 629–32, http://www.pfarrerverband.de/pfarrerblatt/dpb_print.php?id=3267.

[64] "ein kirchengeschichtliches ereignis von aussergewöhnlichen Dimensionen"; translation mine. Kühn, *Die Ergebnisse des II.Vatikanischen Konzils*, 163.

Nevertheless, Protestants in general have understood that the Second Vatican Council opened new ecumenical possibilities. One must be cautious, as Schlink puts it, for "(m)aking these possibilities a reality, ... depends not only on the Roman church but also on the manner in which other churches assess the altered situation and the kind of stance they take in relation to the Roman church."[65] This means that the Council needs to be taken as a question to the other churches.[66] In this way it is the beginning of a dialogue that continues until today and that led to certain results, but that has not yet led to unity. The reason for this situation can be seen in the same ambiguity identified by Protestant commentators in the texts of the Council. But it is obvious that all too frequently both sides in a dialogue are responsible for whether or not progress or stagnation emerges. Therefore one must inquire critically whether the other churches—and especially the Protestants—have taken the Council as also posing questions in relation to their own attitude toward the Roman Catholic Church, a question beyond the scope of this essay.

I would like therefore to conclude with a proposal made by Michael Bünker. He refers to *Unitatis Redintegratio* 4, which talks about the fact that the church cannot have the fullness of catholicity because of schisms. This means that also the Catholic Church suffers from a certain *defectus*. Bünker proposes to reflect together, Catholics and Protestants—and here I would also include the Orthodox—on the meaning of catholicity.[67] In a world with a growing pluralism and individualism, which also affects the churches, it is necessary to gain anew the understanding and awareness of what it means to be Christian—together with others and for others.[68]

---

[65] Schlink, *After the Council*, v.

[66] Ibid., 205.

[67] Michael Bünker, "Öffnung und Grenzen. Das Ökumenismusdekret aus evangelischer Sicht," in *Das Zweite Vatikanische Konzil*, ed. Jan-Heiner Tück (Freiburg: Herder, 2012), 369–82, at 381.

[68] Some reflections on catholicity in this sense have taken place in an academic consultation of *Societas Oecumenica* in August 2014 in Budapest. The Proceedings have been published as *Catholicity under Pressure—The Ambiguous Relationship between Diversity and Unity*, ed. Dagmar Heller and Peter Szentpétery (Leipzig: Evangelische Verlagsanstalt, 2016).

CHAPTER 15

The Russian Orthodox Observers at Vatican II in the Context of Soviet Religious Politics

Anastacia Wooden

Even before any of its documents were adopted, Vatican II initiated a new chapter in ecumenical relations by inviting non-Catholic observers and guests to the Council. Fifty-three observers and guests attended the first session. By the end of the fourth session, the total number of observers and guests grew to one hundred and eighty-two. Although they could not speak or vote at general assemblies, their voices were heard through other venues. This small group of people (when compared to the roughly 2400 bishops present), like a pinch of a precious spice, "seasoned" the Council, giving it its unique flavor.

It is no exaggeration to say that, of all the invited guests and observers, the most surprising and extraordinary were the two observers from the Russian Orthodox Church (ROC), who arrived on the second day of the Council. Their presence was extraordinary considering that the ROC in general, and its international activity in particular, was completely controlled by the Soviet, communist government that was in a long-standing relationship of mutually militant ideological animosity with the Vatican.

A. Wooden (✉)
The Catholic University of America, Washington, DC, USA

© The Author(s) 2018
V. Latinovic et al. (eds.), *Catholicism Opening to the World and Other Confessions,* Pathways for Ecumenical and Interreligious Dialogue, https://doi.org/10.1007/978-3-319-98581-7_15

237

It was also surprising considering that the ROC was the only Orthodox church represented at the Council from the Council's first day.

In this paper, I will not address the processes within the Roman Catholic Church (RCC) which led to the extension of an invitation to the ROC to send observers to Vatican II. The goal of this paper is to briefly outline the complex interplay of various political, ecclesial and national factors that affected the manner in which this invitation was accepted by the ROC and how its observers were able to participate in the work of the Council.

THE RUSSIAN ORTHODOX CHURCH IN THE SOVIET STATE

The attitude of the ROC to the RCC on the eve of the Council was determined in a large degree by the complex interplay of three groups of factors: theological, national and political. In other words, these are the factors that were determined by (a) the ROC's common Orthodox theological stance, (b) its specifically Russian national outlook, and (c) the historically unique political circumstances of its existence in the Soviet state.

"Non Possumus"—Theological Factors

The title for this section is the title of the anonymous article published in the *Journal of the Moscow Patriarchate* in May of 1961.[1] This article, in a succinct and elegant way, presents two theological objections to Vatican II that were shared by all Orthodox Churches.

First, it expresses disagreement with the presumptuous way the council was called "ecumenical." The Orthodox Churches considered the council an internal affair of the RCC. The article posited that the Council could not be called ecumenical since it would be "unthinkable" for Rome to invite Orthodox primates as equals. Such a council would then become the highest organ of power in the Church contradicting the Roman idea of Christian unity as a worldwide unity of all Christians under the power of the Pope. This temptation of monarchical centralization of power, which the anonymous author parallels with the devil's

---

[1] "Non Possumus!" *Zhurnal Moskovskoj Patriarchii* [*Journal of the Moscow Patriarchate*, in Russian Журнал Московской Патриархии] 5 (1961): 73–75.

temptation of Jesus in the desert, should be firmly rejected because no power but love can unite Christians in the Church as the Body of Christ.

Second, the article voices suspicions about the true intentions of the Council. It asserts that the RCC must have vaguely felt that an "ecumenical council" cannot be called without the participation of the Eastern churches and therefore, the coming Council tries to bring them (and representatives of other Christian confessions) in as observers.[2] For that purpose, the RCC even created special committees for Eastern Churches and for Christian Unity, led by Cardinal Augustin Bea. The article interprets the cardinal's statement, in one of his interviews, that the ROC will receive an invitation to send observers if it desires so as a diplomatic way of saying "there will be no invitation but such an initiative will be met positively."

It is for these reasons and "without enmity toward the Catholics," the anonymous author claims, that the Moscow Patriarchate is compelled to reply to Cardinal Bea with a resounding *Non possumus!* (following Peter in Acts 4:20) to any Orthodox participation in the Council.

"Third Rome"—National Factors

Being a Russian national church, the ROC also had its own set of idiosyncratic attitudes reflected in the title of a "third – and final – Rome" given to Moscow. These included traditional long-lasting attitudes of Russian Orthodoxy, such as support of state interests in international affairs and patriotic aspirations, and related to its opposition to unification of the Orthodox Churches around Constantinople.

From the beginning of the sixteenth century, the See of Moscow started to identify itself as the "Third Rome"—the last center of Orthodoxy and a final incarnation of the Christian empire. This messianic claim was born in the conditions of growing self-sufficiency and isolation of the Russian church from the Orthodox East due to "transfer of both the political and the ecclesial centers from Kiev to Moscow, the growth of national unity around this new center, [and] the fall of

---

[2] Illustrating this concern of the Orthodox churches, Charles Napier speaks of "the genuine confusion which existed for a time as to whether the Council was to be a "Council of Union," to which all would be invited, or not." Charles Napier, "The Orthodox Church and the Second Vatican Council," *Diakonia* 1, no. 3 (1966): 175–93.

Constantinople."[3] It is rooted in a belief widespread in Russian ecclesial circles that while in the late-Byzantine period Constantinople succumbed to Latin theological positions, the purity of the Orthodox faith and life was preserved in Muscovite adherence to the traditions of Orthodox Christianity.[4]

In addition to seeing itself as a defender of the Orthodox purity, the ROC also saw itself as a fullest expression and a "guardian of Russian identity," a feature that remained characteristic of the ROC's consciousness even during the Soviet period.[5] Therefore, even amid severe internal persecution of the ROC by the Soviet state, it nevertheless shared with this state its patriotic aspirations in foreign affairs as a continuation of Russian state interests.

"On Ne Nous Permet Pas"—Political Factors

The title for this section is a taken from the words of Fr. Vitali Borovoy,[6] a prominent Russian Orthodox theologian and ecumenist who participated as the ROC's observer in all four sessions of the Council. Borovoy was making a point that the above-mentioned response of *Non possumus* should be actually read and understood as "We are not allowed."[7] These words give a glimpse of the degree of control which the Soviet authorities exercised over the ROC's activities: so complete and restrictive was this control and so severe the accompanied persecution, that it

---

[3] Alexander Schmemann, "Russian Theology: 1920–1972: An Introductory Survey," *St. Vladimir's Seminary Quarterly* 16, no. 4 (1972): 172–94, 173.

[4] George E. Demacopoulos and Aristotle Papanikolaou, "Orthodox Naming of the Other; A Postcolonial Approach," in *Orthodox Constructions of the West* (New York: Fordham University Press, 2013), 12.

[5] Adriano Roccucci, "The Experience of the Russian Orthodox Church during the Soviet Regime," in *The Holy Russian Church and Western Christianity*, ed. Giuseppe Alberigo and Oscar Beozzo (Maryknoll: Orbis, 1996), 60.

[6] Here I follow the way the Russian version of his name *Виталий Боровой* (*Bimaлi Баравы* in his native Belarusian) is transcribed in the entry "Borovoy" in *Dictionary of the Ecumenical Movement* (Geneva: WCC Publications, 1991), 109. The World Council of Churches spells his first name as "Vitaly." Other spellings such as "Vitalij Borovoj" or "Borovoi" are also acceptable.

[7] Dom Emmanuel Lanne quotes Borovoy's words at a meeting in Moscow: "*Non possumus* voulait simplement dire 'On ne nous permet pas.'" See Emmanuel Lanne, "La perception en Occident de la participation du Patriarcat de Moscou à Vatican II," in *Vatican II in Moscow (1959–1965)* (Leuven: Bibliotheek van de Faculteit Godgeleerdheid, 1997), 112.

can be acknowledged that political factors played a decisive role in the final shape of all the ROC's international activities at that point in time. Therefore, to understand and properly evaluate the actions of the ROC surrounding the sending of observers to Vatican II one needs to have a fuller picture of Soviet religious policy and the goals of its foreign policy at the time.

The communist doctrine of the Soviet state dictated its negative attitude toward any religion as "the opium of the masses" and proscribed a variety of means aimed at "liberating" the masses from religion's oppressive influence. In practice this doctrine was carried out continuously with varying degrees of intensity in different forms of physical and ideological destruction of all religious institutions and sentiments. The physical destruction of the ROC's clergy and property began very quickly after the 1917 revolution in Russian and was carried out with a particular intensity during Stalin's regime in the 1930s, making the physical survival of the ROC in the USSR a very real concern.

However, the beginning of the Great Patriotic War in June of 1941 (as World War II is called in reference to German aggression against the Soviet Union) marked a new phase in Soviet religious policy. In the face of the fast advancement of the German troops, the Soviet government had to mobilize all available resources. In this tragic time the oppressed ROC raised its voice calling all people to unite in their struggle against the fascist threat. Already on the first day of the war, June 22, 1941, the head of the ROC, Metropolitan Sergij (Starogorodskij), wrote and sent out to all active parishes his appeal to the Orthodox believers to defend the country. The energetic patriotic activity of the Church also included collections of funds and clothing for the troops and blessing of the troops heading to the war zone.[8] Stalin quickly realized the power the Church had to unite and strengthen the spirit of the nation. To ensure support of the faithful he responded by bringing active persecution of clergy to its lowest level, allowing restoration of the active ecclesial life, and authorization of an unprecedented meeting with a group of the ROC's hierarchs. This last meeting eventually led to the organization in

[8]S. Bolotov, *Russian Orthodox Church and Foreign Policy of the USSR in the 1930s–1950s* (Moscow, 2011), 50. In Russian. [С. В. Болотов. *Русская православная церковь и международная политика СССР в 1930е - 1950е годы*. Москва: Издательство Круцитского подворья, 2011.]

1945 of the first in the history of the USSR Council of the ROC and the election of the Patriarch.

By the end of 1943 as the eventual German defeat was already foreseeable, Stalin started to think about the role of the Soviet Union in diplomatic "remaking" of the post-war world. As the Soviet Union was seeking assistance from its Western allies, abuse of freedom of religion in the USSR was becoming one of the major points of contention. From this point on, the USSR's international engagements and objectives begin to dictate Soviet religious policies alone with its ideology.[9]

Free of theological scruples, Stalin designated the ROC to become one of his major instruments in achieving various international objectives, as Orthodoxy was central not only to Russian identity but to many other nations within the sphere of Soviet foreign interests. The seriousness of this strategy can be illustrated by juxtaposition of the map of historically predominantly Orthodox countries in Eastern Europe and the map of countries that belonged to the so-called "Soviet Block" that was formed after WWII.[10] In fact, after the USSR extended its zone of influence over territories that included the Serbian, Romanian, Bulgarian, Polish, Albanian, and Czech Orthodox churches, it had control over about 85% of the Orthodox population of the World.[11]

To clear the way for its interests, Soviet policy first had to minimize Catholic influence in the above-mentioned regions. This objective was swiftly accomplished by suppressing to a point of physical elimination the Eastern Catholic churches in Ukraine, Romania, Czechoslovakia and the Carpathian region—all within about five years of the end of WWII.[12]

Second, there was a need to counteract the Vatican's anticommunist stance. This was addressed by presenting the Vatican itself as an anti-democratic force in the service of capitalist oppressors while promoting the USSR as a true defender of the people's interests. As the first ambassador of the USSR to the Vatican Jurij Karlov attests, "the dominant opinion of Soviet party leaders at the time was based on the assumption that because of the so-called 'deep general crisis of Catholicism,' the number of Catholics in the world would constantly

---

[9] Ibid., 143.

[10] Ibid.

[11] Ibid., 126.

[12] The anti-uniate campaign in Ukraine was personally coordinated by the future leader of the USSR, Nikita Khrushchev, who reported directly to Stalin. See ibid., 135.

decrease and the Vatican would be constrained to make up for the decline of its religious prestige by active public involvement in international issues."[13] Based on this assumption, ideological warfare was designed to create discontent within the ecclesial hierarchy of the RCC, with a far-reaching goal of breaking the RCC itself into a number of local churches which dissolve their ties with the Holy See.[14]

Last but not least, parallel to the formation of a zone of Soviet influence in Europe, the creation of a system of unity of the local Orthodox churches was planned. Obviously, the center of this unity was reserved for the highly controlled ROC. The outward appearance of this plan was supposed to appeal to world Orthodoxy but the hidden plan was supposed to benefit Soviet interests.[15] This plan included the calling of a pan-orthodox council in Moscow and even election of a new ecumenical patriarch.[16]

To effectively use the ROC's international contacts to achieve all these objectives, Stalin designed what can be called "pragmatic" model of the relations between the ROC and the Soviet state. This model allowed the ROC to exist and function with two stipulations. First, the state monitored and controlled the ROC's activity through an especially designated government agency—the Council for the Religious Affairs and, more specifically, the Council for ROC Affairs—which were staffed with KGB operatives. Second, the ROC was supposed to actively promote Soviet interests through its international contacts and engagements. In summary, "the use of the Church to serve Soviet foreign policy and its propaganda was one of the terms of agreement signed between State and Church in order to guarantee the latter's survival."[17]

Stalin's death brought about changes in the internal Soviet religious policy from a pragmatic to more ideological direction. At the XXII

---

[13] Jurij Karlov, "The Secret Diplomacy of Moscow and the Second Vatican Ecumenical Council," in *Vatican II in Moscow (1959–1965)*, 296–97. As Melloni points out, "the illusion that the Vatican could be used by Communist diplomacy to 'divide' the West was an approach which changed only as a result of contacts and the experience of the Council." See Alberto Melloni, "Between Ostpolitik and Ecumenism," in *The Holy Russian Church and Western Christianity*, ed. Alberigo and Beozzo, 93.

[14] Bolotov, *Foreign Policy*, 200.

[15] Ibid., 145.

[16] Ibid., 197.

[17] Roccucci, "Experience," 51.

Congress of the Communist Party of the Soviet Union (CPSU) the new head of the state Nikita Khrushchev announced a grandiose goal of completing the creation of communist society in twenty years (by 1980). Liquidation of all religious institutions and sentiments had to be intensified in different forms to meet this "deadline."[18] Whereas Stalin's repressions were deadlier but had a nature of an external assault, the new approach aimed at damaging the church from the inside through the ideological pressure on the churchgoers and even meddling with the ROC's canonical structure. The net result of this period can be vividly described by statistics: "On 1 January 1958 the Moscow patriarchate had 13,414 churches, 12,169 ordained priests, 56 monasteries, and 7 hermitages. On 1 January 1966, it had 7523 churches, 19 monasteries and 7410 registered clergymen."[19]

Contrary to what one would expect, this policy was executed parallel to the essentially unchanged doctrine on the use of the ROC in the interests of its foreign policy. Even in the midst of anti-religious hysteria the ROC was still expected to continue its international activity for the benefit of Soviet foreign interests.

THE ROC AND VATICAN II

To complete the account of the USSR's religious policies one should note its unchangeably negative attitude toward the Vatican and the RCC. For a brief time when in the course of WWII Soviet troops entered traditionally "Catholic" territories, Stalin showed some interest in establishing contacts with the Holy See.[20] However, in 1945 the comments of Pius XII against communism and his support of "soft peace" with Germany made it clear that any hopes of friendship with the Vatican were in vain. Therefore, the USSR's policy toward the Vatican—that

---

[18]Aleksij Marchenko, *Religious Politics of the Soviet State in the Years of Rule of N. S. Khrushchev and Its Influence on the Church Life in the USSR* (Moscow, 2010), 264. In Russian [Протоиерей Алексий Марченко. *Религиозная политика советского государства в годы правления Н. С. Хрущева и её влияние на церковную жизнь в СССР*. Москва: Издательство Круцитского подворья, 2010.]

[19]Mikhail V. Shkarovskii, "The Russian Orthodox Church in 1958–64," *Russian Studies in History* 50, no. 3 (2011): 94.

[20]Bolotov, *Foreign Policy*, 87–88.

"double-dealing living corpse"[21]—became one of open confrontation and even an ideological war. Moreover, this attitude spilled onto the ecumenical movement which was perceived as an "epidemic" spread by American Protestantism in order to enslave humanity under the heel of capitalism.[22] This was matched by the equally negative attitude of the Vatican toward communism, the Soviet state and even the ROC as fully controlled by this state.[23]

Obviously, the ROC was expected to maintain the same negative position in its international engagements toward the RCC in general and the upcoming council in particular. Its official attitude toward the council was expressed in the already mentioned article *Non possumus*. Therefore, at a pan-Orthodox conference which took place in September–October of 1961 in Rhodes, the Moscow patriarchate also took a strong anti-Vatican and anti-ecumenical stance. However, at a second such conference in September–October 1963, the ROC's delegation joined Constantinople's delegation in promoting a resolution "to initiate an equitable dialogue with the Roman Catholic Church and to allow any Orthodox church to send observers to the Second Vatican Council."[24]

This radical shift in the ROC's position had to reflect an equally radical change in the Soviet leadership's attitude toward the Vatican. It is a widely-held opinion among the scholars of modern history that this change occurred with the election of Pope John XXIII. The new Pope's down-to-earth personality, his tireless peace efforts, and the role he played in the resolution of the Cuban missile crises earned him a title of the "Red Pope." Since Soviet politicians lacked any understanding of the Vatican's religious motives, they interpreted many of the Pope's actions—like his speech in favor of peaceful settlement of the Berlin crisis (September 1961) and especially of the Cuban crisis

---

[21] Krassikov's essay provides many more colorful expressions that were used by the Soviet propaganda.

[22] See entry *"Ватикан"* [Vatican] in *Bolshaya sovetskaya enciklopediya*, [in Russian *Большая советская энциклопедия*] 2nd ed., vol. 7 (Moscow: BSE, 1951), 53–55.

[23] For example, Moscow Patriarch Alexij was personally attacked in Pius XII's encyclical *Orientales Omnes Ecclesias* of December 23, 1945, following the arrest and sentence to forced labor camps of the Ukrainian Catholic bishops in April of 1945. Pius XII, Encyclical Letter *Orientales Omnes Ecclesias*, AAS 38 (1946): 33–63, no. 57.

[24] Shkarovskii, "Russian Orthodox Church," 88.

(October 1962)—as an indicator of an extremely anti-American stance,[25] which especially appealed to the Soviet leadership. For Khrushchev, it signaled a new opportunity not only to promote Soviet interests by widening the social basis for communist ideas in Western countries, but also to find new sources of financial support for a struggling Soviet economy. He perceived the Vatican's concern for the situation of believers in the USSR to be "more formal than essential in nature and thus could be ignored"[26] and allowed Soviet diplomats and security agencies to reach out to the Vatican.

At the same time, the ROC itself underwent certain changes in attitude toward its international "obligations." In earlier years, its obligations were fulfilled with little enthusiasm or initiative reflecting the ROC's uncooperative attitude toward the Soviet state. However, as the change of generations in the ROC's hierarchy and clergy took place, so did the change in attitude toward the Soviet state.[27] A new generation of priests and bishops were born, raised, educated and found their way to faith within the conditions of the Soviet state. As such, they did not challenge the fact of the existence of this State but looked for the ways "to build the church in the conditions of the Soviet system."[28]

Today this assumed loyalty to the State is often interpreted negatively as collaboration with the State and all its communist goals. Taking into consideration the actual conditions of the ROC's existence in the USSR, such an interpretation is too simplistic. It fails to make a proper distinction between the motives of the ROC's leadership and the motives of the state; instead, it judges the ROC and Soviet government "as a single entity."[29] Those who call the ROC's leaders "collaborators" because they did not choose to fight the state itself do not take into account or even unfairly dismiss their sincere and relentless pursuit to seek "within the rules of the system...places of freedom and the good of the church."[30]

[25] Karlov, "Secret Diplomacy," 297.

[26] Ibid.

[27] Roccucci, "Experience," 57.

[28] Ibid.

[29] Karim Schelkens, "Vatican Diplomacy after the Cuban Missile Crisis: New Light on the Release of Josyf Slipyj," *The Catholic Historical Review* 97, no. 4 (2011): 692.

[30] Roccucci, "Experience," 55–56.

Metropolitan Nikodim (the head of the ROC's Department of External Affairs at the time of Vatican II) personified this new generation. As current Moscow Patriarch Kirill wrote about him:

> Metropolitan Nikodim, while fully admitting the justice of criticism of the existing regime ... used to say to me: "The church ought to seek ways of asserting its physical presence. It must take into account the historical reality in which it exists. It is important to maintain a dialogue with the world around, including the ruling powers. This dialogue will bring victory to those who prove to be spiritually stronger and better equipped and whose convictions are deeper."[31]

Metropolitan Nikodim's strategy was to use the ROC's international engagements as a way to ensure the ROC's physical survival by raising awareness of the international Christian community. During their travels abroad, the ROC's leaders were not allowed to speak openly about the persecution of the Church. Instead, Metropolitan Nikodim wanted to let the world know about the Russian Church as an alive and vibrant Christian community and "about the tens of millions of believers in the USSR who filled the churches to capacity."[32] This new approach was very successful and the ROC's fate "suddenly became of great interest to the world Christianity."[33]

In this way, the preparatory period (1959–1962) of the Vatican II auspiciously coincided with the beginning of direct political contacts between Soviet leaders and the Vatican as well as with the desire of the ROC for international outreach. As Borovoy summed it up, "the high esteem in which John XXIII had come to be held in the eyes of Moscow with his politics of peace and reconciliation had shown the Russian Church the green light in closer relations with Rome."[34] Still, the Soviet state and of the ROC had different reasons and different objectives for their mutual interest. Perhaps the difference in objectives of

---

[31] Kirill of Smolensk and Kaliningrad, "Nikodim (Rotov), 1929–1978," in *Ecumenical Pilgrims: Profiles of Pioneers in Christian Reconciliation*, ed. Ion Bria and Dagmar Heller (Geneva: WCC Publications, 1995), 161.

[32] Shkarovskii, "Russian Orthodox Church," 90.

[33] Ibid., 89–90.

[34] Vitaly Borovoi, "The Second Vatican Council and its Significance for the Russian Orthodox Church," in Alberigo and Beozzo, *The Holy Russian Church and Western Christianity*, 135.

both parties contributed to the complexity of what Fr. Thomas Stransky, C.S.P., an original member of the Secretariat for Promoting Christian Unity (SPCU), called a tangled "mass of events and intentions" that surrounded the process by which the ROC received and responded to an invitation to send its observers to Vatican II.

Prior to sending official invitations, the SPCU initiated contacts with various Christian churches to investigate whether a positive reply to these invitations could be expected. In February of 1961, Msgr. Willebrands visited Constantinople and was assured by the Ecumenical Patriarch Athenagoras of his interest in sending observers provided all Orthodox churches came to agreement about it. The Patriarch informed all the churches, including the Moscow Patriarchate, about his contacts with Msgr. Willebrands. This means that when, in May of 1961, the Moscow Patriarchate's official journal published *Non possumus* it was received by the SPCU as a quasi-official negative response to its initiative. Therefore, when SPCU President Cardinal Bea formally invited Patriarch Athenagoras to delegate observers in July of 1962, similar letters were sent directly to other Patriarchates (such as Alexandria, Antioch, Jerusalem, Greece, Cyprus) but not to the Moscow Patriarchate.[35]

Only through personal contacts between Msgr. Willebrands and Metropolitan Nikodim in August of 1962 at a meeting of the World Council of Church's Central Committee was it clarified that the ROC actually had an interest in sending its observers. To make it possible, Msgr. Willebrands visited Moscow in strictest secrecy in September 27–October 2 of 1962 in his official capacity. In his talks with the ROC's authorities as well as representatives of the Department for Religious Affairs, he received an assurance that an invitation from the Vatican might be positively received. This was a first-ever visit of a Vatican official to Moscow.[36]

To the present day, Rome, Constantinople and Moscow do not agree about exactly how events unfolded following this visit. According to Fr. Stransky, Cardinal Bea sent an invitation to the ROC by telegraph and express mail on October 4 of 1962. On October 6 Patriarch Athenagoras contacted both Cardinal Bea and Moscow Patriarch Alexis to find out whether the ROC will be sending observers, but he did not receive a definitive response. The next day, on October 7, he declined

[35] Thomas F. Stransky, C.S.P., "The Foundation of the Secretariat for Promoting Christian Unity," in *Vatican II by Those Who Were There* (London: Chapman, 1986), 78.
[36] Stransky, "Foundation," 79.

the invitation to send the observers for lack of unanimity between the Orthodox churches. However, on October 11, the opening day of the Council, the SPCU received a telegram from Moscow about sending observers—Protopresbyter Vitali Borovoy and Archimandrite Vladimir Kotliarov. They arrived to Rome the next day.

In an interview given in 1963 one of these observers, Borovoy, gave a slightly different account of events. Borovoy insisted that the ROC received the RCC's invitation on October 10, one day before the opening of the Council. The Holy Synod of the ROC then immediately held a meeting which made a decision to send observers. Borovoy also insists that Athenagoras's decision not to send observers was not made in consultation with the ROC. He says that they received a wire of Athenagoras's decision on October 10, when it was too late to change their mind because on the same day the highest organ of Soviet power, the *Politburo of CPSU*, adopted a resolution proposed by the ministry of Foreign Affairs and approved by the KGB to send the observers to the Council.[37] Borovoy adds that he and his colleague Kotliarov were very surprised upon their arrival to Rome to see no representatives of other Orthodox churches.[38]

It is possible that both accounts are correct in facts but not in assumptions. For example, the fact that a wire was sent from Rome to Moscow on a certain day does not necessarily mean that it reached the intended receiver on the same day. After all, communications between the ROC and Rome and Constantinople were closely monitored and controlled by the Soviet authorities. This hypothesis is in part supported by the

---

[37] Adriano Roccucci, "Russian Observers at Vatican II. The 'Council for Russian Orthodox Church Affairs' and the Moscow Patriarchate between Anti-Religious Policy and International Strategies," in *Vatican II in Moscow (1959–1965)*, 69.

[38] The ROC's representatives were not the only Orthodox at the first session of the Council: there were also present as guest of the SPCU Bishop Cassien from St. Sergius's Orthodox Theological Institute in Paris and Fr. Alexander Schmemann from St. Vladimir's Orthodox Seminary in Crestwood, New York; observers from the Russian Orthodox Church Outside Russia included Bishop Anthony of Geneva, Fr. Troyanoff from Switzerland, and Prof. Grotoff from Rome; the WCC sent Greek Orthodox Nikos Nissiotis as a representative. However, the ROC was the only Orthodox *church* to send its observers. After Paul VI's pilgrimage to Jerusalem where he acknowledged *nostra culpa* of the RCC in the relationships with the Orthodox churches, the Greek Orthodox Church finally consented to sending observers. So at the third session of the Council there were observers from the Greek Orthodox Church as well as the Ecumenical Patriarchate and the Patriarchate of Alexandria.

fact, pointed out by Alberto Melloni, that "already in 1963 an article appearing in *Reforme* argued that the telegram from Constantinople with which the Ecumenical Patriarch informed Moscow of the decision not to send observers to Rome had been blocked by the Communist Party."[39] It would be in keeping with the efforts of the Soviet authorities to act against the unification of Orthodox churches around Constantinople and against Patriarch Athenagoras in particular, whom they called an American puppet and whose actions they interpreted as "intended to increase its influence on Orthodoxy to the detriment of the Moscow Patriarchate."[40] In his report on Msgr. Willebrands' visit to high Party officials, Borovoy appealed precisely to this goal when he noted that "thanks to the decision made in Rhodes for Orthodoxy to act together, Constantinople had not sent its observers yet and the ROC still has a chance to do so and, consequently, be in position of influencing Orthodoxy in opposition to Constantinople's Western orientation."[41] This report played an important role in persuading Soviet authorities to allow the ROC's observers to go to the Council. In it Borovoy talks about two fronts within the Catholic Church: reactionary-conservative and reforming. In his evaluation, the Council was no longer in the hands of the first group. Since the idea of non-Catholic observers belonged to the second group, refusal of the invitation would serve a blow to the reformers.[42]

Needless to say, the arrival of the ROC's observers to Vatican II caused considerable tensions between Rome, Constantinople and Moscow. However, as Fr. Stransky stresses, "in all this muddle and its aftermath, Monsignor Willebrands, Cardinal Bea, Pope John and Patriarch Athenagoras exercised holy diplomacy: all four uttered not a public word."[43] The complicated circumstances surrounding the arrival the ROC's observers were also responsible for the mixed reaction to their presence at the Council on the part of Catholic bishops: from the glad welcoming by Pope John XXIII and the SPCU to the unequivocally

---

[39] Melloni, "Ostpolotik," 100, Note 33.
[40] Roccucci, "Russian Observers," 52.
[41] Ibid., 67.
[42] Ibid., 66.
[43] Stransky, "Foundation," 80.

negative response to this "real misfortune"[44] from the Ukrainian bishops who were "deeply shocked and offended" by the presence of the ROC observers.[45]

The negative reaction to the ROC's observers was mostly fueled by the perception of them as secret KGB agents who arrived to the Council with the single goal of promoting Soviet interests. This perception, as already discussed above, was understandable but not well-balanced and fair. Still, at the Council they had to behave as double agents—officially promoting Soviet interests and in private contacts speaking for the interests of their church. It was well known at the time that the ROC's representatives abroad were constantly monitored by KGB agents who posed as interpreters or secretaries. At the Council, they were Nikolay Afinogenov at the first, second, and fourth sessions and, possibly, Boris Neliubin at the third and fourth sessions. Therefore, any candid discussions had to take place only on a one-on-one basis.[46]

Also, the observers were supposed to submit daily reports to the Kremlin through the Soviet Embassy in Rome. Borovoy refused to go there himself because, as he put it, "already everybody considered us spies." Thus, his colleague Kotliarov was chosen for this task because his image was already tainted in the Italian press, which noted his likeness to Vladimir Lenin.[47]

The observers' daily attempts to "feed the wolf but save the sheep" were risky but nothing was as dangerous as Borovoy's involvement in negotiations with the Soviet government to release Ukrainian Catholic Metropolitan Josyf Slipyj. Slipyj for eighteen years remained in deplorable conditions of a Siberian forced labor camp since his arrest and conviction in 1945 for alleged anti-Soviet activity and cooperation with the Fascist regime. Pope John XXIII, who kept a picture of Slipyj on his desk, was continuously advocating for the Metropolitan's release. The presence of the ROC's observers at the Council provided an opportunity

---

[44] This is how the head of the Ukrainian delegation, Metropolitan Maxim Hermaniuk described it in his diaries of the Council. See *The Second Vatican Council Diaries of Metropolitan Maxim Hermaniuk, C.SS.R. (1960–1965)*, trans. Jaroslav Z. Skira (Leuven: Peeters, 2012), 71–72.

[45] Schelkens, "Vatican Diplomacy," 692.

[46] Theoretically the observers at the Council did not need interpreters as they were provided by the Russicum.

[47] Ibid.

to directly reach out to the Soviet government. According to Stransky, Borovoy played a key role in convincing the authorities to finally grant Slipyj his release in January on 1963.[48] Sadly, even after Slipyj's release, the head of the Ukrainian Catholic delegation at the Council—Metropolitan Hermaniuk—refused to meet with Borovoy even though Slipyj himself did so.[49] Years later Cardinal Willebrands asked Borovoy about the personal risks that he took in securing Slipyj's release. His response beautifully shows that Borovoj's desire to selflessly serve the One Church was a motivation for all his activity on behalf of the ROC:

> je suis convaincu qu'en agissant ainsi j'ai servi l'Eglise, non seulement votre, eglise, mais l'eglise du Seigneur... La liberation du Metropolite Slipyj peut devenir le signe d'un developpement nouveau qui aura une importance tres grande pour la situation de votre eglise dans notre pays et d'une maniere inderecte aussi pour l'eglise orthodoxe. Deux problemes se presentment encore, un grand problem, c'est le development de votre eglise en Russie. Le petit problem, c'est ma part et mon risqué personnel.[50]

CONCLUSION: WHY DID THE PARTICIPATION OF THE ROC'S OBSERVERS MATTER?

There were short-term and long-term implications of the presence of the ROC's observers at the Council for the relations between the ROC and the RCC.[51]

In the short term, the presence of the ROC's observers gave a strong impulse to the establishment of political and ecclesial relations between the RCC and the ROC. Almost immediately, the arrival of the observers

---

[48] Slipyj was granted an amnesty but was not fully rehabilitated. He forever remained an enemy of the Soviet state and could not return to his beloved Ukraine. Ibid., 707–8.

[49] Peter Galadza, "The Council Diary of Metropolitan Maxim Hermaniuk and Turning Points in the History of the Catholic Church: An Interpretation," in *Vatican II: Experience canadiennes/Canadian Experiences*, ed. Michael Attridge, et al. (Ottawa: University of Ottawa Press, 2011), 237–38.

[50] Schelkens, "Vatican Diplomacy," 705–6, Note 83.

[51] Radu Bordeianu offers reflections on how the manner of their initial participation still affects the state of the Orthodox unity today. "Orthodox Observers at the Second Vatican Council and Intra-Orthodox Dynamics," *Theological Studies* 79, no. 1 (2018): 86–106.

allowed the establishment of direct personal contacts between the Vatican, the Moscow Patriarchate and, inadvertently, the Kremlin. These new channels of communication were successfully tested only months after the opening of the Council when the Vatican played an important role in the peaceful resolution of the Cuban missile crisis in November 1963. Also, the release of Metropolitan Slipyj was accomplished precisely through the *personal* appeal of Pope John XXIII, *personally* vouched for by Fr. Borovoy, and *personally* granted by Khrushchev, as a gesture of good will. Overall, these contacts fell short of establishing diplomatic relations between the USSR and the Holy See: full diplomatic relations between the Holy See and Russia were only established after the fall of the Soviet Union in 2009. Nevertheless, they allowed for visits of high-level Soviet officials to the Vatican (Minister of Foreign Affairs A. Gromyko and Chairman of the Presidium of the Supreme Soviet N. Podgorny in 1966 and 1967) and eventually led to the relative improvement of the Catholic Church's position in countries of the Soviet Block (Hungary, Poland, and Romania).

Additionally, in a similar fashion the Council marked the beginning of ecumenical contacts between the RCC and the ROC, such as theological discussions in Leningrad in 1967, and even the presence of ROC representatives at John Paul I's inauguration on September 3, 1978.

Moreover, the personal contacts of the observers with other participants of the Council created not only a concern for the fate of the Christians in the USSR, but also awakened a genuine interest in Orthodox theology. Here, the personality and breadth of theological knowledge of Borovoy played the key role.[52] He is the one credited with drafting the Orthodox opinion included in the New Delhi Statement on Unity (1961) on the Trinitarian basis of the Church's unity. Throughout his fruitful ecumenical career in the World Council of Churches and its Faith and Order Committee he was valued by his colleagues for his theological opinion.[53]

---

[52] For more on Borovoy, see my publication dedicated to the 100th anniversary of his birth titled "'The Agent of Jesus Christ': Participation of Fr. Vitali Borovoy in the Second Vatican Council as an Observer from the ROC." *Occasional Papers on Religion in Eastern Europe*, 36 (2016). http://digitalcommons.georgefox.edu/ree/vol36/iss4/2/.

[53] See for example, "What is Salvation?" *International Review of Mission* 61, no. 241 (1972): 38–45; "Life in Unity" *Ecumenical Review* 36, no. 1 (1984): 3–10.

Although Borovoy did not consider the Council to be "ecumenical" in the historical, canonical and dogmatic sense,[54] he shared its "completely positive valuation" by the ROC.[55] From his perspective, the Council demonstrated positive changes in the RCC, a new welcoming attitude toward Orthodoxy, and the political effectiveness of the 'eastern policy' of Paul VI. Noting that some documents of the Council were written under the influence of Russian Orthodox theology and philosophy, he even expressed hope that its work will be helpful in preparation of the Orthodox council and Orthodox *aggiornamento*.[56] In other words, he maintained that the study of the Council and its documents can be beneficial for the Orthodox Church itself. Fifty years after the Council and twenty years after Borovoy's statement, his opinion is sadly not shared by many. Specific references to the documents of the Council by Orthodox theologians are rare and usually consist of pointing out their deficiencies from an Orthodox perspective. Therefore, from a long-term perspective, the lack of a meaningful reception by the Orthodox Churches has to be acknowledged.

Indeed, based on my personal contacts with Orthodox faithful, I dare to say that the overwhelming majority of those I know do not know that the Council recognized the full ecclesial reality of the Orthodox churches, despite a lack of communion with the Church of Rome (UR 15). One can only wonder how this affects the perception of the RCC's ecumenical gestures toward the Orthodox Churches.

A final point concerns the contemporary evaluation or re-evaluation of the ROC's motives for participation in the Council. In October of 2015, the Belarusian Orthodox Church (of Moscow Patriarchate) conducted a conference commemorating the 100th anniversary of Fr. Borovoy's birth. The conference took place in the Minsk Orthodox Seminary in Zhirovicy, a school that Borovoy helped to rebuilt in the 1940s. It was an official event graced by the presence of four bishops and blessings from Metropolitan Pavel, the Exarch of All Belarus, and Metropolitan Hilarion, the current Chairman of the Department for

---

[54] Borovoi, "Second Vatican Council," 130.

[55] Ibid., 137.

[56] "Ecco il motive per cui molto della riccezza teologica e dell'esperienza conciliare del Concilio Vaticano II ci può essere utile nella fase preparatoria dei nostril Concili e del nostro aggiornamento." Vitalij Borovoij, "Il significato del Concilio Vaticano II per la Chiesa ortodossa russa," in *Vatican II in Moscow (1959–1965)*, 90.

External Church Relations of the Moscow Patriarchate.[57] At some point during this conference a question was raised whether participation in the Council and the whole of ecumenical activity of the ROC would happen at all without pressure from the Soviet state and the ROC's struggle for survival. A few speakers not only doubted the sincerity of the ROC's ecumenical intentions, but also happily denied it. They saw "theological justification" for any inter-Christian relations resting exclusively in witnessing to the truth which only the Orthodox possess and offered their reflections on why it is proper to call *all* non-Orthodox "heretics" even without specific conciliar statements on the matter.[58]

Sadly, it could be suggested that this strand of thought is discernible in aspects of the ROC's present-day teaching and preaching, although I am not qualified to properly evaluate the strength and popularity of such a strand. Personally, I find hope in the fact that this is not a result of deliberate discernment of Catholic teaching but rather a result of the ROC's internal processes and currents. Today, the evidence suggests that the national interests of the Russian state again play an important role in ROC's external affairs. This conclusion can be illustrated by the speech of Moscow Patriarch Kirill presented on November 3, 2009 at the opening of the Third Assembly of the Russian World. In his speech, the Patriarch presented the ROC's programmatic vision of the so-called "Russian World" and the ways for its strengthening and development.[59] By describing the far-reaching limits of the "Russian World," he explained that:

> the Church is called Russian not in accordance with the ethnic principle. This name points out that Russian Orthodox Church fulfills its pastoral mission among the peoples that receive Russian spiritual and cultural tradition as a foundation of its national identity, or, at least, as its significant part.

This definition allowed the Patriarch to extend the definition of the Russian World beyond its traditional "nucleus" of Russia, Ukraine, and

---

[57] In Russian: *Отдел внешних церковных связей Московского Патриархата (ОВЦС)*.

[58] This reasoning is taken from the presentation by Fr. S. Movsesyan, Assistant Rector of the School of Theology of the Belarus State University.

[59] The full text can be found at: http://www.patriarchia.ru/db/text/928446.html. Last modified August 31, 2015.

Belarus all the way to Moldova.[60] Taking into account Russia's territorial disputes with Moldova's region of Pridnestrov'e in 1989 and its more recent territorial claims in Ukraine, one may notice a tendency of the modern Russian state to align its borders with the territories of the "pastoral mission" of the ROC. In my view, therefore, the "Russian World" is at one and the same time both a vision for the potential ecclesial outreach of the ROC and yet also a quasi-official political doctrine behind the expansion of the Russian state.

It is for Orthodoxy itself to decide on the validity of such a mingling of ecclesial and national interests. Today, when a new set of complexities is arising in the ROC's external affairs, it is apposite to recall John XXIII's timeless and *prophetic* words at the opening of the Vatican II "in the present order of things, Divine Providence is leading us to a new order of human relations which, by men's own efforts and even beyond their very expectations, are directed toward the fulfillment of God's superior and inscrutable designs." Therefore today, as in 1963, we may be able to come to see that "everything, even human differences, leads to the greater good of the Church."[61]

[60] An inclusion of Ukraine and Belarus into the "Russian World" is made in the perspective of the Rus' of Kiev, of which modern Russia sees itself an heir. Hence is the title of the patriarch "of Moscow and all the Rus'" adopted by the Moscow Council in 1917.

[61] John XXIII, alloc. *Gaudet Mater Ecclesia*, AAS 54 (1962): 786–96; for an English translation, see "Pope John's Opening Speech to the Council," in *Documents of Vatican II*, ed. Walter M. Abbott (New York: America Magazine, 1966), 710–19.

CHAPTER 16

Vatican II and the Redefinition of Anglicanism

Mark D. Chapman

Anglican self-definition has never been straightforward: there are several competing historical myths as to what constitutes authentic Anglicanism as I have charted in detail, elsewhere.[1] Anglicans from across the world and from across different periods, not least in the Church of England, have expressed (and continue to express) themselves in very different ways: nowadays there are large numbers of Evangelicals, some of whom are charismatics; a substantial proportion of Anglo-Catholics, some of whom adopt traditional forms of liturgy of the most Tridentine kind; as well as many who rest somewhere between the two. Theologically they range from ultra-conservative to ultra-liberal and sometimes whole churches take on a particular theological hue which often depends on the vagaries of missionary history. Because of the high degree of independence which

---

[1] Mark Chapman, *Anglican Theology* (London: T & T Clark, 2012).

M. D. Chapman (✉)
Ripon College Cuddesdon, Cuddesdon, Oxford, UK
e-mail: mark.chapman@rcc.ac.uk

M. D. Chapman
University of Oxford, Oxford, UK

© The Author(s) 2018
V. Latinovic et al. (eds.), *Catholicism Opening to the World and Other Confessions,* Pathways for Ecumenical and Interreligious Dialogue,
https://doi.org/10.1007/978-3-319-98581-7_16

257

has been claimed by Anglicanism from its beginnings in the post-Reformation Church of England, authority and canon law are weak, especially between the member churches (or 'provinces' as they have come to be known). All this means that there are different selections of key authorities, classic texts and representative theologians. Almost everything is contested, partly because, with no authoritative figure such as Luther or Calvin, there is no obvious body of thought to turn to in order to identify what is truly Anglican. Even the Church of England's formularies, particularly the thirty-nine Articles of Religion of 1571 or the liturgies of the Book of Common Prayer of 1552 (and revised in 1559 and 1662), have never carried the weight of the Augsburg Confession.

That said, however, throughout the history of the Church of England and the Anglican Communion it spawned, one characteristic has been more dominant than almost anything else: Anglican identity has been established in opposition to Rome. This formed the core of teaching during the split from Rome during the reign of Henry VIII in the 1530s; it continued through Elizabeth I; and it has persisted well into modern times. Anti-Romanism was further cemented in the seventeenth and eighteenth centuries with the deposition of the Catholic King James II in 1688 and the Act of Settlement of 1701 which ensured that England (and from 1707 the United Kingdom) would always have a protestant monarch (descended from the Electress Sophia of Hannover) and consort.[2] Nevertheless, even though such a monarch would be Supreme Governor of the Church of England and could no longer be a Roman Catholic, he or she did not need to be an Anglican: indeed, the first two of the Electors of Hanover who ruled England from 1714 were neither English-speakers nor Anglican. But it was to them that the English clergy swore their oath of allegiance. Especially during the eighteenth century, but also for a long time afterward, a broad and anti-Roman protestant identity was clearly at the heart of Anglican and broader British identity.[3] It remains strong in certain parts of the Anglican Communion and within certain church parties to this day.[4]

---

[2] The Act of Succession to the Crown of 2013 now allows for a monarch to marry a Roman Catholic.

[3] See Linda Colley, *Britons: Forging the Nation 1707–1837*, 3rd rev. ed. (New Haven: Yale University Press, 2009).

[4] See E. R. Norman, *Anti-Catholicism in Victorian England* (London: George Allen & Unwin, 1968); F. Tallett and N. Atkin, eds., *Catholicism in Britain and France Since 1789* (London: Hambledon, 1996). On the American context see Philip Jenkins, *The New Anti-Catholicism: The Last Acceptable Prejudice* (Oxford: University Press, 2003).

The story of changed relations between Anglicans and Roman Catholics traces its origin to the massive political changes following the French Revolution of 1789. In England, an influx of large numbers of Catholic émigrés including many clergy led to a change in tone.[5] The final defeat of Napoleon in 1815 was met both with repression, but also with modest reforms, even though most were resisted by the churches. Across Europe there were moves in the churches toward a form of neo-confessionalism or Romantic repristination of a seemingly dead past.[6] In England, some Anglicans began to narrate another story of their identity: the pan-protestantism which had been the dominant understanding for most Anglicans from the time of the Reformation was supplanted at least for some by a quite different narrative which established the Church of England on the early Fathers. It was a church, they held, that had survived more or less unscathed through the Reformation. Patristic and, later, medieval sources formed the basis for its identity rather than the writings of the reformers. Historical continuity was emphasized which meant that the Reformation became little more than a purging of some of the worst excesses of the Roman system. The Tractarians, John Henry Newman, John Keble and later Edward Bouverie Pusey re-interpreted the Church of England as a catholic church. But that catholicity was anything but Roman. Indeed, at the heart of the Oxford Movement was a deep-seated antagonism toward Rome, almost as vehement as that of the sixteenth century.[7]

The reasons for this were far from straightforward. With the direct rule of Ireland from London after 1801 the question of Catholic Emancipation became increasingly pressing. The need to govern Ireland led to the conversion of Napoleon's victor and Prime Minister, the Duke of Wellington, as well as Robert Peel, Member of Parliament for the University of Oxford to the cause. Roman Catholics were emancipated in

[5] On Catholicism in the nineteenth century, see E. R. Norman, *The English Catholic Church in the Nineteenth Century* (Oxford: University Press, 1984); Sheridan Gilley, "The Roman Catholic Church in Britain," in *A History of Religion in Britain: Practice and Belief from Pre-Roman Times to the Present*, ed. Sheridan Gilley and W. J. Sheils (Oxford: Blackwell, 1994), 346–62; and John Bossy, *The English Catholic Community, 1570–1850* (Oxford: University Press, 1976).

[6] See R. W. Franklin, *Nineteenth Century Churches: The History of a New Catholicism in Württemberg, England, and France* (New York: Garland, 1987).

[7] See my *Fantasy of Reunion: Anglicans, Catholics, and Ecumenism, 1833–1880* (Oxford: Oxford University Press, 2014), esp. Chapter 2.

1829. Newman and his friends campaigned vigorously in their university to resist such a change, even unseating Peel himself. Anglo-Catholicism, as it came to be known, was a particular form of catholicism; with rare exceptions, it remained anti-Roman, adopting instead a 'branch theory' of the church which gave no particular pre-eminence to Rome.[8] It had no longing for a pope nor any strong sense of authority in the present day: instead, the Church of England, with its catholic bishops, was the true church for England since it derived its authority from the past. This meant others—including Roman Catholics—were usurpers, at least when they practised their religion within the confines of England. Despite sympathies for antiquity and later a revival in medieval forms of worship and architecture, Anglican hegemony remained largely untouched: and it remained resolutely anti-Roman. At the same time, more protestant-minded Anglicans simply continued to maintain that the Roman Church was the Babylon of the Apocalypse and to campaign against what was referred to as the papal aggression, especially around the time of the establishment of an English Roman Catholic hierarchy in 1850.[9]

The unwillingness of Roman Catholicism to countenance any efforts toward reunion, at least at the official level, meant that all parties within the Anglican Churches, however high or low, could rest secure in the sure and certain knowledge that there could be no danger of accidentally falling into the hands of Rome. This had been noted at the early Lambeth Conferences. In 1897, for instance, the Anglican bishops from across the world meeting in Lambeth Palace, the Archbishop of Canterbury's residence in London, deeply regretted the approach of Pope Leo XIII in his Apostolic Letter *Praeclara Gratulationis Publicae* of 20 June 1894, which issued an invitation to other Christians to return to 'the Unity which has ever existed in the Catholic Church and can never fail ... The Church, as the common mother of all, has long been

[8] See esp. Mark Chapman, "Temporal and Spatial Catholicism: Tensions in Historicism in the Oxford Movement," in *The Shaping of Tradition: Context and Normativity*, ed. Colby Dickinson (Leuven: Peeters, 2013), 17–26. On the branch theory see William Palmer, *Treatise on the Church of Christ*, 2 vols. (London: Rivington, 1838).

[9] See, for instance, Christopher Wordsworth, *Union with Rome: Is Not the Church of Rome the Babylon of the Book of Revelation?* (London: Rivington, 1850). See also John Wolffe, *The Protestant Crusade in Great Britain 1829–1860* (Oxford: University Press, 1991); Denis G. Paz, *Popular Anti-Catholicism in Mid-Victorian England* (Stanford: University Press, 1992).

calling you back to her'.[10] The assembled bishops also noted the Bull *Apostolicae Curae* of 18 September 1896 ('On the Nullity of Anglican Orders').[11] Although commending the spirit of the Bull and the Church of England's responses, the

> Committee with deep regret felt that, under present conditions, it was use-less to consider the question of Reunion with our brethren of the Roman Church, being painfully aware that any proposal for reunion would be entertained by the authorities of that Church only on condition of a com-plete submission on our part to those claims of absolute authority, and the acceptance of those other errors, both in doctrine and in discipline, against which, in faithfulness to God's Holy Word, and to the true principles of His Church, we have been for three centuries bound to protest.[12]

The 1908 Lambeth Conference continued in a similar vein even if its tone was rather less bleak. In the Report to the Conference of The Committee Appointed to Consider and Report Upon the Subject of Reunion and Intercommunion, there was a frank admission that even though reunion with the Latin west might ultimately be necessary for any scheme of reunion, '[a]ny advance ... is at present barred by difficul-ties which we have not ourselves created, and which we cannot of our-selves remove'.[13] This meant that the Anglican Communion could still remain together because even those Anglo-Catholics who might have wanted reunion would never find a welcome. Anglican protestants and catholics could therefore live together in a broad if not always comforta-ble church.

Through the twentieth century things began to change, at the very least in terms of the vitriol of the rhetoric. At the 1920 Lambeth Conference, for instance, a famous appeal was issued 'to all Christian people' to reunite, which led eventually to the setting up of the united

[10] Leo XIII, Apostolic Letter *Praeclara Gratulationis Publicae*, ASS 26 (1894): 705–17; English translation available at: http://www.papalencyclicals.net/Leo13/l13praec.htm.

[11] Leo XIII, Apostolic Bull *Apostolicae Curae*, ASS 29 (1896): 193–203.

[12] *Conference of Bishops of the Anglican Communion Holden at Lambeth Palace in July 1897: Encyclical Letter from the Bishops with the Resolutions and Reports* (London: SPCK, 1897), 106–7.

[13] *Conference of Bishops of the Anglican Communion Holden at Lambeth Palace, July 6 to August 5, 1908: Encyclical Letter from the Bishops with the Resolutions and Reports* (London: SPCK, 1908), 171.

churches of the Indian subcontinent from 1947.[14] Yet, despite the dominance of Anglo-Catholicism in the 1920s and the increasing use of Roman forms of worship in Anglican churches in this period, there was little real hope of reunion with Rome. The secretive Malines Conversations of the 1920s[15] could never have resulted in anything concrete. This was proved by the publication of the Encyclical *Mortalium Animos* by Pius XI of 6 January 1928 which forbade Roman Catholics from taking part in any ecumenical assemblies (§8) and affirmed unequivocally that in the 'one Church of Christ no man can be or remain who does not accept, recognize and obey the authority and supremacy of Peter and his legitimate successors' (§11). Therefore, it concluded, let 'the separated children draw nigh to the Apostolic See, set up in the City which Peter and Paul, the Princes of the Apostles, consecrated by their blood'.[16] This meant that, internally at least, Anglicans could debate and discuss their Catholic identity as much as they wanted but without any real hope (or fear) of reunion with Rome. And this remained true even when the success of the Anglo-Catholic Congresses and the extensive controversies over the Prayer Book revealed the extent of Anglo-Catholic domination of the Church of England in the 1920s and '30s.

[14] See Charlotte Methuen, "Lambeth 1920: The Appeal to All Christian People, an Account by G. K. A. Bell and the Redactions of the Appeal," in *From the Reformation to the Permissive Society: A Miscellany in Celebration of the 400th Anniversary of Lambeth Palace Library*, ed. M. Barber, G. Sewell, and S. Taylor (Woodbridge: Boydell & Brewer, 2010), 521–64.

[15] Viscount Halifax, *Notes on the Conversations at Malines 1921–1925. Points of Agreement* (London: Mowbray, 1928); see also R. J. Lahey. "The Origins and Approval of the Malines Conversations," *Church History* 43, no. 3 (1974): 366–84; Bernard Barlow, *'A Brother Knocking at the Door': The Malines Conversations 1921–1925* (Norwich: Canterbury Press, 1996); and H. R. McAdoo, "Anglican/Roman Catholic Relations 1717–1980: A Detection of Themes," in *Rome and the Anglicans: Historical and Doctrinal Aspects of Anglican-Roman Catholic Relations*, ed. Wolfgang Haase (Berlin: Walter de Gruyter, 1982), 143–289 at 195–210.

[16] Pius XI, Encyclical Letter *Mortalium Animos*, AAS 20 (1928): 5–16, no. 12.

THE BEGINNINGS OF ANGLICAN REALIGNMENT: GEOFFREY FISHER'S VISIT TO ROME

The ecumenical situation between Roman Catholics and Anglicans, however, began to change rapidly in the late 1950s and 1960s. I will single out three particular examples connected with John XXIII and the Second Vatican Council that helped reshape Anglican self-understanding as Rome voluntarily renounced its hostility toward protestants and particularly the Anglican Churches. The first example was the visit of Archbishop Geoffrey Fisher to Pope John XXIII on 2 December 1960, shortly after the Secretariat for Promoting Christian Unity (SPCU) had been established under Cardinal Augustin Bea (1881–1968). This was the first visit of an Archbishop of Canterbury to a Pope after the Reformation. Although it was a cautious meeting, it was also deeply symbolic. At first sight it was also somewhat unlikely: Fisher was very much a man of the establishment, a bureaucratic rather than a charismatic leader which made him quite distinct from his predecessor at both Repton and Canterbury, William Temple.[17] He also shared the typical presuppositions of the Church of England: in Adrian Hastings' words he was, 'a firm Protestant, almost intuitively suspicious of Rome'.[18] In 1956 he noted: 'I grew up with an inbred opposition of anything that came from Rome. I objected to their doctrine; I objected to their method of reasoning. ... So I grew up, and I saw no reason for differing from that opinion as the years went by.'[19] Cardinal John Heenan later recalled that Fisher was 'a combination of affection and censure'.[20] Nevertheless, like many

---

[17] Peter Staples, "Archbishop Geoffrey Francis Fisher: An Appraisal," *Nederlands Theologisch Tijdschrift* 28 (1974): 239–63 at 263. On Fisher, see also William Purcell, *Fisher of Canterbury* (London: Hodder & Stoughton, 1969); Edward Carpenter, *Archbishop Fisher: His Life and Times* (Norwich: Canterbury Press, 1991); David Hein, *Geoffrey Fisher: Archbishop of Canterbury* (Cambridge: James Clarke, 2008); and David Hein and Andrew Chandler, *Archbishop Fisher 1945–1961: Church, State and World* (Farnham: Ashgate, 2012).

[18] Adrian Hastings, *A History of English Christianity, 1920–1985* (London: Collins, 1986), 522.

[19] Quoted in Purcell, *Fisher of Canterbury*, 271; see also Andrew Chandler and Charlotte Hansen, *Observing Vatican II: The Confidential Reports of the Archbishop of Canterbury's Representative, 1961–1964* (Cambridge: University Press for the Royal Historical Society, 2011), 1–20.

[20] John Heenan, *A Crown of Thorns: An Autobiography, 1951–1963* (London: Hodder and Stoughton, 1974), 262.

of his generation, Fisher soon became a committed ecumenist, preaching an influential sermon at Cambridge in 1946,[21] but his energies were principally directed toward the World Council of Churches, as well as to Methodists and the other Free Churches and the Church of Scotland and the quest for full organic unity.[22]

The ecumenical mood changed, however, with the election of Pope John XXIII in October 1958. Not long afterward, Mgr. Johannes (Jan) Willebrands (1909–2006) had attended the World Council of Churches Central Committee meeting in St. Andrews, Scotland, in August 1959, where he met Fisher, and where it was rumoured that they had begun to plan a meeting with the Pope (although Willebrands later said that this was a 'falsehood' which would have been an abuse 'of the glorious hospitality of the World Council of Churches').[23] Shortly afterwards, however, it would appear that the Pope had communicated his willingness to meet Fisher in Rome, a formal letter being sent by Willebrands, now secretary of the SPCU, to John Satterthwaite (1925–2014), General Secretary of the Church of England's Council for Foreign Relations from 1955–1970 on 27 October 1960.[24] The visit to Rome was to be part of a wider ecumenical journey that included trips to Jerusalem and to Istanbul to meet the Ecumenical Patriarch. A press release was issued by Lambeth Palace on 3 November.[25] Shortly afterward, speaking in November 1960 to the Church Assembly, Fisher made a plea for the normalization of conversations with Rome, which should no longer be secret like the Malines Conversations. Rather, 'in time it ought not to be more unusual for Christian leaders to meet in this way, just as here at home we had grown accustomed to Anglicans and Freechurchmen speaking together. If there

---

[21] *A Step Forward in Church Relations: Being a Sermon Preached before the University of Cambridge on Sunday, November 3rd, 1946* (London: Church House, 1946); see Carpenter, *Fisher*, 310–13; and Hein, *Fisher*, 72–74.

[22] See Carpenter, *Fisher*, 309–70; Hein, *Fisher*, 74–77; and Chandler and Hein, *Fisher*, Chapter 6.

[23] Carpenter, *Fisher*, 707. This was confirmed by Sattherthwaite in a letter to Willebrands of 7 November. See William Purdy, *The Search for Unity: History of Relations between the Anglican and Roman Catholic Churches from the 1960s to the First ARCIC* (London: Chapman, 1996).

[24] Carpenter, *Fisher*, 708; Staples, "Archbishop Geoffrey Francis Fisher," 260–61.

[25] Purdy, *The Search for Unity*, 26.

was a plot at all, it had been conceived in the study at Lambeth'.[26] Not surprisingly there was some opposition in some protestant quarters. On 21 November Fisher received a deputation from protestant Evangelicals led by the Baptist Labour peer, Albert Victor Alexander, Earl Alexander of Hillsborough and the Ulster Unionist MP Captain Lawrence Percy Story Orr, honorary President and Chairman respectively of the United Kingdom Council of Protestant Churches.[27] There was also criticism from some in the Roman Catholic hierarchy in England and Wales, although other Roman Catholics worked behind the scenes to garner support for the visit (and to ensure that it was not frustrated by conservatives at home). In the end, Archbishop Heenan of Liverpool, who was shortly afterward elevated to Westminster, gave the visit his enthusiastic backing.[28]

Within the Vatican there were different levels of enthusiasm for the visit.[29] There was also widespread ignorance about the Church of England, which led the officials of the new Secretariat for Promoting Christian Unity to ask for further clarification from the English Jesuit Bernard Leeming who supplied a page about Fisher, a page about the history of the Church of England and a page about present-day Anglicanism. About Fisher, with whom he had had some 'personal relations', having dined with him at Christ Church, Oxford, he wrote: 'He is not much of a theologian but I think a very sincere man, more led by feeling than cold reason. He loved his predecessor William Temple, whom he also succeeded as headmaster of Repton.'[30] He also noted the political influence of the Archbishop and his ready access to the monarch.

Despite this, the Secretary of State Cardinal Domenico Tardini, a Vatican official of long experience, was anxious that the visit would be misinterpreted and did his best to ensure a press blackout. He sent four conditions, later described by Fisher as 'astonishing',[31] to Sir Peter

[26] *Commentary on the Church Assembly and on the Convocations of Canterbury and York, Autumn Session, 1960* (London: Church Information Office, 1960), 11.

[27] Owen Chadwick, "The Church of England and the Church of Rome, from the Beginning of the Nineteenth Century to the Present Day," in *Anglican Initiatives in Church Unity*, ed. E. G. W. Bill (London: SPCK, 1967), 73–107 at 102.

[28] Carpenter, *Fisher*, 711–12.

[29] For a detailed account of the visit, see Carpenter, *Fisher*, Chapter 58.

[30] Purdey, *The Search for Unity*, 27.

[31] Purcell, *Fisher*, 281.

Scarlett, British Ambassador to the Holy See: there were to be no photographs; Fisher was not to be granted an official meeting with Cardinal Bea, which Scarlett regarded as a 'preposterous thing'[32]; there was to be no press release; and there were to be no Vatican officials invited to the reception at the ambassador's residence.[33] In addition, Fisher was not to be referred to as Archbishop, but was simply to be known as 'Dr. Fisher'. This meant that the press statement that had been earlier agreed with Cardinal Bea proved unacceptable. However, even though there were to be no official photographs, it proved impossible to silence the press corps who had realized the importance of the visit and who assembled at the airport in large numbers to greet Fisher's arrival.[34] Fisher and his advisors, especially Colonel Robert Hornby his press secretary, handled the diplomacy impressively, ensuring that the visit was not reduced solely to 'una simplice visita di cortesia', which is how it had been billed in *L'Osservatore Romano*.[35] Indeed, with Willebrands' help, Hornby had held a quiet press briefing a few days earlier.[36] Shortly after his arrival Fisher preached a widely reported sermon at the English Church of All Saints' where he somewhat pointedly differentiated between the imperial model of the church and the 'commonwealth' model adopted by Anglicans.[37] There was a degree of brinkmanship till the very end, with Fisher even threatening to depart on the very morning of the visit since the Vatican had not been able to agree a statement.

Nevertheless, the visit took place with a degree of pomp and at 67 minutes was far longer than expected. Both men were practical and wanted to make things work.[38] Pope John had a disdain for theologians. In a conversation with Bernard Pawley, who became Anglican representative in Rome shortly after the meeting, Pope John remarked that theologians 'have got us into this mess, and we have got to get ourselves out

---

[32] SPCU archives in Purdey, *The Search for Unity*, 27.

[33] Purcell, *Fisher*, 281.

[34] See the Pathé newsreel at: http://www.britishpathe.com/video/archbishop-of-canterbury-arrives-in-rome/query/1960+Olympics (accessed 12 August 2015).

[35] Hein, *Fisher*, 78.

[36] Purdey, *The Search for Unity*, 32.

[37] Carpenter, *Fisher*, 731–32.

[38] Staples, "Geoffrey Francis Fisher," 263.

of it; it is practical men like you and me who will deliver us from it'.[39] Fisher said soon afterward: 'We talked like two good Christian gentlemen about anything that came into our minds'.[40] *The Times* reported the following day that after shaking hands, Fisher had begun with the words, 'Your Holiness, we are making history'.[41] There were no official records of the visit, but within twenty minutes of leaving the audience, Fisher dictated an account to Satterthwaite.[42] After some pleasantries the Pope revealed to Fisher that he had arranged a meeting with Bea. They then discussed the Vatican Council, which the Pope explained had the 'R. C. Church as its prime concern'. After Fisher noted that other churches were interested in what was happening, the Pope then said that 'in due course he expected that they would be able to take up matters concerning other Churches' both Orthodox and protestant. It was at this point that Fisher intervened to insert a special 'plea for Anglicans too as falling in neither of these categories'. 'The Pope', he observed, 'readily accepted the distinction of Anglicans having a different position from Protestant bodies generally'.[43]

The mood seems to have been particularly cordial, with the Pope commenting on the happiness that the encounter with the leader of the Church of St Augustine had brought him. At this point, there seems to have been the crucial moment of the whole encounter where Fisher

> pointed out that no-one could return to the past and that it was useless merely looking backwards. What is necessary is that we all advance – that in going forward *together* we will never remain quite the same as we were before.[44]

Later in life Fisher recorded his own recollections of the meeting, which were somewhat livelier than his immediate impressions. The two leaders, he noted, had a 'to and fro' conversation as 'two happy people

---

[39] Cited in Frederick Bliss, *Anglicans in Rome* (Norwich: Canterbury Press, 2006), 44.

[40] Purdy, *The Search for Unity*, 30–31.

[41] "Dr. Fisher Spends an Hour with The Pope," *The Times*, 3 December 1960, 6.

[42] Cited in full in Carpenter, *Fisher*, 734–36.

[43] Ibid., 735.

[44] Ibid.

who'd seen a great deal of the world and of life and of the Churches'.[45] When John XXIII quoted from his own address about the importance of returning to the 'Mother Church', Fisher responded: 'Your holiness, not *return*! None of us can go backward, only forwards. Our two Churches are now running on parallel courses and we may look forward to their meeting one day'. Pope John replied: 'You are quite right', to which Fisher added, 'I never heard him speak again of "returning"'.[46] After the meeting a short statement was finally agreed. The press conference broke no confidences about the meeting, and Fisher's office remained clearly in control. By all accounts, it seems to have been light-hearted and enjoyable. *The Tablet* reporter commented: 'One was reminded of a headmaster taking the sixth form for Greek – there was the same easy authority, the same friendly firmness, the occasional shaft of wit; the occasional recall to relevance'.[47] The communiqué itself however was modest, and merely spoke of Fisher's sharing some of his experiences in Jerusalem and Istanbul, the Pope's desire to increase 'brother feeling among all men, and especially all Christians', and 'personal conversations of a spiritual nature'. It then reported on the exchange of gifts. It concluded firmly: 'It was never intended that this should be an occasion for consideration of particular problems or issues, and the meeting retained throughout the character of a visit of courtesy. It was marked by a happy spirit of cordiality and sympathy, such as befitted a notable event in the history of Church relations'.[48]

The Times reported the following day that Fisher called on Bea at his own initiative and also that his meeting with the Pope was quite different from the earlier visits of the German protestant Bishop Otto Dibelius in 1956, and Mervyn Stockwood, who had paid a private visit to Rome in April 1959 shortly before his appointment as Bishop of Southwark and was unexpectedly granted an audience with John XXIII where they

[45] Ibid., 737. An account is given in *Touching on Christian Truth: The Kingdom of God, the Christian Church and the World* (London: Mowbray, 1971), 187–88.

[46] *Touching on Christian Truth*, 187–88; the text in Carpenter is slightly different, and may be his own transcription from the tape.

[47] See *The Tablet*, 10 December 1960, 1141; for a brief assessment of other reports, see Purdey, *The Search for Unity*, 34–35.

[48] See *The Tablet*, 10 December 1960, 1156.

shared their 'hopes and prayers'.[49] Unlike them, *The Times* noted, Fisher went not privately, but as leader of worldwide Anglicanism.[50] The meeting with Bea lasted 35 minutes and was also attended by Willebrands and Sattherthwaite. It began with an account of the structure of the SPCU given by Willebrands (which was all that was reported in the press), before moving on to more general topics. Fisher spoke of the increasing unity of the Anglican bishops, before announcing that he was ready to form a small group of experts who might advise him on ecumenical matters. He also spoke of the appointment of an unofficial Anglican delegate to Rome, who would act as liaison officer to the Secretariat. He went on to comment on domestic matters, noting that while Heenan was very open to Anglicans, other bishops were less accessible, and he complained against the common practice of rebaptizing Anglican converts to Roman Catholicism. He also felt that the observers at the Council should be chosen by himself after consultation.[51]

One should not underestimate Fisher's role in the change of mood in ecumenical relations, even if the importance of the meeting with John XXIII was downplayed in Rome at the time. *L'Osservatore Romano*, for instance, simply commented: 'Dr. Geoffrey Francis Fisher had an audience with His Holiness.'[52] The lack of photographs meant that the visit was not perhaps as widely reported as it might have been and some felt it was purely tokenistic: on 3 December, *The Daily Mail*, for instance, published a cartoon under which was a headline, 'The picture that could not be taken'. The cartoon itself, by Nicolas Bentley, had a picture of Fisher with the Pope with the caption: 'So long, see you in 2360'. In hindsight, however, the importance of the meeting was profound: it was to have major and lasting implications for the identity of Anglicanism. Quite simply, the foe against which the whole weight of Anglican history coalesced became a more or less willing conversation partner overnight. And it took the courage of both sides to make that happen.

---

[49] Michael de-la-Noy, *Mervyn Stockwood: A Lonely Life* (London: Mowbray, 1996), 105–6.

[50] "Dr. Fisher Spends an Hour with The Pope," 6.

[51] SPCU archive, in Purdy, *The Search for Unity*, 31. The Sunday after the meeting, Heenan engaged in a BBC discussion with Michael Ramsey, "Archbishop of York," *The Tablet*, 10 December 1960, 1144–45.

[52] See Carpenter, *Fisher*, 739.

Fisher had noted the importance of the visit to Rome in his sermon at the English Church: 'The period of the cold war between Churches is not altogether past. But it is passing'.[53] Speaking of the Rome visit in his presidential address to Convocation of Canterbury (the clergy synod of the southern province of the Church of England) on 17 January 1961, Fisher made some references to its 'courteous' nature which are good examples of his dry wit:

> My visit was not concerned with anything other than those courtesies of the Kingdom of God on which our Lord built his Church. These courtesies flourish in part but they should flourish everywhere within the Christian brotherhood, and, indeed, should be shown unceasingly to those outside it, too, without any embarrassment about other questions of doctrine or jurisdiction or religious practice, and still less with any uneasiness about claims or rights or protocol or prestige.[54]

Looking back in retirement, Fisher observed that it was 'without doubt the personality of Pope John' that led to the change of attitude. 'It was quite obvious to the world that Pope John was a different kind of pope, whom I should like to meet, and could meet, on grounds of Christian brotherhood without any kind of ecclesiastical compromise on either side'.[55] Fisher likened Pope John to his friend and predecessor at Canterbury, William Temple: 'Both of these eminently simply and eminently gifted men were examples of the love of God and interpreters of it to their fellow men.'[56] It was such a characteristic in Pope John that allowed them to trust one another: 'It is by such easy conversation between people who trust each other that fixed ideas from the past get unfrozen and liquidated'.[57]

From the SPCU Cardinal Bea gave his judgment in his lengthy and very cautious article in *La Civiltà Cattolica*, the Jesuit periodical. He defended the need for the utmost discretion about the meeting on the grounds that Christian disunity was, 'as it were, gazing in upon the

[53] Chadwick, "The Church of England and the Church of Rome," 104.

[54] *The Chronicle of Convocation Being a Record of the Proceedings of the Convocation of Canterbury: 17–19 January 1961* (London: SPCK, 1961), 7.

[55] Purcell, *Fisher*, 273.

[56] Fisher, *Touching on Christian Truth*, 187.

[57] Ibid., 188.

private sorrow of a mother'. He consequently asked: 'How could one expect a mother to give wide publicity to these first steps toward a new *rapprochement* after so long and sorrowful a separation?'[58] Nevertheless he recognized that it 'was Dr. Fisher who sensed the change of atmosphere; pointed it out; realized the obligations entailed and took the necessary steps to bring the public to a greater awareness of the new atmosphere and to foster their interest'.[59] He also noted the new situation of openness: 'one outcome of the meeting has been for "the thoughts of many hearts to be made manifest"'.[60] Somewhat enigmatically, he concluded: 'We are sincerely convinced that his visit of last December will bear fruit, though we have no wish to specify its nature'.[61] In January 1970 Willebrands, by then a Cardinal and president of the SPCU following Bea's death, reflected on Fisher's meeting in a sermon given at Cambridge University, and definitively reversing any sense of its being simply a courtesy visit: 'For the first time since the Reformation the Archbishop of Canterbury met the Pope. This fraternal encounter in historical perspective so much more than a mere gesture of courtesy, was a stroke of vision pointing firmly to the future.'[62]

Protestant criticism of Fisher did not evaporate after the meeting. In a debate on Christian Unity in the House of Lords in May 1961, for instance, Fisher met with further hostility from Lord Alexander of Hillsborough.[63] But he stuck to his guns. Rome—like Russia thirty years later in politics—could no longer be seen simply as the foe and the focus for a negative identity. The thaw in relations between the churches was further encouraged with the appointment in 1961 of Bernard Pawley, a Canon of Ely, as Anglican representative in Rome,[64] who quickly proved effective at making friends in the Vatican and helping remove some of

---

[58] "A proposito della visita di S.G. il dott. G. Fisher," *La Civiltà Cattolica* 4 (1960): 561–68; see Augustin Bea, *The Unity of Christians*, ed. Bernard Leeming (London: Chapman, 1963), 61–72 at 70–71.

[59] Bea, *The Unity of Christians*, 71.

[60] Ibid., 64–65.

[61] Ibid., 71.

[62] "Diversity Without Separation," *The Tablet*, 24 January 1970, 92–93 at 92; see also *Documents on Anglican/Roman Catholic Relations* (Washington, DC: United States Catholic Bishops' Conference, 1972), 34.

[63] See the debate in the House of Lords, *Hansard*, 10 May 1961.

[64] On Pawley, see Chandler and Hansen, *Observing Vatican II*, 15–19.

the ignorance about the Anglican Communion: 'it is only fair to say,' Pawley remarked, 'that the Pope's lack of objective information about the Church of England was immediately evident' in his audiences.[65] Pawley proved immensely effective in working behind the scenes in the preparations for the Second Vatican Council. During the Council itself, his personal friendships, especially with Cardinal Bea, proved central in helping the assembled bishops come to a better understanding of the other churches.[66]

ANGLICANISM AND THE SECOND VATICAN COUNCIL

Despite its low-key presentation in the press, this major change in Anglican-Roman Catholic relations had an obvious impact on the traditional protestant anti-Romanism of the English churches: if Rome was to be a willing ecumenical partner then this would inevitably lead to a change of heart on the part of Anglicans. For many Anglo-Catholics, of course, this was a moment that they had been waiting for over a very long period. This change in mood can be well illustrated by the course of the Vatican Council itself, especially the modifications to the Decree on Ecumenism. The presence of the ecumenical observers and the unexpected extent of the hospitality extended to them were obviously important in shaping the conciliar debates. These included three Anglicans (plus two other Anglicans who were members of other delegations).[67] The Anglican observers, who were the first to accept the offer,[68] quickly built up a close friendship with members of the SPCU.[69] Although I will

[65] Chandler and Hein, *Fisher*, 108. See Bernard and Margaret Pawley, *Rome and Canterbury through the Centuries* (London: Mowbray, 1974), 335–36.

[66] Purdey, *The Search for Unity*, 37–38.

[67] For the Anglican observers, see Bliss, *Anglicans in Rome*, 62–63. A full list is given by Bernard Leeming, S.J., *The Vatican Council and Christian Unity: A Commentary on the Decree of Ecumenism of the Second Vatican Council, with a Translation of the Text* (London: Darton, Longman and Todd, 1966), 312–17. See also Bernard Pawley, ed., *Second Vatican Council: Some Anglican Views* (Oxford: University Press, 1966); Peter Webster, *Archbishop Ramsey: The Shape of the Church* (Farnham: Ashgate, 2015), 31.

[68] David M. Paton and R. M. C. Jeffery, *Christian Unity and the Anglican Communion*, 2nd ed. (London: Church Information Office, 1966), 45.

[69] See Bliss, *Anglicans in Rome*, 63–69; Purdey, *The Search for Unity*, 58–61. This fullest account is given in Chandler and Hansen, *Observing Vatican II*, 31–404. Personal reflections were offered in *The Second Vatican Council: Studies by Eight Anglican Observers*, ed. Bernard C. Pawley (London: Oxford University Press, 1967).

not discuss the whole process in detail, it is fair to say that through the next few years there was a subtle but profound reshaping of Anglican identity over the course of the Vatican Council: by singling out Anglicans from other protestants in the final Decree on Ecumenism the Council Fathers decisively challenged the historic protestant identity of the Church of England.

Chapter 3 of the draft schema for the second session was circulated in June 1963, which contained three chapters on ecumenism. It generally met with an enthusiastic response from the assembled bishops when it was discussed. For Anglicans, however, there was a problem. While the draft spoke warmly and extensively of the orthodox churches, all the other Christian communities 'arising from the sixteenth century onwards' were lumped together. This offended many Anglicans for whom the idea of continuity was central to their identity.[70] In his recollection of the Council, Bishop John Moorman of Ripon, the most senior of the Anglican observers, noted that those 'who had taken the trouble to find out something about Anglicanism realized that, in spite of its curious habits, it was obviously something quite different from other protestant communities, and that it ought not, therefore, to be lumped together with them in the post-Reformation group'.[71] In the light of such pleading several bishops at the Council sought to change the text. During the three days of debates in the Decree in December 1963, Paul Gouyon, for instance, coadjutor of Rennes and Titular Archbishop of Pessinus, noted that 'we look in vain' in the schema for 'any clear allusion to the great Anglican community, which in its origins is certainly quite distinct and different from the communities of the Reformation'. He continued: 'It would satisfy me better if there were different and separate chapters for the Orthodox Churches, for the Anglican Communion, and for the communions which grew out the Reformation.'[72] The branch theory of the Anglo-Catholics was quietly being accepted by at least one Roman Catholic bishop as what constituted authentic Anglicanism.

Bishop Jean-Édouard-Lucien Rupp of Monaco went as far as quoting Newman's opinion that 'the fact that the Anglican Church had for three

---

[70] See Purdey, *The Search for Unity*, 71–72.

[71] John Moorman, *Vatican Observed: An Anglican View of Vatican II* (London: Darton, Longman and Todd, 1967), 98.

[72] Hans Küng, Yves Congar, O.P., and Daniel O'Hanlon, S.J., eds., *Council Speeches of Vatican II* (Glen Rock, NJ: Paulist Press, 1964), 115–17.

centuries produced so many holy people, and accomplished so much good, [meant] that it could be explained only by a special intervention of Divine Providence'. Rupp also observed that 'in the Anglican Church many beautiful and inspiring things were to be found on bishops and their place in the church'.[73] Bishop Ernest Arthur Green of Port Elizabeth even thought it worthwhile to open up the question of Anglican Orders since 'local secretariats for Christian unity cannot be expected to solve a problem of this magnitude. It must be resolved on the highest level between the supreme authorities of the Roman Catholic and the Anglican Churches.'[74] Similarly, Dom Cuthbert Butler of Downside felt it appropriate to single out the Anglican Church from the others since it was 'so widespread, so devoted to patristic antiquity and which has deserved so well of the ecumenical movement'.[75] Eventually the text noted that 'among those in which the Catholic traditions and institutions in part survive, the Anglican Communion occupies a special place' (UR 13).[76] This amounts to an explicit recognition of Anglicanism as something different from other protestant churches. It was a de facto singling out of one of the competing models of Anglican identity as the authentic voice of Anglicanism. To a limited degree, then, Anglo-Catholicism was vindicated at the Council through this modest insertion: it meant that those 'Catholic traditions and institutions', by which is presumably meant the three-fold ministry, are emphasized as central features of Anglicanism (rather than as accidental and pragmatic survivals as they had been understood by many Anglicans). The insertion of the specific recognition of Anglicans into the Decree provided a significant boost for those Anglicans for whom the historic episcopate was central for a church to be a church (and which was later to prove fatal for the Church of England–Methodist conversations later in the 1960s and early 1970s).

[73] Paraphrase in Chandler and Hansen, *Observing Vatican II*, 282.

[74] See Chandler and Hansen, *Observing Vatican II*, 285.

[75] A translation of the debates has been posted at: https://vaticaniiat50.wordpress.com/2013/12/02/session-nears-end-council-assured-ecumenism-chapters-still-on-agenda/ (accessed 13 August 2015).

[76] Cited in Herring, *The Vatican Council*, 12.

MICHAEL RAMSEY'S MEETING WITH PAUL VI

Finally, I turn briefly to the visit of Fisher's successor, Michael Ramsey to Pope Paul VI in the year after the closing of the Council from 22 to 24 March 1966.[77] Unlike Fisher, Ramsey, who was translated to Canterbury in May 1961 after Fisher's retirement, was a major theologian who had been professor in Durham and Cambridge before his elevation to the episcopate. He was also a relatively liberal Anglo-Catholic whose first major work was *The Gospel and the Catholic Church*,[78] which sought to subject the tradition of the Church to critical scrutiny against what he perceived to be the standards of the Gospel. After he had become Archbishop of Canterbury, he held a 'Requiem celebration of the Holy Communion' for Pope John,[79] which proved challenging to a number of more protestant-minded Anglicans for whom requiem masses were anathema. In his sermon Ramsey spoke of a 'man who touched human hearts with charity', also noting that 'however long the road [to reunion] may be, charity already makes all the difference to it'.[80] Despite his obvious Anglo-Catholic sympathies, however, Ramsey showed a reluctance to visit Rome, partly because of the problems over mixed marriages that had met with intransigence from Catholic authorities. In addition, he had no great desire to upset more protestant-minded Anglicans either in England or other parts of the Communion: some protestants both inside and outside the Church of England felt that Ramsey was in danger of becoming Rome's poodle.[81]

There were also problems from the Catholic side. A few years earlier when Cardinal Bea had visited Ramsey in Lambeth, some in the English Catholic hierarchy felt that the personal warmth of relationships between Ramsey and Rome was holding up the cause for the beatification of the forty Catholic martyrs of the reformation. Others, including Heenan, Archbishop of Westminster from September 1963 and Cardinal from 1965, were anxious that the focus on Rome meant that local ecumenical discussions were being stalled in England. This created something

---

[77] See Owen Chadwick, *Michael Ramsey: A Life* (Oxford: University Press, 1991), 313–23.

[78] Michael Ramsey, *The Gospel and the Catholic Church* (London: Longmans, 1936).

[79] Webster, *Archbishop Ramsey*, 31.

[80] 17 June 1963, in Webster, *Archbishop Ramsey*, 161.

[81] Chadwick, *Michael Ramsey*, 315.

of a temporary conflict between the English bishops and the SPCU.[82] For his part, Ramsey was also keen to ensure that ecumenical relations were international and Communion-wide rather than focused purely on England, which helped expand the role of the Archbishop as leader of an international Communion of Churches. In January 1966 he wrote to Oliver Tomkins, Bishop of Bristol, that dialogue needed to be controlled by the SPCU: 'Of course the English hierarchy has to be involved, but if it is allowed to control, we find our Continental contacts kept out, and the propagandist element strengthened'.[83] A few months after his visit to Rome, Ramsey wrote that what he feared most was a return of what he called the 'siege mentality' of the past, and which he thought was exemplified in the proposals to canonize the English Martyrs.[84] This was, he felt, 'far different from the spirit of the meeting between His Holiness the Pope and myself in March 1966'.[85] Despite his reservations about going to Rome, Ramsey's mind was eventually changed partly because of a sense of expectation in the country at large, and partly because of the character of Pope Paul VI who was something of an Anglophile.[86]

The visit in March 1966 could not have been more different from that of Fisher less than six years earlier. It was almost universally warmly received from both sides, despite some rather ludicrous posturing by extreme protestants including Ian Paisley.[87] During his visit Ramsey also opened the Anglican Center in Rome in the Palazzo Doria Pamphilj, and inaugurated the new Church of England Diocese of Gibraltar, which covered the whole of continental Europe.[88] The venue was far more impressive than in 1960: Ramsey and Pope Paul met in the Sistine Chapel. There were official and very grand photographs. The discussion itself was wide-ranging and had been well prepared for.[89]

---

[82] For details see Purdey, *The Search for Unity*, 92–93.

[83] 26 January 1966, in Webster, *Archbishop Ramsey*, 183.

[84] See Purdey, *The Search for Unity*, 40–41.

[85] Note on the proposed Canonisation of the English and Welsh Martyrs of the Reformation Period, 8 November 1966, in Webster, *Archbishop Ramsey*, 189–90.

[86] Chadwick, *Michael Ramsey*, 315–17.

[87] Ibid., 319.

[88] Bliss, *Anglicans in Rome*, 89–96.

[89] Ramsey made extensive notes on his preparation for the conversation with the Papal Nuncio in London, Igino Eugenio Cardinale, which list the matters that were later addressed. See Purdey, *The Search for Unity*, 94–95.

They tackled the problem of validity of orders as well as mixed marriages and re-baptism. They also moved into the idea of a Commission to tackle difficulties, which eventually became the Anglican-Roman Catholic International Commission. Through the course of the meeting Ramsey formed a respect for Pope Paul, which seems to have been mutual.[90] The following day there was a shared prayer service in the basilica of St. Paul's-Outside-the-Walls. A key part of the symbolism was the gift of an episcopal ring by the Pope after the end of the service which had concluded with a final (joint) blessing by the two leaders, as well as the signing of the Common Declaration which established the ARCIC process which was to address 'not only theological matters such as Scripture, Tradition and Liturgy, but also matters of practical difficulty felt on either side'.[91] The giving of the ring deeply moved Ramsey, who felt as if Paul was 'giving me a piece of himself'. After the press conference Ramsey was asked whether this was a tacit recognition of the validity of his orders. He replied: 'Not at all; but what it does betoken is the official recognition of the Church of England as an official Church with its rightful ministers. That from Rome means a great deal'.[92] Cardinal Willebrands noted the importance of the occasion at an address given at the opening of the Anglican Center in Rome:

> Has there ever been a meeting at Rome so official and so solemn in character which in so limited a space of time gave rise to events of such great importance? I remember that in preparing for this meeting the Pope wished that a very special protocol be worked out which would characterize the events as the visit of one Church to another and not just the meetings of Heads in a consecrated spot.[93]

This was the beginning of what he called 'real dialogue'. The Archbishop of Canterbury had led 'the Anglican Communion into dialogue

---

[90] Chadwick, *Michael Ramsey*, 321.

[91] Paton and Jeffery, *Christian Unity*, 47. The official report was included in the pamphlet, *The Archbishop of Canterbury's Visit to Rome, March 1966* (London: Church Information Office, 1966).

[92] Chadwick, *Michael Ramsey*, 322. It is reported that Ramsey died wearing the ring. See Gordon Wakefield, "Michael Ramsey and Ecumenical Theology," in *Michael Ramsey as Theologian*, ed. Robin Gill and Lorna Kendall (London: DLT, 1995), 63–81 at 63.

[93] Jan Willebrands, "The Ecumenical Significance of the Visit of the Archbishop of Canterbury," *Unitas* 19 (1967): 8–17 at 14.

with Rome which had opened its doors to him. He had brought the Anglican Communion into joint prayer with our church'.[94] At least on Willebrands' view, Anglicans were being treated by Roman Catholics as one member of the species Church.

CONCLUSION

These three examples reveal that the ecumenical openness initiated during the preparations to Vatican II and through its course promoted something of a change in the perception of Anglicanism among both Roman Catholics and Anglicans. To some extent at least, this was to threaten its historic protestant identity, which had already been challenged by Anglo-Catholics even though there was no real hope of ecumenical progress in the pre-conciliar church. The visits by the two successive archbishops as well as the modification of the Decree on Ecumenism had the effect of downplaying the importance of the Reformation in Anglican identity. In practice, Anglicanism was no longer treated as a protestant community like the others but as a church (and the See of Canterbury now possesses an episcopal ring as proof).[95] For most of their history, however, the vast majority of Anglicans in both the Church of England and its daughter churches, would have begged to differ from this sort of understanding. It was their own formulation of 'Anglican' identity that was limited to the four points of the so-called Quadrilateral that had been adopted at the Lambeth Conference of 1888 that made this novel understanding possible. For quite different reasons they had downplayed the centrality of the Reformation and overstressed the 'historic episcopacy' as central to Anglican identity.[96] This meant that Anglicanism could easily be elevated into a kind of ecumenical 'bridge church',[97] which had been reformed but was also Catholic

---

[94] Willebrands, "The Ecumenical Significance," 14.

[95] Archbishop Justin Welby wore the ring for his visit to Pope Francis on 14 June 2013: see http://www.archbishopofcanterbury.org/articles.php/5076/archbishop-justin-meets-pope-francis-in-rome (accessed 13 August 2015).

[96] See my "American Catholicity and the National Church: The Legacy of William Reed Huntington," *Sewanee Theological Review* 56 (Easter 2013): 113–48.

[97] See, for example, Graham Leonard, "Foreword," in *The Panther and the Hind: A Theological History of Anglicanism*, Aidan Nichols (Edinburgh: T&T Clark, 1993), ix; see also 179.

in its structures. In their own way Vatican II and the ecumenical mood that it encouraged thus played their part in re-forging Anglican identity and moving it away from Protestantism. Many Anglicans have been very willing to lose some of their Protestant identity and accept their vocation as a Church that is both reformed and Catholic. This understanding proved immensely fruitful in the early ARCIC dialogues and has much to commend it, however much it might deviate from historic Anglican identity. In the end, it may not prove sustainable against the realignment of Protestant Christianity and the rise of global Evangelicalism that, it seems to me, is shaping Anglican identity far more rapidly than any longing for unity with Roman Catholics.[98]

[98] See my *Anglican Theology*, 199–210.

PART VI

The Fruits and Future of Vatican II's Ecumenical Opening

Surveying the Impact of *Unitatis Redintegratio*: Achieved Convergences— Current Processes—Open Questions

Dorothea Sattler

There are worldly wisdoms only poets can express with few words. One of them was formulated by the Austrian writer Peter Handke: "Before any meeting: Consider the road the other person has taken."[1] Today, some statements from the documents of the Second Vatican Council about the significance of the ecumenical movement do not strike us as very surprising because their concerns in the meantime have been put into action in multiple contexts. However, a closer examination of the doctrinal statements compared with earlier commentaries on the subject matter reveals how thematically comprehensive and methodically fundamental the last Council's new views on ecumenism have been.

---

[1] Peter Handke, *Phantasien der Wiederholung* (Frankfurt am Main: Suhrkamp, 1983), 42.

D. Sattler (✉)
Westfälische Wilhelms-Universität Münster, Ökumenisches Institut,
Münster, Germany
e-mail: dorothea.sattler@t-online.de

© The Author(s) 2018
V. Latinovic et al. (eds.), *Catholicism Opening to the World and Other Confessions*, Pathways for Ecumenical and Interreligious Dialogue,
https://doi.org/10.1007/978-3-319-98581-7_17

283

The ecumenical movement that finds recognition in the documents of the Second Vatican Council began many centuries before this event. The ecumenical movement arose in the end of the nineteenth and the beginning of the twentieth centuries within non-Roman Catholic Christianity. Christians from the Reformed and Orthodox traditions took the initiative in the area of ecumenism. For that, we are grateful today. For many centuries, the Roman Catholic Church regarded these developments with great skepticism. In August 1927, the first "World Conference on Faith and Order" took place in Lausanne. In 1928, Pope Pius XI published the encyclical *Mortalium Animos*[2] with the main objective to dissuade Roman Catholic Christians from the thought of participating in this form of the search for unity. In his encyclical Pope Pius XI labeled those congregating in ecumenical affinity in connection with the establishment of the movement "Faith and Order" derisively as "pan-Christians" and expressed great concern: "And these men, so far from being quite few and scattered, have increased to the dimensions of an entire class, and have grouped themselves into widely spread societies, most of which are directed by non-Catholics, although they are imbued with varying doctrines concerning the things of faith."[3] The Pope admonished that "We should not permit the flock of the Lord to be cheated by dangerous fallacies."[4] Therefore spoke of "avoiding this evil."[5] The words the Council Fathers placed at the beginning of *Unitatis Redintegratio* sound so very different: "The restoration of unity among all Christians is one of the principal concerns of the Second Vatican Council. Christ the Lord founded one Church and one Church only. However, many Christian communions present themselves to men as the true inheritors of Jesus Christ" (UR 1).

In the first part of my essay, I will concentrate my attention on the ecumenical convergences that already have been achieved as a result of statements in *Unitatis Redintegratio*; in part two, I will set the Decree on Ecumenism in relation to current processes; and in part three I will finish by formulating some open questions.

---

[2] Pius XI, Encyclical Letter, *Mortalium Animos*, AAS 20 (1928): 5–16.
[3] Ibid., no. 4.
[4] Ibid., 5.
[5] Ibid.

ACHIEVED CONVERGENCES

Many concerns of the Decree on Ecumenism that were regarded as innovations at the time of its origination have in the meantime become habits we take for granted. They have become standards for ecumenical togetherness. Some of these merit special mention here.

Acknowledging the Need for Reform in All Christian Confessional Communities

"There can be no ecumenism worthy of the name without a change of heart" (UR 7). This sentence from *Unitatis Redintegratio* has developed an effectual history like hardly any other passage, one that certainly cannot be documented on the textual level alone. The readiness for repentance has become a basic attitude within the ecumenical movement. Today's dialogues are vividly conscious of the historical conditionalities of denominational standpoints in the context of world history. All Churches regard the return to scriptural doctrines as their respective task. The Decree on Ecumenism expresses it like this: "All the faithful should remember that the more effort they make to live holier lives according to the Gospel, the better will they further Christian unity and put it into practice" (UR 7).

Acknowledging the Already Existing Unity Through Common Baptism

"Baptism...establishes a sacramental bond of unity which links all who have been reborn by it" (UR 22). Since the time of the Second Vatican Council there have been various efforts to achieve a new appreciation of the one baptism from an ecumenical point of view. Especially in periods of crisis, both individuals and larger communities seek confidence in the present by remembering a meaningful origin. With time-specific characteristics, the history of the celebration of the remembrance of baptism reflects the challenge, felt again and again by the Christian community of faith, to make sure of the beginning in order to be able to face the present and form the future. The remembrance of baptism can be regarded as an admonition to be sincere in Christian discipleship. Today, the remembrance of baptism can be considered the probably most hopeful perspective of the current ecumenical efforts.

Open and Willing to Engage in Processes of Ecumenical Dialogue

"We must get to know the outlook of our separated brethren. (...) Most valuable for this purpose are meetings of the two sides - especially for discussion of theological problems - where each can deal with the other on an equal footing (*par cum pari agat*)" (UR 9).

Since the Second Vatican Council, the Roman Catholic Church has primarily conducted bilateral dialogues with all Christian confessional communities. Even experts find it hard to keep track of the specific events. Today, everybody talks to everyone about everything across the globe. In this regard, *Unitatis Redintegratio* calls for the fundamental attitude that the counterpart should be met in discussions on an equal footing. The effectual history of this admonition cannot be valued highly enough.

CURRENT PROCESSES

For quite some time various events on different levels within the ecumenical movement have been happening at the same time. Coordinating resources are needed to direct the different phenomena towards a common goal. It is necessary to show the unifying concern in all efforts. In this regard, the Decree on Ecumenism has formulated groundbreaking thoughts.

Christological-Soteriological Concentration of Ecumenical Questions

After being lifted up on the cross and glorified, the Lord Jesus poured forth His Spirit as He had promised, and through the Spirit He has called and gathered together the people of the New Covenant, who are the Church, into a unity of faith, hope and charity, as the Apostle teaches us: "There is one body and one Spirit, just as you were called to the one hope of your calling; one Lord, one faith, one Baptism" (Eph 4:4-5). For "all you who have been baptized into Christ have put on Christ... for you are all one in Christ Jesus" (Gal 3:27-28). It is the Holy Spirit, dwelling in those who believe and pervading and ruling over the Church as a whole, who brings about that wonderful communion of the faithful. He brings them into intimate union with Christ, so that He is the principle of the Church's unity (UR 2).

The anamnesis of Jesus Christ is the mission of the entire ecumenical movement. Recent outlines on Christian-theological soteriology try to approach the concept of the redeeming meaning of Jesus Christ's death, the theology of the cross, by describing Jesus Christ's death as the final consequence of his life. "Men killed Jesus Christ, but God raised him up"—this is what the Acts of the Apostles keep impressing upon the early Christian communities.[6] God brings his Son back to life in a new way, He agrees with his message, He lets the witnesses of the resurrection experience that the love, Jesus Christ lived, is eternally valid and everlasting because it shows God's own willingness to remain faithful to the community, just and loving when He is met by murderous rejection. If one lives in the spirit of this Jesus Christ, one will be a human being with the desire to reconcile—provided one has sufficient strength for it. An ecumenical attitude, therefore, is in high accordance with the nature of Christian discipleship.

Addressing the Concerns of the Spiritual Ecumenism of Life

This change of heart and holiness of life, along with public and private prayer for the unity of Christians, should be regarded as the soul of the whole ecumenical movement, and merits the name, "spiritual ecumenism." (UR 8)

Spiritual experiences are consciously registered events where human beings by the power of the presence of the spirit of God are led to the depths of their existential questions and can recognize and grasp a trustworthy and faithful answer. Those who ever have experienced that other human beings can express the answer, they themselves have found to the common questions of life, in a credible and appealing manner will no longer want to elude the attraction of spiritual togetherness. Life leaves a lot to be desired. Together, we find it easier to enter the gloom of existence, to deliberate our unavoidable death and the burden of sin. The light of confidence in the God of life can only be guarded in the community.

We obviously live in a period of ecumenical history where ecumenical-theological dialogues alone do not lead us closer to each other. The ecumenism of life assumes that already today the spirit of God leads

---

[6] Acts 3:15, 4:10, and passim.

human beings to live a form of ecumenical affinity that fulfills the mission of Christian discipleship—by actions of service (*diakonia*), missionary work, celebrations of faith. Today, not everything that is possible is practiced already in the sense of ecumenism within the spheres of activity of the Churches.

Necessity for Comprehensive Ecumenical Education

We must get to know the outlook of our separated brethren. To achieve this purpose, study is of necessity required, and this must be pursued with a sense of realism and good will. Catholics, who already have a proper grounding, need to acquire a more adequate understanding of the respective doctrines of our separated brethren, their history, their spiritual and liturgical life, their religious psychology and general background. (UR 9)

These considerations of the Council had groundbreaking character. The consideration that all disciplines of theology in the future also should be taught from an ecumenical point of view (cf. UR 10) had an influential effect on the academic reforms after the Council.

OPEN QUESTIONS

The open questions of ecumenism today mainly concern the understanding of Churches and ministry. One principle is very important in this connection.

The Hierarchy of Truths

When comparing doctrines with one another, they should remember that in Catholic doctrine there exists a "hierarchy" of truths, since they vary in their relation to the fundamental Christian faith. (UR 11)

In the period after the Council the term "Hierarchy of truths" attracted great attention and also was a subject under discussion in ecumenical dialogues. The Council Fathers showed openness for the concept of a legitimate multiplicity of Christian traditions and at the same time provided a criterion that can help us distinguish between more important and less important doctrinal traditions—the connection with the foundation of faith.

In many areas, the consideration of the varying closeness of a doctrinal tradition to the middle of the Christian confession has proved to be helpful in ecumenical dialogues. This effort consequently incorporates the Council's main concern of a christological-soteriological orientation of the ecumenical questions. At the same time, even today the question in which form the Roman Catholic Church would be able to support the model of a unity of the Churches in reconciled diversity, a model rather rooted in reformatory thoughts, remains open. Which criteria must be met before we can speak of an existing unity of Churches that then also would pave the way for new answers in the area of the joint celebration of the sacraments? What precisely do the Council Fathers mean with the wording:

> All in the Church must preserve unity in essentials. But let all, according to the gifts they have received enjoy a proper freedom, in their various forms of spiritual life and discipline, in their different liturgical rites, and even in their theological elaborations of revealed truth. In all things let charity prevail. (UR 4)

Incorporation of the Question of Ministry in Its Larger Contexts

The mentioning of an existing *defectus ordinis* in the Churches that emerged from the Reformation has developed an effectual history like hardly any other passage from the Decree on Ecumenism:

> Though the ecclesial Communities which are separated from us lack the fullness of unity with us flowing from Baptism, and though we believe they have not retained the proper reality of the eucharistic mystery in its fullness, especially because of the absence of the sacrament of Orders, nevertheless when they commemorate His death and resurrection in the Lord's Supper, they profess that it signifies life in communion with Christ and look forward to His coming in glory. Therefore the teaching concerning the Lord's Supper, the other sacraments, worship, the ministry of the Church, must be the subject of the dialogue. (UR 22)

Today, the state of ecumenical discussions regarding the question of the recognition of ministries is by no means unpromising. There is a common conviction that the spirit of God guarantees the connection between the apostolic time and the present of the Church. Documents from dialogues speak of the chain of imposition of hands as a visible sign of the efforts for the apostolicity of the Church. Historical studies have demonstrated that the reference to an uninterrupted episcopal succession has been apologetically motivated from the beginning. Together we ponder the relevance of the episcopate. From my point of view, it is in accordance with the main concerns of the Second Vatican Council to argue pneumatologically and *via empirica* with regard to the doctrine of ministry. The witness to Jesus Christ lived by Protestant Christians, including readiness for martyrdom, can be regarded as proof of their foundation in the apostolic succession.

The Social-Ethical Dimension of Ecumenism

In these days when cooperation in social matters is so widespread, all men without exception are called to work together. ... All believers in Christ can, through this cooperation, be led to acquire a better knowledge and appreciation of one another, and so pave the way to Christian unity. (UR 12)

The Council Fathers set special accents with their appeal for common social service in the world's crisis regions in the battle against hunger, poverty, housing shortage, and analphabetism. The ravaged human face of Jesus Christ, again and again, reappears in all human beings suffering from the various forms of violence. Ecumenism, remembrance of Jesus Christ in the spirit of God, has a deeply diaconal, caritative dimension. It relies on the thought that all human efforts to preserve human beings' livability are inspired and supported by the spirit of God. The ethics founded on the creation theology, the cry for justice for all human beings, concern about the preservation of livability, resistance against any form of violence—these tasks belong very deeply to the mission of ecumenism.

It will never be too late to address the concerns of the Council. For the Council Fathers it may have been like for the writer Peter Handke who confesses: "The *wish* to write does not suffice for me, I also have to feel the *need*."[7]

---

[7] Handke, *Phantasien der Wiederholung*, 69.

CHAPTER 18

A Patroness for the Council? Building a Movement for Our Lady of Perpetual Help in Aid of Church Unity

Patrick J. Hayes

Almost immediately after he learned of Pope John XXIII's call for the Second Vatican Council, given in the Basilica of St. Paul Outside-the-Walls on January 25, 1959, Father John V. Maguire, a Redemptorist of the Baltimore Province, set to work on a campaign to secure Our Lady of Perpetual Help (OLPH) as the patroness of the twenty-first ecumenical council. The purpose of the Council would be for greater unity in and among the Christian fold. Pope John's statement underscored "a renewed invitation to the faithful of the separated communities that they also may follow us amiably in this search for unity and grace."[1] Thus, this moment was not merely for Catholics in communion with Rome, but for other Christians as well. When asked whether room would be

[1] See Pope John XXIII, alloc. *Questa festiva*, AAS 51 (1959): 65–69 at 69.

P. J. Hayes (✉)
Redemptorist Archives, Philadelphia, PA, USA

© The Author(s) 2018
V. Latinovic et al. (eds.), *Catholicism Opening to the World and Other Confessions*, Pathways for Ecumenical and Interreligious Dialogue,
https://doi.org/10.1007/978-3-319-98581-7_18

291

made for those who came to be called "separated brethren," the head of the Council's ante-preparatory commission, Cardinal Domenico Tardini, stated that he anticipated representatives of other faiths to be present at the Council as observers for, he said, "we have nothing to hide."[2] Pope John made his plea for the Council through "the intercession of the Immaculate Mother of Jesus and our Mother." It could hardly have escaped McGuire's attention that a unity council was beckoned with the assistance of the Blessed Virgin. At the time of the pope's announcement, Maguire was the editor of *Perpetual Help Magazine*, a publication designed to promote the icon of OLPH and to bring news of Redemptorists engaged in missionary work around the world. He did not succeed in making OLPH the Council's patroness, but the story of the effort is instructive, albeit almost entirely absent from the literature on Vatican II.

In this essay I want to do two simple things. First I intend to lay out the history of the grassroots movement to install OLPH as the Council's patroness. Second, I want to propose that a failure is not the end of the story, but can actually be a vehicle for future discussions among ecumenical partners. That the Vatican Council admonished all Christians to engage in ecumenical understanding and to work for unity is now a given, but it left open precisely how this could come about. I wish to suggest that this can be greatly facilitated by the meditative posture one takes before the icon of Perpetual Help.

JOHN V. MAGUIRE, C.Ss.R. AND PERPETUAL HELP MAGAZINE

Father John McGuire, a Brooklyn native ordained in 1944, edited *Perpetual Help Magazine* for five decades, from 1953 until 2003, the year of his death. During this time he proved himself an exceptional editor and publicist. Just as quickly as the pope made his announcement, McGuire sprang into action to place the Mother of Perpetual Help icon on the world stage. He went to his typewriter and tapped out the following lines: "Since such great hopes for the reunion of the Christian world are today entertained everywhere, it is most desirable that no means be left untried that is capable of bringing God's blessings upon the sessions

---

[2] See the Cardinal's remarks in Giovanni Caprile, ed., *Il Concilio Vaticano II, vol. I, part 1: L'Annunzio e la Preparazione, 1959–1962* (Rome: Edizioni "La Civiltà Cattolica," 1966), 177.

of the Council. Certainly among these means must be counted the choice of a heavenly patron whose good offices may be counted upon to intercede with the Most Blessed Trinity for the restoration of that unity." For McGuire, that patron was Mary under the title of Our Lady of Perpetual Help. He marshaled the magisterial teaching of the previous seventy years, which instructed the faithful that Mary was both conciliatory toward the Church as well as the highest advocate before her divine Son.[3]

Maguire laid out several theological arguments for placing the Council's work under her protection. Among these was the potential for establishing unity between Rome and the separated Churches of the East. He called attention to the fact that the Perpetual Help icon was one that was familiar to all in the East and had been throughout the early twentieth century. It was classed among the *Strastnaia*—the Sorrowful Mother icons—depictions so named because of seventeenth century versions, one of which was ensconced in the monastic convent of Strastnoi, the Monastery of the Passion, destroyed by the Soviets in the 1930s.[4]

---

[3] McGuire's choice of magisterial texts all point to a moment when the unity of the Church would be recognizable, that is, when all Christians not in communion with the Roman Pontiff returned to the Church by accepting his authority. Thus in Pope Leo XIII's *Adiutricem Populi* (1895), he notes that "Mary will be the happy bond to draw together, with strong yet gentle constraint, all who love Christ, no matter where they may be, to form a nation of brothers yielding obedience to the Vicar of Christ on earth, the Roman Pontiff, their common father." He cited Pope Pius XI, who in *Lux Veritatis* (1931) begged Mary to prohibit "the people of the East" from "unhappily wandering and still separated from the unity of the Church and thus from her Son whose Vicar on earth we are." Finally, he cites Pope Pius XII's *Fulgens Corona Gloriae* (1953), where that pope calls out to all "those also who are separated from Us by ancient schism and whom nonetheless We love with paternal affection." Invoking her help, he asked that Mary "look down on all those who are proud to call themselves Christians, and who, being united at least in the bond of charity, humbly raise to her their eyes, their minds, and their prayers, imploring that light which illumines the mind with heavenly rays, and begging for that unity by which at least there may be one fold and one shepherd." Leo XIII, Encyclical Letter *Adiutricem Populi*, ASS 28 (1895): 129–36, no. 17; Pius XI, Encyclical Letter *Lux Veritatis*, AAS 23 (1931): 493–517, part III, p. 515; and Pius XII, Encyclical Letter *Fulgens Corona Gloriae*, AAS 45 (1953): 577–92, no. 44.

[4] See Marie Joseph Rouët de Journel, "Marie et l'iconographie russe," in *Maria: Études sur la Sainte Vierge*, ed. Hubert du Manoir, 7 vols. (Paris: Beauchesne, 1949–1964): II, 445–81. For the ecumenical reach of this icon, see also William McLoughlin and Jill Pinnock, eds., *Mary for Earth and Heaven: Papers on Mary and Ecumenism Given at International Congresses of the Ecumenical Society of the Blessed Virgin Mary at Leeds (1998) and Oxford (2000) and Conferences at Woldingham (1997) and Maynooth (2001)* (London:

Its fame spread throughout Russia. The icon was found in Siberia by Redemptorist missionaries who went there in 1908, and in some parts of India no home could be found without it.[5] As care packages to starving Russian children were assembled in 1922, Pope Pius XI directed that pictures of Perpetual Help be included among the foodstuffs. In 1928 he sent a copy in mosaic to the Coptic monarch Empress Zeoditu [Taitou] of Ethiopia.[6] In 1931, when Archbishop Mar Ivanios, the Malankara Syrian Catholic leader of Kerala, came into communion with Roman Catholics, he noted that "Perpetual Help could unite East and West. She is equally known to both."[7] At the Marian Congress of 1950, the icon was commended by participants as the "Imago Unistica."[8] During the early stages of the Cold War, she became a bulwark against Communist infiltration in South Asia.

BUILDING COLLABORATION: 1959

In February 1959, McGuire wrote to the Redemptorist Rector Major in Rome, Father William Gaudreau, proposing a movement to make OLPH the Council's patroness. The General wrote back on March 11 with enthusiastic approval. Fueled by this cooperative spirit in the Redemptorists' General Curia, McGuire then wrote to each provincial around the globe advocating for the proposal. Gaudreau believed the movement should be from the ground up and not from the top down, however, and so begged off making a general appeal to the world's bishops. Instead, McGuire immediately wrote to confreres around the world whom he believed would be sympathetic to his plan. This consisted of inviting people to pray, collecting petitions from the Bishops to the Holy

Gracewing, 2002). For Mariology emerging from Vatican II, see most recently Aidan Nichols, *There Is No Rose: The Mariology of the Catholic Church* (Minneapolis: Augsburg Fortress, 2015).

[5] See *Analecta Congregationis SS. Redemptoris* [hereafter *Analecta*] 1:5 (1922): 200–6.

[6] *Analecta* 9:1 (1930): 39.

[7] As quoted in John V. McGuire, C.Ss.R., "Our Lady of Perpetual Help and the Ecumenical Council," reprint from *Perpetual Help Magazine* (June–July 1959): 18, a copy of which is in the Redemptorist Archives of the Baltimore Province [hereafter RABP], OLPH Files: Vatican II (1959).

[8] Ibid., 23.

See, and securing petitions from the laity as well. He contacted an Indian confrere, Father Cyr Puthenangady, who had been publishing short books on OLPH since 1951. This proved to be an invaluable source of enthusiasm for the project on the Asian sub-continent.[9]

More locally, McGuire was joined by Father Henry Goetten, who ran the Perpetual Help Center in the Bronx, a ministry which promoted devotion to the icon in "mission kits" sent to dioceses around the world. Goetten maintained an extensive listing of dioceses that received these kits and so with every new package sent, he enclosed an appeal letter to the local bishop. Goetten's extensive network of associates around the globe promoted the idea, especially in remote places. Each was requested to forward a note to him about any action taken. From Columbo, Sri Lanka, Goetten received a letter from a priest named Herat, who wrote that every Wednesday at All Saints Church in that city 35,000 people gathered for the OLPH novena. At least a third of these were non-Christians, he said, including "Hindus, Muslims, Parsis, Buddhists and a sprinkling of 'non-descripts.'"[10] Other confreres in India, especially Bangalore, promised to spread word throughout the country to get local churches engaged in the campaign.

In Africa, the Apostolic Delegate stationed in Mombasa, Kenya, Archbishop Gastone Mojaisky Perrelli, wrote directly to Pope John requesting permission to join in the campaign. He explained that in Africa the image of Our Lady of Perpetual Help was very diffuse, especially between indigenous and Indian populations.[11] Other nunciatures were enlisted as curriers for the sentiments of local bishops. From Chittagong, East Pakistan, Bishop Raymond Larose asked the nuncio in Karachi to convey his support for the campaign.[12] Goetten received notes from bishops in Auckland, New Zealand, Gulu, Uganda, and Cape Town, South Africa, promising to consider the appeal. Another prelate, Bishop Frederick Hall of Kisumu, Kenya, wrote him indicating that he

---

[9] McGuire urged Puthenangady on April 24, 1959, to write to Father General William Gaudreau in Rome to push the cause for a conciliar patroness. In RABP, OLPH Files: Vatican II (1959).

[10] Herat to Goetten, May 12, 1959, in RABP, OLPH Files: Vatican II (1959).

[11] Perrelli to Beatissimo Padre, May 18, 1959, Prot. No. 2580, 1959, in RABP, OLPH Files: Vatican II (1959).

[12] Larose to Archbishop Emanuele Clarizio, June 1, 1959, in RABP, OLPH Files: Vatican II (1959).

would be placing pictures of OLPH in every church in his diocese.[13] Another from Maitland, Australia, Bishop John Toohey, commended the campaign but confessed a certain bias—his own diocese already had OLPH as its patroness.[14]

Redemptorist bishops or dioceses that were hosting Redemptorist ministries naturally warmed to the idea. Bishop Thomas Reilly, C.Ss.R., a Boston native and head of the See of San Juan de la Maguana in the Dominican Republic, felt the project would meet with success.[15] Bishop Joaquim de Lange Tefé in the Amazon—a prefecture of the Diocese of Manaus, where Redemptorists had worked for many years, was also on board. He wrote directly to Pope John exhorting him to place the Council under the protection of OLPH. Archbishop James Davis of San Juan, Puerto Rico, where Redemptorists had worked for nearly a century, asked the Pope directly to consider making OLPH the conciliar patroness.[16] The Provincial of the Redemptorist Vice-Province of Campo Grande, Brazil, noted that the project could count on petitions being sent from two archbishops and four bishops from Brazil and one archbishop and another bishop from Paraguay. "These are the Bishops under whom we are working and they are very cooperative."[17] Some bishops took the initiative to write directly to members of the Roman Curia to suggest that OLPH have a universalizing role.

---

[13]Goetten referred to Bishop Frederick Hall of the Diocese of Kisumu. See the letter of Goetten to Archbishop Owen McCann of Cape Town, South Africa, May 26, 1959, in RABP, OLPH Files: Vatican II (1959) as well as Bishop Hall's own letter, with enclosure of a copy of his petition to Pope John, dated May 21, 1959, in RABP, OLPH Files: Vatican II (1959).

[14]See Bishop John Toohey to Goetten, May 20, 1959, in RABP, OLPH Files: Vatican II (1959).

[15]See Reilly to Goetten, May 19, 1959, in RABP, OLPH Files: Vatican II (1959).

[16]De Lange to "Beatissime Pater," June 3, 1959, in RABP, OLPH Files: Vatican II (1959) and Davis to "Beatissime Pater," May 31, 1959, which Davis sent to the Holy Father through Cardinal Gaetano Cicognani, in RABP, OLPH Files: Vatican II (1959).

[17]See Vice-Provincial Father Francis Freel to McGuire, October 9, 1959, in RABP, OLPH Files: Vatican II (1959). In a subsequent letter, dated November 7, 1959, in RABP, OLPH Files: Vatican II (1959), Freel identified the bishops alluded to in his October 9 missive to McGuire. These were: Dom Ladislau Paz (Corumba, Mato Grosso); Dom Antonio Barbosa (Campo Grande, Mato Grosso); Dom Orlado Chaves (Archbishop of Cuiaba, Mato Grosso); Dom Jose Ferreira (Dourados, Mato Grosso); Dom Monoel de Silveira D'Elboux (Archbishop of Curitiba, Parana); Dom Aemilius Sosa Gaona (Concepcion, Paraguay); Juan Bogarin (Archbishop of Asuncion, Paraguay).

In the Archdiocese of Jaro, the Philippines, the chancellor, Monsignor Ciceron Alberto Tumbocon wrote to Cardinal Pietro Ciriaci, prefect of the Sacred Congregation of the Council, that by placing the Council under the icon's gaze, it would be "an additional means of bringing together the East and the West."[18] Similar letters were sent to Ciriaci from Bishops Peter Kobayashi of Sendai, Japan, Epifanio Surban of Dumaguete in the Philippines and Jose Cuenco, the Archbishop of Jaro, in the Philippines.[19]

At least two prelates wrote early in the campaign to Cardinal Domenico Tardini, the Secretary of State to the Holy See. Bishop Francis Esser, O.S.F.S., the ordinary in the Diocese of Keimos in South Africa, implored him to place the prospect of the Madonna as conciliar patroness directly before the Pope. She was, he said, "our one Hope."[20] Additionally, the metropolitan of the Greek Melkite Catholics, Archbishop Mikhayl Assaf stated that Pope John was reigning as "le Pape de l'Unité Chrétienne" and that with the expectation of Christians of every race, the ecumenical council should have the Blessed Virgin's advocacy in heaven. In light of the world's problems, he wrote, the Helper of Christians should be invoked for her protection. "The Virgin Mary should be the natural patron of the Council of Unity, as she is the Mother of Christians and all humanity redeemed by the blood of her Divine Son. But perhaps Our Lady of Perpetual Help, whose miraculous icon has been venerated for centuries in Rome, at the church of the Redemptorist Fathers, should be appointed the patroness of the unity of the Council." Assaf also urged Tardini to bring the matter to the Pope.[21]

Few replies from the Holy See were collected by the Redemptorists, but Archbishop Assaf was kind enough to forward a typescript of Cardinal Tardini's reply to his request. Dated June 4, Tardini's letter acknowledged the archbishop's suggestion and thanked him for bringing it to his attention. He also mentioned that he brought the matter

[18] Tumbocon to Ciriaci, May 19, 1959, Prot. No. 497/59, in RABP, OLPH Files: Vatican II (1959).

[19] Kobayashi to Goetten, May 21, 1959, Prot. Nos. 216/59 and 217/59, in RABP, OLPH Files: Vatican II (1959); Cuenco to Goetten, May 21, 1959, in RABP, OLPH Files: Vatican II (1959). For Cuenco, the proposal was willingly accepted, given the prominence of OLPH devotions in his own diocese.

[20] Esser to Tardini, May 19, 1959, in RABP, OLPH Files: Vatican II (1959).

[21] Assaf to Tardini, Mary 20, 1959, in RABP, OLPH Files: Vatican II (1959).

before the pope in accordance with his wish. Pope John gave thanks for the information and sent the apostolic blessing to the archbishop, but no further comment on the pope's thinking was provided.[22] Nevertheless, it spurred the Redemptorists on knowing that word had reached the ear of the pope that the campaign was underway.

In June and July, McGuire wrote the two most important essays of his career for *Perpetual Help Magazine* on "Our Lady of Perpetual Help and the Ecumenical Council." It was copiously reprinted as a single pamphlet and sent with each appeal to bishops around the globe, including the apostolic delegates of each country. By August, McGuire and his fellow editor on the magazine, Father James Galvin, C.Ss.R., wrote to every Redemptorist provincial in the world in multiple languages, asking them to promote the movement by explaining the case to the press, urging the prayers of the faithful for the campaign particularly at the weekly novenas, and requesting the Apostolic Delegates, bishops and presidents of seminaries to forward petitions to the Holy See. A form letter was worked up in Latin and all the modern European languages to be sent to the Holy Father from all corners of the Earth. By August 21, 1959, McGuire stated in a reply letter that already about twenty bishops from around the world had sent personal letters to Rome supporting the campaign.[23] Eventually, notification reached McGuire that entire groups of

---

[22] Assaf to Goetten, June 8, 1959, relaying the content of a letter from Cardinal Tardini, Prot. No. 4938/59 and dated June 4, 1959: "Monseigneur, J'ai bien reçu l'aimable letter (Reg. XII, No. 517/59) que Votre Excellence m'adressait en date du 20 Mai dernier, et je la remercie vivement des felicitations et des voeux qu'elle voulait bien y formuler pour ma personne. La suggestion de Votre Exellence, à propos du Concile Oecuménique, a retenu aussi mon attention, et je n'ai pas manqué de la porter à la connaissance de Sa Sainteté, comme vous en exprimez le désir. Le Souverain Pontife vous en remercie par mon entremise et accorde de grand coeur a Votre Excellence et aux fideles confies a ses soins la benediction Apostolique. Etc." In addition to this reply to Archbishop Assaf, Archbishop Pericles Felice, Secretary of the Council's Ante-preparatory Commission, wrote the Abbott of St. Procopius Monastery in Lisle, Illinois, stating that the commission had received his petition. But Abbot Ambrose Ondrak, O.S.B., had addressed his letter to the Pope, which signaled that it had been referred to the agenda-making body in charge of the conciliar process. See the copy of the letter from Felici to Ondrak, August 17, 1959, Prot. No. 47/59, in RABP, OLPH Files: Vatican II (1959).

[23] McGuire to Wright, August 21, 1959, in RABP, OLPH Files: Vatican II (1959).

bishops had sent in petitions, as with all the bishops of Japan and a good many from Bolivia.[24]

Many American bishops responded positively when contacted. Among them were the bishops of Providence, Rhode Island (Russell J. McVinney), Trenton, New Jersey (George Ahr), Erie, Pennsylvania (John Mark Gannon and auxiliary Bishop Edward P. McManaman), Wheeling, West Virginia (Thomas J. McDonnell), and the Archbishop of Philadelphia of the Byzantine Rite (Constantine Bohacevskyj). Similarly, the bishops of Harrisburg (George Leech), Buffalo (Joseph Burke; together with auxiliary Bishop Leo Smith), Syracuse (David Cunningham, auxiliary Bishop), Hartford (Archbishop Henry O'Brien, together with auxiliary Bishop John Hackett) and Columbus (Clarence Issenmann) were also compliant.

Confreres in Canada were eager to lend a hand in the effort and their diligence proved fruitful. No less than 21 of the English-speaking bishops, including Cardinal James McGuigan of Toronto, replied favorably and sent petitions either to Cardinal Tardini or to the Pope. The Cardinal's letter was used in every subsequent communication with the hierarchy. "Born of the East and loved in the West," he wrote, "it seems singularly fitting that our Mother of Perpetual Help be chosen as the happy Mother of the Ecumenical Council that has as one of its great prayers and objectives the union of the East and the West in the one true Church."[25]

Father Timothy O'Sullivan, C.Ss.R., then based in Toronto at Our Lady of the Assumption, was enlisted to spearhead the work in Canada. He broached the subject with Father Lucien Gagné, C.Ss.R., of the Province of Ste. Anne-de-Beaupre and each agreed to try to influence Canadian bishops in their respective areas. Both men asked the secretary of the Canadian Conference of Catholic Bishops, Bishop Charles-Omer Garant, auxiliary Bishop of Quebec, to put the petition on the agenda of the Conference, which would be convened in January 1960. Meanwhile, all English-speaking bishops in Canada were sent McGuire's pamphlet. O'Sullivan was so taken with this pamphlet, he ordered 300 more

---

[24] For the Japanese response, see the letter of Father J. Fuller, C.Ss.R., to Father James Galvin, C.Ss.R., February 1, 1960, in RABP, OLPH Files: Vatican II (1960). At the time, Fuller was stationed in Suita-shi, Osaka-fu, Japan.

[25] McGuigan to Father Timothy J. O'Sullivan, C.Ss.R., February 8, 1960, in RABP, OLPH Files: Vatican II (1960).

copies for distribution beyond the bishops' conference.[26] By September 1, 1960, Father Gagné had had an interview with Cardinal Paul-Émile Léger of Montreal. Subsequently, the cardinal wrote a letter of commendation for the project and signed the petition. Gagné had also taken the cardinal's letters to the International Marian Center in Nicolet, Canada. There he met the ordinary of that diocese, Bishop Joseph Albert Martin, who promised to send an appeal letter of his own to all the bishops of the world in support of the cause. When the Apostolic Delegate to Canada met Gagné at the Shrine of St. Anne during her festal celebrations that summer, he promised the Redemptorist that he would personally raise the prospect of making OLPH patroness of the Council with the Holy Father and urge him to approve the request. He was scheduled to visit Rome on September 15.

Among European provinces that supported the idea of a conciliar patroness, the Spanish province of Madrid sent letters to all of the country's bishops, asking them to return their petitions to then-Father Luis Franco, C.Ss.R., the future bishop of San Cristobal de La Laguna, or Tenerife.[27] These in turn were given directly to the Secretary of State. Some high-ranking prelates bypassed the Secretariat altogether. Cardinal Franz Koenig of Vienna, while on his *ad limina* visit, put the matter on his agenda when he visited Pope John.

By mid-June, 1960, McGuire had received notification that nearly a hundred bishops from around the world had been enlisted as supporting the Madonna of Perpetual Help as patroness of Vatican II. When he wrote the American bishops indicating that this movement was gaining steam, he invited any who had not yet considered it to jump on the bandwagon. He managed to secure additional petitions from Archbishop Patrick O'Boyle and auxiliary Bishop Philip Hannan of Washington, D.C., Robert Joyce of Burlington, Vermont, John Russell of Richmond, Virginia, and Bishop James Gerrard of Fall River, Massachusetts. Joining them was the Vicar General of the Archdiocese of New York, auxiliary

---

[26] O'Sullivan to McGuire, December 14, 1959, in RABP, OLPH Files: Vatican II (1959).

[27] See the form letter of Franco to "Excmo. y Rvdmo. Sr. D.," May 1, 1960 in RABP, OLPH Files: Vatican II (1960). Luis Franco Cascón was appointed a bishop in February 1962 and attended three sessions of the Council. The only evidence for any response of the Spanish hierarchy came from the Bishop Daniel Llorente y Federico of the Diocese of Segovia, who replied affirmatively that he supported the initiative. See the bishop's letter to Franco, May 2, 1960, in RABP, OLPH Files: Vatican II (1960).

Bishop John McGuire, and Bishop Nicholas Elko of the Pittsburgh Ordinariate of the Byzantine Rite.

WANING OF THE MOVEMENT

With these names having expressed their support, McGuire, Goetten, and confreres on several continents had reason to be optimistic. Some tried to temper the plan but reduce neither the momentum nor the enthusiasm. A letter from Father Ray Miller, C.Ss.R., one of the general consultors in Rome but a member of the St. Louis Province, wrote McGuire that he thought his campaign was going very well. However, another thought occurred to him in examining McGuire's petition for use by the bishops at least from the perspective of the general government. "I noticed one thing which interested me especially: you refer to Our Lady as Patroness of Reunion and enclose the clipping about the SJ's and the Apostleship of Prayer. How would it be if we would stream in our campaign more the idea of Our Lady Patroness of *Reunion* than Patroness of the *Council?*"[28] This may have had more persuasive power, especially among critics, though this was hardly the approach favored by anyone other than Miller.

Among the most detailed negative responses to McGuire came from His Beatitude, Patriarch Maximos IV Saigh of Antioch (Melkite Greek). A vocal participant in the Second Vatican Council, Maximos was a powerful advocate and ally for the OLPH cause during his years a missionary for the Society of St. Paul and later as Patriarch. By his own account, he helped spread devotion to OLPH in missionary houses in Syria, Lebanon, and Egypt. He was initially introduced to the plan through the good offices of the Redemptorist superior of the Lebanese mission to the Chaldeans, Father Mauritius Demarey, C.Ss.R., who was based in Beirut. Yet, while he was sympathetic, the Patriarch roundly refused to endorse any introduction of the patronal aspect of the icon for the Council. The current reality demanded a more nuanced analysis. First, given that the numerous ecumenical and provincial councils—some of which dealt with pressing Marian questions—had not seen fit to place themselves under the particular patronage of Mary, it would not be fitting to break that simple tradition today. Second, Maximos was not inclined to favor

---

[28] Miller to McGuire, September 3, 1959, in RABP, OLPH Files: Vatican II (1959).

petitions that elicited from the Pope a proclamation for this or that devotion because they amounted to a "campaign of propaganda." Third, Redemptorists show no proof that the project would achieve its aims, namely, to bring about unity with the Greeks and Russians. In fact, it would cause some confusion for them and widen the gulf of separation that already existed.[29]

In fact, other bishops also refused to support the notion of a conciliar patroness. Some were reticent of choosing one Marian image over another.[30] The majority of those who thought ill of the idea came from the United States. Bishop John Wright of Pittsburgh, who later came around to support McGuire, was initially puzzled by the notion of a conciliar patroness and prompted a letter from McGuire denying that the campaign was importunate or attempting to pressure the hierarchy. The Apostolic Delegate of the United States backed out of the process entirely, asking that he be excused because "usually Papal Representatives are not supposed to send a petition of this type; such petitions are rather to be sent by the Bishops themselves."[31] Among the most pointedly negative letters received by McGuire was from Bishop Jerome Hannon, then of Scranton. "I state my own reaction to your suggestion that I petition our Holy Father to designate Our Lady of Perpetual Help as the Patroness of the Ecumenical Council. I think it would be adversely received and commented on by Protestants who charge Catholics with Mariolatry. I admit that this *scandalum pusillorum* could be ignored if there were an overwhelming reason for doing so. But I do not think there is. We can all pray to Our Lady of Perpetual Help for the success of the Council without rubbing Protestants in a sore spot."[32]

---

[29] See the packet of letters from Father Mauritius Demarey, C.Ss.R., including his correspondence with Patriarch Maximos, a copy of the Patriarch's reply to him, and Demarey's analysis for McGuire and Galvin, in RABP, OLPH Files: Vatican II (1959). Demarey was dismayed to explain that Maximos's mentality was typical of the responses he had been getting from bishops in his area.

[30] Thus the Bishop of Meerut in India countered that "perhaps the Orientals may be venerating Our Lady under some other title, well known and loved by them. In such supposition, perhaps it would be better to try to bring them back to Rome under the motherly lead of that icon." See Bishop Joseph B. Evangelisti, O.F.M. Cap., to Fr. Henry Goetten, May 9, 1959, in RABP, OLPH Files: Vatican II (1959).

[31] Apostolic Delegate Eugenio Vagnozzi to McGuire, September 1, 1959, Prot. No. 58/59, in RABP, OLPH Files: Vatican II (1959).

[32] Hannan to McGuire, August 24, 1959, in RABP, OLPH Files: Vatican II (1959).

The project may have hit its lowest point when the Provincial of the London Province of the Redemptorists wrote that he was declining to approach Britain's bishops because they feared the episcopate would accuse them of being publicity hounds should the effort succeed. Redemptorists at Clapham, therefore, were oddly opposed.[33]

Despite these voices, which by the documentary evidence were largely in the minority, the drive for a conciliar patroness went forward over the course of the next year. Yet on September 8, 1960, a letter was sent to Father Goetten at the Perpetual Help Center. Written in Italian and dispatched from the Central Commission for the Preparation of the Second Vatican Council, only a carbon copy survives in the Baltimore Province Archives.[34] The letter does not display a signature, though the author is likely Archbishop Felici, the secretary of the Commission. In short, it brought to an abrupt halt any future petition-gathering. It said that Cardinal Franz Koenig had submitted a similar petition and so accepting anything further would not be convenient. Moreover, there were numerous other petitions for titles for the Madonna. What precisely the Koenig petition stated is unclear and what other petitions existed has not come to light. Additionally, the rationale is not made available for declining to choose OLPH over other Marian images. Yet the message was indubitable: cease and desist.

It is difficult to link the Roman response with any additional denials placed upon movements working toward a new Marian definition (either as *mediatrix* of all graces or *co-redemptrix*) but officials were following the papal admonitions to avoid anything that smacked of a dogmatic council. It may be that isolating the Marian role in the proceedings to anything more than a general set of statements (or the outright elimination of her presence in the Council's interventions) was predetermined, if not a foregone conclusion. If one looks at the genesis of the schema *De Beata Virgine Mariae*, which eventually was almost completely abandoned for the final text on Mary within the final chapter of *Lumen Gentium*, the prospect of presenting the Church with a new Marian dogma was doomed from the start, even in a capacity to serve

---

[33] See the letter of Provincial Father Wilfred Hughes, C.Ss.R., to James Galvin, C.Ss.R., September 17, 1959, in RABP, OLPH Files: Vatican II (1959).

[34] See the unsigned letter to Goetten, September 8, 1960, Prot. No. 88 CE/60, in RABP, OLPH Files: Vatican II (1960).

as the vehicle for better ecumenical relations. Yves Congar, O.P., gave a typically cogent analysis:

> One has to consider also the general situation of Mariology in important parts of the Catholic Church, if not everywhere. It is a situation of over-bidding. Very powerful groups have expressed interest in "raising" it still higher and in such a way that tomorrow's bid will only be a step toward higher bids the day after tomorrow. I am afraid that a conciliar text, with its high authority, even if it is not *de fide*, will serve as a trampoline for the acrobats of an exaggerating and maximizing Mariology, even if the text itself is not maximizing (and it isn't, as a whole), and that these acrobats will use various expressions in the text to exaggerate it and push it further.[35]

By September 24, 1960, Father O'Sullivan in Toronto had gotten word that there was opposition to their work. He laid blame for the slow down on the doorstep of the Jesuits whose Legion of Mary and widespread sodality movements seemed to be edging out the OLPH petitions. He doubted that the Bishop of Nicolet would send out petition forms to all the world's bishops, but he wondered whether this might be a project that could be carried forward at the Redemptorist Generalate in Rome.[36] In fact, this had little traction. Writing from the General Curia, Father Ray Miller told McGuire pointedly that "now it seems that the Holy Father has decided on something else; that is, Our Lady is to be Patroness all right, but under the title of the Immaculate Conception. Along about the first of December he made one or two statements to this effect, not solemnly or officially, but as it were in passing." Miller said he had noticed a line in *L'Osservatore Romano* recently that said the pope had decided to put the Council under the protection of the Blessed Virgin—"*omnino in genere*, no particular title at all." Then Miller laid out his own rationale for the pope's change of mind: "When Pope John raised Sant'Alfonso to be a Cardinalitial [sic] church, and confided it to

---

[35] See Congar's white paper prepared for Bishop Weber, "Remarques sur le Schéma *De B. Maria Virgine*," in the Congar Archive, Le Saulchoir, and cited in *History of Vatican II, vol. 1: Announcing and Preparing Vatican Council II, Toward a New Era in Catholicism*, ed. Giuseppe Alberigo and Joseph A. Komonchak (Maryknoll: Orbis; Leuven: Peeters, 1995), 260.

[36] O'Sullivan to McGuire, September 26, 1960, in RABP, OLPH Files: Vatican II (1960).

Cardinal Ritter, there was a rumor that one reason why he did so was because he had not made Our Lady of Perpetual Help in Sant'Alfonso the Patroness of the Council!"[37] Clearly the pope's intention was not to marginalize Mary. In fact, for the opening of the Council and on his expressed wish, a depiction of the Mother of God was placed in a place of prominence in the aula of St. Peter's. A large tapestry with a crowned Madonna hung behind the papal throne, above Bernini's baldachin.[38]

An Anniversary and an Opportunity

While the history of the Redemptorists' campaign to make the OLPH icon a focal point for church unity met with resistance and eventually was brought to a halt, it has to be acknowledged that the image was invoked in a manner that did not square with the ecumenical aspirations of either the Roman church or the churches of the East. In the end, the ecumenism advanced by the Council was one of mutual respect, one that adopted language that decried the anathemas of the past, and one that honored the validity and truth that was to be found in their respective polities. It was not one based on a demand to acknowledge papal primacy or unity of sacramental life. Instead, the advocates for making OLPH the Council's patroness sought to make her the means by which the Eastern churches somehow would come to "see the light" about their past errors and return to the one, true Church. In all honesty, this was a non-starter.

As the Redemptorists recently celebrated a jubilee year commemorating Pope Pius' commendation of the OLPH icon to the order in December 1865, which carried with it by April 1866, the papal admonition to Redemptorists to "make her known"[39] throughout the world, the question of the value of the icon for ecumenical work remains prescient. I think it can be useful. The initial theological rationale remains potent for Mary as one who draws the faithful deeper into the mystery of the Incarnation, as one who is intimately linked to the Second Person of the Trinity, and as one who consoles us in our longings and pain. The miraculous icon is a manifestation of these realities and so is still valid

---

[37] Miller to McGuire, February 26, 1961, in RABP, OLPH Files: Vatican II (1960).

[38] See *History of Vatican II*, vol. 1, 483.

[39] See Matthias Raus, *Circular Letters of Redemptorist Generals with Introductory Study of The Spirit of St. Alphonsus and His Institute* (Milwaukee: Bruce, 1932), 288.

for contemporary theology and spirituality. We all operate in a fractured state and we need heavenly assistance to reconcile. If there is to be hope of repairing our broken communion, the Madonna is without doubt our common advocate. What is necessary to abandon, however, is a tendency to seek her intervention with the warped intention to absorb the other in some triumphalist manner. Growth in understanding and mutual respect should be the goal. Humility before these tasks will pave the way.

The worldwide Redemptorist congregation has begun jubilee celebrations commemorating Pope Pius IX's decision to commend the icon to their care.[40] Much will be made of their involvement in its promotion, but this timely anniversary affords us a chance to revisit the possibility of keeping the icon before us in our ecumenical relations. It is not merely a monument or pious picture, but a global symbol of what was so captivating about the Council's spirit and potentialities. If we acknowledge that the icon is not meant to restore the churches of the East to the so-called Mother Church of Rome and if we eschew any pretense to such use, we find that the Holy Mother has already done her job.[41] The icon bridges Christian divisions in both appearance and symbolism. It also speaks to a variety of cultures, as was seen by the large and diverse number of bishops who supported the Redemptorists in their cause.

At the end of November, 2014, Pope Francis traveled to Turkey on a pastoral visit to "his brother Andrew"—the Ecumenical Patriarch of Constantinople Bartholomew I. The pontiff made his intentions plain: "I want to assure each one of you here that, to reach the desired goal of full unity, the Catholic Church does not intend to impose any conditions except that of the shared profession of faith. Further, I would add that we are ready to seek together, in light of Scriptural teaching and the

---

[40] See the letter of the Superior General Very Rev. Michael Brehl to "Dear Confreres, Sisters, Lay Associates, and Friends," April 26, 2015, Prot. No. 0000 073/2015, in RABP, Provincial Files: Paul Borowski, 2015.

[41] Thus Pope Francis made a proposal of a union with the Orthodox Church during his meeting with Patriarch Bartholomew I in November 2014. According to *La Civiltà Cattolica*, "The Pope picked up on a motion made in 1982 by the then Cardinal Joseph Ratzinger: Rome should no longer ask of the East what was formulated and lived in the first millennium. This was the restoration of an old formula from the Council of Florence in 1439: A reunification of the Latin Church and the Greek Church on the basis of equality, and not a return to the 'mother Church.'" See Giancarlo Pani, "Per giungere alla piena unità: Dal Concilio di Firenze all'abbraccio di Istanbul," *La Civiltà Cattolica*, no. 3951 (February 7, 2015): 209–312, available at www.laciviltacattolica.it.

experience of the first millennium, the ways in which we can guarantee the needed unity of the Church in the present circumstances. The one thing that the Catholic Church desires, and that I seek as Bishop of Rome, 'the Church which presides in charity,' is communion with the Orthodox Churches."[42] Fifty-six years after Pope John expressed his desire for greater unity, his successor is now on the precipice of a true communion.

[42] See the remarks of Pope Francis, given at the end of the Divine Liturgy in the Patriarchal Church of St. George in the Phanar, "One single profession of faith," *L'Osservatore Romano* (December 3, 2014): 9–10.

CHAPTER 19

The Ecumenical Imperative After Vatican II: Achievements and Challenges

Susan K. Wood, S.C.L.

Too often, in recent decades, one would hear the lament that the churches were in an ecumenical winter. The enthusiasm and hope experienced on the heels of the Second Vatican Council seemed to some to have cooled. As some obstacles to unity were overcome, new fissures seemed to appear in the dry, cracked earth. Yet, I prefer to think that the fruits of more than fifty years of dialogue have slowly and inexorably formed into buds like those of the peonies that grow each spring by my back porch. They are full and compact, pregnant with promised blossoms, only awaiting the warmth of sunlight to burst into color and fragrance.

The ecumenical movement seeks no less than full visible unity of separated Christian churches. Approximately fifty years of dialogue since the promulgation of *Unitatis Redintegratio*, the decree on Ecumenism of the Second Vatican Council (21st November 1964), have produced significant agreements. Although ecumenism has become a subset of theology with ecumenical documents filling volumes, much of this work resides on shelves awaiting reception. Rather than an ecumenical winter, these results

S. K. Wood, S.C.L. (✉)
Marquette University, Milwaukee, WI, USA
e-mail: susan.wood@marquette.edu

© The Author(s) 2018
V. Latinovic et al. (eds.), *Catholicism Opening to the World and Other Confessions*, Pathways for Ecumenical and Interreligious Dialogue,
https://doi.org/10.1007/978-3-319-98581-7_19

of dialogue represent an ecumenical springtime, with the buds nourished by years of effort swelling and on the verge of bursting into bloom. I will summarize some of the major achievements of the past fifty years, some of them existential rather than doctrinal, will identify some major challenges to ecumenism, and will conclude with an ecumenical wish list.

To assess these achievements, it is first necessary to identify the benchmarks of ecumenical progress, to know what demonstrates progress and what does not. First, progress does not mean uniformity and therefore is not measured by uniformity. The type of visibility sought in full visible communion does not demand the sacrifice of that which is distinctive in various ecclesial traditions. The Roman Catholic *Directory for the Application of Principles and Norms on Ecumenism* states the goal of the ecumenical movement: "This unity which of its very nature requires full visible communion of all Christians is the ultimate goal of the ecumenical movement. The council affirms that this unity by no means requires the sacrifice of the rich diversity of spirituality, discipline, liturgical rites and elaborations of revealed truth that has grown up among Christians in the measure that this diversity remains faithful to the apostolic Tradition."[1]

Diversity, which must exist within full visible unity, is not a concession to division, but an expression of the very catholicity of the church. The *Ecumenical Directory* expands on this principle: "The unity of the Church is realized in the midst of a rich diversity. This diversity in the Church is a dimension of its catholicity. At times the very richness of this diversity can engender tensions within the communion. Yet, despite such tensions, the Spirit continues to work in the Church calling Christians in their diversity to ever deeper unity."[2]

When we look for achievements, we look for actions that are respectful of our dialogue partner. Dialogue is not a negotiating process, toward a lowest common denominator of agreement. Nor is it simply a revisiting of our historical past to clear up misunderstandings, although this can constitute one component of dialogue. In situations where dialogue partners must take account of "binding positions" which explicitly condemn the other, it can be helpful to clarify exactly what

[1] Pontifical Council for Promoting Christian Unity, *Directory for the Application of Principles and Norms on Ecumenism*, AAS 85 (1993): 1039–19, no. 20; the *Directory* cites *Unitatis Redintegratio* 4 and 15–16.

[2] Pontifical Council for Promoting Christian Unity, *Directory for the Application of Principles and Norms on Ecumenism*, 16.

the "binding position" of the church is, and in what ways it sought to preserve the integrity of the gospel in a particular context. In dialogue we search for new entrances into old divisions, such that we discover new ways forward. Seeking formulae that express the common faith of both partners in mutually acceptable language blazes a new way forward towards unity.

Major Achievements

Perhaps the greatest ecumenical achievement of the twentieth century is the awareness of the *need* for Christian unity, itself, and the admission that the lack of unity wounds all ecclesial traditions. John Paul II, in his Apostolic Letter *Tertio Millennio Adveniente* spoke of the wounds of division requiring repentance and conversion that are a scandal to the world:

> Among the sins which require a greater commitment to repentance and conversion should certainly be counted those which have been detrimental to the unity willed by God for his people. In the course of the 1,000 years now drawing to a close, even more than in the first millennium, ecclesial communion has been painfully wounded, a fact "for which at time, people of both sides were to blame" (UR 3). Such wounds openly contradict the will of Christ and are a cause of scandal to the world. (UR 1)[3]

The first major achievement of ecumenism is confession of the sin of division, the confession that we are wounded and that the Catholic Church shares the blame for this wound of division. This division prevents the church from realizing full catholicity (UR 4). Recognition of this fact graces the church with a humility that replaces a former triumphalism of the Post-Reformation era symbolized by Robert Bellarmine's description of the church as a perfect society. At the same time it challenges the present state of division as the status quo where division simply offers opportunities for individual choice and is no longer seen as a violation of Christ's prayer for unity.

A second major achievement is that ecclesial communities continue to talk to one another. As simple as this may seem, it cannot be overestimated. The cost of dialogue is considerable, both in terms of financial

---

[3] John Paul II, Apostolic Letter *Tertio Millennio Adveniente*, AAS 87 (1995): 5–41, no. 34.

resources on the part of the participating ecclesial communities, but also in terms of human resources. Ecumenical dialogue is essentially a conversation, a speaking and a listening, between partners. Each partner speaks from his or her context, from his or her perspective of hearing the Gospel and from his or her perspective of viewing the world. Dialogic speech seeks to enter as much as possible into the experience of the other and so to see the other's perspective through their eyes. A successful ecumenist can articulate the partners' perspective not only so that they recognize it as their own, but also sometimes better than they can articulate it themselves. This dialogue involves receiving the ethos of the other and those aspects of the Christian tradition that have been preserved in the heritage of the other. This is what *Unitatis Redintegratio* means by the words "we must become familiar with the outlook of the separated churches and communities" (UR 9). Here "outlook" is a weak translation of the Latin, which is "*animus*," the "spirit," "seat of feeling," or the "heart" of the dialogue partner.

A third achievement of the ecumenical movement is the development of an ecumenical spirituality. As the Decree on Ecumenism stated, "There can be no ecumenism worthy of the name without a change of heart" (UR 4). As we work towards Christian unity, we become more converted to Christ. Conversely, the more deeply we are converted to Christ, our center, the more closely we will approach one another in Christ, much like the closer a spoke of a wheel is to the hub, the closer it is to the other spokes. We promote unity among Christians best when we live holier lives according to the Gospel (UR 7).

John Paul II names the concrete implications of a more radical conversion to the Gospel: "an increased sense of the need for repentance: an awareness of certain exclusions which seriously harm fraternal charity, of certain refusals to forgive, of a certain pride, of an unevangelical insistence on condemning the 'other side', of a disdain born of an unhealthy presumption."[4] Conversion does not mean that we become other than what we are, but that we become more authentically what we are. When we speak of a "willingness to change" as a result of dialogue, what is called for is the willingness to see the other in a different way, to change our patterns of thinking, speaking and acting toward the other. Our understanding of other should resist the temptation to subsume the

---

[4] John Paul II, Encyclical Letter *Ut Unum Sint*, AAS 87 (1995): 921–82, no. 15.

other into our own a priori theory of them, and perhaps be open to the development of a more inclusive narrative. Thus we are called to explore theologies of healing and forgiveness in the search for openness to a transformed and reconciled relationship.

A fourth ecumenical achievement is the identification of new paradigms in which to examine old divisions. Developing from a former methodology of comparative theology, ecumenical dialogue has now entered a new era of constructive theology that seeks to propose new lenses to look at ecumenical relationships. Within the mutual and reciprocal exchange of ecumenical dialogue we allow ourselves to experience a fusion of horizons with our dialogue partner enabling us to heal our divisions, strengthen our common witness, and engage in the shared mission of furthering the reign of God. These new lenses and the fusion of horizons constitute a paradigm shift in how we view certain theological issues dividing our churches. This faithfully follows John Paul II's view of ecumenism when he says that we ought to change our way of looking at things and that "contemplation of 'the mighty works of God' has been enriched by new horizons."[5]

The document entitled "The Church as Koinonia of Salvation: Its Structures and Ministries," of round ten of the US Lutheran-Roman Catholic Dialogue, incorporates such a paradigm shift.[6] The dialogue analyzes various interdependent levels of church life and ministry, namely, the diocese/synod with its bishop and the parish/congregation with its pastor or priest. It evaluates ministry by how it witnesses and serves the communion of the church and discovers that "our ordained ministries are wounded because the absence of full communion between our ecclesial traditions makes it impossible for them adequately to represent and foster the unity and catholicity of the church."[7] Similarly, it notes, "our communities are wounded by their lack of the full catholicity to which they are called and by their inability to provide a common witness to the gospel."[8] Thus the dialogue recommends that each church recognize that the other realizes, even if perhaps imperfectly, the

---

[5] Ibid.

[6] Randall Lee and Jeffry Gros, F.S.C., eds., *The Church as Koinonia of Salvation: Its Structures and Ministries, Lutherans and Catholics in Dialogue—X* (Washington, DC: United States Conference of Catholic Bishops, 2005).

[7] Ibid., para. 103.

[8] Ibid.

one church of Jesus Christ and shares in the apostolic tradition, and that the ordained ministry of the other effectively carries on, even in perhaps imperfectly, the apostolic ministry instituted by God in the church. It further recommends "that Roman Catholic criteria for assessing authentic ministry include attention to a ministry's faithfulness to the gospel and its service to the communion of the church, and that the Latin phrase *defectus ordinis* as applied to Lutheran ministries be translated as "'deficiency' rather than 'lack'."[9] The use of the lens of *koinonia* to view church structures and ministries really amounts to a paradigm shift enabling significant progress in our understanding of ministerial identity and tasks.

A fifth achievement is the development of ecumenical methodology, perhaps best illustrated in the Joint Declaration on the Doctrine of Justification (1999). In addition to the doctrinal agreement represented by the JDDJ, the document also represents an achievement in ecumenical methodology, namely, a differentiating consensus, which is now a model and method available to future ecumenical agreements. "Differentiating consensus" offers a common understanding of a doctrinal point while acknowledging differences of formulation by the two traditions. A common statement is followed by a statement: "When Catholics say 'x', they do not exclude 'y', and when Lutherans say 'y', they do not exclude 'x'." The differences within the two traditions are acknowledged, but they are subsumed under a broader agreement.

MAJOR ECUMENICAL AGREEMENTS

Achievements on the way to full visible unity are measured in numerable agreements on significant differences, each agreement being another step towards full visible unity. Although the Roman Catholic Church engages in multiple dialogues, ecumenical achievements are ultimately measured by official Vatican reception of the results of these dialogues in formal joint agreements with its dialogue partners. The practice of the Vatican is not to officially respond to national dialogues. When the results of these dialogues as well as the international ones reach a critical mass warranting discernment on the part of the Vatican that ecumenical consensus has been achieved, the Vatican enters into a joint agreement with its dialogue

[9] Ibid., para. 109.

partner. The most notable achievements of this kind have been with the Orthodox with respect to Christology and with the Lutheran World Federation on the doctrine of justification.

Agreements with the Eastern Christian Churches

Major achievements with Eastern Christian Churches include a number of Christological agreements.[10] In most cases these joint confessions of faith were able to state mutually shared faith in the person of Christ while avoiding language, which for one reason or another, was offensive to the dialogue partner. These joint statements follow the common pattern of confession of sins against unity, purification of memories, and movement towards restoration of ecclesiastical communion. In addition to these Christological agreements, there have been numerous joint statements between various leaders of Eastern churches and popes reaffirming their resolve to continue ecumenical dialogue.

An example of an ecumenical achievement still waiting to bloom is an agreed statement of the North American Orthodox-Catholic Theological Consultation, "*The Filioque: A Church-Dividing Issue?*" released October 25, 2003.[11] To put this document in context, it should be noted that a committee sponsored by the Faith and Order Commission of the World Council of Churches had extensively studied the *Filioque* in 1978 and 1979, issuing the "Klingenthal Memorandum" (1979). However, there had been no thorough new joint discussion of this topic until this study of the North American Orthodox-Catholic Theological Consultation.

[10]These include the common Declaration of Paul VI and Patriarch Athenagoras I (December 7, 1965); the Joint Declaration of Paul VI and Ignatius Jacob III, Patriarch of Antioch of the Syrians (October 27, 1971); the Joint Declaration of Paul VI and Shenouda III, Patriarch of Alexandria, Egypt (May 10, 1973); the Joint Declaration of John Paul II and Ignatius Zakka I 'Iwas, Syrian Orthodox Patriarch of Antioch, accompanied by a common profession of Christological faith (June 23, 1984); a common declaration signed by Mar Dinkha IV, the patriarch of the Assyrian Church of the East, and Pope John Paul II (November 1994); and a formal theological statement signed by Pope John Paul II and the Armenian Catholicos Karekin I indicating their shared belief in the unity of Christ (December 13, 1996).

[11]The text is available on the web site of the United States Conference of Catholic Bishops under the Department for Ecumenical and Interreligious Affairs at: http://www.usccb.org/beliefs-and-teachings/ecumenical-and-interreligious/ecumenical/orthodox/filioque-church-dividing-issue-english.cfm.

This statement notes that "Although both of our traditions profess 'the faith of Nicaea' as the normative expression of our understanding of God and God's involvement in his creation, and take as the classical statement of that faith the revised versions of the Nicene creed associated with the First Council of Constantinople of 381, most Catholics and other Western Christians have used, since at least the late sixth century, a Latin version of that Creed, which adds to its confession that the Holy Spirit 'proceeds from the Father' the word *Filioque*: 'and from the Son'." This addition has been a source of contention since the eighth century both on account of the Trinitarian theology it expresses and also because of the unilateral insertion of the phrase by the Western church into the canonical formulation of a received ecumenical council with the corresponding issues of Church structure and authority that this implies.

This study includes the following recommendations among others:

- that in the future, because of the progress in mutual understanding that has come about in recent decades, Orthodox and Catholics refrain from labeling as heretical the traditions of the other side on the subject of the procession of the Holy Spirit;
- that Orthodox and Catholic theologians distinguish more clearly between the divinity and hypostatic identity of the Holy Spirit, which is a received dogma of our Churches, and the manner of the Spirit's origin, which still awaits full and final ecumenical resolution;
- that those engaged in dialogue on this issue distinguish, as far as possible, the theological issues of the origin of the Holy Spirit from the ecclesiological issues of primacy and doctrinal authority in the Church, even as we seriously pursue both questions together;
- that the theological dialogue between our Churches also give careful consideration to the status of later councils held in both our Churches after those seven generally received as ecumenical;
- that the Catholic Church, as a consequence of the normative and irrevocable dogmatic value of the Creed of 381, use the original Greek text alone in making translations of that Creed for catechetical and liturgical use;
- that the Catholic Church, following a growing theological consensus, and in particular the statements made by Pope Paul VI, declare that the condemnation made at the Second Council of Lyons (1274) of those "who presume to deny that the Holy Spirit

proceeds eternally from the Father and the Son" is no longer applicable.

This consultation concludes that the different ways of understanding the procession of the Holy Spirit need no longer divide Roman Catholics from the Orthodox.

John Paul II celebrated the Eucharist a number of times on the occasion of visits by Orthodox patriarchs where he proclaimed the Creed in Greek without the *Filioque*.[12] On September 13, 1995 the Vatican published the document "The Greek and Latin Traditions Regarding the Procession of the Holy Spirit" in which it states: "The Catholic Church acknowledges the conciliar, ecumenical, normative and irrevocable value, as the expression of one common faith of the Church and of all Christians, of the Symbol Professed in Greek at Constantinople in 381 by the Second Ecumenical Council. No confession of faith peculiar to a particular liturgical tradition can contradict this expression of faith taught and professed by the undivided Church."[13] The North American Consultation remarks on the significance of this statement even though the Catholic Church does not consider the *Filioque* to be a contradiction of the creed of 381. Finally, the document from the Congregation of the Doctrine of the Faith, *Dominus Jesus: On the Unicity and Salvific Universality of Jesus Christ and the Church* (August 6, 2000), includes the text of the creed of 381 without the addition of the *Filioque*.

Is it possible for the Orthodox and the Catholics to reach a compromise position whereby both creedal formulations would be tolerated? Ideally, Catholics would at times refrain from the use of the *Filioque* out of ecumenical sensitivity, and many Orthodox might concur with the hypothesis[14] that its addition to the Creed was historically not in opposition to the Orthodox, but in response to a specifically Western threat to Christology posed by Arian beliefs. Both would need to acknowledge that the alternative formulations of the relationship of the Spirit to the Son were seen to be not church-dividing. Some kind of reception of the

---

[12] The creed was recited in Greek with Patriarch Dimitrios I (December 7, 1987), Patriarch Bartholomew I (June 1995), and in Romanian for the visit of Romanian Patriarch Teoctist (October 13, 2002).

[13] Cited in "The *Filioque*: A Church-Dividing Issue?"

[14] Scholars from multiple traditions, admittedly, have challenged this hypothesis in more recent times.

ecumenical work done on this topic needs to occur on the part of both the Orthodox and Catholics.

Agreements with Reformation Churches

The Joint Declaration on the Doctrine of Justification (JDDJ), signed by Vatican officials and the Lutheran World Federation, represents the first official reception on the part of the Vatican of the results of ecumenical dialogue with ecclesial communities issuing from the Reformation. The key agreement states: "Together we confess: By grace alone, in faith in Christ's saving work and not because of any merit on our part, we are accepted by God and receive the Holy Spirit, who renews our hearts while equipping and calling us to good works."[15]

By signing the Official Common Statement the two partners in dialogue confirm two points. First, Lutherans and Roman Catholics confirm that they have reached a high level of consensus in basic truths regarding the doctrine of justification. Second, they declare that the mutual condemnations from the time of the Reformation concerning the doctrine of justification do not apply to the teaching on justification as set forth by Lutherans and Roman Catholics in the Joint Declaration. For the first time the intention is for the Roman Catholic Church and the Lutheran churches of the world "to declare in a binding manner that an understanding has been reached on a question of faith and doctrine which has been divisive for centuries."

The significance of this event is evident when we recall that a "doctrinal condemnation" is the highest degree of escalation in theological controversy within a church or between churches: the authoritative declaration that a difference with regard to a particular teaching is of such grievous nature that it divides the church. Doctrinal condemnations are the confirmation and seal of church division. On the other hand, the declaration of non-applicability of a doctrinal condemnation means that the ecumenical dialogue has reached a point where the difference with regard to a particular teaching has lost its cutting edge so that this difference is no longer church dividing.

The JDDJ represents an agreement on the doctrine that for Lutherans is a criterion that provides the norm for all other criteria. For Lutherans,

---

[15] The Lutheran World Federation and the Roman Catholic Church, *Joint Declaration on the Doctrine of Justification* (Grand Rapids: Eerdmans, 2000), no. 15.

the doctrine of justification by faith alone stands in an essential relation to all truths of faith and serves to orient all the teaching and practice of the churches to Christ. The question lingers in Catholic minds as to whether it can be seen as *the* criterion. The final draft of the proposed declaration addresses this concern in §18 where it notes that Catholics see themselves bound by several criteria, but do not deny the special function of the message of justification. The core of the doctrine is the confession of "Christ, who is to be trusted above all things as the one Mediator through whom God in the Holy Spirit gives himself and pours out his renewing gifts." At the same time that Lutherans emphasize the unique significance of this criterion they do not deny the interrelation and significance of all truths of faith.

GENERAL ECUMENICAL CHALLENGES

In spite of many ecumenical agreements, a number of challenges prevent these achievements from fully passing into the life of the church and contributing to ecumenical unity.

Misinterpretation of Ecumenical Agreements

Misinterpretation of ecumenical agreements represents a major challenge of ecumenical dialogue. Dialogue seeks to overcome old divisions by approaching these divisions through the use of new categories. However, we often listen to the results of this work through the lens of our accustomed categories since that is the only language we have. For example, we may judge ecumenical agreements on ordained ministry through the juridical category of validity. Validity is a kind of all-or-nothing category as is the concept of church membership. Something is valid or invalid; a person is either in or out of the church. The language of communion, as used by the US Lutheran-Roman Catholic dialogue, allows for varying degrees of fullness. Roman Catholics are in a relationship of imperfect communion with their Lutheran brothers and sisters. The work of the dialogue demonstrated that just as our faith communities are in imperfect communion with each other, so, too, ministers are in a relationship of imperfect communion.

Church Identity

In the 1950s Henri de Lubac wrote: "It is a pity to have to learn your catechism against someone else." Unfortunately, in the past this has been all too true. We tend to define ourselves contrastively by what someone else is not. There is a fear that if the differences between churches are overcome, we will lose our ecclesial identity and cease to be either Catholics or Lutherans, to name one example. This fear has the potential to evoke powerful existential anxieties concerning not only ecclesial identity, but ecclesial survival.

To succeed ecumenically, we must be able to articulate our identity positively rather than oppositionally. It is necessary to distinguish between confessional identity as a sign of fidelity to faith, and *confessionalism* as an ideology constructed in enmity to the other. Respect for another tradition is not a betrayal of one's own. As our engagement with our dialogue partners deepens, we may be led into an experience of appropriating patterns of thinking and witnessing of the partner—being able, in a sense, to think like they do, without thereby losing our own rootedness in identity. Catholics should not fear to sound too much like Protestants, while Protestants should not fear to adopt ecclesial structures that look Catholic. It is only reasonable to think that this convergence will occur as we both mine common historical sources and explore new lenses through which we can fuse our horizons. This experience is a spiritual fruit of dialogue, and also a gift for the sake of further dialogue. Yet, too often such a convergence seems to spark an existential nausea, occasioned by a fear of loss of identity, and we hastily pull back and strengthen our fortifications against the other as precisely as other. This is not so much fear of the other as it is a fear of losing our very selves.

Or, somewhat differently, ecumenical agreements are viewed as "lowest common denominator" Catholicism, Lutheranism, Anglicanism, etc. Such sentiments fail to recognize that among separated Christian communities, a common in belief in Christ and the Gospel far exceeds what separates them. Ecumenical convergence does not ask ecclesial traditions to give up their identity or forget their particular histories.

Church Structures

Our various church structures can be obstacles to ecumenical agreement. For some, the question is "Who is empowered to speak on behalf of the church?" In the case of the Joint Declaration on the Doctrine of Justification, the Lutheran World Federation facilitated the ascertainment of a consensus among its member churches, but did not speak in their stead. However, not all ecclesial groups have an organizational structure that can do this. The very autonomy of congregations, synods, and confessional groups impedes mutual agreements with each other as well as with those with whom they have major differences. Since the Reformation, in particular, differences within congregations have led to a splintering and multiplication of churches as dissenters leave their parent church to found another one. For others, such as the Catholic Church, the impact of ecumenical statements at the level of national episcopal conferences is not always evident.

Ecumenism with Evangelicals and Pentecostals

Evangelical and Pentecostal churches are expanding rapidly and account for a significant portion of the world's Christians. Thus it is imperative that Roman Catholics and mainline Protestant churches enter into dialogue with these groups. Yet this dialogue is fraught with difficulties. First, there is no organization empowered to speak for them as a group. Dialogue is more difficult, because more fragmented, with groups comprised of essentially independent congregations. Furthermore there has been little participation of evangelical and Pentecostal churches in the Faith and Order Commissions. A more basic obstacle to church unity with these groups is that some of them do not recognize members of other churches to be Christian if these individuals were not baptized as adults and have not had the "born again" baptismal experience of the Holy Spirit. However, one notable achievement is the decision of the US Conference of Catholic Bishops in November 2004 to join the ecumenical organization, Christian Churches Together, which includes evangelical voices.

The Challenge of Witness to Christ in a Non-Christian World

The ecumenical movement was born with the World Missionary Conference at Edinburgh in 1910 where a number of Protestant churches discussed their mutual problems in witnessing to Christ within a divided Christianity. Today the churches find themselves in a similar situation. The need for a common Christian witness within a secular world is greater than the divisions within the churches. Seen from outside the walls of these churches, outside the commonality that labels these communities "Christian," belief in Christ and the Trinity is a much greater commonality than what appears from the outside to be intramural bickering about technical issues of which the common believer knows little.

Ecumenical efforts toward Christian unity provide a powerful witness to peace and reconciliation in a violent, war-torn world. As Vatican II's Pastoral Constitution on the Church in the Modern World states: "We are also mindful that the unity of Christians is today awaited and desired by many non-believers. For the more this unity is realized in truth and charity under the powerful impulse of the Holy Sprit, the more will it be a harbinger of unity and peace throughout the whole world" (GS 92).

Wish List

Even as old divisions are mended through long and patient dialogue, new differences emerge in contemporary times. Different Christians see a number of points of division as potentially church-dividing, including the ordination of women, questions of sexuality, moral matters such as abortion and end of life issues, etc. Despite these challenges, on the basis of ecumenical work already done, a number of initiatives towards unity could be taken to show the will for unity on the part of Catholics. In the list that follows, much of the background work has been done through ecumenical dialogue. In many cases, ecclesiastical authorities need only take action. In the spirit of breaking through ecumenical impasses, I offer this wish list, which is stated briefly rather than argued at length.

Filioque. I wish that the Catholic Church, as a consequence of the normative and irrevocable dogmatic value of the Creed of 381 and the ecumenical work on the issue, use the original Greek text alone in making translations of that Creed for catechetical and liturgical use.

Papacy. Pope John II invited discussion and study on the practice of the papacy in his encyclical letter, *Ut Unum Sint* (25 May 1995). In this encyclical he asked theologians and church leaders to engage in dialogue with him on how the papacy could better fulfill its mission and service of love for the unity of the church in openness to a new situation. I wish that under Pope Francis that the hopes of John Paul II might be fulfilled and that substantive work on revisioning the exercise of the papacy could be encouraged and implemented so that Catholics could invite their dialogue partners to recognize in some fashion the papacy as a ministry of unity for the worldwide church.

Mutual recognition of churches. I wish that the Roman Catholic Church be more generous in acknowledging dialogue partners as *churches*. Since *Unitatis Redintegratio* there has been a hardening of how to interpret the ecclesiality of these groups, so at the very least we need to retrieve the original intention of the Council, where the use of the phrase "ecclesial communities" was meant to be inclusive of those communities that do not self-identify as church rather than exclusive of all communities that do not have an historical episcopacy.

Evaluation of orders of separated churches. That the Latin word *defectus ordinis* as applied to Lutheran ministries be translated as "deficiency" rather than "lack."[16]

Recognition of apostolicity. The theological literature and the International Lutheran-Catholic document, *The Apostolicity of the Church*, acknowledge that apostolicity is carried by the whole church and not only by its episcopal ministry even though that ministry, where it exists, is charged with helping to maintain the church in apostolicity.[17] I wish that the Catholic Church would acknowledge that apostolicity is not an all-or-nothing category and recognize the attribute of apostolicity present in our dialogue partners. This will facilitate the mutual recognition of their ministry.

Eucharist as sign and means of unity. Acknowledging that since that we cannot keep an absolute equilibrium between the character of the Eucharist as both a sign of unity and a means of unity, I hope that expanded opportunities for Eucharistic sharing be permitted with those dialogue partners that share Catholic faith in the sacrament, mutually recognize one another's baptism, and have grown in communion with the Catholic Church through dialogue and shared ecclesial elements. This would be determined on a case-by-case basis both in terms of the ecclesial community and in terms of the expanded occasions such as funerals, ecumenical gatherings, mixed marriages etc. We have built so

---

[16] Lee and Gros, *The Church as Koinonia of Salvation*, para. 109.

[17] The Lutheran World Federation and the Pontifical Council for Promoting Christian Unity, *The Apostolicity of the Church*. Study Document of the Lutheran-Roman Catholic Commission on Unity (Minneapolis: Lutheran University Press, 2006; John J. Burkhard, *Apostolicity Then and Now: An Ecumenical Church in a Postmodern World* (Collegeville: Liturgical Press, 2004).

many fences around the eucharist that perhaps it is time to contemplate Jesus's practices of table fellowship and evaluate our own ecclesial practices accordingly.

To achieve this ecumenical step, Catholics must be able to affirm that Christ is substantially present in the dialogue partner's Lord's Supper. This affirmation has usually been tied to a recognition of ministry, arguably the major roadblock to mutual eucharistic sharing. Future work towards on this may build on the US Lutheran-Catholic dialogue's observation that the judgment on the authenticity of Lutheran ministry need not be of an all-or-nothing nature.[18] The dialogue pointed to developments in *Unitatis Redintegratio*, the Decree on Ecumenism from the Second Vatican Council, which affirmed:

> Our separated brothers and sisters also celebrate many sacred actions of the Christian religion. These most certainly can truly engender a life of grace in ways that vary according to the condition of each church or community, and must be held capable of giving access to that communion in which is salvation. (UR 3)

The dialogue found that the category of validity, as traditionally determined, might be too restrictive to evaluate the Eucharistic presence within churches in a relationship of imperfect communion with the Catholic Church. The dialogue cited a letter that Joseph Cardinal Ratzinger, at that time prefect of the Congregation of the Faith, wrote in 1993 to Bavarian Lutheran bishop Johannes Hanselmann:

> I count among the most important results of the ecumenical dialogues the insight that the issue of the eucharist cannot be narrowed to the problem of "validity." Even a theology oriented to the concept of succession, such as that which holds in the Catholic and in the Orthodox church, need not in any way deny the salvation-granting presence of the Lord [Heilschaffende Gegenwart des Herrn] in a Lutheran [evangelische] Lord's Supper.[19]

---

[18] Lee and Gros, *The Church as Koinonia of Salvation*, para. 107.

[19] "Briefwechsel von Landesbischof Johannes Hanselmann und Joseph Kardinal Ratzinger über das Communio-Schreiben der Römischen Glaubenskongregation," *Una Sancta* 48 (1993): 348, cited in *The Church as Koinonia of Salvation*, para. 107.

The dialogue concluded:

> If the actions of Lutheran pastors can be described by Catholics as "sacred actions" that "can truly engender a life of grace," if communities served by such ministers give "access to that communion in which is salvation," and if at a eucharist at which a Lutheran pastor presides is to be found "the salvation-granting presence of the Lord," then Lutheran churches cannot be said simply to lack the ministry given to the church by Christ and the Spirit. In acknowledging the imperfect koinonia between our communities and the access to grace through the ministries of these communities, we also acknowledge a real although imperfect koinonia between our ministries. (§ 107)

Even though ministry may be the most neuralgic issue in ecumenical dialogue today, the question of the Eucharistic presence of the Lord and the ability to expand opportunities for Eucharistic sharing should not have to wait on a "all-or-nothing" mutual recognition of ministry.

Will for unity. John Paul II, in his Apostolic Letter *Orientale Lumen*, 20 said: "Today we know that unity can be achieved through the love of God only if the Churches want it together, in full respect for the traditions of each and for necessary autonomy. We know that his can take place only on the basis of the love of Churches which feel increasingly called to manifest the one Church of Christ, born from one Baptism and from one Eucharist, and which want to be sisters (cf. UR 141)."[20] I wish that the will for unity be more evident among all Christians to impel us to greater ecumenical efforts.

Grand ecumenical gesture. On 31st October, 2016, Pope Francis offered an enormous grand ecumenical gesture when he took part in a Joint Commemoration of the Reformation in the cities of Lund and Malmo, Sweden, alongside prominent Lutheran leaders, including Bishop Munib Younan, then President of the Lutheran World Federation. This historic visit included a Common Ecumenical Prayer service and a Joint Declaration committing both churches to further work toward unity from both leaders. So, finally, I wish from Pope Francis still further grand ecumenical gestures such as this, which can leap over obstacles to unity and help bring the budding peonies into the warm sunlight so that our ecumenical spring may blossom.

---

[20] John Paul II, Apostolic Letter *Orientale Lumen*, AAS (1995): 745–74, no. 20.

PART VII

Conclusion

CHAPTER 20

Remembering the Future: Church and Churches *Toward Multifaceted Unity*

H. E. Cardinal W. Kasper

THE ECUMENICAL VISION: GOD'S UNIVERSAL PLAN OF SALVATION

Remembering the future is for us humans a difficult—for all but certain saints and visionaries, a seemingly impossible—task. In spite of that, the burning question for all Christians remains: What will the future bring for the Church and for the churches? What will the future of ecumenism be in the twenty-first century? The twentieth century brought a good deal of progress and aroused great hopes, but in the twenty-first century by contrast, we also see clear signs of fatigue.[1]

---

[1] Regarding the contemporary state of ecumenism, see: Walter Kasper, *Wege zur Einheit der Christen* (WKGS 14), (Freiburg i. Br.: Herder, 2012), especially pp. 17–34; K. Koch, "Ökumene im Wandel. Zum Zukunftspotential des Ökumenismus-Dekrets *Unitatis redintegratio*," in *Erinnerung an die Zukunft. Das zweite vatikanische Konzil*, ed. Jan-Heiner Tück et al. (Freiburg i. Br.: Herder, 2013), 403–336; and Dirk Ansorge, "Sichtbare oder versöhnte Verschiedenheit? *Unitatis redintegratio* und der ökumenische Dialog," in *Das zweite vatikanische Konzil: Impulse und Perspektiven*, ed. Dirk Ansorge (Münster: Aschendorf Verlag, 2013), 160–98.

H. E. Cardinal W. Kasper (✉)
Catholic Pontifical Council for Promoting Christian Unity, Rome, Italy

© The Author(s) 2018
V. Latinovic et al. (eds.), *Catholicism Opening to the World and Other Confessions*, Pathways for Ecumenical and Interreligious Dialogue,
https://doi.org/10.1007/978-3-319-98581-7_20

329

A theological response to the notion of remembering the future is only possible if we remember that the future dawned once and for all with Jesus Christ. This is the path taken both by the Second Vatican Council, and by the recent document of the World Council of Churches Commission on Faith and Order, *The Church: Towards a Common Vision*, which grounds the *Oikomene* in God's *Oikonomia*, summing up all things in Christ (Eph 1:10).[2]

In Jesus Christ, God was reconciling the world to himself and entrusting to us the message of reconciliation (2 Cor 5:19). According to a foundational statement of the Second Vatican Council, the Church is in Jesus Christ the visible and effective sign of unity with God and between all humanity (LG 1, 9, 48). Unfortunately, the world often fails to perceive this sign.

In order that the paradoxical Biblical testimony may still inspire belief in view of the unreconciled condition of the world we Christians must be reconciled human beings—we must be reconciled with one another. To that end, the night before His death, Jesus prayed "that all may be one... so that the world may believe that you sent me" (Jn 17:21). Ecumenism itself is based and grounded in this "*ut unum sint*" prayer of Jesus. It is not a marginal issue; it is anchored in God's plan of salvation; it is the way of the Church for the salvation of the world.[3]

The Second Vatican Council adopted this idea in Pope John XXIII's memorable opening address *Gaudet Mater Ecclesia*, in which he proposed the theme of the Council; Pope Paul VI also confirmed it with his opening address at the beginning of the second session of the Council. The Council Fathers programmatically adopted ecumenism in the very first document, the Constitution on the Liturgy (SC 1), as one of the goals they set for the Council. The Decree *Unitatis Redintegratio* then declared ecumenism to be one of the major tasks of the church assembly (UR 1).

The foundation for the Church's embracing of ecumenism was laid in the Dogmatic Constitution on the Church *Lumen Gentium* (LG 8, 15). Upon this foundation, ecumenism became *cantus firmus* that the

---

[2] See UR 2; see also John Paul II, Encyclical Letter *Ut Unum Sint* AAS 87 (1995): 921–82, no. 5ff; WCC Commission on Faith and Order, *The Church: Towards a Common Vision* (Geneva: WCC Publications, 2013), esp. pp. 1–4, among many other documents by the commission.

[3] John Paul II, *Ut Unum Sint*, 7.

Council repeatedly addressed in many documents and bindingly passed on to the post-conciliar Church as a sign of the way in which it should move ahead.

Just two words suffice to describe this ecumenical breakthrough: *subsistit in* (LG 8; cf. UR 4). In these two words the entire ecumenical problem of Church and churches is implied *in nuce*.[4] Unfortunately, just after the Council ended a controversy arose as to its precise meaning.[5] The Congregation for the Doctrine of the Faith saw itself on two occasions constrained to intervene in the controversy.[6]

---

[4] Gérard Philips, *L'Église et son mystère au deuxième Concile du Vatican. Histoire, texte et commentaire de la Constitution Lumen gentium*, vol.1 (Paris: Desclée, 1967), 119.

[5] Alois Grillmeier, S.J., "Vatikan II," in *Lexikon für Theologie und Kirche* Supl., vol. 1 (Freiburg i. Br.: Herder, 1996), 170–76; Medard Kehl, S.J., "Die eine Kirche und die vielen Kirchen," *Stimmen der Zeit* 219 (2001): 3–16; Peter Hünermann, *Herders Theologischer Kommentar zum Zweiten Vatikanischen Konzil*, vol. 2 (Freiburg i. Br.: Herder, 2004), 368f.; Karl Josef Becker, S.J., "Subsistit in," *L'Osservatore Romano* 5/6 December 2005, 6–7; Francis A. Sullivan, S.J., "Quaestio diputata. A Response to Karl Becker on the Meaning of 'subsistit in,'" *Theological Studies* 67 (2006): 395–409; Sullivan, "Further Thoughts on the Meaning of 'subsistit in,'" in *Theological Studies* 71 (2010): 133–47; Donato Valentini, S.D.B., "Subsistit in," in *Dizionario di ecclesiologia* (Rome: Città Nuova, 2010), 1383–1408; Walter Kasper, *Katholische Kirche. Wesen, Wirklichkeit Sendung* (Freiburg i. Br.: Herder, 2011), 234–38; Alexandra von Teuffenbach, *Die Bedeutung des* subsistit in *(LG 8): zum Selbstverständnis der katholischen Kirche* (München: Utz Verlag 2002), in connection with Sebastian Tromp, S.J., secretary of Vatican II *Preparatory Theological Commission*. One must also note the relevance of the opinion of the prepatory commission itself. On this, see Giuseppe Alberigo and Franca Magistretti, eds., *Constitutionis dogmaticae Lumen gentium. Synopsis historica* (Bologna: Istituto per le scienze religiose, 1975), 38, 440. For a different approach see: Joseph Ratzinger, "Die Ekklesiologie der Konstitution *Lumen gentium*," in *Weggemeinschaft des Glaubens. Kirche als Communio* (Augsburg: Paulinus, 2002), 127, who tries to explain that *subsistit in* should be understood in the sense of scholastic *subsistentia*, which only exists in the singular and not in the plural. In my opinion, beside the fact that the term *subsistentia* is not a coherent term in scholasticism (see 'Subsistenz,' *Historische Wörterbuch der Philosophie* 10 (1998): 486–93), the word used in *Lumen Gentium* is not *subsistentia* but *subsistit in*. This was an ad hoc term, and from the proceedings it is not clear that the term should be understood in this technical sense; the phrase has more to do with the practical solution removing the strict identification of the Catholic Church with the one Church of Christ. See the above quote from Dirk Ansorge, pp. 179–182, referring to Karl Lehmann.

[6] Congregation for the Doctrine of the Faith, Declaration *Dominus Iesus*, AAS 92 (2000): 742–65; "Responses to Some Questions Regarding Certain Aspects of the Doctrine on the Church," AAS 99, no. 7 (2007): 604–8.

Nonetheless, even 50 years after the end of the Council, many questions still remain open. As the far-sighted Karl Rahner, S.J., saw immediately after the Council, it was only the beginning of a beginning; the
reception of the Council has only just begun.[7]

One thing is indisputable though: the *subsistit in* of the final text replaces
the *est* of the previous drafts. While *est* declares the Catholic Church to be
identical with the one Church of Jesus Christ, *subsistit in* annuls this strict
identification and—notwithstanding the claim of the Catholic Church that
the church of Christ is concretely present in her—means to make room
outside its institutional boundaries for churches and ecclesial communities
in which elements of sanctification and truth are to be found, which as gifts
belonging to the Church of Christ urge catholic unity (LG 8, 15; UR 3).[8]

Thus, there is no ecclesiological vacuum outside the Catholic
Church.[9] Through one baptism, all the baptized are members of the
one body of Christ (UR 13), deeply wounded by existing divisions.
The interpretation of the statements of the Council must take place on
the basis of the totality of the Council's statements and of the conciliar
vision of the Church *ad intra* and *ad extra*.

Ad intra the Church is the reflection of the unity of the Triune
God (LG 4; UR 2), which is a unity in the variety of churches. The
one Church exists in and of local churches (LG 23) that make the one
Church present in legitimate diversity (LG 13; CD 11; AG 6, 15).

This insight led to the rediscovery of the original meaning of catholicity (LG 13).[10] According to Ignatius of Antioch, the Catholic Church is
where Jesus Christ is.[11] Since Jesus Christ is present in all local churches,
the Catholic Church is concretely present in the *communio* of all local
churches.[12] Since Jesus Christ also works in and through the other

---

[7] Karl Rahner, S.J., *Das Konzil—ein neuer Beginn* (1965), new ed.: Karl Lehmann, ed.
(Freiburg i. Br.: Herder, 2012). On the history of this reception see Jan-Heiner Tück,
Erinnerung an die Zukunft (as quoted above in footnote 1).

[8] John Paul II, *Ut Unum Sint*, 10–14.

[9] Ibid., 13.

[10] About the re-discovery of the original meaning of catholicity by Karl Adam, Henry
de Lubac, S.J., Yves Congar, O.P., Avery Dulles, S.J., and others see Walter Kasper,
Katholische Kirche, 254–65.

[11] Ignatius of Antioch, *Ad Smyr.* 8, 2.

[12] A summary of the discussion on this issue with Joseph Ratzinger can be found in:
Medard Kehl, S.J., "Zum jüngsten Disput um das Verhältnis von Universalkirche und

churches (UR 3) and these often give clearer expression to individual elements of being church than the Catholic Church (UR 15), the complete realization of catholicity is only possible in ecumenical exchange and reciprocal enrichment. "Catholic" and "ecumenical" are therefore not opposites, but are two sides of one and the same coin.

Furthermore, this view of the Church *ad intra* opens *ad extra* to the other churches, the religions and the world in the variety of its cultures. The Church has been sent out to the ends of the earth (Mt 28:19) in order to leaven all, like yeast, and in order to take shape in diverse languages and cultures, social orders and national forms as well as in all honorable life patterns of all the people (AG 15).

Unfortunately, divisions hinder this mission (UR 1; AG 6). Therefore, ecumenism and world mission belonged indissolubly together at the beginning of the ecumenical movement and they belong together in our time. Only ecumenically can the Church as a messianic people of God be a sign of joy and hope (*gaudium et spes*) for all mankind, and in particular for the poor and those oppressed in any way (GS 1).[13]

The relationship between ecumenism and world mission today demands an ecumenism that is not limited to academic theological dialogue, but is rather an ecumenism of real life, a down-to-earth ecumenism. That does not mean replacing questions about truth with questions about practical matters. Doing so was a wrong turn in the ecumenical movement that has proven to be illusory.[14] But it does indeed mean that to consider the conflicts of the eleventh and sixteenth centuries we must ask about their significance regarding life and salvation in our missionary situation here and now. That involves ecumenism in the original sense of the term, the "*oikumene*," in the sense of the whole of the inhabited world. It involves the concern that the earth remain inhabitable; that

---

Ortskirche," in *Kirche in ökumenischer Perspektive (FS Walter Kasper)* (Freiburg i. Br.: Herder, 2003), 81–101; Walter Kasper, *Katholische Kirche*, 387–92.

[13] Karl Lehmann, "Die Heilsmöglichkeit für die Nichtchristen und für die Nichtglaubenden nach den Aussagen des 2. Vatikanischen Konzils," in *Heil für alle?. Ökumenische Reflexionen* (Dialog der Kirche 15), ed. Dorothea Sattler and Volker Leppin (Freiburg i. Br.: Herder, 2012), 124–52.

[14] Against this notion (rightfully) see Joseph Ratzinger's 1995 essay "Zur Lage der Ökumene," in *Joseph Ratzinger Gesammelte Schriften* (JRGS 8/2) (Freiburg i. Br.: Herder, 2010), 744–47.

humanity has a shared future in justice, peace, and freedom; and that all can find salvation in Jesus Christ.

This task was entrusted to us fifty years ago by the Council as one of the "signs of the times" (Mt 16:3; LG 1; UR 4). In view of the signs of the times today, including the global ecological, economic, cultural, social, religious and political crises, this task has, if anything, become more urgent. The unity of the Church and the unity of humanity are in our time fatefully interwoven with one another. Therefore, it is our sacred duty that for the sake of world peace and the salvation of humankind we no longer tolerate divisions between Christians.

THREE BASIC TYPES OF CHURCH DIVISIONS

Human sin can all too often stand in the way of God's desire for humanity and the Church. The Church, which is holy, also includes sinners at its heart (LG 8). This involves not only the sins of individual members, but also structures of sin within the framework of the Church itself.[15] The divisions within the Church itself are such structures of sin because they are obstacles in the way of God's plan of salvation, contradict the will of Christ Jesus, and are an offence to the world as well as an obstacle to the most essential mission of the Church (UR 1; AG 6). They are deep wounds in the body of Christ.

The blame lies equally on all sides (UR 3). From the standpoint of visible unity, the present state of Christendom does not present a very attractive sight, with 340 member churches in the World Council of Churches alone, as well as many others that are not represented there. The Catholic Church, which is not a member, though numerically the largest church, constitutes only about half of the world's Christians. This situation must be a reason for unrest (*Unruhe*). The situation is highly complex since it involves not only a quantitative multiplicity of churches but also three qualitatively different types of division.

In the New Testament, we encounter the word "church" (*ekklesia*) in the singular and in the plural. Even the New Testament already reports on tensions and splits within the local churches as well as between them. The resulting estrangements led to the schism between whole groups of local churches such as the one that occurred in the fourth–fifth century

---

[15] John Paul II, *Ut Unum Sint*, 34.

with the Oriental-Orthodox churches or in the eleventh century between the Eastern and Western Church.[16] Those divisions took place between local churches that had from the outset taken up the one Apostolic legacy in different forms and in different ways (UR 14, 16). Due to a lack of understanding and love, they came to a schism, but remained sister churches in nearly full communion. Full ecclesial communion between them can therefore only occur through mutual recognition of different individual liturgical, institutional, and disciplinary manifestations, through a patient process of the renewal of mutual recognition.[17]

The sixteenth-century Reformation resulted in a new form of division that today is generally considered to be the birth of denominationalism.[18] The confessional churches came about not—as in the first centuries—on the foundation of local churches, but founded upon distinctive confessions of faith (in the first instance the Augsburg Confession of 1530). This gave rise to churches of a new type. The Catholic Church has never understood itself as a confessional church, but through the decrees of the Council of Trent, the Trent Confession, and the Trent Catechism, it adopted characteristics of a confessional church. This resulted in a situation that had never existed before: confessional churches existing alongside one another which differed and differ not only in the individual questions of the confession of faith, the sacraments and the understanding of their ministries, but also in their ecclesial self-understanding.

In their formal confessional statements, all these reformed churches retained the term *catholic*,[19] so the Catholic Church increasingly sought to distinguish itself from them by calling itself "Roman Catholic." The Second Vatican Council finally sought to move beyond such confessional constrictions to catholicity. Because of this breakthrough one could say

---

[16] Yves Congar, O.P., *Neuf cents après. Note sur le schisme oriental* (Paris: Éditions de Chevetogne, 1954); German translation: *Zerrissene Christenheit - Wo trennten sich Ost und West?* (Wien: Herold-Verlag, 1959).

[17] Joseph Ratzinger, "Prognosen für die Zukunft des Ökumenismus," in *JRGS* 8/2, 717–30.

[18] Walter Kasper, *Barmherzigkeit: Grundbegriff des Evangeliums - Schlüssel christlichen Lebens* (Freiburg i. Br.: Herder, 2012), 105; *Das Evangelium von der Familie* (Freiburg i. Br.: Herder, 2012), 55f.

[19] For one example, see the Augsburg Confession, especially Article XXI and conclusion.

the Council signified the end of the confessional age and the beginning of an ecumenical era.[20]

When we commemorated the quincentenary of the Reformation in 2017, we did not stand in the same place that we did in 1517 and the period that followed. Far-reaching efforts have achieved rapprochement regarding many divisive questions, so we can now look together to the future and address the fundamental issue of differing ecclesial self-perceptions.[21] The ongoing challenge that remains today is to ask once more what *catholic* unity in the original sense of the word really means, and how we can make it a concrete reality today. I will return to this question later.

The twentieth century was not only an ecumenical century but at the same time the century of the rapid spread of a third form of church division. When one speaks of the evangelical movement, one needs to know that *evangelical* is a term with many meanings and many faces. Precursors are found already in the Anabaptist and spiritual movements of the Reformation period, in the Revival movements of Methodism and Pietism. At the same time, there are charismatic evangelical movements within the traditional churches: they sparked the Ecumenical Movement and its missionary orientation, and have decisively influenced it.

Alongside there are independent evangelical and Pentecostal communities who reject the idea of unity within a "super-church"—as they express it—with a remote or dismissive attitude toward the ecumenical movement. Only in recent years, through the Global Christian Forum, has it become possible to involve them, however loosely, in the

---

[20] John Paul II, *Ut Unum Sint*, 4.

[21] See Karl Lehmann und Wolfhart Pannenberg, eds., *Lehrverurteilend kirchentrennend? Rechtfertigung, Sakramente und Amt im Zeitalter der Reformation und heute* (Dialog der Kirchen 4) (Freiburg i. Br.: Herder – Göttingen: Vandenhoeck & Ruprecht, 1986); The Lutheran World Federation and the Pontifical Council for Promoting Christian Unity, *Gemeinsame Erklärung zur Rechtfertigungslehre* (Frankfurt am Main: Verlag Otto Lembeck, 1999); English translation: *Joint Declaration of the Doctrine of Justification* (Grand Rapids: Eerdmans, 2000); Walter Kasper, *Harvesting the Fruits* (New York: Continuum, 2009); John A. Radano, ed., *Celebrating a Century of Ecumenism. Exploring the Achievements of International Dialogue* (Grand Rapids: Eerdmans, 2012); The Lutheran World Federation and the Pontifical Council for Promoting Christian Unity, *From Conflict to Communion: Lutheran-Catholic Commemoration of the Reformation in 2017* (Leipzig: Evangelische Verlagsanstalt GmbH, 2013); see also Footnote 18 above.

ecumenical movement. Pope Francis above all has energetically opened the door to a new encounter.

It is not easy to define the various charismatic, evangelical and Pentecostal communities with a single denominator. They are all very different, and their differences range from their ecumenical and indeed not seldom anti-ecumenical orientations to their interpretation of Scripture, which can often be described as fundamentalist. This last approach makes dialogue difficult. In contrast to the typical confessional churches, they are bound neither to a confessional foundation nor to an institutional constitution. They perceive the Church mainly as an event. In this, they very much correspond to a situation in which traditional social orders and milieus—including denominational milieus—are breaking down. They equate to the postmodern process of individualization, or to express it in modern terms, they are digital networks to which each person can log on individually.[22]

It is therefore understandable that for a growing number of people, evangelical movements are able to satisfy their hunger and thirst for personal religious experience better than the traditional churches, which can appear to be doctrinally and institutionally rigid and inflexible. While many mainline churches are declining, the evangelical and Pentecostal communities experience growth. Certainly, one can ask whether they can have a future in the long term without ultimately developing some (new) forms of ecclesial institutions. But in a similar way, the traditional churches need to ask themselves how they intend to effectively counter the new challenges, and whether they themselves may not be in need of a profound spiritual renewal.

NEW CHALLENGES FACING ECUMENISM

The ecumenical movement of the twentieth century was without doubt the response of the Holy Spirit to the signs of the times, as a counter movement to the constantly renewed process of division (UR 1, 4). Also in previous centuries, there had been conversations and prayer for unity, but nevertheless, the ecumenical movement of the twentieth

---

[22] See Henk Witte, "Is Catholicity Still an Appropriate Concept in a Postmodern World?" in *Catholicity Under Pressure: The Ambiguous Relationship Between Diversity and Unity.* Proceedings of the 18th Academic Consultation of the Societas Oecumenica, ed. Dagmar Heller and Péter Szentpétery (Leipzig: Evangelische Verlagsanstalt, 2016), 155–70.

century was in this respect something new: a focus on dialogue instead of controversy, the endeavor to overcome misunderstanding and prejudice, the desire to learn from one another and the search to recognize what Christians had in common despite their differences.[23]

The most important fruit of ecumenism is not the multitude of documents but the rediscovery of Christian fraternity and the mutual recognition of one another as Christians.[24] In this time, we realized that what we have in common is greater than that which divides us. That has already led to a new ecclesial reality that has so far been too little considered: a still incomplete but nevertheless profound spiritual community in one God and Father, in the Lord Jesus Christ and in the one body of Jesus Christ.

Anyone who has experienced the previous denominational estrangement as I did in my childhood and youth, in my time as a student, or even in my first years as a priest, can only be amazed at all that has grown in recent decades and be immensely thankful for it. We were of course not able to simply fill in the trenches between the churches, but we have succeeded in building bridges over the trenches which are passable on both sides and through which people can encounter one another.

Significant questions remain, questions of a doctrinal nature and more recently ethical questions that directly affect human lives. The fundamental question for some, yet for many others the dead end, is the question: What is the concrete goal of the ecumenical endeavor? What does unity mean, or what does full communion mean in concrete terms? What is necessary for unity, and what is legitimate diversity? Or in the framework of our topic in this present volume: How can we concretely be the one Church of Jesus Christ within the many churches?[25]

In response, the various churches have developed different models of unity on the basis of their different ecclesiologies, and agreement between them is nowhere in sight. This situation could also prove to be extremely dangerous: if we do not agree about where we are going,

---

[23] See *Dokumente wachsender Übereinstimmung*, 4 vols. (Paderborn-Frankfurt am Main: Bonifatius, 1983–2012); John Borelli and John. H. Erickson, eds., *The Quest for Unity. Orthodox and Catholics in Dialogue* (Crestwood, NY: St. Vladimir's Seminary Press, 1996).

[24] John Paul II, *Ut Unum Sint*, 41.

[25] Harding Meyer, *Ökumenische Zielvorstellungen* (Göttingen: Vandenhoeck & Ruprecht, 1996).

we risk diverging in different directions and in the end finding ourselves further apart than we were at the beginning of the entire process.

With disappointment, one must say that the great expectations following the Council have in large measure not been fulfilled. We have neither fully implemented the Council's decisions nor truly received the post-conciliar documents; most of them have remained without consequence. It is obvious that we are at a standstill. There are even signs of a regression into the old self-satisfied denominationalism. Often we are so anxious for, and concerned with, our own denominational identity that we forget that this identity is only possible in ecumenical co-existence.

In recent times, we have seen how some of the old sensitivities that we had believed were overcome long ago instead have risen up from their graves again like ghosts. An ecumenism of love, of encounter, of listening and of friendship is what we need the most at this moment. Without a hermeneutic of trust the entire results of the dialogue that have been achieved so far, no matter how positive, will be downplayed and the bar for the agreement will be raised ever higher.

To make things worse this "neo-denominationalism" does not meet the needs of most people in the reality of their lives. We live in a world in which denominational milieus are increasingly disappearing. Members of various denominations and different religions, believers and non-believers, today often live next door to one another and even co-exist within the same family. Even within the denominations themselves, there is a pluralism of liberal-progressive, traditional-conservative, and evangelical-charismatic Christians.

We also witness a strange phenomenon that conservatives with church affiliations in all denominations are often closer to one another than the conservatives may be to the progressives within their own ranks. Confessional boundaries are only partially valid, church and denominational affiliation have become flexible and porous.

On the other hand, all churches continue to be confronted with the shared challenge of the growth of secularism in the wider societies in which our churches live, and churches are also now faced with new forms of the persecution of Christians that we are experiencing today. Such persecution of Christians does not discriminate between Catholics, Protestants, or Orthodox: Christians are oppressed, persecuted, and murdered simply because they are Christians. Thus, the twentieth and twenty-first centuries have given rise to an ecumenism written not in printer's ink but with the blood of martyrs. We Christians travel together in one boat on stormy seas.

What does this new situation mean for our subject of church and churches? That question leads me to the last portion of my deliberations. I have no ready-made solution. I can only point toward several innovative elements that I have discovered in encounter with Pope Francis. In my opinion he communicates to us original Gospel-oriented perspectives for a hopeful future.

GOSPEL-ORIENTED PERSPECTIVES ON THE FUTURE OF ECUMENISM

Pope Francis, in his thinking and in his language, is an evangelical pope through and through. In his programmatic apostolic exhortation *Evangelii Gaudium* (2013) he proceeds from the primary biblical concept of the Gospel, referring back to Paul VI's *Evangelii Nuntiandi* (1975).[26] That earlier apostolic exhortation states: "Evangelizing is in fact the grace and vocation proper to the Church, her deepest identity. She exists in order to evangelize."[27]

This appeal to the Gospel has always been the fundamental motif of renewal movements: in the monastic renewal of the Early Church, in medieval renewal movements, especially the Franciscans, as well as in the Reformation and in more recent evangelical movements. Today some very respectable scholars say that the Catholic Church of the twenty-first century will have a charismatic face.[28]

Pope Francis has intuited the heartbeat of the contemporary Church. At the same time, he is no innovator. He stands in the best tradition of renewal movements, which have all drawn their strength and inspiration from the Gospel itself. Among his key reference points is Thomas

---

[26] For discussion, see Walter Kasper, *Papst Franziskus—Revolution der Zärtlichkeit und der Liebe. Theologische Wurzeln und pastorale Perspektiven* (Stuttgart: Katholisches Bibelwerk, 2015).

[27] Paul VI, Apostolic Exhortation *Evangelii Nuntiandi*, AAS 68 (1976): 5–76, no. 14.

[28] Philip Jenkins, *Die Zukunft des Christentums. Eine Analyse der weltweiten Entwicklung im 21. Jahrhundert* (Brunnen: Brunnen-Verlag 2006); John L. Allen, *The Future Church* (New York: Doubleday, 2009).

Aquinas, who himself came out of that great period of Catholic evangelical movements begun by Francis of Assisi and Dominic.[29]

Since both doctrines and sacramental orders have been drawn from the source of the Gospel, they must be interpreted according to the hierarchy of truths (UR 11) in the light of the core of the Gospel. The evangelical message also throws light on our aforementioned question of Church and churches. Four points of view seem significant to me according to the four *Notae ecclesiae*:

1. *The vision of unity.* Jorge Bergoglio referred to Oscar Cullmann's "reconciled diversity" already at an early stage of his pontificate.[30] In doing so he addressed a fundamental concern of the Orthodox and Reformation churches. He does not see unity as a puzzle that is simply pieced together out of many parts. Rather, the whole is greater than the parts and is not the sum of its parts.[31] Therefore, the path to unity is not a path of the institutional merger. The Pope proposes a model for unity different than the image of concentric circles familiar to many Catholics. He has spoken of the contemporary relationship among differing churches as a *polyhedron*, a multifaceted body in which all the parts form a whole but participate in the whole in different ways. Precisely because they maintain their uniqueness, these various parts contribute to the beauty and attractiveness of the whole.[32]

The idea of a *polyhedron* is an image. If one wishes to translate the image into conceptual language, one can learn best from Johann Adam Möhler (d. 1838),[33] the great precursor of ecclesiological and

---

[29] Thomas Aquinas, *ST* I/II, Q. 106, A. 1–2. Regarding the origins of the evangelical movement, see Marie-Dominique Chenu, O.P., *Das Werk des Hl. Thomas von Aquin* (Heidelberg: Kerle, 1982), 39–46.

[30] Oscar Cullmann, *Einheit durch Vielfalt. Grundlegung und Beitrag zur Diskussion über die Möglichkeiten ihrer Verwirklichung* (Tübingen: Mohr Siebeck, 1986). See the positive appraisal of this work in Joseph Ratzinger, "Zum Fortgang der Ökumene," *JRGS* 8/2, 734–36.

[31] Francis, Apostolic Exhortation *Evangelii Gaudium*, AAS 105, no. 12 (2013): 1019–1137, nos. 234–37.

[32] Pope Francis refers to the image of a polyhedron only generally in *Evangelii Gaudium* 236, but at the encounter with one Pentecostal community in Caserta on 28 July 2014, he used it as an example for ecumenical unity.

[33] Johann Adam Möhler, *Die Einheit in der Kirche oder das Prinzip des Katholizismus. Dargestellt im Geiste der Kirchenväter der drei ersten Jahrhunderte* (Darmstadt: Wiss. Buchgesellschaft, 1957), 152–57 (§ 46). See also Walter Kasper, "Einheit in versöhnter

ecumenical renewal. Möhler understood the Church as, from the very beginning, a unity in diversity in the Holy Spirit. Over time, the lived diversity which was once taken for granted has become instead a series of contradictions, because individual aspects of diversity have, in what persons involved wrongly perceive as their self-interest, become absolutized. But while the whole has not been utterly destroyed, it has developed deep cracks, and each of its distinctive parts have become poorer and less attractive as a result. Healing becomes possible when one extracts and removes the poison of mutually exclusive self-centeredness from the individual parts, so that they can form a harmonic whole once more in a new way. The newfound reconciliation in a new deliberate mutually enriching unity in reconciled diversity presupposes conversion on all sides.

2. *Conversion of the churches*. The Church, which our creed professes to be holy, is in constant need of renewal and reform; she is an *ecclesia semper renovanda* (LG 8; GS 43; etc.). To use an image: the polyhedron must be polished so that it becomes a jewel reflecting the light that strikes it in a wonderfully varied way. There is no ecumenism without conversion, renewal, and reform (UR 4).[34] The Groupe des Dombes pointed to the importance of this ecclesial reality in the very important document "For the Conversion of the Churches" (1993).[35]

Every conversion begins with individual persons. One must consider, however, not only the sins of the sons and daughters of the Church, but the structures of sin.[36] Sins may be grounded in the past but they can also reach into the present via hardened structures. Therefore,

Verschiedenheit," in *Wege zur Einheit der Christen*, ed. Kasper, 230–32 (including extended references).

[34] John Paul II, *Ut Unum Sint*, 15–17, 33–35.

[35] Groupe de Dombes, *Pour la conversion des églises* (Paris: Centurion, 1991); English translation: "For the Conversion of the Churches," in *For the Communion of the Churches: The Contributions of the Groupe des Dombes*, ed. Catherine E. Clifford (Grand Rapids: Eerdmans, 2010), 149–223.

[36] John Paul II, *Ut Unum Sint*, 34. The recognition that Catholic Church bears part of the blame for the Reformation came already from Pope Hadrian VI at the Imperial Diet of Nuremberg in 1522. Pope Paul VI also offered a plea for forgiveness at the opening of the second session of Vatican II in 1963. Finally, Pope John Paul II prayed for forgiveness for sins of the Church during the great jubilee year 2000. See also the document of the International Theological Commission: *Memory and Reconciliation: The Church and the Faults of the Past (2000)*.

Pope Francis speaks—in an unusually open manner for a pope—of the conversion of the episcopacy and the conversion of the papacy—even the conversion of the exercise of papal primacy—in the context of a broad pastoral conversion.[37] He has offered concrete proposals for this and leads the way through his own good example.

Ecumenism involves the turning of all Christian partners in dialogue to discern anew the way of Jesus Christ. To the extent that we are one in Christ, we will also be one with one another. Without such a conversion to Christ, all structural reforms, no matter how necessary they may be, will be like a threshing machine that is working away furiously and yet is empty of straw.

The ecumenical movement began in the nineteenth century through shared ecumenical prayer. This suggests that prayer and penitence must constantly be the soul of ecumenism (UR 8).[38] In the end, we cannot bring about unity simply through, programmatic or organizational forms alone. The unity of the Church is the Pentecost gift of the Holy Spirit who invites, enables and urges us to become collaborators with God (1 Cor 3:9).

The Holy Spirit is the primary initiator, agent and soul of all our activities, so we only can pray that the Spirit's storm may bring down the walls that divide us. We pray that the Spirit's fire may inspire us and burn out our prejudices, faint-heartedness, narrowness, inner resistance and hesitation. We pray that the Spirit fill us with the spirit of reconciliation and love, the magnanimity that perceives the great horizon of God's universal design for his Church.

3. *Concrete catholicity.* Conversion to God and conversion to our neighbor belong indissolubly together. Conversion to the Gospel, therefore, includes opening up to other Christians and other Churches. Only in this way is the full realization of the Church's unique catholicity and the realization of her mission possible.

Catholicity includes all: women and men, young and old, clergy, and laity. The laity are not merely recipients, but active participants; not only objects, but above all subjects in the Church. So the doctrine of the *sensus fidei* given by baptism to all is important.[39] This aspect was

---

[37] Francis, *Evangelii Gaudium*, 25ff., 30, 32, 51.

[38] John Paul II, *Ut Unum Sint*, 21–24.

[39] See International Theological Commission, *Sensus fidei in the life of the Church* (2014).

emphasized by the Council but was then unfortunately suppressed again. Francis now wishes to bring about a renewed concrete validity for the *sensus fidei* throughout the entire Church.[40] He desires a *listening magisterium* that enables the Church to reach decisions only after it has sought to discern what the Spirit may be saying to the churches (Rev 2:7, etc.).

Catholicity for him Pope Francis therefore means the reinforcement of the synodal elements in the Catholic Church. Following the model of the Apostolic Council in Jerusalem (Acts 15), Church tradition has recognized synodical traditions in all churches and this throughout both the first and the second millennium. Effective leadership in the Church at every levels—local, regional and universal—is not mutually exclusive to synodality, quite the opposite. They should complement one another. The realization of this signifies a particularly great step closer toward the Orthodox ecclesial traditions and also toward the differing understandings of the Church among Protestant Christians. With this in mind, Francis has taken up the offer made by John Paul II and renewed by Benedict XVI to enter into a conversation regarding new ways of exercising papal primacy.[41]

Since the Council the word *dialogue* has become common parlance for such initiatives. But dialogue can sometimes be taken to primarily mean an encounter between two individuals. For a constructive, creative encounter between ethnic, social, cultural and religious groups, the broader category of *transversal* has in the meantime come into common interdisciplinary use in order to signify the diverse range of partners in the conversations and other forms of exchange throughout the differing parts of the human family.[42] This term does not signify hierarchical thinking, but rather "lateral-thinking" which unites identity and plurality creatively.

---

[40] Francis, *Evangelii Gaudium*, 119, 139, 198.

[41] John Paul II, *Ut Unum Sint*, 95; Address of Pope Benedict XVI during his visit to the Phanar on November 30, 2006, AAS 98, no. 12 (2006): 913–17. Pope Francis seems to follow the lead of Archbishop John R. Quinn on this matter. See *The Reform of the Papacy: The Costly Call to Christian Unity* (New York: Crossroads, 1999); see also James F. Puglisi, S.A., ed., *How Can the Petrine Ministry Be a Service to the Unity of the Universal Church?* (Grand Rapids: Eerdmans, 2010).

[42] This way of thinking can also be found in Enrique Dussel, *Der Gegendiskurs der Moderne. Kölner Vorlesungen* (Wien: Turia + Kant, 2012) who comes from Argentina, and in the German-speaking world by Wolfgang Welsch, *Unsere postmoderne Moderne* (Berlin: Oldenbourg Akademieverlag, 2002); Welsch, *Vernunft. Die zeitgenössische Vernunftkritik und das Konzept der transversalen Vernunft* (Frankfurt am Main: Suhrkamp Verlag, 2007).

It is very important to say that one can neither concede individual identity in favor of a post-modern relativism in which all things are equally valid, nor withdraw into oneself and declare that identity the sole norm. One must be open to value others, seeking commonalities and entering into a process of reciprocal learning and creative collaboration. It would be desirable to reflect upon what this *transversal method* means ecumenically for the realization of a *polyhedric catholicity*.

4. *Apostolicity of the church*. Some criterion is necessary so that processes of transversal communication do not result in an indefinable amalgam. The Apostles' Creed serves in all churches as the standard set once and for all (*depositum fidei*). There can be no *new* or *other* Church, but only a *renewed* Church on the basis of the original apostolic foundation laid down once and for all (1 Cor 3:11; Gal 1:6–9; Jud 3; DV 7).

The Gospel is the same at all times and in all places, and yet it is always profoundly new. Francis speaks of the eternal novelty of the Gospel and means by that its inexhaustible riches, which in its original freshness bursts all categories and clichés.[43] Again and again, we can and must allow ourselves to be surprised by God and his Spirit. In this sense, ecumenism occurs not through standing still but in moving forward. Only water that flows remains fresh, while standing water becomes stagnant.

In this sense, remembering the origins of our faith, of our churches, can provide what has been termed a "dangerous memory" (Johannes B. Metz) which can bring forgotten traditions back into the light of day and energize us to go forth, moving beyond from comfortable and even cherished habits. A church that returns to its apostolic origins also goes forward to the future. Pope Francis calls it the "Church that goes forth"[44]: by that he means a missionary journey, an apostolic Church and a Church in permanent mission.

Apostolicity must be lived apostolicity, the *vita apostolica*, as a poor Church for the poor. Thus, the criterion of apostolicity is freed from a historicizing constriction and can be understood in a holistic sense. Apostolicity signifies both apostolicity of origin and apostolicity of missionary journey, and ultimately, apostolicity concretely lived.

---

[43] Francis, *Evangelii Gaudium*, 11.
[44] Ibid., 20–24.

Ecumenically this concept seems greatly significant to me, since it reframes the subject of continuity with apostolic origins that is fundamental for all churches but evokes among the churches a controversial response. The hermeneutic of continuity must for the sake of the future sustainability of Christianity always be a hermeneutic of reform.[45] As John XXIII said, we must hand on not the ashes but the glow. We must cast aside the ashes that have accumulated, including some denominationalist ashes, so that the fire of the Gospel can glow more brightly and so that its glow can warm hearts.

All of this does not constitute a complete program for ecumenism's future nor even a neat conception of such: these are only thoughts identifying some important and life-giving elements toward shaping a new vision of ecumenism oriented toward the Gospel in view of the signs of the times. Vatican II, itself, sought to clear and follow such a path and thus the Council retains an abiding ecumenical relevance to this very day. But the Council was, as Karl Rahner told us long ago, only the beginning of a beginning. With the current pontificate, a new phase of its reception has begun, perhaps even that great leap forward toward *aggiornamento* that John XXIII considered both possible and necessary. To have the courage to take a leap of faith toward a Gospel-oriented ecumenical future is to show fidelity to the Gospel.

Allow me to close this essay with the prophet Isaiah (Is 43:19): "See, I am doing something new! Now it springs forth, do you not perceive it?" Let us not be robbed of hope, the hope and courage for the new. "Unity has already begun."

---

[45] See the famous speech Benedict XVI delivered on December 22, 2005 on the hermeneutics of continuity as hermeneutics of reform, widely seen as a nod to John Henry Newman's (d. 1890) notion of the development of doctrine. Benedict XVI, "2005 Christmas Address to the Roman Curia," AAS 98, no. 1 (2006): 40–53.

Epilogue

Brian Flanagan

At the meeting that generated the papers in this volume, after a rich morning of papers on ecumenism and the address by Cardinal Walter Kasper that immediately precedes this epilogue, the attendees reconvened for a further moment of remembering both the past and the future. As the Great Organ of the Washington National Cathedral came to life around us, we gathered not only as scholars or theologians, but as Christians and others of good will in thanksgiving, repentance and hope for the future.

Our midday prayer service was designed to commemorate an ecumenical Liturgy of the Word service held on December 4, 1965, just before the close of the Second Vatican Council, at the Basilica of St. Paul Outside the Walls in Rome—the church where, during the Week of Prayer for Christian Unity in 1959, Pope John XXIII had surprised his cardinals, and the world, by announcing his plans for the Council. Presided over by Pope Paul VI and attended by many Council Fathers as well as the observer delegates from other churches and communities, the 1965 prayer service marked the first time a pope had publicly taken part in ecumenical worship.

B. Flanagan (✉)
Marymount University, Arlington, Virginia
e-mail: brian.flanagan@marymount.edu

© The Editor(s) (if applicable) and The Author(s),
under exclusive licence to Springer Nature Switzerland AG,
part of Springer Nature 2018
V. Latinovic et al. (eds.), *Catholicism Opening to the World and Other Confessions*, Pathways for Ecumenical and Interreligious Dialogue,
https://doi.org/10.1007/978-3-319-98581-7

347

Back at the National Cathedral, as we lifted our voices in lament and repentance for our separation and in petition for our unity, we were reminded that the foundation of the ecumenical movement, both historically and structurally, is prayer. In particular, that foundation involves prayer to the Holy Spirit, that Spirit of God might inspire the Church of Christ to express its unity more fully and visibly. As Cardinal Kasper writes in the preceding essay:

> The Holy Spirit is the primacy, the initiative, the main agent and the soul of all our activities, so we only can pray that the Spirit's storm may bring down the walls that divide us. We pray that the Spirit's fire may inspire us and burn out our prejudices, faint-heartedness, narrowness, inner resistance and hesitation. We pray that the Spirit fill us with the spirit of reconciliation and love, the magnanimity that perceives the great horizon of God's universal design for his Church.

And so, as the Taizé setting of the *Veni sancte spiritus* echoed off the stone pillars and vaults of the Cathedral, I was filled with a great sense of hope and awe, and also with a reminder of why so many scholars, writers, pastors, and others, had journeyed from around the world to Washington to spend time in scholarly dialogue: not for their own personal benefit, nor simply to move up another step in the academic *cursus honorum*, but out of their commitment to put their gifts at the service of the church and the world. To draw upon the deconstructed and reconstructed cliché from the essay by John O'Malley, S.J., our conference was as "pastoral" as the council that it commemorated, that is, it concerned itself with learning and teaching in order to "serve to help people live their lives in holiness and to increase their faith."

The wisdom and insight of many colleagues, friends, and, most importantly, sisters and brothers in Christ are on display in the volume that you have just finished reading. Incomplete without its companion volume's focus upon the relationship of the Christian church to members of other religious traditions, this volume nevertheless sets forth a broad and deep reception of the Second Vatican Council in a variety of ways. The essays presented here correspond, broadly, with the three readings from the conciliar documents we heard proclaimed in our common prayer, from *Lumen Gentium* on the universal call to holiness, from *Unitatis Redintegratio* on Christian unity, and from *Gaudium et Spes* on the church's presence in and with all of humanity.

This volume's essays on the opening to the world focus upon the reception of the Council's teaching in the portion of *Gaudium et Spes* that we heard in prayer, where Vatican II taught that "the Church, at once a visible association and a spiritual community, goes forward together with humanity and experiences the same earthly lot which the world does." (GS 40) Charles Curran's essay above highlights that opening to the world in terms of the Council's more theological approach, the centrality of the person to its teaching, and its inductive methodology. In his essay and the others in Part One, we can see both the reception of the past and the re-reception towards the future of the Council fifty years on, after "the beginning of the beginning."

In Parts Two and Three, we see the reception of Vatican II's teaching in *Lumen Gentium* that "all Christians in any state or walk of life are called to the fullness of Christian life and to the perfection of love" (LG 40). In our essays on women and Vatican II, we see the occasional successes but also the recurring failures to receive women's experiences of holiness and teaching authority, the call of all Christians "to the fullness of Christian life," within the Roman Catholic Church and within the wider Church of Christ. In Part Three, the experiences of reception of Vatican II in Papua, Indonesia, in the Philippines, Korea, and elsewhere in Asia, and in 1960s Hollywood, all highlight the local churches and virtual "places" that historically North American and European scholarship have considered marginal to the "real" reception of the Council in the churches and academies of the global north. Both of these parts indicate the global, intercultural dialogue of our conference itself and provide just a hint of the rich mosaic of voices and testimonies of reception that broadened attendees' memory of both the past and the future.

Finally, the Fourth and Fifth Parts of this volume focus upon ecumenism, and can be seen as a reception of the Council's teaching in *Unitatis Redintegratio* that the division of the church "openly contradicts the will of Christ, scandalizes the world, and damages the holy cause of preaching the Gospel to every creature" (UR 1). The Council Fathers' commitment to the ecumenical movement and their statement that "the restoration of unity among all Christians is one of the principal concerns of the Second Vatican Council" (UR 1) was one of the most radical breaks in Roman Catholic teaching and practice from previous centuries, and yet one most taken for granted today by us, the inheritors of that great leap forward of the Holy Spirit. Part Four's essays on the reception and reading of Vatican II by other Christians provides some of the evidence for the impact of the Council not only on Roman Catholic faith, life, and practice, but also on that of all of the churches. Part Five, and Cardinal Kasper's concluding essay, focus more explicitly on the effects and reception of the Council's teaching on ecumenism and on the future towards which the churches, and the scholars gathered together at the National Cathedral that day, are working. Susan Wood's "ecumenical wish list" and Cardinal Kasper's call for a renewed Gospel-oriented ecumenical future under the leadership of Pope Francis both point back to where I began—with the need for both continuing research and continuing prayer in our growth towards the visibly united church of Christ that God dreams about and that the Holy Spirit will enable.

It is impossible now for me to think about our 2015 meeting and this prayer service without thinking of a still more recent and larger ecumenical prayer service that took place on October 31, 2016, in Lund, Sweden. At the Lutheran Cathedral in Lund, Pope Francis, Lutheran World Federation President Munib Younan, and LWF General Secretary Martin Junge co-hosted a common prayer service with which the Lutheran World Federation began its year-long commemoration of the five-hundredth anniversary of the beginning of the Lutheran Reformation. The service, prepared by a joint Lutheran-Roman Catholic task force, was rooted in a study document of the Lutheran-Roman Catholic Commission on Unity and was replicated in numerous joint Roman Catholic-Lutheran commemorations of the Reformation throughout the world. Just more than five decades after the end of the Second Vatican Council, Catholics and Lutherans, along with many other Protestant Christians, were able to join together in shared commemoration of the events of 1517. Like our service, these common prayer services emphasized thanksgiving for our growth in unity, repentance for our past mistakes, and re-commitment to greater growth in mutual love and full unity around the table of Christ. But, as in Susan Wood's essay in this volume, we should see in these services the early blossoms of the full buds of ecumenical dialogue springing forth after what was once described as an ecumenical winter. Remarkably, Catholics and Lutherans were able to come together in commemoration of 1517 as part, not of one church's heritage alone, nor as another church's tragedy, but as part of our joint heritage and tradition, part of what makes us, the one church of Christ in an ecumenical age, who we are.

The essays in this volume similarly lead the way in our ability to claim the Second Vatican Council as an event in the history of the Great

Church, as part of *our* heritage, whether Roman Catholic, Orthodox, Protestant or Evangelical, whether African, Asian, European or Central, Southern or North American, or from Oceania; whether male or female. God willing, in five hundred, two thousand, or ten thousand years the Christian Church will look back at what we learned about ourselves and about our world in our time of separation and in our attempts to be open to the Holy Spirit's re-uniting love. The Second Vatican Council was a crucial moment in our shared journey towards that hope, and it is through both the scholarly effort evident in this volume, and in the prayer and action we can hope that these efforts will inspire, that we will be able to remember the future and the past of the Church of Christ fully.

INDEX

© The Editor(s) (if applicable) and The Author(s),
under exclusive licence to Springer Nature Switzerland AG,
part of Springer Nature 2018
V. Latinovic et al. (eds.), *Catholicism Opening to the World and Other Confessions*, Pathways for Ecumenical and Interreligious Dialogue,
https://doi.org/10.1007/978-3-319-98581-7

A Partridge on a Par Three

The Unexpurgated Golf Letters of Mortimer Merriweather

Inspired and Collated

by

Clive Agran

To Rose, who hates golf but loves me, I think.

Foreword

Mortimer is busy ironing his plus fours at the moment and has therefore asked me to pen this foreword. As you can tell from the number of pages that you will shortly have to plough through, the old boy has fired off a fair-few letters of late and his gnarled old fingers will therefore benefit from a break.

Before I go any further, there are a few things I should perhaps explain to you about Mortimer. Reading his letters, you might form the impression that here is a grumpy old geezer with too much time on his hands and nothing better to do than vent his frustration at his increasing inability to reach a fairway or escape from a bunker by annoying those in authority with his daft ideas and ridiculous suggestions. Well, you would be absolutely right because that succinctly sums him up.

As his age and handicap inexorably rise, Mortimer is undoubtedly becoming somewhat disenchanted with the world. However, although some of his letters display what appears to be intolerance, please don't be offended. A combination of gout and the yips has undoubtedly warped his mind but the upside of that is he has developed an entirely original perspective that has endowed him with a unique outlook. He's very much a man of his time ill-equipped to cope with political correctness, woke awareness or anything originating much after 1957.

But I don't want to sound too negative as, when you eventually get around to reading his letters, you may well be impressed with his originality and forthrightness. He thinks of things that would almost certainly never occur to any right-minded person.

Now might be a good time to explain why there aren't any replies to be found in the following pages. Well, with one or two honourable exceptions, they were just too dull.

Mortimer concentrates on golf because that has been the main focus of his life ever since his great grandfather Egbert left him a mashie-niblick in his will. Golf, together with Madeira wine and the occasional port, is what he lives for. Not content with having won two monthly medals and one mid-week seniors' Stableford in his four-score years, he has sought to bolster his legacy with the letters contained in this book.

Whether the name Merriweather rightfully belongs alongside Old Tom Morris, Ben Hogan, Jack Nicklaus and Tiger Woods in the pantheon of golfing greats is for you to decide. It might sound a preposterous notion now but just wait until you've read this book before you decide whether Mortimer Merriweather is a genius or buffoon.

Clive Agran

(cliveagran@btinternet.com)

Contents   Page

Section 1

Somewhat Offensive

2

Dear British Trust for Ornithology,

I desperately need your help in persuading the golf authorities around the world to adopt new nomenclature for describing how many shots have been taken over par. In case you're not familiar with the Royal and Ancient game, I should explain that par is what a good player on a good day should score on any particular hole. For a short hole it's three, for a medium length hole it's four and for a very long hole it's five.

Exceptionally good players can, of course, score lower than par. One below par is a birdie, two below par is an eagle and three below par is an albatross. Because you know pretty well everything there is to know about birds, you will note the avian nature of the terminology.

Good, bad and average players frequently take a lot more shots than they should on a hole ... one, two, three, four, five or more. Bogey is not a particularly nice word but it's the one used to describe a score of one over par. Thereafter, the game betrays a paucity of originality by describing two over par as a double bogey, three over par as a triple bogey, etc., etc.

There is clearly scope for a more imaginative nomenclature here and continuing with the avian theme is clearly both desirable and easily achieved. Having given it a great deal of thought, I have come to the conclusion that one-over-par, which is presently a bogey, should instead be called a 'partridge'. I like it for two principal reasons: 1) It's just a bit more than par. In fact, it's a 'tridge' more than par. And 2) It will enable players who score a four on a short hole to say, "I had a partridge on the par three", which I think will cause much merriment.

What should also provide a lot of laughs is 'Great Tit', which I think is an apt name for what is currently called a double bogey. Thereafter, I'm hoping for suggestions from you. In case you can't think of any, I've drawn up a provisional list of what I think would work well:

Three over par – presently triple bogey – a 'Shag'.

Four over par – presently quadruple bogey – a 'Ruddy Duck'

Five over par – presently quintuple bogey – a 'Fluffy-backed Tit Babbler"

Although with golfers anything is possible and former British Open champion David Duval recorded a nine-over par 14 on a par five in The Open at Royal Portrush a couple of years ago, I think we should probably stop at the "Fluffy-backed Tit Babbler", don't you? At least golfers will be able to say things like, "I had a couple of Great Tits on the front and finished with a Shag up the last."

Well you'd look tired if you'd had two shags down the back nine!

Dear Deposed President Donald Trump,

Having had a bike nicked from outside my flat in West Hampstead 30 years ago, I can understand how you must feel about having an election stolen from you. The worst thing about it all is that it undermines your faith in humanity and you probably don't feel you can trust people anymore. It must be especially hard for you coming as it does after so many of your aides, assistants and advisors , not to mention that dodgy lawyer of yours, all jumped ship. You gave them respectable jobs in the White House and a chance to move on from their previous involvement in fraud, tax evasion, money-laundering and general criminality and they 'thank you' by dumping you in it. No wonder you get on so well with that nice Mr Putin, who also has good reason to be somewhat paranoiac.

Anyway, my advice is to abandon any idea of running again, forget the whole presidential thing and move on to something for which you have a real passion … golf. I think you'll find that, relieved of the responsibility of leading the western world, your short game will benefit and the time saved by not having to attend boring cabinet meetings and tedious summit conferences will allow you to work on your swing. In the fullness of time you might well look back at the humiliation of not being granted a second term as a blessing.

Because you're in the hotel and hospitality industry, you will also be able to claim any green fees, trolley hire and range balls against tax. Oops, I was forgetting you don't pay tax. Never mind, not claiming any tax relief on these items can only enhance your image and silence those miserable critics within the golf industry – almost certainly high handicappers - who claim you're a megalomaniac just because you acquired Turnberry, Doonbeg and Doral and

re-christened them Trump Turnberry, Trump Doonbeg and Trump National Doral.

Finally, there is an under-exploited course on the east coast of Scotland that is simply crying out for a massive makeover. Not only that but it also regularly hosts the British Open and is so embedded in the rota that even those snotty suits at the R&A won't be able to deny you the thrill of hosting the greatest golf tournament in the world. How does, "The Open at St Trumps" sound to you?

****

Dear Monty,

I've long been a huge fan of yours and would love to see you cap a magnificent career by capturing at least one major title. After all, Phil Mickelson, who can't be much younger than you, just snaffled another one. What's more, I think I can help.

There's nothing I can usefully contribute on the playing front as, frankly, I struggle off a handicap of 19. But my mother taught me a valuable lesson early on in life, which I've always found useful and would like to pass on to you now. She used to say: "Mortimer, no matter what happens, smile and be grateful you're alive." And you know what, it truly helps.

Like most other folk I've been through a lot in my life. What with never having passed the driving test, redundancy and piles, but I've always smiled and considered myself a lucky man. Frankly, with everything you have - a great talent, pots of money and a beautiful family - you ought not to be

so grumpy, especially as you probably never have to pay a green fee or rake a bunker.

Okay, you're allowed the odd scowl when you miss a short putt, but the rest of the time you should try to appreciate the glorious scenery and be happy that you're playing golf. Millions of others can't, because their wives won't let them. When was the last time Mrs M. said: "Colin, you're not off playing golf again! You played Thursday, Friday and yesterday and now you want to play on Sunday as well."?

To golf as often as you do, travel all over the world, stay in the finest hotels, have all your equipment supplied free and be able to watch the best players close up, makes me very jealous. Whenever you feel fed up, just remember Agnes Merriweather and her splendid philosophy on life.

****

Dear Mr Disney,

Below is the synopsis of a feel-good movie I think you should make. It has the working title 'Caught Cheating'. I don't want millions for it, just a modest $100,000 and a decent part in the film.

The action takes place in Surrey, England in 2019.

To the outsider, Charles Salisbury's life seems perfect. Married to the lovely and very much younger Linda, he has two delightful children, a secure job with a bank and is considered a pillar of the local community. His crowning moment comes at a dinner at his golf club held to celebrate his appointment as captain. However, his world starts to fall apart when, minutes before he is due to make his acceptance speech, he is caught literally with his pants

down in the locker room with Geoffrey, the new assistant greenkeeper.

He's thrown out of the marital home by his humiliated wife, sacked by the bank, expelled from his club and, worse still, he finds his favourite Ping putter (product placement opportunity) broken and stuffed in a dustbin. Although almost broken himself, this last act of wanton vandalism motivates him to fight back.

With what little money he has, he buys a caravan and camps on a strip of wasteland adjoining the local municipal golf course. Unlike the toffs at his old club, the less stuffy working-class members of the municipal club welcome him. Driven by a burning desire to revenge his humiliation and with little else to do, he practices golf for hours every day and improves bit by bit. He captains the team at his new club in their annual match against his old club and, fired by all that has happened, his inspirational leadership helps his team to their first ever success in the fixture.

Charles, however, doesn't stop there. Despite being over 40, his handicap tumbles to scratch but, because of what happened that night, he's never picked to play for his county. Then, against the odds, he comes through both a pre-qualifier and qualifier to earn a spot in the British Open. Despite a double-bogey six at the first hole, he has rounds of 69 and 67 to comfortably make the cut. After each round he returns to his caravan, which he tows behind his beaten-up old car. Alone, he stares at photos of his ex-wife, son and daughter, and sobs.

Another 67 in the third round puts him in contention and he tees off on the last day in the final pairing, still symbolically eschewing a caddy and pulling a trolley. As he holes a 20-foot putt on the 18th to clinch The Open, he sees his wife, son and daughter cheering in the stands and he lifts the claret jug as the end credits roll.

I think Brad Pitt would make an excellent Charles Salisbury and Keira Knightley would be ideal as his wife. I'm not fussed about which part I'm given so long as I get to play a bit of golf.

****

Dear Sunningdale,

It is on a matter of the utmost delicacy that I write to you and I would seriously be most grateful if you would kindly respect the privacy of all its parts.

My uncle, Sheik Rashid Binami Al-Binami, is presently living in Dubai but he is hoping to be living in the UK quite shortly if only for the most pleasing summer months. A suitable estate with top-notch facilities has been found for him in very lovely Surrey. He will be most happy there especially as he will be close to the famous Sandown Park where he will enjoy watching the horses.

Horses are his number one pleasure. Golf is his number two pleasure and so I ask what he must do to join your Great Club. He plays very frequently in Dubai and tells me he is averagely good at the golf game. He is most proficient from bunkers perhaps because there is much sand where he can practice.

My English friends tell me that there are often dress rules in such a famous club as the Great Sunningdale. My uncle is comfortable in western suits but his wives only wear traditional costume. Would they be allowed in or would they be obliged to wait in the car park while he is being friendly after doing his holes? Which brings me on to the question of family membership. My uncle has five wives

9

and 12 children. Presumably they would be covered by one family membership.

May Allah allow your putting greens to flourish and bear fruit.

****

Dear Mohammed Al Fayed,

I know you're a huge fan of football, but I have no idea if you play golf. It's an expensive game but great fun. With your excellent contacts you should have no difficulty in getting into a club. Some are a bit sniffy about foreigners, but I seem to recall that you've applied for a British passport, which should speed things up a bit. Anyway, my purpose in writing to you now is to alert you to a great business opportunity connected with golf. Those who love the game are suckers for anything to do with it, particularly the famous courses where punters will pay ludicrous sums for monogrammed sweaters and even golf balls. Why should the golf clubs nick all this valuable business?

What I'm suggesting we do is make available to the public through your world-famous Harrods store, a range of products that are both unusual and yet have historic associations. For example, an egg timer filled with sand from one of the world's most famous bunkers, such as the one guarding the 17th green at St Andrews. By the way, that's a course in Scotland, not Birmingham's home ground.

Then there could be bottles of perfume based on water extracted from such famous hazards as the Swilken Burn, also St Andrews, and Rae's Creek at Augusta National in

the USA. Aftershave, too, could be distilled from mowings shaven from the fairways of Carnoustie in Scotland and Pebble Beach in the States. The possibilities are endless.

The real genius is that these products only need contain <u>some</u> sand, water or whatever from these famous places. One grain per million or one drop per 1000 gallons would be sufficient to enable us to rightly claim that they contain the genuine article. Each packet would include a certificate of authenticity, signed by a respected individual widely acknowledged as someone of proven stature, honesty and integrity… you? Harrods, frequented as it is by wealthy toffs, would be an ideal outlet for our gear and I can see the egg timers being knocked out for something like £29.99, the aftershave for £69.99 and the perfume for £99.99.

****

Dear Dustin Johnson,

May I first of all congratulate you on your excellent golf. From tee to green you are undoubtedly one of the top players around at the moment. And, if you continue to practice conscientiously, I see no reason why you shouldn't improve and put yourself up there alongside some of the all-time greats like Jack Nicholson.

However, watching you on Sky television playing in a recent tournament in the US, I couldn't help but notice that you were tending to bend your right arm as you neared the top of your backswing. In this respect, you've got the same problem as my mate Reg, who plays off 21.

Both you and he tend to spray the ball a bit when you do this. Frankly he does it more than you do but, there again, you take the game a lot more seriously than he does.

It helps Reg to imagine he's got a broom handle stuffed down the right sleeve of his shirt. You might care to try this and see if it makes a difference.

Lastly, I understand that you're finally about to get married to Paulina Gretzky. Congratulations. However, don't make the mistake I did and not tell your intended about your fondness for golf. I suggest you sit down quietly one evening, explain that you play a lot of golf and that this means you will be away quite a bit. In this way, you'll prepare her a bit better than I did my wife and avoid the ridiculous arguments every time you go off to play.

****

Dear Scottish Tourist Board,

I'm thinking of taking my wife and two children to Scotland this year for a holiday. We've never been there before and, although I gather it can be very cold, even in summer, I would like to give it a try if for no other reason than to find out what the kilted people really think of Nicola Sturgeon. By the way, I don't hear anything of Alex Salmond these days. Whatever happened to him? Probably gone to live somewhere warm, sunny and tax-free like that other Scottish patriot, Sean Connery.

Back to business. I took up golf about 10 years ago and, due to a combination of natural talent and sheer determination, have steadily reduced my handicap to the 19.4 it is today. Anyway, I'm considering taking my half-set of Petron

Impalas with me to Scotland but don't want to use up precious space in my little Fiat if there aren't any decent courses up there. Do you know if there are?

I appreciate it's unfair to compare countries but we went to Croatia last year and found a couple of real beauties right next to the Adriatic. Are there any in Scotland next to the sea?

A couple of other things. Do you know if the rules are the same in Scotland as they are in England? I would hate to embarrass myself by accusing some poor jock of cheating if he's only doing something that's allowed north of the border. For example, I expect you're given more time to find the ball up there.

Finally, I understand Scotland has its own currency and bank notes. Would I do better changing my money in England or is the exchange rate no different in Scotland?

****

Dear Executors of the late Sir Bruce Forsyth,

As a very keen golfer, Brucie must have encountered the problem of trying to lift a ball off a bare lie with the attendant risk of sculling the ball. Not anymore. Thanks to the new club I've developed, bare lies will no longer cause concern.

With an almost razor sharp leading edge, made from cobalt-coated tungsten, this club is set to transform the scores of average handicap golfers and will enable even the humblest hacker to have and I quote, "a good game… good game". Geddit?

Why, you might wonder, am I writing to you? Well, designing and manufacturing the club was comparatively easy as compared with thinking up a name for it. To be honest I needed one that suggested that the problem of a lack of natural growth - whether grass on the course or hair on the head - was one that could easily be overcome.

Brucie demonstrated that a lack of natural hair need not be an obstacle in life, but something that can easily be dealt with; in his case, with a discreet hairpiece. In the same way, a lack of grass under the ball can be overcome when you use "The Brucie Scalper." I like the word scalper because it not only implies surgical-like precision (scalpel) but links in almost seamlessly, if that's the word, with "scalp", which in turn connects with hair.

The informal research I've conducted at my golf club suggests that the name is still a popular one that will help sell the product. Although "Brucie" is not a registered trademark, and because his image will not appear on either the packaging or the advertising (unless you'd like it to), I understand that I'm not strictly required to seek your permission to use it. However, as a courtesy, I thought I should at least alert you to the existence of the product and enquire as to whether you would like to be involved in its marketing or promotion.

If nothing else, it will help sustain his memory for thousands of years to come and permanently link his name to the game he loved.

Dear Jimmy Tarbuck,

To be honest, I've never thought you were particularly funny, but my mother liked you a lot and thought you funnier than your compatriot, Billy Connelly.

Anyway, whether you're funny or not is irrelevant. What matters is you're a well-known name and that you play golf because I've developed a really exciting club that I know will interest you.

Called the 'Tarby Tosser', it's a speciality club specifically designed to cope with those awkward little flop shots over bunkers and the like where getting the ball to rise quickly is the priority and not much distance is required.

The 'secret' is the 78 degrees of loft, which enables the player to strike the ball really hard without fear of flying it through the green. The only serious problem we've encountered in the research and development stage is that sometimes the ball flies almost vertically off the face of the club and has on occasions struck the player both on the way up and, less frequently, on the way down.

To overcome this and obviate the risk of someone getting badly hurt and suing us, we've had to incorporate a shield. Originally this was made of the same steel/titanium alloy as the clubface, but we soon discovered that, being opaque, it prevented the player from seeing the ball both at address and impact. We therefore switched to Perspex, which works fine except that occasionally the ball strikes the screen, which is good insofar as it protects the player but bad in that the ball bounces straight back down either onto the ground or, worse still from a scoring point of view, back onto the clubface, which technically constitutes a double hit and incurs a penalty stroke.

My real purpose in writing to you is to enquire as to whether you would wish to become involved in this project as an investor and promoter.

Dear Lloyds of London,

I presume most, if not all, of your members are golfers. Even the women! That's a good thing because golfers more than any other category of human being understand the tricky business of risk/reward. For example, there's a pond guarding the green on a par four and to carry the pond and reach the green is a distance of, say, 148 yards. Do you take out a wood and go for it or lay up with something safe like a five iron? That's the sort of tricky risk/reward calculation we golfers have to make somewhere in the region of 18 times a round.

And golfers understand the nature of insurance better than, say, tennis players because, 1) an errant golf shot can do a lot more damage than a mistimed volley, and 2) tennis players can't score a hole-in-one and are therefore never required to buy a round of drinks for a large bunch of thirsty strangers.

The other factor that I know will enhance the appeal of the proposal I'm about to make is that golf club membership is ridiculously expensive and, if you join an absurdly posh club with top-notch facilities such as fresh towels in the changing room, it can run into thousands of pounds. But what happens if, as we have discovered to our considerable cost recently, there's a global pandemic? You can't play golf and nor can you claim a refund. An extended lockdown, in effect, costs you a considerable sum of money but not if you have taken out a pandemic policy.

Someone who has shelled out, say, £2000 on his annual golf club membership surely won't baulk at paying a modest £100 on top to insure himself against not being able to play because of some nasty virus. It will be hugely profitable not only because these things only occur on

average about once a century but also because, as we all know, you boys are hugely adept at finding reasons for not paying out. You could, for example, shove a clause in the small print that says, *inter alia*, that you're only liable if the lockdown lasts for more than three months, which is most unlikely, and the first two months aren't covered anyway. Kerching!

All I ask is for a modest 10% commission on all the premiums. Interested?

****

Dear Professional Golfers Association of America,

I appreciate that in some energetic sports a build-up of phlegm in the mouth can occur that, where the individual concerned is reluctant to swallow aforementioned unpleasant substance, he or she may feel it necessary to spit. However, even when played quite quickly, which is, sadly, never the case in your events, golf isn't one of those sports and it is therefore complete unnecessary for the participants to do it. And so why do they, especially when millions of people all over the world are watching? What sort of example is that setting children? During the final round of the USPGA this year, I counted no fewer than seven, full-blown gobs, as we call them in the UK. Tiger Woods, Dustin Johnson... the bigger the name, the more it seems they feel the need to spit.

Although I don't want to make too big a thing of it, it's dramatically less prevalent among European golfers. For example, I've never seen Justin Rose, Rory McIlroy or even the slightly wild Tommy Fleetwood indulge in this disgusting practice so there is evidently a cultural element involved here.

Having thought long and hard about the subject, I have rejected the idea of installing spittoons next to each tee and green as this would add unsightly clutter. Instead, I have come to the conclusion there is no alternative but to penalise players: one shot if the offence takes place on the tee, fairway or in the rough; two on the green and three if anyone is audacious enough to gob into the hole. That would pretty soon put a stop to it!

As I suspect you will be too pusillanimous for such decisive action, I have an alternative proposal. The scorers who accompany each group should be tasked with the responsibility of noting down every time a player spits. Then, at the end of the tournament, the 'winner' could be presented with the 'Silver Spittoon'; in other words, publicly humiliated.

****

Dear St George's Hill,

Those of us who love sport appreciate what a marvellously civilizing influence it can be. There are so many lessons that sport can teach us; self-discipline, magnanimity, confidence, graciousness, getting along with team-mates and accepting decisions. And there really is nothing like the delicious pleasure of crushing opponents, is there?

'Sport in the Community' deals with what are commonly termed 'problem children'. Almost exclusively from deprived backgrounds, they are simply kids who, through no fault of their own, find themselves at odds with society. Mostly they are just petty criminals who thieve and deal in drugs because they've never been shown a better way. Frequently disowned by their families and shunned by society, there's a real danger they will be consigned to life's

waste-bin unless something dramatic is done to encourage them to mend their ways and change their lives.

Those of us involved in 'Sport in the Community' passionately believe we can rescue these children through sport. With responsibility for most of south-east London, I have so far managed to persuade various providers of sporting facilities to contribute at least some time to our youngsters. They include a ten-pin bowling alley, roller-skating rink, gym and swimming pool. Having identified golf as a suitable activity, I'm very much hoping you will be willing to help as well.

All we ask is that our boys and girls are welcomed at your club on, say, one or two days a week – preferably including a Saturday and/or Sunday – and are made to feel at home. Although to the best of my knowledge none has played golf before, most are willing to experiment and give it a go. If you could lend them the sticks and balls, I'm sure they would be happy to take it from there. We wouldn't presume to ask that you supervise them but it might be as well to keep a general eye on proceedings.

It would, of course, be wonderful if we discovered the next Mick Faldo but I'm much more concerned that our kids understand that success has to be earned; a lesson I hope they will learn observing and mixing with your high achieving members.

Dear Prostatitis Sufferers' Association,

Normally large is a good thing. For example, a large portion of chips is better than a small portion, unless you're trying to lose weight, of course. But an enlarged prostate is, as we all know, really bad news as, apart from any other considerations, it means you have to wee far more often than normal blokes.

Life can become awkward and embarrassing. One tip you might care to pass on to your members is only wear dark trousers; the darker the better. But it's with regard to sport in general and golf in particular that I'm writing to you now. Not unnaturally, men with prostatitis want to live as normal a life as possible and that includes participating in sport. But not all sports are prostatically friendly, so to speak. Take athletics, for example. Some events are clearly not as inclusive as they should be and, in effect, discriminate against those with enlarged prostates. The 10,000 metres can take well over half an hour, particularly if you're a bit slow. And that might be just too long for some. So why not persuade the athletic authorities to pause the race half-way so that those that need to can go to the toilet.

Tennis has been leading the way in this regard by allowing players to more or less go to the loo whenever they want. Sadly this progressive policy has led to a fair bit of abuse where players claim to need the toilet but are just leaving the court in an attempt to break their opponent's concentration. I would suggest to the LTA and ATP that they should furnish each player with a sample jar that has to be filled by those requesting a break. Failure to fill it should cost offenders at least a game.

The only sport that really caters for prostatitis' sufferers is golf. Even though a round can take upwards of four hours,

there are innumerable opportunities for players to relieve themselves in the trees and bushes. Links courses, which are in any case hugely over-rated and frequently prohibitively expensive, offer little cover in this regard and are therefore best avoided.

In conclusion, therefore, I would urge you to adopt golf as the official sport of the Prostatitis Sufferers' Association

Section 2

Hugely Controversial

Dear Penguin,

Love him or hate him, undoubtedly one of the most influential characters of the last century was Adolf Hitler. There have, I know, been an awful lot of books written about him but none so far has explored what I think was a critical influence on him ... golf. My book, "Golf and the Rise of Fascism", examines the psychologically damaging effect of frequent defeats at Munich Municipal golf course at the hands of a number of Jewish players, principally Sol Sternberg, Moshe Levinsky and Abe Horowitz.

Unflinchingly honest, my book examines in some detail Hitler's strong grip which caused him to hook the ball, especially off the tee, much to the amusement of Steinberg, Levinsky and Horowitz. Their laughter and Hitler's embarrassment fuelled a sense of grievance that led first to his giving up the game and then, by stages, to the Second World War and the Holocaust.

Among the many issues explored in the book is the role of Uwe Pretzel, the assistant pro at the Munich course. Had he, the book speculates, persuaded Hitler to move the thumb on his right hand further round the shaft thereby weakening the grip, maybe the Second World War would have been avoided and over 20 million lives spared.

Painstakingly researched, the book includes observations from, amongst others, Albert Speer, Field Marshall Rommel and Arnold Palmer. Particularly revealing are some comments made by former President Roosevelt, who notes how any reference to golf in the diplomatic exchanges with Hitler met with a frosty response.

Prime Minister Neville Chamberlain made the mistake of inviting Hitler to play in a fourball partnering Goering against himself and Lord Halifax at Wentworth. Hitler

couldn't be tempted, not even when Chamberlain suggested Poland as a side-stake. When the Prime Minister accused the German Chancellor of being a "scaredy-cat", Hitler went into a rage, slammed his putter onto the cabinet table and vowed to "play through" Poland as if it were a "single player with no standing".

Would you be interested in publishing my book?

****

Dear Prince Andrew

First of all, thank you for the good work you're doing promoting golf. Too often the game is regarded by the general public as an elitist game that is the sole preserve of toffs, but you've done a great job demonstrating to the masses that everyone can play.

My purpose in writing is to ask you how a golf club goes about the business of having 'Royal' added to its name. I presume that someone royal like you has to come down to inspect the place and pass it as suitable for Royals generally. Is that right?

If there's an application form that has to be completed perhaps you would be kind enough to get one of your staff to post one to me.

The other thing of course is how much does it cost? Is there a one-off joining fee and then an annual subscription or what?

Finally, would it matter if the course only had nine holes?

The people I've spoken to at my club are all agreed that it's a great idea and that it would considerably enhance our reputation, both in the area and nationally, as well as boost our green fee revenue thus helping to keep our subscriptions down.

By the way, if you were able to help us, we would be both honoured and privileged to offer you free lifetime membership, a club tie and possibly a reserved space in the car park. Can you imagine how good it would look if there was a sign that read: "Reserved for HRH The Duke of York." That should be worth a couple of quid on the green fee, eh?

Now that you're not opening fetes, visiting hospitals, dishing out medals and all that nonsense, presumably you've got plenty of time to work on your swing. And you might like to know there's a couple of cracking young girls employed in the pro shop who I'm sure you're going to like.

****

Dear Nigel Farrage,

I don't blame you for the appalling mess Brexit turned into because I don't suspect you had any idea when you were out there on the hustings whipping up xenophobia that it would degenerate into such a complete fiasco.

Even if the economy is wrecked, millions lose their jobs and we struggle to find the resources to do all the things we want to do for the NHS, education and social welfare, I'm sure we will all be a lot happier without any interference from abroad. Anyway, I'm writing to you now because I fear that in your understandable eagerness to distort the facts and generally dissemble, you may have overlooked an

important area of human endeavour where dastardly Europeans may yet cause more havoc.

Because I lack your enormous self-confidence, which some say borders on supreme arrogance, I can't be certain but I believe golf's Ryder Cup is unique in fielding a team that represents Europe. Since it has not only enjoyed considerable success in the biennial matches against the USA but has also fostered a tremendous camaraderie amongst players of different nationalities, I presume you will want to put a stop to it as it risks undermining the distrust and mutual suspicion that are such important elements of your xenophobic philosophy.

You should therefore be made aware that the next proposed Ryder Cup match is fast approaching, which means there's not a great deal of time for you to put a stop to it. Inevitably, millions of golf fans will be disappointed, but I assume you will think that a small price to pay for pursuing your goal of isolating us as far as is possible from the rest of Europe. To help stifle the inevitable outcry, you could explain that you're merely restoring the Ryder Cup to what it was pre-1978 when it was a Great Britain and Ireland team that took on the USA. I don't imagine for a moment that the fact we hardly ever won will bother you in the slightest.

Dear Head of Bombing, 48th Fighter Wing, RAF,

I'm considering building a brand-new golf course and have an option to purchase what is presently a sheep farm on Romney Marsh, Kent. However, I'll need some help and that is why I'm writing to you.

The 150-acre farm is ideal for golf in every respect other than it is almost completely flat. Although flatness might be a significant advantage in an airfield, it is quite definitely a disadvantage in a golf course.

I've looked at the landscaping option and, frankly, it is simply too costly to move hundreds of tons of earth about.

It was whilst watching 'Apocalypse Now' that the idea came to me. Presumably you are always looking for new areas on which to practice your bombing. So, how about dropping a few cluster bombs and daisy cutters on my proposed golf course? Although it would be nice if they could be precisely targeted to create, for example, suitable greenside bunkers, frankly it wouldn't matter too much where they landed, provided, of course, that they didn't stray onto the nearby housing estate or main road as collateral damage is probably best avoided.

In return for your help, I'm happy to offer the pilots who actually drop the bombs complimentary membership of my club and all other USAF and RAF personnel, 50 per cent off the usual green fee.

****

Dear Supreme Leader of North Korea (may I call you Kim?),

When you were growing up, wasn't it a bit confusing having the same first name as your father? If your mother shouted, "Kim, would you keep the noise down as I'm trying to watch television?" would you immediately know whom she was addressing? And that hyphen in your surname is rather exotic. Here in the UK, it used to be that only the aristocracy had hyphens, but nowadays it seems more prevalent among black footballers than it is among toffs.

Anyway, I'm writing to you about a subject that I know is close to your heart – world peace. Like you, I'm a great believer in it and believe I have found a way to turn it from a dream into reality. From my experience of playing golf

for more than 40 years, I appreciate what a great opportunity it presents to make new friends and discuss things in a relaxed and calm environment.

Your dad, of course, was evidently a natural at the game and shot the proverbial lights out in the first round he ever played. Even if the six holes-in-one are possibly a slight exaggeration and, for argument's sake, he only had five, it's still sensational stuff. Thirty-eight under par is, quite frankly, incredible scoring.

My idea is for you to host a huge golf tournament (The Kim Classic?) on the Pyongyang course. Apart from anything else, an event such as this will help promote North Korea as a holiday destination. Instead of pros, you could invite world leaders to participate, nearly all of whom play golf, albeit not as well as your old man.

I would suggest a maximum of 72 players, a Stableford format (which should speed up play) and a complimentary bar. To mix things up a bit and reduce the risk of inadvertently aggravating an old border dispute, you could endeavour to go for a geographical spread and put, for example, a European prime minister in with an African tribal chief, a South American dictator and an Asian despot.

Selling the valuable TV rights to, say, Amazon Prime should generate sufficient revenue to pay for at least half-a-dozen rockets.

Dear Secretary of Royal St George's,

I am a film producer who would very much like to use your famous clubhouse and course for a movie that is presently in what we call the 'development stage'. At the moment, we're working on a script and preparing budgets and I'm hoping that you might be willing to help.

To be absolutely honest with you, the film is not the sort you're likely to see at your local cinema. But there again that sort doesn't often make money. Ours is what is popularly termed an 'adult movie' and distribution will be by mail order and through specialised outlets only.

With the working title "Confessions of a Golf Pro", it tells the story of a rather handsome golf professional who seduces his female pupils and most of the women's section at his club. He also employs two gorgeous Swedish assistants who keep the club members happy. As luck would have it, the pro-shop backs onto the men's showers, which makes life exciting for everyone.

The climax of the film, if that's a suitable term, comes when the golf pro is caught in bed with the captain's wife and the captain is similarly embarrassed when he's discovered in a bunker with one of the assistant pros by the club secretary, whose wife is next door having it away on the snooker table with the head greenkeeper.

Although there's a lot of sex and a fair bit of nudity, it's essentially a comedy that belongs somewhere in the 'Carry On' tradition. Assuming you're happy for us to use your facilities - it would only be for three or four days in the summer - because budgets are necessarily tight, we would rather have some sort of contra deal than pay for the facility. In return for letting us use your clubhouse, I'm prepared to

offer your members a unique opportunity to star in the film as extras and receive a complimentary DVD copy of it.

It might also be possible to hold the premiere at your club and invite all your members to attend. In view of the subject matter, it might be as well not to invite wives and girlfriends. Royal St George's will also be acknowledged in the film's end credits. For your information, the total crew including cameras, lighting, sound, makeup, director, actors and actresses should number no more than 30.
Are you 'up' for it?

****

Dear Jeremy Corbyn,

Although it's quite likely that you perceive golf as a rather bourgeois activity, nevertheless I sense you would welcome an opportunity to metaphorically smack a seven-iron against the backside of all Zionists, Israelis and Jews. Harold Wilson, one of your predecessors of course, was a very keen golfer and a member of Hampstead Golf Club, which is quite near your home in upmarket Islington. I believe he left the club in protest against their policy of not admitting Jews, which doubtless you would regard as something of a plus!

Even if you don't follow the game closely, you will have no doubt heard of the British Open Golf Championship, which has been going even longer than the Labour Party. But did you know that ever since the first Open was held in 1860, it has never been won by a Palestinian? And I think we all know who is to blame for that – yes, Israel of course.

Quite simply, very few Palestinians play golf because there are no courses for them to play on. Why, when the terrain, particularly around the sand dunes in Gaza, is ideally suited to golf? There's not even a nine-holer! Again, Israel is to blame because it has done absolutely nothing to encourage Palestinians to take up the game. What is Israel frightened of? That they will use the bunkers for military purposes? Or that they will thump long drives over the border fence without shouting 'fore' thereby threatening Israel's security?

Anti-Semites throughout the UK are looking to you, Jeremy, to highlight the appalling apartheid that exists between golfers and non-golfers in the Middle East and, of course, to blame Israel for absolutely everything that's wrong in the world.

****

Dear League Against Cruel Sports,

I'm not sure if golf is on your list of cruel sports. If it isn't, it certainly should be.

It would be hard to overestimate the enormous amount of psychological damage that golf has inflicted on me. Formerly a calm and placid person, I'm now irritable and twitchy.

The unrelenting mental pressure starts on the first tee when you have to drive off in front of a whole load of strangers and doesn't stop until you've attempted to hole a testing, six-foot, downhill putt with a touch of left to right break to halve the match on the 18th.

Then there are all manner of other horrors that can strike at any time and are perfectly capable of reducing even the toughest of grown men to a gibbering wreck. I hate to even think it, let alone, type the dreaded word ... shank, aaaaaaaaaarrrrgggghhhhhhh!

If you don't play the game you will almost certainly be unfamiliar with the most awful shot in golf, which flies off the clubface at the most appalling of angles. The worst thing is that it can strike anyone at any time. And after it has happened once, you know that it can happen again. Consequently, every shot thereafter is an ordeal. And God forbid if it does happen again, then you're as good as dead.

And then there's putting and the dreaded yips... yeeeeeeeeeeeeeekkkkkksssssss!

In case you don't know, the yips are an involuntary muscle spasm that twitches the putter head in your hand and causes you to miss comparatively short putts by embarrassingly huge distances. I've seen grown men reduced to tears and almost driven to suicide by this appalling affliction. As well as the psychological damage, golf can also ruin a perfectly good back and a perfectly good marriage.

Frankly foxhunting, hare coursing, and stag hunting, although somewhat messy, are comparatively benign activities. At least they only harm animals.

I'm planning a protest demonstration outside the main entrance at the next Open Championship. However many people you're able to send in support would be most welcome. And please hurry up and add golf to your list of cruel sports.

Dear Pope Francis,

Let me make myself clear from the outset, I'm not Roman Catholic. Apart from anything else, my dodgy hip makes it difficult for me to kneel, which would render praying rather problematic. And praying is clearly an important part of your religion. Not that I would be required to do anything about it unless I had ambitions to be a monk, celibacy is something else which, frankly, has little or no appeal.

Although, as I say, Catholicism doesn't grab me by the cassock, so to speak, I remain open-minded about religion generally and could possibly be persuaded to join your lot if it could be demonstrated to work. Doubtless that sounds a bit unreasonable to someone like you who obviously has enormous faith, but I'm a practical and pragmatic man who needs concrete evidence that a thing works before I'm prepared to give up my Sunday mornings to sit on an uncomfortable bench in a an absurdly spacious and draughty building. Those candles don't give off a great deal of heat, do they?

What is it, you might reasonably ask, that I do on a Sunday morning that's more important than saving my soul? Well, unless it's raining, I would ordinarily be playing golf at Dale Hill Hotel and Golf Club, which is just to the south-east of Tunbridge Wells. I don't know whether it's the close proximity to nature or just the sheer fun of it all but, curiously, I believe there is a spiritual aspect to golf that undoubtedly has a religious dimension, although not perhaps in a conventional way. How else do you explain my friend Harry's ridiculous hole-in-one where the ball hit two trees and a waste-paper bin on its way into the hole? Harry, who was 78, had been playing golf for over 50 years and never had a hole-in-one before, died two days later. At last he was at peace.

Now to the main point of my letter. My putting has completely gone to pieces. I shan't try and explain the 'yips' to someone who doesn't play golf and is too preoccupied looking after the welfare of an estimated 1.2 billion people to worry too much about a poor 19 handicapper for whom three-putting is an enormous source of anguish, but it's a nightmare. The club pro hasn't been much help and so, forgive me asking, but do you know of a prayer that could sort it out? Or do you think, say, dipping my putter head in holy water might do the trick? Last question; is there a patron saint of golfers to whom I could appeal or stick a replica of him on my golf bag?

If you are able to help and my handicap drops below, say, 15, I promise to convert.

He did, he just prayed to
end a golfers Yips problem...

Section 3

Simply Preposterous

Dear Ewen Murray,

Forgive me writing to you as I've no doubt you're being approached the whole time by people wanting you to play at their club, open fetes or support their charity. Well, I've got a proposal that I believe will make me rich and you even richer.

As a nuclear physicist with a background in engineering, I'm peculiarly well qualified to conduct research into golf club design and construction. For the past four years I've been working on a revolutionary putter that tests have confirmed is five times more likely to hole a putt than a conventional putter. Unbelievable, I know, but true.

My handicap has tumbled from 19 to 10 in the 12 months I've been testing my new 'Krypton' putter. Why have I improved so much? Look at the stats. I'm hitting no more fairways than before (averaging 3.2 a round), reaching no more greens in regulation (2.8 a round) or registering more sand saves (lifetime average seemingly stuck on 0.27%) but I now regularly take fewer than 23 putts a round (my record is an astonishing 19!).

Working at a Ministry of Defence research laboratory gives me access to material and facilities denied to most civilians. Anyway, all conventional putters are primarily reliant on good balance. You might be surprised to learn that mine isn't. All it does is literally impart a massive positive charge that effectively magnetises the ball so when it approaches or passes near the hole, it is attracted to the negative charge in the metal of the cup and is pulled towards it until it inevitably disappears into it.

Field tests have highlighted just a couple of minor problems that I feel obliged to disclose to you. Firstly, as it has an even stronger electrostatic field than the cup, the flagstick

has to be removed well away otherwise the ball may adhere to it and be virtually impossible to remove. Secondly, there is a slight health and safety issue due to the depleted uranium core that is in the putter head. However, using a putter-cover impregnated with copper and a lead-lined golf bag, significantly reduces radiation levels. Mind you, finding a caddy who can lift a 225-pound golf bag can be a challenge.

In return for a modest percentage of the profits, would you be willing to endorse the 'Krypton' and mention it on Sky every time you get the chance?

****

Dear St Andrews,

I am reliably informed that the British Open will be played on the Old Course next year (2022), which I think will give you sufficient time to instigate the improvements outlined below.

Although St Andrews is undoubtedly steeped in history, what strikes me most of all whenever I watch golf being played there on TV is how featureless it is compared to the great American courses like Augusta National and Pebble Beach. Frankly, it's rather dull and so what can be done to improve it? It came to me like a well-struck seven-iron. What's the most important hole on a golf course? Why, the 18th of course, the finishing hole. So, perversely, this is where I suggest you start.

At the moment it's a rather uninteresting, short, par four. Goodness me, it's almost driveable! The Swilken Burn doesn't present enough of a hazard to worry the better

players and, let's face it, most of the guys teeing it up at the British Open are more than averagely good. So what you must do is dam up the Swilken Burn and let the water flood the surrounding area until you've got a decent lake. It's a shame that the pretty stone bridge will be lost but you can easily find an alternative spot to dump it somewhere on the course. Or you might prefer to flog it to some rich Yank such as Donald Trump and the proceeds would help pay for the landscaping.

A nice big lake would make the competitors think more carefully on the tee. The trouble with the hole at present is that nothing very exciting ever happens apart from some poor sucker missing a short putt.

To top it all off tastefully and provide some visual interest, I suggest you install a really big fountain. A statue in the middle of, say, an old man stooped under the weight of his golf bag could be very effective, especially if there were jets of water streaming out of his clubs and into the sky. And a few Koi carp in the lake wouldn't do any harm either. They're not cheap but if you can persuade visitors that their golfing luck will improve if they empty their pockets into the lake, the fish will pay for themselves in no time.

The St Andrews fountain could become the most famous fountain in the whole of golf, which you might care to use for branding purposes on your merchandise.

Since I've probably given you enough to think about for now, I'll leave my idea on how to divide those ridiculous double greens with the careful use of Leylandii hedging for another time.

Dear TaylorMade,

Once a gifted 17 handicapper who was solid both off the tee and around the greens, I'm now struggling to break 100. Why? To put it bluntly, my body is letting me down. More specifically, it's my left hip. Arthritis has taken its toll and the nice people at my local hospital are now telling me that I need to replace it, presumably with a shiny new one, which is where you come in.

Instead of any old 'off-the-shelf' hip, I'd like a customised one specifically designed to, yes, improve my golf! Why, I thought to myself as I sat in the hospital waiting-room, can't my hip match my clubs? If I can play with forged-iron, cavity-back clubs, why can't I walk on a similarly designed hip with the same level of performance and forgiving properties? If, for example, my hip had the same coefficient of restitution as my driver, is it not reasonable to assume that I could sit down, get up and walk around with the same assuredness with which I drive off the tee?

And a graphite shaft connecting my hip to my femur should ensure I recover the sort of flexibility my body enjoyed 30 years ago. And what a psychological boost it would be to know that my hip and clubs were not only totally compatible but were manufactured by the very same people.

I appreciate that producing body parts is not an area into which you have ventured but, given the worrying decline in the number of people playing golf, wouldn't it be sensible to diversify? I'm sure all those white-coated boffins you presently employ to expand the sweet-spot, could easily turn their educated hands to reducing human suffering whilst at the same time rescuing veteran golfers from the indignity of a 20+ handicap.

If it encourages you to take up my suggestion, I would happily let you fit me with the very first TaylorMade hip in the world and have my game monitored to see what, if any, improvements followed.

Although I'm not sure whether or not you could sell them in pro shops, I am absolutely certain that artificial hips are a booming market that will surely continue to expand as the population ages.

Dear Hassan Rouhani,

I'm not a Muslim and therefore don't really understand, a) what the difference is between the Sunnis and Shias, or b) why you appear to be at each other's throats the whole time. To an outsider it seems crazy that one lot of Muslims doesn't get on with another lot. Presumably, as is often the case, there was an incident some while ago that caused a bit of ill-feeling and no one can bring themselves to apologise and say sorry. I had an Uncle Alf who fell out with my Auntie Gladys during a game of bridge because she bid three spades when she should have passed. To my knowledge, they never spoke to each other again. How silly is that?

Well, my suspicion is that your spat with the Shias is equally daft and could easily be resolved with a bit of goodwill on both sides. The problem often is that, fearing loss of face, neither side wants to make the first move. So let me be the one to propose something that could start the blessed process of reconciliation.

Sport unites where politics divides. So, rather than shouting, politicians should be playing. My suggestion is that the Sunnis and Shias should have an annual golf match alternately in Iran and, say, Saudi Arabia. Although I know the latter are building several decent courses I have no idea whether there are any suitable tracks in Iran. If I may say, it's not really my fault I don't know as you are rather a secretive lot, aren't you? Take nuclear weapons for example. Although everyone suspects you're building them, no one knows for certain because you seem keen to conceal stuff. Anyway, it could be that you regard golf as a decadent imperialist game. If that's the case, you're completely wrong. Just take a look at China and all the courses they're building there.

Back to the match. I suggest you start modestly with just one fourball; you and a friend against, say, King Abdullah and one of his (many) sons. If that goes well, you could gradually expand it to maybe a dozen a side. Then, who knows, you could copy the Ryder Cup format of foursomes, fourballs and singles over three days. Sky television might be interested in covering the event and, before you know it, a whole generation of young Sunnis and Shias will grow up thinking that they just belong to two opposing golf teams rather than implacably hostile enemies.

One final nice touch you might want to consider is inviting Israelis to referee the matches. In that way, you'd be taking another virtuous stride in the direction of world peace.

****

Dear Dr Ping,

You will be thrilled to learn that I have one of your putters. I got it cheap on eBay but am delighted with it. Every so often it seems to miss a bit on the right-hand side but, to be honest, it could very well be my fault and not the putter's.

I'm writing because I've had what I think is a very good idea and would be interested to hear what you think of it. To take advantage of the twilight rate at a nearby course, I frequently tee off in the early evening. The place is blissfully quiet and the only downside is the light frequently fails towards the end of the round. Because I don't drive the ball very far, the poor visibility is less of a problem on the tee than it is on the green. I find reading the line of the putts increasingly difficult as the sun sinks while my putts don't. But, rather than moan, I've done something about it.

It's very simple really as it's essentially nothing much more than a torch that can be easily attached to the shaft of the putter. To distribute the weight more evenly, I've located the battery in the grip with a wire going down the interior of the shaft. Incidentally, the same battery supplies power to a small coil heater that keeps the grip warm on a cold evening.

The torch is adjustable, as is the beam, so that I can illuminate a specific spot either on the line of the putt or on the hole itself. As a courtesy to my opponents, I always turn it off when they're putting. It really works incredibly well and the only negative is that it attracts annoying moths that can be an unwanted distraction and so I'm presently developing a device that emits a high-pitched screech that I'm hoping will scare them off.

My idea is to sell the kit that would enable golfers to convert their existing putters. All customers would need is a power drill, soldering iron and rudimentary knowledge of applied electro-physics. I'm hoping you will be willing to endorse my product along the lines of: "As recommended by Dr Ping."

GCSE-Level Examination – submitted to the Qualifications and Curriculum Authority

I'm encouraged that modern education extends beyond the three R's and that children are leaving school with a broader understanding of the world. However, there is one vital area of human activity that is still largely being ignored... golf.

I believe the Royal and Ancient game is a legitimate area of study and should be included in the national curriculum. So, in a bid to start the ball rolling so to speak, I've drafted a dummy GCSE level golf examination paper that will give you a good idea of what I'm about. Perhaps have a go at it yourself and let me know what you think.

Golf (Theory) GCSE Examination.

Although this paper should take no more than three-and-a -half hours to complete, it will probably take longer.

Candidates should be aware that if they fall more than one question behind the candidate in front of them, they should call through whoever is sitting behind.

Write an essay on one of the following:

1. Ben Hogan has a better swing than Nick Faldo but the Englishman wore more interesting sweaters. Discuss.

Or

Was what happened in the Ryder Cup at Brooklyn, Massachusetts, an indictment of matchplay golf or simply a few boozed up Yanks misbehaving themselves?

Or

Golfers have no dress sense. Discuss

2. Match up the golfers in column **A** with the most appropriate description in column **B**.

A)	B)
Tommy Fleetwood	God-fearing
Bernard Langer	Pissed
Bryson DeChambeau	Phenomenally rich
Shane Lowry	A Nutter
Tiger Woods	Needs a haircut
Nick Faldo	Not Very Popular
John Daly	Should go on a diet

3. Your ball lands in a cowpat. Do you:

    a) Claim relief, on the basis that playing it as it lies is just too disgusting?

    b) Nudge it away gently with your shoe when your playing partners aren't looking?

    c) Drop it under penalty of one stroke?

4. A member of your regular fourball never buys a round of drinks. Without recourse to physical violence, explain how you would deal with the situation.

5. Which is the odd one out and why?

St Andrews, Royal Troon, Carnoustie, Royal Birkdale, Royal St. George's and Dale Hill Hotel and Golf Club

6. Your club car park is full except for the space reserved for the Captain. Do you:

    a) Find somewhere else to park?

    b) Reverse into the Captain's spot and accidentally knock down the sign so that you can claim that you didn't realize it was his?

    c) Park alongside the 18th green by way of protest at the inadequate parking provision and be prepared to join another club?

7. Using diagrams, explain what happens when you shank a ball.

****

Dear Mr Callaway,

Golf equipment is, I know, a very competitive business. Because the only thing that matters to the overwhelming majority of golfers is smashing the ball further, this rivalry must be particularly acute when it comes to drivers. Irons are all very well and wedges certainly have their place but I suspect the driver is the flagship in your fleet. If you can outgun the opposition, then you're well on the way to the top of the pile and I'm certain I can help you achieve that.

Ever since I was a young lad, I've been interested in explosives. As a boy, I would take fireworks apart and then put them back together so that they behaved differently to the way the manufacturers intended. I would change the colours around, make rockets fly further and increase the decibel level of the bangs. This background in explosives

has helped me in my recent quest to develop a driver that will really hit the ball immense distances, and I mean IMMENSE.

You'll understand, I know, that for commercial reasons I'm not in a position to reveal the details but I have developed a club I call the 'Howitzer' that consistently hits the ball comfortably over 400 yards. My record to date on flat terrain with no following wind is 518 yards. Imagine driving the green on a par five! And the best thing about it is that anyone can achieve these distances because club head speed is almost totally irrelevant.

As with all new technology there are one or two teething problems. The principal headache, and I choose the word advisedly, that I'm wrestling with at the moment is the almost unbearable noise. Unsurprisingly, the club at impact sounds not unlike a very loud shotgun, which can be quite a problem when, as is often the case, the tee is adjacent to a green that may or may not have people putting on it.

The other challenge is trying to eliminate the near blinding flash that accompanies the bang. During trials, I've been wearing goggles and ear-muffs and there is clearly a commercial opportunity in selling these accessories along with the 'Howitzer'. Because there are so many conservative elements in the golfing establishment, I would be lying if I said everyone will welcome the 'Howitzer'. But you have experience of these and doubtless an expert legal department that will help you overcome these reactionary elements.

In conclusion, what I'm hoping for is some form of joint venture with you that married my technical genius with your considerable experience to our great mutual advantage.

Dear Boris Johnson,

I don't know whether or not you play golf but, either way, I'm certain you are going to like the incredible idea I've had.

It came to when riding upstairs on the 88 bus travelling along the Bayswater Road. Looking out at the enormous expanse of grass that is Hyde Park, it surprised me how few people there were enjoying this excellent facility. Then it came to me; what a wonderful opportunity exists for developing a truly, world-beating golf course right in the centre of the world's greatest city.

So excited was I by the idea that I immediately jumped off the bus and took a good look around. And the more I looked, the more excited I became. For example, the Serpentine could, with a little imagination and re-shaping, make a wonderful water feature guarding the green of a tricky par three.

Although I appreciate there are still a few royals knocking about in Kensington Palace, I'm sure they wouldn't mind being confined to, say, the top floor to enable the balance of the building to be converted into arguably the greatest and most historic clubhouse in the world. Possibly the only negative I can identify in the whole scheme is that there's no way to avoid felling a few old trees. But I would estimate no more than four or five hundred would need to go.

The big plus from both your and the Treasury's point of view would be the enormous income that would be generated. At present there's just the deckchair rental and a modest revenue from the Serpentine café but I'm talking tens of millions of pounds. Membership of the incredibly exclusive Royal Hyde Park Golf and Country Club (Patron: HM the Queen) would be hugely sought after by all those

fat cats who live in Kensington, Belgravia and Knightsbridge. Even at half-a-million quid, I'm certain you would have no difficulty enrolling, say, 1000 members.

Then there are the corporates! How much do you think a Japanese bank would pay to join? Five million? The revenue would be fantastic and we've not even considered bar sales and the pro shop. And what about the worldwide merchandising possibilities? The income could make good your extravagant election promise to boost the NHS and there would be enough left over to fund a significant tax cut in the next budget to satisfy your rich friends. Handled properly and provided your daft Brexit doesn't bugger everything up, it could on its own almost guarantee you another four years in the top job.

Dear Brother or Sister Chairperson of the Communist Party of Great Britain,

The last couple of decades have been pretty depressing for those of us who have been eagerly anticipating the imminent collapse of capitalism and the long awaited take over by the oppressed proletariat. On the other hand, the weather seems to be steadily improving and Spurs are still in the Premiership.

Although I'm completely confident that brother Karl more or less got it right when he predicted the inevitable demise of capitalism, I believe that the irresistible forces of history might need to be gently encouraged if this particular working-class hero is to be around to witness the revolution.

Somewhat weary of working within the system to bring about its collapse (I had a temporary job at my local newsagent and deliberately creased copies of the Daily Telegraph) I now recognise that there is no alternative to direct action. I believe the time is right to strike at the soft underbelly of capitalism and hit the exploiters where they gather in great numbers to orchestrate their oppression. I'm referring, of course, to golf clubs.

Although destroying all the clubhouses has considerable appeal, a more subtle approach might be less confrontational.

What I propose, therefore, is that we metaphorically tear down the symbols of power by moving to a distant corner of the car park all the spaces reserved for the Chairmen, Captains and Lady Captains. Apart from the enormous psychological impact to be gained from striking at the undemocratic symbols of elitism and power, the practical chaos that will be wrought when BMW, Mercedes, and

other flash motors are ousted from their regular spaces will almost certainly throw the oppressors into disarray. At that moment, while they are all looking for somewhere to park, we'll move in and seize control of the means of production, the media and whatever else we need in order to liberate the masses.

****

Dear Thomas Bach, Chairman of the International Olympic Committee,

The Olympics are fast becoming one of the undoubted highlights of the sporting calendar, spanning so many different sports and involving so many athletes. It's too bad the winter Olympics have to take place in winter but I don't suppose there is anything you can do about that. Anyway, the summer Olympics are unbelievably popular and have a global appeal that's right up there with the University Boat Race and Greyhound Derby.

However, as you know better than most, it's fatal to become complacent and the Olympics must continually evolve if they are to maintain their pre-eminence. And so it was that I began thinking what I could do to improve things. Because of a personal obsession I have about energy conservation and global warming, I wonder sometimes about the example being set by having the Olympic flame burning so extravagantly the whole time. I appreciate its symbolic importance but feel that it could at least be reduced in size or, better still, switched off between events. Another thing, is anyone really interested in either dressage or synchronized swimming?

I'm so pleased you finally caved in to financial pressure from the likes of Nike, Titleist and Ping and re-instated golf. However, do we really need yet another 72-hole, strokeplay tournament that is hardly distinguishable from any other golf event?

So here's what I suggest. Each country that wishes to participate should enter a fourball team made up of a professional golfer, a businessman, a showbiz celebrity and a prominent politician. The US dream team, for example, could be made up of Tiger Woods, Bill Gates, Jack Nicholson and Donald Trump. Imagine both the enormous interest that would be generated and the opportunities it would create for world leaders to sort out their problems in a relaxed atmosphere over a pint of beer in the clubhouse afterwards.

The two best balls of the four to count and, because I very much doubt whether the celebrities and politicians have much stamina, it probably should be an 18-hole event.

****

Dear Messers Royal and Ancient,

First of all, may I congratulate you on a wonderful game. I took up golf just over 12 months ago and just love it. My wife says I spend more time at my club than I do with her. If you met her, you would understand why! Just kidding.

Anyway, my point in writing is not to make jokes at the expense of the old trouble and strife but to suggest how the game might be improved. Even with the reduction in the time allowed to look for balls, too many minutes are wasted thrashing around impenetrable undergrowth. Why?

Because the 'shot and distance' rule is far too harsh. Instead, I think a player who has either lost a ball or can't be arsed to look for it should be allowed to drop another one more or less where he was aiming the original ball at the cost of just one shot.

Also, escaping from bunkers is far too difficult for the ordinary man or woman, especially when the ball is in an awkward spot. Without penalty, I suggest a player be allowed to kick the ball just once in a bunker to a more reasonable position provided that it remains in the bunker.

Where a player accidentally hits a ball out of bounds but there was no intent on his part to secure an advantage by, say, cutting a corner, he may play the shot again with no penalty. Since golf is an honourable game played by honourable men and women, the final decision as to whether there was intent or not rests solely with the player.

Finally, to make putting both more exciting and fairer, a putt that lips out should count as one-and-a-half shots but the putt should be deemed to have been holed. For example, a player putting for a four whose ball lips out should score four-and-a-half not five. In matchplay, obviously four-and-a-half beats a five but in strokeplay all half shots are rounded up at the end to avoid awkward scores such as 104-and-a-half, which of course would count as 105.

Dear William Hill,

Not since Oxo won the Grand National quite a few years ago have I had a bet. However, I fancy a tickle on a forthcoming competition at Dale Hill Hotel and Golf Club, which is where I've been a member since 1986 but still haven't been invited to be club captain. Perhaps you can give me odds on that happening before I move on up to the Great Clubhouse in the Sky. Another time, perhaps.

The July Mid-Week Stableford is the competition I have in mind. It normally attracts a modest field that barely reaches double figures but that need not concern you as the somewhat complicated bet I have in mind has nothing do with the result.

As usual, I shall be playing with the same group I've played with every week for the past 27 years – Martin, Peter and Guy. I appreciate that I ought to make a greater effort to get to know more of the members but somehow can't be arsed. To be honest, although Guy's okay, the other two are incredibly dull. Martin moans the whole time about his arthritic hip while Peter has to be among the slowest golfers on the planet.

Anyway, I would like an accumulator on the following. To make it easier for you since you obviously don't know the people involved, I have inserted what I honestly consider are fair odds next to each leg of the bet. If you would like to conduct further research, I can let you have the mobile phone numbers of the other three so that you can chat to them and make up your own mind.

1) Martin being the last to turn up   5/4

2) Guy forgetting a pencil to mark the card   1/1

3) My drive down the first being the longest in our group   2/1

4) Me hitting the green on all four par threes   4/1

5) Me not going into any bunker the entire round   5/2

6) Me not three-putting at all   4/1

7) Guy hitting at least one T-shot out of bounds   4/6

8) Martin uttering at least two audible expletives on each nine   1/1

9) Peter losing at least one ball on each nine   4/5

10) My nett score being the lowest   11/4

11) Peter offering to buy the first round of drinks   7/4

By my reckoning, but I think you should do your own calculation, the cumulative odds of all the above happening is 65,780 to one. If so, I should like to put the enclosed fiver on to win £328,904.

Finally, I noted in a recent promotion of yours that you were offering to return punters' stakes in the event of one leg of an accumulator going down. Is that still valid? In which case, if only 10 of the above 11, come good, do I get my fiver back?

Section 4

Utterly Ridiculous

Dear Head of Titleist,

Although I don't buy any, I'm always pleased if I find a Titleist so your advertising clearly works, even if it doesn't always necessarily result in increased sales. And it's about the issue of lost golf balls that I'm writing to you.

As an environmentalist, I'm rather concerned that they are polluting the planet. It's not your fault because it's not you who are losing them. However, as the manufacturer, I believe you have a social responsibility here. My worry is that your balls contain a number of toxic substances that contaminate both the soil and water, thereby harming mammals, fish, birds and even often forgotten insects.

Instead of simply complaining, I have come up with an environmentally friendly alternative. Called the Ecoball, it's made entirely of vegetable matter - mostly a blend of crushed walnut shells and shredded acorns. It's non-toxic and biodegradable.

Lost Ecoballs simply rot and, far from doing damage, actually enrich the soil. My research also shows that they are positively liked by certain species of fish, particularly carp, which eagerly feed on the decaying matter.

In a world of increasing environmental awareness I believe that there are a growing number of people, and golfers are not very different from ordinary people, who would willingly pay a small premium for a product that was environmentally benign.

The only significant drawbacks I've so far encountered with the Ecoball are: 1) Their tendency to dissolve in water renders them impractical in wet weather; 2) You can't leave them too long on a damp fairway whilst, for example, looking for your playing partner's ball, because they will

start to take root; and 3) They travel a little under half the distance of a conventional ball. Regarding the last point, I believe responsible golfers would willingly trade a little length in return for not harming the planet, don't you?

Would you be interested in some form of joint venture, which combined your manufacturing and marketing might with my pioneering concept?

****

Dear Wentworth,

Three years ago, GLOVE was formed. It stands for Growing Lovely Organic Vegetables Everywhere. We have, appropriately, a five-point program that we believe will help combat the world food shortage, whilst at the same time doing no harm to the environment.

The first of these five points is to identify suitable sites for planting, growing and harvesting our vegetables. These sites can be anything from railway embankments and motorway verges to waste tips and roundabouts. They come in all shapes and sizes.

What they have in common is that they are otherwise unproductive. At our recent AGM, one of our Surrey members came up with an enormously interesting suggestion that we investigate the possibilities that exist on golf courses. She lives quite close to you and thought that you might be willing to help.

Although I don't play the game myself, I understand that the only important bits of the course are what you call the fairways and greens.

Apparently, there are substantial tracts of land elsewhere that are almost entirely unused. These, I gather, are called the rough and strictly speaking shouldn't be visited by the players.

This is how GLOVE works. One of our people will survey your site, carry out soil tests and identify suitable areas. We will then draw up a planting program tailor-made for you.

Our people are trained to be unobtrusive but, so that you can readily identify them, they wear bright yellow overalls with a big red GLOVE logo on the back.

They will prepare the land, plant the seeds, tend to plants and harvest the crop. Because they are mostly volunteers who have regular jobs during the week, they'll mostly be on your course at weekends, which I assume would be best for you anyway.

Our intention is to inconvenience you as little as possible. In fact, you won't have to do anything. All we ask is that you desist from using any insecticides, weed killers or other chemical treatments within 400 yards of any of our plots. We would also appreciate it enormously if when you mow the fairways and greens that you pile the clippings onto a convenient compost heap. In return for your help, we are happy to offer you 10% of everything we grow. Should you want more we'll gladly sell it to you at a 25% discount on our normal prices.

As we will need to move quickly if we are to get our parsnips established before the soil dries out, perhaps you would be kind enough to let me have a speedy response to this appeal.

Dear Early Man Department at the British Museum,

You may or may not be aware that there is some confusion and dispute about the origins of golf and in which country it was first played. The Scots would have you believe that they invented it, as would the Dutch, American Indians, Mongols, Greeks and many others. Considerable national prestige is the prize to be won by the country that can prove that it's the only true originator of the game.

All the above leads me on to a rather extraordinary find I made last month whilst playing in my club's midweek Stableford. Rather uncharacteristically for me, since I tend to draw the ball rather than fade it, I sliced my drive into the trees on the right of the fairway on the par four 14th. My suspicion is that I probably took the club back outside the line and failed to bring it back to square on impact.

Since the ball was a pretty decent one, I ventured into the woods in search of it. Although I never in fact found it, what I did discover was indeed quite remarkable.

First of all, there was a very old bone that had been fashioned into something akin to a lob wedge. There will, I know, be sceptics who will say that it is just an old bone that happens to resemble the shape of a golf club. However, close inspection of the top of the bone reveals heavy scratch marks. The significance of these is quite clear to me. If indeed what I found was an early, say Neolithic, golf club, it would have been used during a particularly wet period in the earth's history. Heavy rain will have rendered the club slippery and early man, without the benefit of modern all-weather grips, will have needed to improve adhesion by effectively roughing up the top of the club. This will have given him a competitive edge and, who knows, improved

his chances of capturing the Club Championship and mating with whoever he chose from the women's section.

Before you dismiss this as pure speculation, you should examine the "ball" I found nearby. Although considerably heavier and with far fewer dimples than the modern equivalent and almost certainly less responsive around the green, it would undoubtedly have done the job.

It occurred to me that an ancient predecessor of mine might have entered the self-same wood, searching for his ball, some several thousand years earlier and been attacked by a sabre-toothed tiger.

Given the likely historical significance, I'm reluctant to post the objects. Would it be possible to bring them along and show them to an expert?

****

Dear American Golf,

Before I introduce you to my amazing invention, may I ask whose side you are on in the Ryder Cup? Your name suggests you support the Yanks. Is that right?

Never mind, my purpose in writing to you now is to introduce you to the incredible Pentapole which, as the name suggests, is five things in one; all of which every golfer should take with him or her onto the course.

Okay, you've hit your opening tee shot into a fairway bunker. After you've knocked the ball back onto the fairway, there's a problem... no rake. Don't panic, simply pick up your Pentapole, flick the control to 'R' and out will pop a rake with a reach of just over two metres. Finished

with it? Simply press 'R' again and the rake will withdraw back into the Pentapole.

As you wedge-it to the green, you take a significant divot which flies 10 feet in front of you. You don't have to walk forward to retrieve it and then back to replace it, just flick the switch on your Pentapole to 'D' and a five-pronged, metal 'hand' will extend up to three metres, scoop up the divot and return it to you. Incidentally, the divot returner doubles as a ball retriever to recover wayward shots that, for example, plop into a water hazard or on the wrong side of a barbed-wire fence.

Your next tee shot lands three-quarters of the way up a hill and leaves you with a blind shot to the green. Is there anyone on the green? And where on the green is the flag? Don't trudge up the hill to look, just press 'P' on your Pentapole and an eight-metre long periscope will extend upwards to give you a clear sight of the green.

Now you're on the green and worried that the group behind, because they can't see you, might hit up and cause you injury at best and to miss the putt at worst. Press 'F' on the Pentapole control and the periscope will once again rise eight metres in the air but this time a red flag will spring out of it which emits a high-pitched alarm so you will be both visible and audible to the group behind.

Finally, as you stride up the 18th, a threatening cloud looms up behind the clubhouse. Could it be a thunderstorm? Don't panic, just press 'L' on your Pentapole control and a 15-metre lightning conductor will soar skyward. Plant it in the ground and then stroll to the clubhouse knowing that any lightning in the vicinity will strike it and not you.

Final point, don't forget to go back out and retrieve your Pentapole before driving home as they cost £99.99. Cheap for an item that saves you money and energy while

protecting you from being struck both by other golfers and God. How many Pentapoles would you like to order for your shops?

****

Dear Armitage Shanks,

Like many with a handicap as high as mine, I get rather nervous before commencing a round of golf and almost invariably have to visit the gents. That in itself is not a problem but for the fact that your toiletware (is that the correct word?), which in all other respects is fine, causes me considerable anguish simply because of the name, 'Armitage Shanks'. Because it's displayed quite prominently on the urinals, doubtless for marketing purposes, I tried switching to the cubicles but there it was again on the toilet bowls. There really is no escaping it.

I have no problem with Armitage, which is indeed an elegant name, but 'Shanks' is very problematic for those, like me, who have an unhappy history of occasionally hitting golf balls almost sideways. In the UK we call that unmentionable shot a – I can hardly bring myself to type the word – shank ... aaaarrrrgggggghhhh!. It's horrible and incredibly destructive. It got so bad with me that I paid a fortune to see a sports psychologist who said I must obliterate all thoughts of it from my mind. How can I do that when your company's name screams out at me before I have even walked to the first tee? There are some bushes at the back of the car park but, although there's nothing in the Rules of Golf about it, old-fashioned golf clubs, and mine is one of those, frown on that sort of thing. If caught I could be suspended or even thrown out.

May I therefore respectfully urge you to re-brand your products in the UK. Having given it considerable thought, I believe I have an altogether better and more acceptable name. 'Flush' is a good positive word in golf that means to strike the ball perfectly. And, of course, it's appropriate to your industry. And so 'Armitage Flush' would ensure continuity whilst at the same time avoiding distressing anxious golfers like me.

****

Dear Golf Museum in St Andrews,

Because it was raining so heavily when I visited St Andrews in February (unusual for Scotland, eh?), I wasn't able to achieve my life's ambition of playing the Old Course and so I instead wandered around your museum. Although quite interesting, it was no substitute for the Road Hole or taking on the Swilken Burn. Never mind. Anyway, I have an idea for 'beefing' up your exhibits which I'm hoping you will like.

Next month I'm having my left hip replaced, which set me thinking. I have very little idea of what my left hip or, for that matter, my right hip, looks like. The same is true of the rest of my joints and all my internal organs. Since the purpose of museums is to educate and entertain, don't you think it would add enormously to the appeal of yours if you could display body parts in an attractive and interesting way?

Although I've not formally asked, I've no doubt the Conquest Hospital in Hastings would be happy to post you my old hip. However, I recognise that, despite the fact that I'm still the only member at Hendon Golf Club to have won

70

three consecutive, monthly, mid-week, Stableford competitions (1976 - September, October and November), my hip isn't of huge interest to many people. The same, I don't think, could be said of, say, Jon Daly's liver or Tiger Woods's back.

In the same way that we're all being asked to carry organ donor cards, perhaps you could persuade the top players to do something similar so, in the event of their death, you would have first dibs on their body parts. It may sound a bit grisly but it would be very educational.

****

Dear Sotheby's,

Because you hold regular auctions, you should be in a good position to advise what I should do with my tee pegs. If you don't play golf, you might not know that tee pegs are the little structures upon which you place your ball when teeing off.

Ever since I started playing golf back in the early 1970s I've collected them. Today I have somewhere in the region of 25,000.

My collection is held in over 100 shoe boxes which are filed away according to material: 'wood', 'plastic', and 'other': by height: 'very tall', 'tall', 'moderately tall', 'average', 'below average', 'short' and 'very short': and by colour: 'red', 'blue', 'green', 'yellow', etc. So, for example, if I need a moderately tall yellow one made of plastic I know precisely in which box to look.

Some of the tee-pegs bear the names of companies and golf courses on the stem, while others are blank. Although I

don't know, because I haven't been able to find any information anywhere, my suspicion is that my most valuable ones will be those bearing a company name that, for whatever reason, is not around anymore. For example, I have a few with "BCCI" on them, "Thames TV Golf Society", "Maxwell Communications", and my most prized one of all "Fly Concorde", although the last named is a bit damaged.

How do I go about selling them through your auction? Would they be auctioned individually or by the box, or do you think they would fetch more as a collection?

Although I know it's difficult to say, do you have any idea what they might be worth?

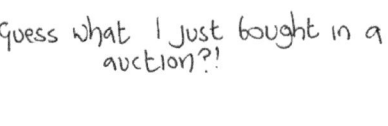

Dear Head Greenkeeper of Royal Troon,

Like every other greenkeeper in the world, no doubt one of your biggest headaches is keeping your greens looking good and playing well. Members and visitors alike expect the greens to be smooth and true throughout the year and whatever the weather. Well, you will be thrilled to learn that your prayers have been answered and there's now a product that will both save you enormous amounts of money and provide the finest, truest greens in the world.

Although it looks and feels just like bentgrass, Omniturf has the enormous advantage in that it requires zero maintenance and is guaranteed to last for 25 years! Manufactured from a secret blend of some of the finest artificial fibres known to man, Omniturf behaves just like grass, looks just like grass and, thanks to our amazing boffins, even smells just like grass!

I'm sure you're now thinking this is just too good to be true. Well, what is even better is that we're willing to give – yes, GIVE – you a free demonstration. Here's the deal. Choose any one of your greens and, provided it's no bigger than 2500 square metres, we'll remove it and replace it with Omniturf to give you a chance to test if for yourself. The whole operation only takes a week.

We're extremely confident that after you've tried it, you'll want us to come back and do the lot. To give you some idea of cost, 18 average-sized greens generally works out at somewhere in the region of £1m. You'll probably save that in fertiliser, weed-killer and fungal treatments inside 24 months. And there's more money to be saved by firing most of the overpaid green staff and instead getting the comparatively cheap cleaners who look after the clubhouse to vacuum the greens about once a fortnight.

Dear Golf Equipment Wholesaler,

As distributors of golf equipment, you will appreciate the spectacular technological improvements that have been made in recent times. Titanium, graphite and other high tech materials have taken over from wood and steel. Consequently, today's clubs and balls bear little resemblance to those our grandfathers used. Every facet of golf, including the bag, trolley and ball has undergone dramatic changes. Even the humble shoe spike has recently been transformed.

However, there is one tiny area where there has been absolutely no change at all. The tee-peg is precisely the same humble piece of wood it has always been. But I believe its days are numbered as I have developed the next generation of tee-peg.

Called the "Eterni-tee", it has a number of remarkable features that its predecessor lacks. Firstly, it is a precision piece of equipment that can set the ball at precisely the same height off the ground every time. Secondly, it has a memory that will adjust that height to whatever is appropriate for the club you're using.

Thirdly, since it sits on the ground rather than in it, it reduces club deceleration on impact. Finally, because of an audible signal it emits five seconds after the shot, and every five seconds thereafter, it simply can't be lost. Hence, "Eterni-tee".

It works like this. The telescopic stem is controlled by a small chip in the base. The cup is also the dial, which turns so the arrow points to the number of whichever club is being used. The peg is most extended for a driver and most retracted for a lob wedge.

One of the chief advantages it has over the present peg is that you only need one instead of a number at different heights. Also, being made of titanium and virtually indestructible, you don't have to carry more than one in your pocket so no more embarrassing moments trying to locate your ball-marker in amongst a jumble of pegs.

Also worth mentioning is the fact that the battery is automatically recharged by the action of being struck. So, although at £49.99, it might seem expensive, it will last for years and save money in the long run.

Finally, by slashing the number of broken pegs littering the tees, it will help keep courses tidy whilst saving the planet by reducing waste.

****

Dear Lewis Hamilton,

As you know better than most, speed is a wonderful thing. And what impresses me about F1, even more than roaring down the straight at 200mph or thereabouts, is the speed with which they change your tyres. Compare the six or seven seconds they do it in with the one-and-a-half hours my local garage took to switch over my spare with the nearside front left about a fortnight ago.

Anyway, I gather you play golf and probably agree with me that it provides a far greater adrenaline rush than driving a car ever can. Going round and round the same circuit over and over again must be so dull that staying awake has to be a problem, surely. Whenever I feel a bit drowsy behind the wheel I switch on Radio 5 Live, which helps. Do you have a radio in your Mercedes or does all the clever technology

take up so much space there's no room on the dashboard for the knobs?

Back to golf. For busy people like you and me, what we least like about the game is the inordinate amount of time it takes to play a round. Part of the problem is, of course, slow play but I'm afraid there is not a lot we can do about that. However, there is one area which I believe offers enormous scope and that is the buggies. Why do they have to be so slow? Probably because they don't want you to know how slow they really are, there's no speedometer but I would be surprised if their top speed was more than about 10mph. If you could raise that to, say, 50mph, think how much time that would save.

Why don't you have a word with the technical team at Mercedes and persuade them to design a sort of F1 golf buggy. We could call it the 'Hurry-up Hamilton', flog it to golf clubs all over the world and become obscenely rich, if you're not that already.

****

Dear PGA of Europe,

Although the Ryder Cup is undoubtedly one of the outstanding sporting occasions ranking alongside such other iconic events such as the University Boat Race, the Grand National and the Eurovision Song Contest, I think it's beginning to get just a tiny bit out of hand. Remember Brookline?

It's no good just wringing our hands, we must do something about it. What I'm proposing is a number of minor modifications to the format that I'm confident will ensure

the event's survival as a wonderful, international, sporting occasion whilst at the same time eliminating some of the less desirable aspects of it.

The problem, as I see it, is the matchplay format with its inherent confrontational character. Put two or four red-blooded blokes in a head-to-head game and, inevitably, aggression is generated which eventually turns unpleasant. Then the crowd gets involved and things get out of hand. I've seen it in WWE wrestling on Sky and I fear we will witness it at a forthcoming Ryder Cup unless something is done. Fortunately, it's not too late.

So here's what I propose. On day one, instead of foursomes in the morning and fourballs in the afternoon, I suggest we kick off with a long-driving competition. Unlike the existing arrangement where only some of the guys get to play on the first two days, all 24 players hit three balls. Each hits one ball in turn with the USA and Europe going alternately. To make it easier for the spectators and TV, the two sides could hit differently coloured balls. Only one ball from each player to count with the longest hitting scoring 24 points and the shortest just one point.

Although I've not yet worked out all the details, other contests could include crazy putting, a nearest-the-pin competition, a Texas scramble, etc. Instead of three days of cut-throat matchplay, you would have three days of fun and games. Instead of harsh words and mutual recrimination, you would have happiness and laughter. And at the end, the winners will lift the trophy and the losers will have had a good time. Finally, let's hope the Yanks get stuffed!

Section 5

Pure Fantasy

Dear Augusta National,

You will recall the little Welshman who won the US Masters quite a while back, Ian Woosnam. Well, by extraordinary coincidence he designed one of the two courses at my club, Dale Hill Hotel and Golf Club in East Sussex, England. So, in a sense, our two clubs are already inextricably bound together. My hope is to further strengthen the bonds between us so that despite the fact that we are separated by a great ocean and little bits of land at either end, we may forge a partnership that will survive for centuries, and, incidentally, strengthen my bid for captaincy.

If I may explain that last bit. For some time now, I have felt that I should be elected captain at Dale Hill but, because of what I'm sure is nothing other than racial prejudice - something I'm sure Augusta National would never tolerate - I have been passed over. So I need to pull off an amazing coup, or something similar, to convince members that I should be captain.

May I suggest the following reciprocal arrangements as the first tentative couple of steps towards establishing closer ties between our clubs.

1) The winner of the US Masters be exempted from qualifying in the usual way for our biggest tournament, The Higginbottom Trophy (a scratch competition ordinarily restricted to those who have won either a medal or Stableford competition in the previous 12 months). To even things up, I think The Higginbottom Trophy winner should then automatically qualify for the following year's US Masters.

2) Both sets of members be offered the courtesy of the other's course so that Augusta National members visiting this country can play Dale Hill for nothing; while our members, who might find themselves in Augusta, can play

your course for free. I feel compelled to warn you, however, that you'll find our greens are pretty quick, especially in summer.

****

Chairman of The Open Championship Venue Selection Committee,

The British Open is undoubtedly one of the biggest events in the golfing calendar. However, I think there is a real danger of it becoming a bit stale. What do I mean? For example, it always seems to be held on a seaside course. These are pleasant enough and, watching the waves crashing on the shore, doubtless helps players relax. But what worries me is that foreigners watching on television will think Britain is no more than just a length of coastline. What about all the pretty inland courses? Why are they never chosen to host the event?

Take my own club Dale Hill Hotel and Golf Club, just south of Tunbridge Wells. Apart from the fact that they use builders' sand in the bunkers, what's wrong with it? It has what I believe they call "the necessary infrastructure", including a sauna and well stocked pro-shop.

Although the A21 is a bit slow in places, there's a 50-bedroom hotel which, assuming they are prepared to double up, could accommodate most of the field. There's a modest swimming pool, two dining rooms and a large selection of beers.

The carpark presently only holds about 200 vehicles but it could be extended if necessary around the back of the greenkeeper's shed. What's more, and this is where it has

the edge over, say, Muirfield, it has two courses. Splitting the field would make life a lot easier for you and remove the need for ridiculously early tee off times.

I've spoken informally to the general manager and he has no objections in principle, although he didn't like the sound of a tented village "flattening the grass", so we may have to look at that one. And care would have to be taken regarding dates so as not to clash with one of Dale Hill's biggest events, the July Cup. However, with goodwill on both sides, I see no reason why these obstacles can't be overcome.

Bringing the British Open to this part of East Sussex will not only provide the local economy with a much-needed boost, I believe it will also refresh what is in danger of becoming a rather tired tournament and give the pros an exciting new challenge. Is it too late for next year?

****

Dear Roland McDonald,

Rather than try and fight this vegan thing, I would urge you to embrace it as you would a wounded cauliflower. Although vegetables aren't anywhere near as tasty as lovely meat, undoubtedly there is scope for producing dishes which are borderline edible. Combining my love for the great game of golf with a passion for cooking, I believe I have come up with something that will both appeal to your many customers as well as encourage them to take up golf.

To answer your anticipated question as to why McDonald's should encourage its clientele to take up golf, I would urge you to look at the size of some of them and think how

desperately they need the exercise. By subtly encouraging them to take up a healthy sport, you can claim to be doing your bit to combat obesity whilst continuing to flog essentially very unhealthy burgers.

Called the McBunker, for reasons that will become apparent in a moment or two, my imaginative creation is something that you might care to promote at around the time of the Open Championship. Traditionally held in the middle of July, it is the undoubted highlight of the golfing calendar.

Okay, I sense you want to know the recipe. Well, between the two halves of your bog-standard bun, you first slap down a bed of boiled cabbage. This represents the grass on the fairways and greens. In a scooped-out bit in the middle, you plonk a large spoonful of scrambled eggs, which of course represents the sand in the bunker. As for the ball, a single egg of cod's roe would do. If anyone complains that cod's roe isn't very white, you should explain that golf balls aren't always white and the one in their McBunker is one of those that isn't.

Although I experimented with a number of various ingredients to represent the rake, including trying to bend soggy twiglets, in the end what I thought worked best was shoving a plastic T-shaped toothpick into the top of the bun that was both fun and, by holding the whole thing together, was functional as well.

And so there you have it – a significantly less unhealthy burger that promotes healthy exercise.

Dear Desert Island Discs,

What's happened to Roy Plumtree? I ask because I was listening to Desert Island Discs the other day for the first time in quite a while and there was some woman asking all the questions. I've nothing against women *per se*, you understand, but it just didn't sound right.

Anyway, my point is the programme is sounding rather tired, worse even than I do after 18 holes of golf. The problem, as I see it, is there are far too many what you might call celebrities and far too few ordinary people. Look back over the last 50 years or thereabouts and you could hardly claim your guest list is composed of a representative sample of humanity. Showbiz grotesquely outnumbers every other area of human endeavour while my extensive research has failed to reveal even one golfer. Mind you, I can't blame you for not inviting Sir Nick Faldo onto your show because he is irredeemably dull.

The problem with celebrities is they are rather inclined to bang on about their glitzy lifestyle leaving us Radio 4 listeners feeling like failures just because we never starred in a movie, had a number one hit, wrote a best-selling novel or won a Nobel Prize. The other thing about them is they choose music they think will impress listeners. We don't want dreary classical rubbish. Most people like music you can dance to or singalong with.

Assuming you're persuaded by the strength of my argument that you need more ordinary people to be marooned on your desert island where, you might wonder, will you find a decent cross-section of the nicer elements in our society? The answer might surprise you. Having spent a fair bit of my life in there, I can tell you that you need look no further than the spike bar at my local golf club.

There are all sorts in there... scratch golfers, high handicappers, single figure players, the lot. There are even women!

To kick things off, you might care to invite me as I've a fund of riveting anecdotes and golf stories that I'm confident will amuse your listeners. That and some great music from the likes of Freddie and the Dreamers, the Monkees, the Yardbirds and Billy Fury should make for a brilliant show. How about it, BBC?

****

Dear Talent Agency,

Although you may well not have heard of me, I am something of a celebrity at Dale Hill Hotel and Golf Club. It's impossible to be precise but I would estimate something like 63.8% of the members would recognise me. A weekday member for nearly 20 years, by conscientiously competing in most of the medals and virtually all the mid-week Stablefords, I have assiduously developed a high profile to the extent that I am generally regarded – and forgive me if I sound immodest - as one of the club's most popular characters.

My rise to fame, if I may call it that, climaxed around Christmas 2019 when I was asked if I would present the prizes at the Ladies Annual Dinner. Rumour has it that Colonel McDuffy had been booked but his gout flared up two days before the event, which would explain why I was given such short notice.

Despite that, my speech went down rather well. It's not easy to encapsulate a lifetime's adventures on the links in

one short address and I thought I did well to keep it down to just three-quarters of an hour. It didn't help that a projector wasn't available and so I couldn't show slides of my golf trips to the Costa del Sol and North Wales but I soldiered on and didn't allow the distinctly audible snoring emanating from the Lady Captain to distract me.

Anyway, having compiled such an extraordinary collection of riveting anecdotes, witty bon mots, sparkling jokes and fascinating observations on the nature of golf and life, it seems a great shame that, as things stand, it's highly unlikely that they will ever be aired again. Unless, that is, you can add me to your roster of outstanding speakers and secure me a string of engagements. Although golf is my greatest passion, I do know a great deal about, and can speak authoritatively on, a number of diverse topics including cheese labels, bee-keeping and breeding budgerigars.

Money has never been my god but I gather huge sums can be earned on the speaking circuit. Tony Blair, apparently, commands a six-figure fee. Well, three, or preferably four, figures will be enough for me, initially at least. Perhaps I could start with golf clubs and work my way up to massive corporate occasions.

Dear Met Office,

Have you ever heard of Bryson DeChambeau? Don't worry if you haven't as I suspect he won't have heard of Michael Fish, Carol Kirkwood or Tomasz Schafernaker. Anyway, although he's rather slow when playing golf and, frankly, a bit of a 'nutter', he's nevertheless a very successful American golfer who's won quite a few important tournaments.

Rather like a lot of the boffins that I suspect work at the Met Office, he's something of a mad scientist. Anyway, he approaches golf in much the same way as you do the weather. For example, I don't suppose that you hang bits of seaweed outside your office or believe it's going to rain just because the cows are sitting down. Well, DeChambeau analyses all the data before taking a shot, which is one of the reasons he plays so slowly.

Although he's a bit creepy, you can't argue with his performances. At the time of writing, I think he's about number five in the world. Anyway, one of the vital variables he takes into account is air density and I'm wondering if there might be any commercial benefit to you in producing air density forecasts. You needn't bother with the whole country just places like St Andrews, Sunningdale, The Belfry, Sandwich, Muirfield, etc.

I don't want to be paid for the idea, all I ask is that I be allowed to audition for the job of presenting the daily air density forecasts on TV.

Dear António Guterres,

What with wars, famine and disease, not to mention global pandemics, I appreciate that you've got your work cut out at the United Nations and I therefore hesitate to involve you in something which might at first glance appear to be quite trivial. However, because of the international nature of the problem I honestly believe that you are in an ideal position to sort it out.

Although I respect that different countries have different traditions and different ways of doing things, there are times when uniformity would be to everyone's benefit. Take plug sockets for example. If every country could agree to have the same number and shape pins, travelling would be much easier and you could take your hairdryer all over the world.

Since I'm an old man with very little hair, I'm less concerned about hair dryers than I am about golf. The specific problem that I've encountered on the golf courses of the world that you might be able to fix concerns the markers that indicate how far you are from the green.

Firstly, there are all sorts of different colours. Secondly, the markers are at varying distances from the green. Thirdly, they can be in either yards or metres. And, finally, sometimes they indicate the distance to the front of the green and sometimes to the centre.

As a result, the poor visiting golfer is utterly confused. (As indeed might you be if you're not a golfer and can't altogether appreciate the problem I'm trying to describe.) Although you might presume that this is something that the various governing bodies of golf should sort out I fear that, because of petty rivalries and jealousies, they won't. It

therefore needs a respected global figure of great stature to intervene.

Initially, however, it might help if someone were to visit the principal golfing nations of the world, play on the main championship courses and report back to you. Now that I am more or less retired, I have the time and would be happy to take on this awesome task as an official UN Ambassador.

Perhaps after you've raised the issue in the General Assembly and/or Security Council, you could let me know how much I'm going to earn and what sort of bar expenses would be considered acceptable.

****

Dear Rolex,

Although I know it sounds ridiculous, nothing in this world is more important to me than punctuality. Take this letter for example. The letterbox at the end of my road is emptied daily (except Sundays) at 4.45pm and so there I will be at 4.44pm this afternoon dropping it in. Because they care less about punctuality than I do, the Royal Mail often don't empty the box until after 5pm; I know because I can see it from my bedroom window.

Not only am I a remarkably punctual person, I am also a keen golfer. The two are not entirely unrelated as timing is a key component of the golf swing and turning up on the tee on time is absolutely vital, which brings me seamlessly onto the need to replace my present timepiece.

Unfortunately, the black plastic strap broke on my present watch at the top of my backswing hurling the important bit straight into the ball-washer thereby dislocating one of

Mickey's arms. Sod's law dictated it was the right arm which, since you're in the business, you probably already know indicates the hour. So although I now know it's, say, 20 minutes past something, I don't know what that something is. Consequently, I can be an hour early or, much worse, an hour late, which is absolutely hopeless.

From reading your advertisements, I gather that you have struck deals with a number of top golfers. My suspicion is you probably give them a decent wedge (not lofted ☺) as well as one of your watches. Well, if you were to enrol me as a Rolex ambassador, you would only have to supply a watch as I wouldn't demand any money. Not only would I wear your watch with pride but I believe ordinary handicap golfers would also more easily identify with me than they would with a bunch of self-satisfied, super-rich, smug bastards who just so happen to be exceptionally good at golf.

****

Dear Senior Producer of the Archers,

I must confess that I don't listen to The Archers very often. However, on those infrequent occasions when I do, I quite enjoy it.

Having said that, I feel that the time has come to shift the social focus away from The Bull. Apart from anything else, I worry that you might, in some subliminal way, be encouraging the consumption of alcohol. Although I don't think it should be demolished to make way for an Ambridge bypass or be destroyed by a meteor, I do think that another regular venue should be found that has a healthier and more wholesome appeal.

Having given it a great deal of thought, I believe I have come up with the perfect solution. Since agriculture is almost certainly in terminal decline in this country, alternative uses must be found for farmland. And what better use could there possibly be than recreational?

So I suggest you convert a chunk of Home Farm (about 250 acres should be sufficient) into "Ambridge Golf and Country Club".

Golf is a great game and offers enormous opportunities for characters to interact. Then there are the competitions. Provided we can find a way to persuade the bulk of Ambridge inhabitants to quickly reach an acceptable standard of play, you could have sworn enemies meeting in the final of, say, the Walter Gabriel Memorial Trophy.

Mixed foursomes matches, traditionally rather fraught affairs, offer scope for all sorts of intrigue and naughtiness. If you decide to take-up my idea, by way of thanks, would you kindly audition me for the part of the club professional. Incidentally, if he's still alive, I think Jack Woolley would make an ideal club captain.

Section 6

Completely Daft

Dear Pfizer,

Before I go any further, would you kindly settle an argument that broke out in the spike bar of my golf club recently between myself and Harvey 'Three Putts' Harrison as to whether or not you pronounce the 'P' in Pfizer. My argument was that you **do** pronounce the 'P' otherwise why would it be there?

Before I go even further still, may I congratulate you wholeheartedly on discovering a vaccine for that appalling Coronavirus thing that not only has killed dozens of people all over the world but caused the postponement of the US Masters, the cancellation of The Open and basically ruined the last two summers. I'm just hoping that I'm not among the unfortunate 10 per cent, or thereabouts, for whom your remedy apparently doesn't work.

Having dealt the pandemic a mortal blow, doubtless you are looking around wondering what to do next. After all, you can't afford to have all those white-coated boffins sitting around in your well-equipped laboratories twiddling their scientific thumbs while waiting for the next nasty bug to escape from one of those disgusting Chinese markets where they sell all manner of diseased wild animals, can you? In retrospect, I think my mother was absolutely right in refusing to ever eat in a Chinese restaurant. "You never know what's lurking beneath those huge piles of rice," she used to say.

Back to business. For some years now I have suffered from an affliction that blights the career of many a golfer for which, as yet, there is no known cure. Called the 'yips', its name suggests it might also have originated in China. Without going into too much detail, it's a sort of involuntary muscle spasm that renders putting an absolute

nightmare. Golfers suffering from it would, I'm certain, pay vast sums to be cured.

If you would approach the problem with the same commitment, enthusiasm and determination you so admirably displayed when battling Coronavirus, I'm confident you could have a pill, vaccine or whatever available in all good pro shops before very long.

Finally, with regard to enrolling volunteers, I would happily put myself forward on condition you promise not to fob me off with some worthless placebo.

****

Dear Headmaster of Eton College,

I'm writing to enquire as to whether you would consider offering golf to your pupils as an alternative to the Wall Game. From the little I've seen of the latter, it seems decidedly rough and dangerous.

Not only is golf safe and civilised by comparison, it is also absolutely ideal for young toffs looking to make their way in the world of banking, stock broking, insider trading, money laundering and the like.

If you are prepared to consider it, I should like to offer my services as head golf coach. A 19 handicapper with an elegant shoulder turn but a rather strong grip, I honestly believe I could have won a couple of majors if only I had taken up the game earlier instead of wasting my time playing football. At the dodgy school I went to there was no choice. Now I'm keen to give others the chance that I never had.

Eton is fortunate in having plenty of playing fields, one of which could be used as a sort of driving range. And then I would hope there is a possibility that we could borrow the nine-hole course I understand the infamous Prince Andrew has in a corner of Windsor Great Park.

No doubt you're quite chummy with the Royals and so a request from you will stand a much better chance of succeeding than one coming from me.

****

Dear European Tour,

In a world of finite resources where we all have a duty to conserve energy and reduce waste, how can professional golfers justify teeing up a brand new golf ball every couple of holes? Surely this is just profligate nonsense that flies in the face, not so much of bunkers, but of responsible behaviour. From my own considerable experience as a 19-handicapper, I can say with some authority that new balls behave no better and fly no further than averagely scuffed balls. So why do pros frequently discard a perfectly decent ball to tee up a new one? One obvious explanation is that they are given an endless supply of them for which they don't have to pay and so there's no incentive for them to be less wasteful.

Furthermore, the manufacture of golf balls clearly contributes to golf's carbon footprint and thus to climate change. Although my club (Dale Hill Hotel and Golf Club) is thankfully nearly 300 feet above sea level, the same is not true of the dozens of magnificent links courses stretched around our glorious coastline. Muirfield, Turnberry, Royal St George's, Rye, Royal Portrush, Trevose, Troon and

dozens of others are extremely vulnerable to even a modest rise in sea level. Do we really want the Old Course at St Andrews only to be playable at low tide? Will we be happy that greenkeepers will not only rake the bunkers but drag seaweed off the greens as well? Of course not and so this is why the European Tour must introduce a rule that requires pros to only use one ball per round. If they lose it, they are out of the tournament.

Although this may sound harsh, in my opinion it will have the very beneficial effect of discouraging players from hitting the ball too far. For some time now the authorities have been worried about courses being overwhelmed by the 'bombers' but have been frightened to act for fear of being sued by the equipment manufacturers. Well, this could be the answer!

In recognition of helping to save both the planet and the game of golf, all I ask is that the new rule that requires players to only use one ball be called "Mortimer's Rule". In that way, although I've never won a major, my name will be immortalised so long as the game of golf is played.

Dear Guinness,

When people think of Ireland, which three things immediately spring to mind? Well, I believe they are Guinness, golf and dodgy priests doing unmentionable things to young children. Well, discarding the last one for reasons of good taste, let's focus on the other two - your magnificent beer and the greatest game on earth.

A creative thinker who makes a modest living by coming up with wholly original ideas to sell to large companies such as yours, I have what I believe is a genius proposal that I'm confident will boost consumption of Guinness wherever the game of golf is played.

Called the 'Guinness Golfball Giveaway', it's remarkably simple really and works like this. Whenever a customer orders a pint of Guinness, the barman or barwoman asks them, "Do you want to tee-off?" If the customer says "yes", the barman or barwoman proceeds to ask them a question about the Irish Open Golf Championship, such as, "Who won it in 1927?" If they answer, "George Duncan" and provided they buy another pint of Guinness, they go through to the next round.

In round two they have to answer a simple question on the rules of golf. For example, "If the player lifts his or her ball at rest or causes it to move, the ball must be replaced on its original spot (which if not known must be estimated) (see Rule 14.2), except in two specific circumstances, can you give me either of them?" The correct answer is either when the player lifts the ball under a Rule to take relief or to replace the ball on a different spot (see Rules 14.2d and 14.2e), or when the ball moves only after the player has begun the stroke or the backswing for a stroke and then goes on to make the stroke. It's entirely at the discretion of

the barman or barwoman to decide whether the customer's answer is correct. If it is and provided they buy another pint, they can proceed to the third and final question on famous Irish golfers. Here the questions inevitably are a tad harder such as, how old was Christy O'Connor Snr when he died in 2016? The correct answer, of course, is 91. Everyone who gets three correct answers in a row wins a golf ball.

One of the great attractions of the 'Guinness Golfball Giveaway' is that it can easily be adapted to any country simply by tailoring the questions to that country. For example in Kazakhstan, question one would be about the Kazakhstan Open; question two would be about the rules of golf and question three would be about famous Kazakhstan golfers.

I'm happy to research and script all the questions for which I would ask a modest €10,000 per country.

****

Dear Sky Sports,

Until Sky appeared there was very little golf on TV and so I say 'well done' for bringing us so much great golf from around the world.

My purpose in writing is to make a suggestion that I think will improve your coverage considerably. Unlike football, where Sky has come up with a number of exciting innovations, the golf coverage has remained pretty much the same. One camera on the tee, another behind the green and occasionally one on the fairway with a sound man picking up the tedious discussion between player and caddie as to which way the wind is blowing.

Why not insert cameras into the heads of the putters of the main contenders? Then as the player lines up to stroke the ball, we at home will get a unique view of the putt. Admittedly, things might go a little awry as the player follows through after the putt but staying with it might provide some unusual shots of cloud formations and the like. You're not called Sky for nothing!

To anticipate a rather obvious concern that players won't welcome bulky cameras and attendant wires hanging off their putters, you know as well as I do that cameras these days are very small so that even the most sensitive players will hardly notice them.

If, as I expect, this proves enormously popular, you could extend the experiment to include other clubs such as drivers and sand wedges. And another place they could be sited is in the flagsticks. A recent rule amendment allows players to leave the flag in when they putt. Perhaps you could lobby to make leaving the flag in compulsory and train the caddies to turn the stick so that the lens is facing whoever is putting. Caddies generally are accommodating chaps and would, I'm sure, be happy to cooperate, especially if you bung them a few beers after the round.

Ultimately, of course, a camera inside the ball offers the unbelievably exciting prospect of a totally fresh perspective on the game. But that, like the players' prodigious drives, might be way off in the distance.

Dear FootJoy,

The traffic is horrific and it looks like you're going to be late on the first tee and incur a two-shot penalty or, worse still, be disqualified. You pull up in the car park but you've not yet changed your shoes. Don't panic because you're wearing a pair of Kwikswitcher shoes. Just leap out of the car and clip a pair of spiked soles onto them – soft or hard spikes depending on the conditions. And then crunch an imperious drive down the first.

On the tricky par three, you hit your tee-shot a bit fat and just fail to carry the stream that guards the green. Your ball is lying in shallow water and is distinctly playable but you don't want to play the rest of the round with wet feet. Nor do you want to take a penalty drop. Fortunately, you've remembered the 'growtall' attachment is in your bag and so you simply unclip your spiked soles and snap on the six-inch platform soles. After you've splashed out, you stick your spikes back on and hole the putt for par. (Incidentally, I tried installing the platforms inside the shoes so that they would automatically inflate when they made contact with water, in much the same way as do lifeboats in aircraft, but I experienced too many mishaps when simply striding down slightly soggy fairways).

Back to our story. You win the match and, as you walk off the 18th green, your dejected opponent shakes your hand and then disappears into the locker-room to change his shoes whereas all you have to do is unclip your spikes and, hey presto, you're now back into town shoes and ready for that celebratory pint.

You will be aware of how expensive shoes are these days, especially decent golf shoes. What shall we say, £100? So three pairs will cost £300. Instead, a pair of Kwikswitchers

will only set you back a modest £125, thus saving you £175! And you can save a whole lot more when you buy any of the numerous accessories including snap-on ice-blades, crampons, football boots, ballet shoes and roller-blades.

Since my knowledge of the boot and shoe industry is somewhat limited, I'm wondering if you would like to buy my patented design and take over the entire project. Does £250,000 all-in sound reasonable?

****

Dear Andy Murray,

First of all, belated congratulations on winning so many tennis matches during your extremely illustrious career. My sister, Audrey Meriweather, is a huge fan of yours and, frankly, has been inconsolable since your decision to more or less semi-retire. As I, too, have a dodgy hip, I can probably empathise with your plight more than she can. Incidentally, may I politely enquire as how you were able to have your recent hip operation organised so quickly when I've been waiting ages for mine? Perhaps the NHS queue north of the border is shorter than it is in Sussex. Well, I suppose it's only fair there are compensations for living in such a bleak place with such awful weather surrounded by the likes of that dreadful Alex Salmond and having to listen to dreary bagpipes.

Anyway, while you're considering what you're going to do in the future, may I make a suggestion? Although you will doubtless be tempted to take up commentating or coaching, I would urge you to continue competing, but at golf not tennis. Golf is so much better than tennis; it's much

friendlier, apart from the occasional 'fore!' no one yells and it's a lot less tiring.

I read somewhere that, although Jamie was better, you were a half-decent single-figure player in your youth until you foolishly switched to tennis. With a few lessons, I'm sure you would soon be playing well enough to compete on the European Tour. Remember, golfers traditionally don't peak until their mid-30s and so time is on your side. To the best of my knowledge, no one has ever won a tennis grand slam AND a golf major. By becoming the first, you would secure your place in the pantheon of great British sportsmen and, because I know you're a bit funny about it, sportswomen.

As you are already fairly well-known, I'm absolutely certain that, if you did become a pro golfer, you would receive dozens of sponsors' invites to play in the very best, most lucrative tournaments. You would only need to make a few cuts and secure the odd top-ten finish to earn enough to retain your card and stay on the tour.

To help keep the cost down, I'd be willing to carry your bag for free, for the first couple of years at least. "Merriweather and Murray", has a ring to it, don't you think?

Come on, Andy – let's do it!

****

Dear Michael O'Leary,

"Mr O'Leary is a commercial genius," I told my friend when we were flying with Ryanair from Shannon to Gatwick after a lovely golfing holiday in County Clare. To be precise, because we were sitting 15 rows apart as a result of your inspired policy of separating travelling companions unless

they're prepared to stump up the extra, I said it to him as we were walking into the south terminal at Gatwick.

Of all your innovations, I think extorting a penal charge from suckers who, for whatever reason, don't have a boarding pass is perhaps your single greatest contribution to modern travel. Anyway, I have a suggestion which, if implemented, should provide a fitting boost to what appears to be your sagging bottom line.

Not that it matters to you one grimy Euro how rich or poor are the customers you fleece but there is, perhaps, a tad more satisfaction in ripping off the rich. Anyway, golfers generally are fairly well off and so could be regarded as legitimate targets. Although you already charge a fair bit for carrying clubs in the hold, there is undoubted scope for squeezing a bit more from the unwary hackers. Since no golfer has a clue as to what the circumference of his bag is, you could apply a maximum limit of, say, 25 inches which, although sounding generous, would catch out all but the smallest bags. Trust me, very few would slip through the net. Alternatively, you could stipulate a maximum of 13 clubs which, since nearly every golfer has a full-set of 14, should generate substantial extra revenue. Or why not do both and enjoy a double bonanza?

Doubtless you have a 'Fleecing Unit' which could assess my suggestions and I hardly need advise you, or them, of the need to slip something in very small type somewhere near the bottom of the terms and conditions. Renowned for respecting the rules, golfers should take whatever penalty you decide to extract on the chin.

Dear DJ Spoony,

As a black man yourself, you will be aware of the awful prejudice that exists in many sectors of our society. And, as a golfer, you know that, to its enormous shame, the game which we both love has hardly blazed the progressive trail in recognising the fundamental equality of human beings. Sadly, we still can't claim that all golfers will be welcome everywhere regardless of race, creed, colour, religion, sex or handicap. A black woman playing off, say, six should be just as welcome at any golf club as a white, middle-aged man with a dodgy grip and a handicap in the 20s. However, golf remains a bastion of reactionary forces who seem determined to resist much-needed change.

As a very respected club member, I'm frequently shocked both by the appalling prejudices manifested by my playing partners and, even more insulting, the casual assumption they make that I must share their ugly attitude. To my considerable shame, rather than disabuse them, I simply say nothing and hope that they might cotton on to the fact that I don't agree with them.

What I've been searching for is a discreet but effective way of indicating to those with whom I play golf that I'm not bigoted and I'd rather they kept their unfunny racist jokes to themselves. The solution came to me on the short 15th at Dale Hill Hotel and Golf Club ... a black ball. Because it symbolises rejection, a black ball would, in my opinion, be a particularly appropriate method of conveying the message, "Shut up, bigot!"

What I'm suggesting, therefore, is that an approach be made to one of the major golf ball manufacturers urging them to produce a ball and make a modest donation to Black Lives Matter for every one they sell. After fairly

extensive field tests with a few that I painted myself, I found them perfectly satisfactory in every respect other than they are fiendishly difficult to follow in flight and then to find. Still, I'm confident "we will overcome" this slight obstacle.

Your support in this venture would be greatly appreciated.

****

Dear Head of Research and Development at Phoenix Office Furniture,

You will be aware, I'm sure, of the strong liking our captains of industry and business leaders have for the game of golf. Even the very briefest of glances through "Who's Who" and the hobbies of the rich and famous reveals an astonishing fondness for it.

Furthermore, I believe that this fact can be commercially exploited by a combination of my considerable knowledge of the game and your well-deserved reputation in the exciting world of office furniture.

I therefore propose that we jointly examine the feasibility of reproducing some of the most famous greens in the world in the offices of some of the most powerful men and women on the planet.

If you've ever watched golf on television, you will have seen the computer-generated graphics that are often used to illustrate the slope on a green. All the information that we need, therefore, is already available and I don't suppose it would be much of a problem to persuade the relevant TV companies to release it to us.

All we would need to do is convert this information into three dimensional carpets with some form of foam supporting the raised areas. This foam would need to be fairly resilient in order to create an authentic turf-like feel and care would need to be taken to ensure that the texture of the surface material, the carpet if you like, possessed similar qualities to a close-cut lawn so that putting on it would be just like putting on a green. We could even check the speed of the carpets with the same device used by tournament officials, a stimpmeter.

The only problem I can foresee is making adjustments to the rest of the office furniture to allow for the slope. For example, three of the legs on the desk might need to be shortened to ensure that the top was horizontal. Because this furniture might get moved around, rather than simply saw off legs at the bottom, it would perhaps be desirable to make the legs adjustable.

And I would suggest the hole itself be movable to even out the wear and tear and to provide the occupant with a variety of challenging putts. I suggest we start with a range of 18th greens taken from such great courses as St Andrews, Wentworth, Carnoustie, Pebble Beach and Augusta. These could be split into ranges. How about the British Open, Ryder Cup and US Open with six in each?

Clearly with offices being predominantly rectangular and of different sizes, we would simply take a rectangular chunk out of each green. Bunkers in the form of sunken sofas could be an optional extra.

Section 7

Absolutely Crazy

Dear Dalai Lama,

As I understand it, you are the spiritual leader of all the Buddhists in the world. Although they're relatively thin on the ground as compared with the more common Christians and Muslims, there are, I've discovered, over 500 million of your lot. Why then do I not meet more Buddhists? I know a lot of Christians, a surprising number of Jews, a sprinkling of Muslims and quite a few atheists but I can't claim to know even one, actual, practicing Buddhist. They're certainly not down the Dog and Duck on a Friday night and so, where are they all? They make up seven per cent of the world's population and so, statistically speaking, one in 14 of the people I bump into shopping in Sainsbury's on a Thursday evening, should be Buddhists; and even more in the organic fruit and vegetable section. Because they don't all wear the gear you do, I suppose it's possible there are more around than I realise.

Let me move swiftly on to **my** religion… golf. I don't suppose either the topography or the climate is suitable up there in Tibet for the Royal and Ancient game but, from what I know of Buddhism, it strikes me as the ideal game for your followers. It's very Zen, you see. And being outside in the fresh air with glorious scenery and so close to nature, it stimulates all sorts of profound communing with the natural forces that govern everything. Not only that but golf also has its mantras such as, "Keep your head down", "Left arm straight", "Swing smoothly" and "Don't miss for God's sake." And a belief in reincarnation brings hope to those of us who dream of coming back as a scratch golfer.

So what I'm proposing is running a series of retreats at Dale Hill Hotel and Golf Club near Ticehurst in East Sussex exclusively for Buddhists wishing to both come to a greater

understanding of life whilst at the same time lowering their handicaps. Called 'Birdies for Buddhists' it would be a week-long retreat. Each day would begin with a quiet period of calm and refection followed by a short-game clinic, a veggie burger and chips for lunch, a round of golf in the afternoon, a peaceful session in the spike bar before a bit of chanting and an early night.

It would certainly help me sell the package if you would be willing to endorse it. Something like, "Improve both your golf and your chances of a better life next time around with 'Birdies for Buddhists'" - D Lama.

****

Dear JP McManus,

Although a couple might have dropped dead since the article was written, I read somewhere that you presently own 550 racehorses. It might be a fun idea to organise an enormous race for all your horses to find out which is the quickest. Imagine 550 horses thundering down an especially widened track. Wouldn't that be an amazing spectacle? Apart from finding a wide enough racecourse, one problem might be getting hold of 550 sets of your distinctive green and gold silks. And I don't envy the racecourse commentator identifying all the runners and riders. Anyway, I'm contacting you as one golfer to another in the hope that you might be able to help me.

Presumably thinking up names for all your horses must be quite a headache. Well, I have a readymade name that I would be absolutely thrilled for you to use. To be completely straight with you, the idea behind it is to send a very clear message to the committee at my golf club, Dale

Hill, that there is one man who has been repeatedly overlooked for the captaincy and that man is me! And so the name that I would be delighted for you to use is Captain Merriweather, which I think sounds rather good, don't you?

Assuming you like the name as much as I do, may I ask that you save it for one of your better nags? Although it might sound a little unreasonable, how disappointing it would be for me if it ended up running in low grade races at, say, Newton Abbot or Bangor-on-Dee. And how much more impact it would have on the committee if it, say, won the Grand National or the Cheltenham Gold Cup. If it did win a big race, I would happily grab the horse's head on one side while you took the other so that we could jointly lead it into the winner's enclosure.

Although I recognise my idea is a 25/1 shot, stranger things have happened in racing. Remember Foinavon? Which wasn't one of yours, I don't think.

****

Dear Mr Djokovic,

Although I'm not a world number one, or ever likely to be, I believe I understand what I think is your problem. It's certainly not your backhand, which is pretty solid, but rather it is your astonishing lack of popularity. You would think, wouldn't you, that the greatest tennis player in the world would be hugely popular. But you're obviously not, which evidently upsets you because, like most of us, you want to be loved.

I've not conducted a formal survey but, supplied with three alternative answers to the question, 'Which of the following

most accurately describes Novak Djokovic?' my hunch is that that here in the UK (obviously in Serbia things are somewhat different) the answers would roughly be as follows:

a) A brilliant tennis player and a worthy champion whom I much admire 5%

b) An arrogant and ill-tempered tosser who behaves like a spoilt child 30%

c) A complete cock 65%

What I suspect you want to know is how do you go about improving your image and popularity rating? Well, let me tell you about a bloke at my golf club, Dale Hill. Let's call him Roger. A scratch golfer who has won the club championship no fewer than 20 times and nearly all the other club competitions for which he is eligible, he is always magnanimous in victory and gracious on those rare occasions he loses. He never sulks nor has he ever thrown a club in his life. Considering how good he is, he is remarkably modest and friendly to everyone, even the very high handicappers! I sincerely believe you should try and be more like Roger.

There is one more thing I would like to suggest and that is to cut out that ridiculous nonsense when you win and point to the ceiling and then throw your arms out to the four corners of the arena. What the f*** is that all about? It looks like you're reaching up to God and acting as a conduit to draw down his love to then share it with the spectators. It might be as well to remember that you're just a professional tennis player and not the frigging messiah!

Dear LGBT Foundation,

I would very much welcome your advice as to how I should go about changing my gender from male to female. Is it just a case of me simply self-identifying as a woman? If that's all it is and there's no requirement to undergo any unpleasant surgery, I'm up for it.

To be honest, it's not a question of always having felt myself to be a woman as I never have. In case you're curious to know why an octogenarian gentleman and lifelong misogynist would want to switch sides, so to speak, I shall explain.

I'm a very keen, if not terribly accomplished, golfer. As I get older, I'm increasingly finding the par fours are not, as they're supposed to be, reachable in two. Anything over 350 yards is frankly way out of my range. Sure, I could get on in three and then hole the putt for par but my putting is pretty awful and so I very rarely single putt.

I have therefore come to the conclusion that the only way I could reach most of the par fours in regulation is to shorten the holes by playing off the forward red tees. However these, as I'm sure you are aware, are reserved for women. Ah, now do you understand my situation?

Another worthwhile benefit I would enjoy if I switched over is a significantly reduced membership subscription at my club, Dale Hill. For some arcane reason, women pay less.

Finally, the women's section is very much smaller than the men's and so the odds of me being elected Women's Captain would be significantly shorter than they are of being elected Men's Captain which, frankly, seems increasingly unlikely.

And having stumbled into the women's locker room one evening after a particularly boozy session with the boys, I appreciate how much more fragrant and appealing it is compared to the men's.

****

Dear President Bolsonaro,

I've always wanted to visit Brazil (why some people spell it with an 's' baffles me). Any country that produces outstanding footballers such as Pele must be doing something right, eh? More than anything else, I would love to explore the Amazon Basin which, thanks to your enlightened 'slash and burn' policy, must be far more accessible now.

I appreciate that the primary purpose of burning so many millions of hectares was to provide your farmer friends with cheap land but now that so much impenetrable jungle has been eliminated, there exists a unique opportunity to build hundreds of decent hotels and top-notch visitor attractions. And there should be more than enough space left over to create dozens, if not hundreds, of first-class golf courses. Providing them will help Brazil attract more of the right sort of tourist and fewer Sir David Attenboroughs, if you know what I mean.

As things stand, apart from the carnival in Rio and the odd sandy beach, Brazil hasn't a great deal to offer today's discerning traveller. Furthermore, golf courses would provide suitable employment – caddies, greenkeepers, bar staff and the like - for those who have inadvertently been displaced. By introducing them to the joy of golf, it might even stop them dwelling on the destruction of their former

way of life. As a further sop, you might care to use your considerable influence to persuade the courses to offer genuine indigenous folk a 15% discount on the regular green fees.

From a political perspective, by helping to establish your country as an appealing destination that offers exceptional golf in a unique jungle-like setting, you will create a legacy as a visionary leader rather than the arsehole who never took Covid seriously and thus contributed significantly to the death of over half-a-million of his people.

Dear European Tour,

Why is golf's popularity waning? Is it because it's virtually impossible for ordinary people to hit the ball straight or is it because golf clubs are horribly stuffy places that positively discourage visitors? Well, after giving the matter considerable thought I believe that I at least have an explanation as to why the viewing figures for European Tour events on TV are dropping while, if you'll forgive my joke, my putts aren't?

The explanation in a word is 'technology'. While other sports featured on TV have embraced it, golf hasn't. Take tennis for example. The loathsome Djokovic hits a backhand that appears to land very close to the base line. Is it in or out? The tension mounts as Hawk-Eye follows the ball's trajectory and … it's out! Yippee!

Moving onto cricket and England are once again struggling with only the likeable Joe Root seemingly capable of stopping the horrible Aussies from bowling us out for a miserably low score. And then he's hit on the pad. The horrible Aussies all leap in the air and appeal. Oh no, the umpire has raised his finger and the horrible Aussies are ecstatic. Root thinks for a moment and then gives the 'T' sign indicating he wants the decision reviewed. The whole of England holds its breath as DRS (Decision Review System) swings into action. Bad news as a combination of 'Snicko' and 'Hot Spot' reveal the ball didn't touch the bat. Will Hawk-Eye save our captain? One red light, two red lights but the third red light fails to illuminate as the predicted path of the ball is just clearing the off bail. Joe's not out and the horrible Aussies are gutted. Yippee!

Although not universally popular, the Video Assistant Referee (VAR) has certainly added another dimension to

watching football on TV. It increases the tension and contributes considerable controversy whilst relieving the linesmen (no-one calls them assistant referees) of the awesome responsibility of deciding whether or not a goal-scorer was offside.

Sadly, golf has nothing to compete with the above and so I suggest you adapt VAR to determine whether or not a player was in front of the marker when teeing off. For example, the extremely unlikeable Bryson DeChambeau hits what appears to be a magnificent tee-shot on a par three that finishes just a few inches from the hole. His unattractive face lights up. But hang on, was his left foot a fraction in front of where it should have been? Yes, VAR indicates it was and it's a two-shot penalty. DeChambeau goes purple with rage. Yippee! How entertaining is that?

****

Dear Black Lives Matter,

Can anyone tell me why professional golfers don't 'take a knee' by kneeling down when hitting their opening tee-shot in tournaments? Not only would that make a bold statement about how much black lives matter but it would also reveal who are the genuinely gifted ball strikers.

You might be interested to learn that I was going to suggest that all competitors 'take a knee' before teeing off in the Veterans' December Mid-Week Stableford at my club Dale Hill before it was pointed out to me by Toby 'Please Don't Make Me Putt That' Atkinson that at least half the field would struggle to get up again.

But it's about another related matter that I'm writing to you now. Have you by any chance heard of Old Tom Morris? (By the way, in no way is he connected to the main character in 'Old Tom's Cabin'). Well, Old Tom Morris is a revered figure in golf and is widely regarded as the sort of 'Grandfather' of the game credited with doing more than anyone else to establish it back in 19th century Scotland. There are loads of books about him and dozens of historic golf courses designed by him. In other words, he's a formidable target that I believe I have the ammunition to thoroughly discredit. And what a significant coup it would be for BLM if you could expose him as an evil and exploitative man.

After considerable research in his home town of St Andrews, I have uncovered scandalous revelations that will send enormous shock waves reverberating around the ordinarily genteel world of golf. In the middle of the 19th century, Old Tom Morris established his own golf equipment business manufacturing balls and clubs. And what were the latter made of do you think? Hickory wood. And where did it come from? The southern states of the USA where it was almost certainly harvested by slave labour. And so there you have it, golf's most legendary figure exposed as little better than a slave trader!

As well as tearing down all the statues of him, I think we should demand that all the courses he designed, including the Old, New and Jubilee courses at St Andrews, be immediately closed with a view to being comprehensively redesigned in due course by a contemporary golf course architect, preferably one of colour.

Dear Head of the Nobel Prize Committee,

Looking through the list of Nobel prizes, I note that you dish them out for Physics, Chemistry, Physiology or Medicine, Peace, Literature and Economics. How often, if ever, have you reviewed this list since you were set-up in 1900? My suspicion is that you haven't and are consequently out of touch with current trends. Stuck in Sweden, it's perhaps hardly surprising you're unaware of what's going on in the world.

Frankly, very few of my friends or family are in the least bit interested in either Physics of Chemistry. You should do what I did at school about 65 years ago and drop them both immediately. Medicine is critical to the wellbeing of mankind and so you should definitely retain that. As a published author myself, I certainly recognise the importance of great literature but does Economics contribute anything to the sum total of human happiness? Peace is a very good thing so that should definitely stay.

Chucking out the unpopular stuff will leave you room to add some fresh subjects that are more in tune with the age. At present, you don't reward anything sporty, which is a great shame as sport is an area of human endeavour that really interests people in a way that Physics and Chemistry never can or will.

There are, of course, a lot of sports from which to choose. In your part of the world there is, for example, skiing. But winter sports are only really of interest in those places where it snows a lot. Golf, on the other hand, is played in pretty well every country on the planet. And so I urgently suggest you start a Nobel Prize for Golf. But don't give it to one of the famous players, who neither needs the money nor the recognition. Instead, give it to an unsung hero who,

for example, has spent a considerable amount of time making inspired suggestions as to how the game could be improved.

One last question; is it okay to nominate oneself for a prize?

****

Dear Principal Trainer of Sniffer Dogs,

Am I right in assuming that a decent dog with effective nostrils can be trained to sniff out anything from drugs to dynamite, bodies to bullets and gorgonzola to golf balls? The other thing I need to know is at what age do you retire your animals – 10, 20, 30?

The reason I ask these questions is that I believe I can offer a 'second career' to one of your ageing hounds that will enable him or her to employ their olefactorial talent to good effect as well as keeping him or her active right up until the moment he or she drops down dead.

My research has confirmed a long-held suspicion of mine that there is big money to be made in finding lost golf balls. The problem has always been how to locate them when they are often buried in the deep rough. I experimented with drones but too many golfers complained they were an unwanted distraction.

Dogs are ideal hunters because they are comparatively easy to train, cheap to feed and no problem to look after as compared with, say, dolphins. Because of their boundless energy, they also ought to be able to keep going for at least ten hours at a time. Assuming it takes them no longer than about 30 seconds to locate and retrieve a lost ball, they could recover somewhere in the region 1200 balls a day.

Since a quality second-hand golf ball is conservatively worth about 50p that means a decent dog could earn its handler about £600 per day or £3000 for a five-day week. Allowing for two weeks holiday a year that's £150,000 per annum less, say, £250 for dog food, which leaves £149,750.

Would I be correct in thinking that you would be only too happy to let one of your retiring dogs go to a caring home for free?

Sorry he's yet to learn if a ball is lost or not.

Dear Queen,

First of all may I say what a pleasure it has been to be one of your humble subjects for the past 70 years. I honestly couldn't have asked for a nicer monarch to reign over me and my only regret is that, although I lived just the other side of Hyde Park from you for a number of years when working at the Ministry of Agriculture and Fisheries in Westminster, we never met. Sadly, unless I receive a knighthood for services to golf, and pretty sharpish because neither of us is getting any younger, it is extremely unlikely that we ever will.

However, I haven't given up all hope of seeing your regal smile close up and the Platinum Pudding competition would appear to offer what I suspect will be my very last chance. Since I hate cooking and have no significant experience of preparing puddings, I must confess it's something of a long shot – a bit like a hole in one.

And it's that almost mythical phenomenon that is the inspiration behind my recipe for 'Merrriweather's Mess' which, incidentally, only uses ingredients that you might encounter either directly on a golf course or, at the very least, in a shop or off licence close to a golf course. The ingredients are as follows:

Two pounds of raspberries

Half-a-dozen free-range eggs

One pound of self-raising flour

Half-a-pound of castor sugar

Four tablespoons of treacle

Three milk chocolate bars

Five fluid oz of gin

Five fluid oz of kirsch

Five fluid oz of whisky

Five fluid oz of kummel

Two pounds of green marzipan

One Twiglet

Wash the raspberries and put them in a large bowl. Melt the chocolate bars on a low heat and then pour the chocolate onto the raspberries before slowly adding all the other ingredients except the marzipan. Stir with a large spoon until the mixture is reasonably firm and can be moulded into a large thick disc. Create a small round hole in the middle and then cook in a pre-heated oven at 195 degrees Celsius for half-an-hour or thereabouts. Remove from the oven and roll the marzipan flat before spreading it evenly over the top so that it resembles a green. For the final touch, shove a twiglet in the hole to represent the flagstick.

****

Dear Xi Jinping,

Before I explain the principal purpose of this letter, would you kindly settle an argument I'm having with my friend Dave? He thinks the 'XI' in your name means you should properly be referred to as Jinping the 11th in the same way that Louis X1V, the King of France in the middle of the 17th century, was Louis the 14th and David Love III is Davis Love the Third. But for that to be the case, I think China would have had to have been occupied by the Romans and Chinese school-children obliged to learn Latin, which I'm pretty sure never happened.

The other thing I would like to know is whether or not you have ever been mistaken for a cricket team. Although a left-arm wrist spinner's delivery that is the equivalent of the googly is sometimes called a 'Chinaman', I suspect you're unfamiliar with the game. Anyhow, because there are 11 players in a cricket team and XI, as explained above, is 11, cricket teams often have X1 after their name as in, for example, the Chinese National XI or the Ignore Human Rights XI.

Anyway, since I take a keen interest in what's going on in the world, I'm aware that China is seeking to expand its global influence, and why shouldn't you? Apparently, you've been doing so for quite some time mainly through offering seemingly soft loans to poorer countries to finance infrastructure projects that Chinese firms undertake. In this way, you not only make huge profits but also increase the dependence of these third world countries on you. Very clever!

Penetrating more advanced western countries has presented a greater challenge, I suspect. Okay, we know that Huawei phones are monitoring all our conversations but transcribing them and then filing them away is a ridiculously labour-intensive operation even for a country of nearly one-and-half billion people.

What I believe you should be doing is taking over key components of the social and economic fabric of these 'target' nations. Unfortunately, you've just missed out on Newcastle United which has been grabbed by the Saudis but there are other trophy assets to be had in the UK and I would urge you to despatch your Overseas Control Minister to take a look at Dale Hill Hotel and Golf Club. For a tiny fraction of what the Saudis coughed up for Newcastle, you could secure one of the finest golf resorts in the south-east

of England with two courses and no fewer than 50 bedrooms, all of which have en-suite bathrooms.

If you take my advice and buy Dale Hill, all I ask in return is that you support my bid to become club captain.

****

THIS IS THE LAST WILL AND TESTAMENT OF MORTIMER WINSTANLEY FORTESCUE BERTRAM MERRIWEATHER

Being of sound mind and body I hereby bequeath the following:

£1000 to Dale Hill Hotel and Golf Club to fill in that intensely annoying little bunker just in front of the 13th green.

£500 to Dale Hill Hotel and Golf Club to pay for a bench to be situated behind the 5th tee and a further £100 to pay for a plaque with the following inscription: "On July 18th, 1991 Mortimer Merriweather came the closest he ever managed to a hole-in-one when striking a five iron from this tee with the ball finishing a mere three inches (7.62cms) from the hole."

My Taylor-Made set of clubs together with the attached umbrella, pitch-mark repairer, towel and folding trolley to the Golf Museum at St Andrews.

All my golf balls, including the three unopened sleeves of Top-Flites, to the driving range at Dale Hill Hotel and Golf Club.

All my golf clothes including several pairs of plus fours, numerous Argyll sweaters and far too many flat caps to be

returned from whence they came, the Help the Aged charity shop in Tunbridge Wells High Street.

All my golf magazines dating back to 1954 with their useless advice on how to cure a slice, to the wastepaper skip at Mountfield Recycling Centre in East Sussex.

The 100+ equally useless instruction videos and CDs into the household waste skip at Mountfield Recycling Centre.

All my golf books including, "How to Break 100 without Breaking Sweat", "Cure the Shanks", "Don't Ever Yip Again", "Say Goodbye to Three-Putting" and "The Secrets of Club Captaincy" to Tunbridge Wells Lending Library.

After I've expired, my body will be cremated and the ashes delivered to Dale Hill Hotel and Golf Club by Hermes and split into three roughly equal portions and disposed of as follows:

1) One lot to be deposited in the big bunker guarding the sixth green. I always struggled to escape from it. Having been responsible for removing so much of the sand it would be nice to give something back, as it were.

2) Another lot should be unceremoniously dumped in the lake to the left of the ninth fairway to join the vast number of balls I deposited there over the course of more than half a century.

3) The final lot should be scattered on the green of the par five 11th, upon which I so nearly sank the only putt for eagle that I ever had in my entire life. In asking this I recognise that, from the perspective of the rules of golf, I may for evermore be deemed a loose impediment and dealt with accordingly.

Dear Editor of the Times,

Although I read the Telegraph, I think it would be altogether more fitting if, when the time comes, my obituary were to appear in your paper which, albeit a bit left-wing for my taste, is a respected journal of record. My birth appeared in the Times in 1936 as did my ill-fated marriage in 1960 and so it would be appropriate if, following my death, you carried an authoritative account of my life.

To make it easier for you, I have drafted my own obituary, which I affirm is both fair and accurate.

Born in Bagshot in 1936, Mortimer Winstanley Fortescue Bertram Merriweather was the only child of Colonel Archibald Merriweather of the King's Royal Hussars and Cecilia Mablethorpe. Following somewhat reluctantly in his father's illustrious footsteps, Merriweather attended Eton College before going on to East Basildon Polytechnic where he gained a Diploma in Woodwork and was voted 'Toff of the Year' by his fellow students in 1957.

The following year he joined the Civil Service as a clerical officer at the Ministry of Agriculture and Fisheries, a post he held for 43 years without ever being seriously considered for promotion. Although enormously frustrated at work, his loyalty to the Crown was so strong that he never considered leaving.

Away from his cramped office, Merriweather devoted most of his time to the game of golf without ever achieving much in the way of progress. His handicap stubbornly hovered in the low to mid 20s. Nevertheless, his fertile imagination resulted in a number of original ideas to improve the game but, much to his regret, none of these ever came to anything.

Another huge disappointment was his failure to be elected captain of his beloved golf club, Dale Hill. Despite campaigning tirelessly throughout his more than half-century at the club, the closest he came in the ballot was third out of four when the person he just edged into last place was exposed as a convicted paedophile.

****

THE END

The manufacturer's authorised representative in the EU is Springer
Nature Customer Service Centre GmbH, Europaplatz 3, 69115 Heidelberg,
Germany. If you have any concerns regarding our products, please
contact ProductSafety@springernature.com

Printed and bound by CPI Group (UK) Ltd, Croydon, CR0 4YY

10/11/2025

01994631-0001